THE BEST OF
JOHN CALVIN

Compiled by
Samuel Dunn

BAKER BOOK HOUSE
Grand Rapids, Michigan 49506

Reprinted 1981 by Baker Book House Company
ISBN: 0-8010-2467-6

First published in 1837 by Tegg and Son (London)

First printing, September 1981
Second printing, May 1983

PHOTOLITHOPRINTED BY CUSHING - MALLOY, INC.
ANN ARBOR, MICHIGAN, UNITED STATES OF AMERICA

PREFACE

THE opinions of Calvin are much better known than his writings. The former, for the last three hundred years, have occasioned unparalleled discussion; while the latter have not been so generally read as those of some other authors. His works, published at Geneva, comprehended twelve volumes in folio, which the edition of Amsterdam reduced to nine. His sermons and lectures, which have been published since his death, amount to about five volumes more. The manner in which these have been preserved, is thus stated in the preface to a volume which the deacons of the Genevese church published in 1567; " From the year of our Lord 1549, the late M. Dennis Raguenier being fled hither, gave himself to the gathering of the sermons, word for word, which M. John Calvin did ordinarily make; and that with such swiftness and cunning through the use of certain notes and shapes, as few words escaped him even from the beginning, which thing, when they saw who had the charge of the poor strangers at that time, although they had not any great sum of money wherewith to relieve the present needs, yet failed they not to take such order, that the same writer was entertained, after a sort, with some part of the same money, to the intent he might have wherewith to maintain himself and his small family, while he gave himself wholly to the gathering of these sermons, and to the engrossing them fair again afterwards, because he should spare no time to any other business than that. He undertook the charge, with condition that he should copy out all the sermons fair, into books of a certain scantling or size, whereby they should be made, which he should deliver to one of the deacons, to be faithfully kept as a peculiar benefit belonging to the poor strangers. Copies were afterwards given to those who had not an opportunity of hearing them, that they might profit themselves by the doctrine of them. In consequence of this, imperfect editions of some of the sermons were printed, which induced the deacons to publish a correct one."

The whole works, then, of Calvin amount to about fourteen folio volumes. Shortly after their first appearance, many of them were translated into English; but for the last two hundred years, all his writings that have been published in our language would, perhaps, not occupy two such volumes. And as the early translations have become extremely scarce, his writings are now known to very few English readers. This consideration has induced me to prepare the present volume. I am aware that many are not partial to selections or abridgments; but they do not show unto us a more excellent way. That the voluminous works of other times are not read in the present day is acknowledged. I knew but of one person who had read the writings of John Goodwin which were recently condensed into one volume; and with the individual who has read all the works of John Calvin I have not yet been fortunate enough to meet. What, then, in such cases is to be done? Are the works, for instance, of our author to be left to sink into utter oblivion? Their value entitles them to other treatment. Is it recommended that they be published in a complete and uniform edition? The speculation would be a bad one, for modern readers would not be very ready to plod their way through such interminable pages. An abridgment, or a condensation, seems then the only alternative. But to do any thing like justice to Calvin in an abridgment would require at least twelve or fourteen such volumes as this, nor would he then, as some other authors, appear to advantage.

The present volume has not been prepared without some labour and expense. In giving these four hundred pages of selections to the public, I have had to read of our author what would be equal to twenty thousand pages of the same size. While thus plodding, the following remarks of one of the most eloquent writers of the present day have not been without their influence :—

" There is something pious, we think, and endearing, in the office of thus gathering up the ashes of renown that has passed away ; or rather of calling back the departed life for a transitory glow, and enabling those great spirits which seemed to be *laid* for ever, still to draw a tear of pity, or a throb of admiration, from the hearts of a forgetful generation."

These selections have been made in good faith, and will be found, I trust, in every instance to give the real meaning of our author. They have been chiefly taken from his commentaries and sermons, and are remarkably practical ; for my object was to prepare a useful volume, and not a controversial one.

The talents of our Reformer have been so frequently extolled, that it may seem unnecessary to introduce any testimonies here ; but a few quotations from the works of distinguished individuals will, perhaps, not be uninteresting to the reader :—

" He was a reverend father and a worthy ornament of the Church of God."—BISHOP JEWEL.

" Calvin was an illustrious person, and never to be mentioned without a preface of the highest honour."—BISHOP ANDREWS.

" Two things of principal moment there are which have deservedly procured him honour throughout the world ; the one his exceeding pains in composing the Institution of the Christian Religion, the other his no less industrious travails for the exposition of Holy Scripture." RICHARD HOOKER.

" Calvin's commentaries abound in solid discussions of theological subjects, and practical improvements of them." —MATTHEW POOLE.

" I know no man since the Apostles' days, whom I value and honour more than Calvin, and whose judgment in all things, one with another, I more esteem and come nearer to."—Richard Baxter.

" I hold the memory of Calvin in high veneration—his works have a place in my library, and, in the study of the Holy Scriptures, he is one of the commentators whom I frequently consult."—Bishop Horsley.

" I believe Calvin was a great instrument of God, and that he was a wise and pious man."—Rev. John Wesley.

" His Commentary upon the Old and New Testament is a production that will always be esteemed on account of its elegant simplicity, and the evident marks it bears of an unprejudiced and impartial enquiry into the plain sense of the sacred writings, and of sagacity and penetration in the investigation of them."—Dr Archibald Maclean.

" Calvin himself was both a wise and a good man—inferior to none of his contemporaries in general ability, and superior to almost all in the art as well as elegance of composition, in the perspicuity and arrangement of his ideas, the structure of his periods, and the Latinity of his diction."—Dr Laurence, *Archbishop of Cashel.*

" He was an eloquent, wise, and learned man."—James Nichols, F.A.S.

The Memoir contains the leading incidents in Calvin's life; and the sketch of his character, it is hoped, will be found a faithful representation. The Chronological List of his publications, with their translations, so far as they have been ascertained, cannot fail of being acceptable to many readers; while the whole-length portrait of our author, which has been correctly taken from the edition of his works published at Amsterdam in 1667, will be, it is presumed, an additional recommendation of the volume.

Edinburgh, *June* 10, 1837

CONTENTS

THE LIFE

OF

JOHN CALVIN

SINCE the days of the Apostles there have been few names that have occupied a more prominent place on the page of ecclesiastical history, than that of John Calvin. He was born July 10, 1509, at Noyon, a city of France, about sixty miles north-east of Paris. His parents, Gerhard Calvin, and Jeanne Franc, were persons of moderate fortune and of unblemished character. His father had a sound judgment, and was so judicious in giving advice, that he was highly respected by the neighbouring gentry, in consequence of which his son received a liberal education, though at the expense of the father, with the children of the Mommors, a family of the first rank in that place. He afterwards accompanied them to Paris, where he had for his tutor, in the College de la Marche, Mathurin Cordier, a man of eminent piety and learning, and who spent upwards of fifty years in the tuition of youth at Paris, Nevers, Bourdeaux, Geneva, Neuchatel, and Lausanne. He was indebted, under God, to Robert Stephens, for his complete deliverance from the errors of Popery, and died at Geneva, September 8, 1564, six months after his distinguished pupil, at the advanced age of eighty-five.

On leaving the College of La Marche, Calvin went to that of Montaign, where he studied logic and other liberal arts with great success, under the care of a Spanish master. Having from his youth shown great seriousness of mind, and often sternly reproved the vices of his companions, his father destined him for the church, and, according to the corrupt practice of the times, obtained for him the chapelry of La Gesine, in the Cathedral of Noyon, to which he was preferred in May 21, 1521, when he was scarcely twelve years of age. September 27, 1527, he was presented to the parochial cure of Marteville, which he exchanged on July 5, 1529, for Pont l'Eveque, a village near Noyon, where his father was born. Here he is said to have delivered some sermons to the people, though he had not received ordination under the papal hierarchy, in any other way than by tonsure, which is the first step of holy orders, and may be had in that corrupt church at the age of seven years. The course, however, on which he had entered, was soon interrupted; his father, thinking that the law was a more certain path to wealth and fame than the church, obliged him to relinquish his theological studies. Calvin informs us that at this time he was strongly " addicted to the superstitions of the papacy ;" it was not however long before he saw the gross errors of the Romish Church, and was so disgusted with her corruptions, that he determined to withdraw himself from her communion. It would be highly interesting to know the several stages of his conversion to the reformed religion, and the helps of which he made use, but these it is now impossible to discover. He attentively read the Holy Scriptures, and was indebted to the instructions of his relative, P. R. Olivetan. This individual published at Neuchatel, in 1535, the first French Bible ever printed in Switzerland, and translated from the Hebrew and Greek. He was banished from Geneva, where he was tutor in a gentleman's family, in consequence of his defending the

Lutherans against the attack of a Dominican friar.   He
died at Ferrara, in 1536 or 1538, having, it is supposed,
been poisoned, on account of his activity as a reformer,
and translator of the Scriptures.   Calvin wrote the Preface to the Old Testament, addressed to "all the emperors,
kings, princes, and nations, subject to the dominion of
Christ."

When Calvin left Paris he removed to Orleans, where
he studied the civil law under the direction of Peter de
l'Etoile, the most distinguished of the French civilians ;
and his progress was so great that he not unfrequently
supplied the chairs of the professors in their absence.   On
leaving the university a doctor's degree was unanimously
offered him by the proper authorities.   In the midst of
his various employments, he now more diligently studied
the sacred volume, and such was his proficiency that many
persons who wished to be instructed in the reformed religion applied to him for information, and were equally impressed with his learning and zeal.

There is a letter of Calvin's, which is supposed to
have been written in 1530, on the marriage of Henry
VIII. and Catharine, in which it is stated that the marriage is null, and that the King ought to part with the
Queen, upon the law of Leviticus.   But as the letter is
without date or name, and as Calvin could not then have
been above twenty-one years of age, it is thought that a
matter of such importance would not be referred to so
young a man ; and that, consequently, it is doubtful if
he wrote the letter.

His application to his studies was now so intense that
after a light supper, he continued reading till midnight,
and in the morning was employed while in bed, in reviewing what he had read the night before.   These late
studies no doubt materially impaired his health, and
brought on that weakness of the digestive powers with
which he was afflicted all his life, and which at length
shortened his days.   Just two hundred years after this,

the Rev. Samuel Wesley, April 20, 1732, thus speaks of his brother John :

> " Does John seem bent beyond his strength to go,
> To his frail carcase literally foe ?
> Lavish of health, as if in haste to die,
> And shorten time, to ensure eternity ?

From Orleans Calvin went to Bourges, to attend the lectures of Andrew Alciati, an eminent Milanese lawyer, who had been invited thither by Francis I. to promote the knowledge of the civil law in the university, where the fame of his abilities drew from different parts a great number of students. While in this city Calvin became intimately accquainted with Melchior Wolmar, a native of Rothweil, in Germany, a man of extensive learning, and deep piety, and the sole preceptor of Beza, from childhood to mature age. He had imbibed the principles of the Reformation, and was now professor of Greek in the university at Bourges, under the patronage of the Duchess of Berri, afterwards Queen of Navarre. He died at Eisenach in 1561, aged sixty-four. To him Calvin was indebted for his acquaintance with Greek literature. But while he diligently pursued his professional studies, divinity was not neglected by him, for he occasionally preached at the neighbouring town of Ligniers, in the presence, and with the approbation of the governor of the district.

In 1532, his father died, and he returned to Noyon ; but after a very short stay, he removed to Paris, where, when he was only twenty-two years and nine months old, he commenced authorship, by publishing a commentary on Seneca's Treatise on Clemency, which has been commended for its learning and eloquence. While at Paris, Calvin became acquainted with the zealous supporters of the reformed religion, among whom was Stephen Forgeus, an eminent merchant, to whom he was strongly attached, and who afterwards sealed the truth with his blood. From this time Calvin resolved to abandon all other studies, and devote himself entirely to the service of God ; a resolution peculiarly gratifying to those pious individuals in the city, who held private meetings for mutual edification, in the things which belonged to their peace.

But Paris was not to be the scene of his labours. Nicholas Cop, whose father was physician to the King, was appointed Rector of the University. Calvin prepared for him an oration, to be delivered, according to custom, on All Saints' day ; and introduced into it some remarks on Popery, that gave great offence to the doctors of the Sorbonne. The consequence was that the rector, informed by his friends of the danger to which he would expose himself if he attended to the summons which he received to appear before the Parliament, immediately fled out of the kingdom to Basle. A party proceeded to Calvin's lodgings, but not finding him at home, they seized his papers,—among which, they found many letters from his friends,—several of whom were, in consequence, exposed to the greatest danger. He was protected by the Queen of Navarre, only sister of the King of France, distinguished for her learning, piety, and firm attachment to the Protestant cause. She died, December 2, 1549, aged fifty-five years. After the interview with the Queen, Calvin went to Saintonge, where he became acquainted with Louis du Tillet, at whose request he wrote some short homilies, which were read by the neighbouring clergymen to their congregations. He is also said to have administered the sacrament in caves and gardens to some Protestants of Poictiers ; and shortly after, he removed to Nerac to visit a very interesting character — James le Fevre, who was so pleased with the behaviour of his young friend as to express his confidence that God intended him for important service in the church. This venerable man had been tutor to the children of Francis I., and professor of mathematics in the University of Paris,

where, in consequence of the improvements he had introduced in several of the sciences, as well as his opposition to the scholastic theology, the hatred of the other
doctors was so strongly excited that he with difficulty
escaped the Inquisitors, and retired to Nerac. He never
actually left the Romish Church, though he evidently
approved of the Reformation; but he seems to have
wanted courage openly to avow his sentiments. "How
shall I stand," he said to the Queen of Navarre, "before
the bar of God—I who have preached the gospel of his
Son to so many who have followed my doctrine, and met
a thousand torments, nay death itself, with constancy—
while I, their teacher, fled—fled from persecution, and
have lived to the age of 101; although death, even in
its most appalling horrors, ought never to have excited
even a shudder in my frame. Yet feeling and knowing
this, I privately withdrew myself, and basely deserted
the post assigned me by the Lord of glory." After the
Queen and her friends had comforted him by assurances
of Christ's readiness to forgive; "Nothing," he added,
"remains for me but to depart to God, as soon as I have
made my will; nor ought I to delay, for I think that
God has called me. I appoint you my heir; I bequeath
all my books to your chaplain; my clothes to the poor;
and I commend the rest to God." "What," said the
Queen, smiling, "shall I get by being your heir?"
"The office," he said, "of distributing to the poor."
"Be it so!" repled the Queen, "and I declare, this inheritance is more pleasing to me than if my brother, the
King of France, had nominated me to all his possessions."
The countenance of the old man brightened, and he
said,—"Now, O Queen! I require some rest. May you
be all happy! Mean while, farewell!" He lay down on
a couch, and fell into a gentle doze. One of the party,
after a little time, went to awake him; but his spirit had
departed.

Calvin returned to Paris in 1534, and found Servetus

disseminating his opinions. They agreed to have a public discussion, the time and place were appointed, but Servetus did not make his appearance. During this year some individuals having circulated through the city certain papers against the mass, the king was so enraged that he appointed a public procession. The sacrament was carried through the city in great pomp; Francis walked before it, bearing a torch in his hand; his three sons supported the canopy over it; the nobles marched in order behind. In the presence of the numerous assembly the king declared that if one of his hands was infected with heresy, he would cut it off, and would not spare even his own children, if found guilty. As a dreadful proof of his being in earnest, eight martyrs were that day burned alive in four principal places in the city.

The violence of persecution induced Calvin to determine on quitting his native country; and, accordingly, after publishing his " Psychopannychia," a small treatise against the sleep of the soul from death to the resurrection, he departed with his friend Tillet for Basle, one of the largest towns in Switzerland. Near Metz a servant plundered him, and fled with one of the horses; but the other servant having ten crowns, they were enabled to proceed to Strasburg, and thence to Basle. Here he contracted a particular friendship with Grynæus and Capito, diligently applied himself to the study of Hebrew, and published his celebrated " Institutes of the Christian Religion." His design in commencing this work was to supply his countrymen, the French, with an elementary compendium for their instruction in the principles of religion. But by the time it was finished, he had another reason for publishing it. Francis I. of France, desiring the assistance of the Protestant princes of Germany, and knowing their abhorrence of the persecutions he had carried on against his subjects of the reformed religion, endeavoured to excuse his conduct by alleging, that he

caused none to be put to death but some rebellious fana-
tics. Calvin, to meet such foul aspersions, determined
on the immediate publication of this treatise. In the
dedication to Francis, he boldly and triumphantly refutes
the calumnies, and then concludes in the following language :—" Thus have you, O king, the venomous injustice of the slanderers largely enough declared, that you
may not with an ear of too easy belief bend to their reports. I fear, also, lest it be too largely set out, forasmuch as this preface is in a manner come to the quantity
of a whole book of defence, whereby I intended not to
make a defence indeed, but only to mollify your mind
before hand, to give audience to the disclosing of our
cause ; which your mind, though it be now turned away
and estranged from us, yea, and inflamed against us, yet
we trust we shall be able to recover the favour thereof,
if you shall once have without displeasure and troublous
affliction, read over this our confession, which we wish to
be instead of a defence for us to your Majesty. But if
the whisperings of the malicious do so possess your ears,
that there is no place for accused men to speak for themselves ; and if those outrageous furies do still, with your
winking at them, exercising cruelty with imprisoning,
tormenting, cutting, and burning ; we shall, indeed, as
sheep appointed to the slaughter, be brought to all ex-
tremities ; yet so that in our patience we shall possess
our souls, and wait for the strong hand of the Lord,
which shall without doubt be present in time, and stretch
forth itself armed, both to deliver the poor out of affliction, and to take vengeance on the despisers, which
now triumph with so great assuredness. The Lord the
king of kings establish your throne with righteousness,
and your seat with equity, most noble king. Basle,
August 1, 1536." This was Calvin's chief work ; it was
written both in Latin and French, and translated into
Dutch, Italian, and Spanish. Mr Norton translated it
into English so early as the year 1561, and it passed

through six or seven editions during his life. The translation of Mr Allen, which made its appearance in 1813, is more elegant than Norton's, but not so faithful.

After publishing the Institutes, Calvin took a journey into Italy, and visited the celebrated Renée, Duchess of Ferrara, and daughter of Louis XII., who was distinguished for her piety and cordial attachment to the Reformation. " He received," says Dr M'Crie, " the most distinguished attentions from the Duchess, who was confirmed in the Protestant faith by his instructions, and ever after entertained the highest respect for his character and talents." Calvin, however, soon returned to France, and, having settled his affairs there, and taking his brother Anthony with him, he prepared to return to Basle or Strasburg, but the wars obliging him to take his route through Dauphine and Savoy, he was thus unexpectedly conducted to Geneva. Here he soon visited Farel and Viret, two eminent reformers. Farel was very anxious that he should remain and assist him at Geneva. Calvin, however, was not disposed to comply, when Farel thus addressed him :—" You have not any other pretext to refuse me than the attachment which you profess for your studies ; but I denounce to you, in the name of Almighty God, that if you do not share with me the holy work in which I am engaged, his curse will rest upon you for seeking your own, and not the things of Jesus Christ." Calvin, terrified by this denunciation, surrendered himself to the disposal of the Presbytery and Magistrates, by whom he was appointed Professor in Divinity, in August, 1536, and shortly after, with the consent of the people, a pastor of one of the churches.

This year was remarkable for a close alliance between Geneva and Berne, and for the establishment of the gospel at Lausanne, where a public disputation was held between the Protestants and Papists, which Calvin attended. Farel published a formulary of Christian doctrines, suited to the state of the Genevan church, which was then only just emerging from the errors and super-stitions of Popery ; and Calvin added a short Catechism on the chief articles of religion, and then, in conjunction with his colleagues, he attempted to induce the people to abjure Popery, and swear to observe the scheme of doctrines and order thus prepared for them. Many refused to do it, but on July 20, 1537, this object was effected. The city, however, was far from being in a state of peace. Party spirit ran high, and violent feuds existed between individuals and families. During this year Calvin and his colleagues held a public disputation with the Anabaptists, and the Council denounced a sentence of banishment for life against all who should attempt to teach their doctrines at Geneva. The consequence was, that this sect there soon disappeared. Peter Caroli next attacked Farel, Viret, and Calvin, charging them with holding erroneous notions concerning the Trinity. A very full synod was held at Berne to consider the truth of the accusation, and afterwards a council at Lausanne, where he was proved guilty of calumny, and received sentence of banishment. Calvin this year wrote two letters to the Protestants in France, to confirm them in their faith : one of them directed to Cheminus, was against idolatry, the other to Gerard Ronsel, against the Popish priesthood.

Geneva at this time was in a very unsettled state. Popery was expelled, but violent contentions and flagrant immoralities were awfully prevalent. Calvin and the other ministers lifted up their voice like a trumpet, and showed the people their transgressions, declaring that while things were in such a state they could not consent to administer the Lord's Supper. This was violently resisted by the syndics or chief magistrates, and the people ; and as the ministers had refused to comply with the direction of a Synod held at Lausanne, to restore the use of unleavened bread, the baptismal fonts, and the festivals, which they had abolished, the council, April

23, 1538, passed an order for the banishment of Calvin, Farel, and Courault. When Calvin was informed of this decree, he said, "Had I been in the service of men, this would have been a bad reward ; but it is well that I have served Him, who never fails to repay his servants whatever he has once promised." He retired to Strasburg, where he met with a cordial welcome from Bucer, Capito, and Hedio, and was appointed Professor of Divinity, with a very liberal stipend. He also, with the sanction of the senate, established a French Church, for the benefit of his countrymen resident in the city.

The following year, as the Genevese were still contending among themselves, the Romanists began to entertain hopes that they might be regained to the Papal Church; and the eloquent Cardinal Sadolet, Bishop of Carpentras, was employed to make the attempt. He addressed to "his dearly beloved brethren, the magistracy, council, and citizens of Geneva," an artful letter, in which he omitted nothing that might induce "the wandering dove to return unto the secure ark of the true Church." There was no one in Geneva capable of writing a suitable answer to this epistle. But when Calvin got a copy of it, he immediately wrote to the Cardinal with such eloquence and judgment, that the project was abandoned.

Calvin now published an enlarged edition of his Institutes, and a Treatise on the Lord's Supper, as well as his Commentary on the Epistle to the Romans. In the dedication of this work to " Simon Grynée, a gentleman of the most tried worth," Calvin says, " Philip Melancthon, on account of his singular learning, industry, and skill in every kind of knowledge, has cast more light upon this epistle than any of his predecessors." After noticing the various excellencies in Bullinger and Bucer, he adds, " To wish to contend with writers of such unrivalled excellence, as it would, I confess, be a proof of too presumptuous an emulation, so it never entered even my mind that I should deprive them of the least portion of their celebrity. Let their favour and authority with the public, which all good men acknowledge they deserve, remain unimpaired. This, I hope, will be granted me, that no production of man ever attained such consummate perfection as not to leave room for the industry of their successors to improve, either by polishing, or adorning, or illustrating." He then bears the following testimony to his friend : " The more intimately I am acquainted with you by familiar intercourse, which generally diminishes something of the high opinion we form of others, the more is my value and esteem of you heightened. All men of learning also agree in regarding you with distinguished honour and estimation. Farewell.—Strasburg, October 18, 1539."

Calvin was also useful in reclaiming many Anabaptists ; among others, Paul Volse, to whom Erasmus had dedicated his " Manual of the Christian Soldier ; " and John . Storder, who subsequently fell a victim to the plague, and whose widow, Idolette de Bure, a person of great virtue and gravity, Calvin, by the advice of Bucer, married. As the Reformers entered into holy matrimony to show their conversion from Popery, the Papists reproached them, as if they warred against Rome for the same reason that the Grecians warred against Troy. " Our adversaries pretend," says Calvin, " that we wage a sort of Trojan war for a woman. To say nothing of others at present, they must allow myself at least to be free from this charge ; since I am more particularly able in my own case to refute this scurrilous reflection. For notwithstanding I was at liberty to have married under the tyranny of the Pope, I voluntarily led a single life for many years." And in a letter to Farel he observes, that " he was not of that passionate race of lovers, who, when once captivated with an external form, eagerly embrace also the moral defects which it conceals. I expect chastity, frugality, patience, and solicitude for my personal health and prosperity, in that lady who delights me with her beauty."

In 1541, the Emperor Charles V. appointed a conference to be held at Worms, and afterwards at Ratisbon, to settle the differences which had arisen in Germany. Calvin attended, at the desire of the ministers of Strasburg, and was of no small service, especially to the French churches. Melancthon was much pleased with him, and often called him "the Divine." And Jasper Cruciger, minister of Wittemberg, had a profitable conversation with him on the subject of the Lord's Supper.

As several of the magistrates who had banished the ministers from Geneva, were now dead or removed, a way was made for their return. To this Calvin at first was strongly opposed. March 1, 1541, he writes thus to Viret, " The further I advance, the more sensible am I how arduous a charge is that of governing a church ; and there is no place under heaven that I more dread than Geneva." And in a letter to Farel he says, " Hear my mind in this matter. If I consulted my own inclination, I would rather do any thing than obey you in this ; but as I am regardless of my own right, I offer my heart as a sacrifice to God. You have therefore no room for suspecting that I deceive you. I give you my promise from the heart. Even though I am not very ingenious, yet excuses are not wanting by which I might free myself, so as easily to stand excused before men. But I know that I have to do with God, who detects any deceit of this nature. Therefore I subject my mind, tied and bound, to the obedience of God, and since I am destitute of wisdom myself, I deliver myself up to the guidance of those through whom I hope God himself will speak to me."

April the 4th, the ministers of Zuric wrote to him,

urging his return, and a deputation was sent from Geneva to Strasburg to obtain the consent of its citizens for his removal. They were very reluctant to part with him, but at last consented to do it for a limited time. Still he could not be persuaded to yield, until Bucer denounced the severe judgment of heaven against him, and pressed upon him the consideration of the example of Jonah. But as he was now engaged to attend the conferences at Ratisbon, between the Papists and Protestants, he had to procure Viret from Lausanne to undertake the charge at Geneva, till he should be able himself to repair thither. This took place Sept. 13, 1541, when he met with a cordial welcome from the council and citizens, who rested not until the temporal grant of his services, by Strasburg, was changed into an entire surrender. He was then urged to retain the privileges of a citizen, and his stipend. The former he accepted, the latter he refused, " there being nothing," says Beza, " that he less desired than riches."

Calvin could not but be gratified at the reception he met with at Geneva. " I had intended," he remarks, " on my return, to address the people, entering into a review of the past, and a justification of myself and my colleagues ; but I found them so touched with remorse, so ready to anticipate me in the confession of their faults, that I felt that such a proceeding would not only be superfluous, but cruel." They even passed a decree, acknowledging the great injuries they had done him, and imploring forgiveness of Almighty God. He represents most of the ministers whom he found in possession, as " arrogant, fierce, destitute alike of zeal and learning, and secretly counteracting the measures in which they professed to concur ;" and adds, " I might have gained applause by severity towards them, and have put them all to rout with ease ; but I abstained ; and I pray God to preserve me in the same moderation."

He now diligently applied himself to the correction of

public morals, and procured the establishment of the consistory, an ecclesiastical court, composed of ministers and laymen. This tribunal had no power to inflict corporal punishment ; but it could censure or excommunicate the disorderly, while it referred the more important cases to the council, with its own judgment upon them. Some writers have represented this court as savouring too much of Popish tyranny ; while others have said that its operations were attended with the most beneficial effects, contributing greatly to the prosperity and preservation of the liberties of the republic.

That Calvin was not disposed in any way to connive at the vices of the Genevese is sufficiently plain from the following address which he delivered to the Council :— "If you desire to have me for your pastor, correct the disorders of your lives. If you have, with sincerity, recalled me from my exile, banish the crimes and debauchery which prevail among you. I certainly cannot behold, without the most painful displeasure, within your walls discipline trodden under foot, and crimes committed with impunity. I cannot live in a place so grossly immoral. Vicious souls are too filthy to receive the purity of the gospel, and the spiritual worship which I preach to you. A life stained with sin is too contrary to Jesus Christ to be tolerated. I consider the principal enemies of the gospel not to be the pontiff of Rome, nor heretics, nor seducers, nor tyrants, but such bad Christians ; because the former exert their rage out of the church, while the latter, by their innumerable and abominable vices, overthrow my doctrines, and expose it, defenceless, to the rage of our enemies. Rome does not constitute the principal object of my fears. Still less am I apprehensive from the almost infinite number of monks. The gates of hell, the principalities and powers of evil spirits, disturb me not at all. I tremble on account of other enemies, more dangerous ; and I dread abundantly more those carnal covetousnesses, those debaucheries of the tavern, and of gaming; those infamous remains of ancient superstition, those mortal pests, the disgrace of your town, and the shame of the reformed name. Of what importance is it to have driven away the wolves from the fold, if the pest ravages the flock? Of what use is a dead faith without good works? Of what value even truth itself, where a wicked life belies it, and actions make words blush? Either command me to abandon a second time your town, and let me soften the bitterness of my afflictions in a new exile, or let the severity of the laws reign in the church. Re-establish there the pure discipline. Remove from within your walls, and from the frontiers of your state, the pest of your vices, and condemn them to a perpetual banishment."

The labours of our reformer at this period were extraordinary. It is said that he preached twice every other Sabbath; gave weekly three lectures on theology; on the Thursdays he presided in the consistory; and on the Fridays collated and expounded the Holy Scriptures to what was called the congregation. His correspondence was very extensive, and his advice was frequently sought by the Council. He was one of the Commissioners appointed for revising the laws of the city, a work which received the sanction of the state in 1543.

So many duties now devolved upon him, that he earnestly desired, but in vain, to obtain the assistance of Farel, and was very anxious to have that of Viret rendered permanent. He said, " If Viret is taken from me, I am ruined, and cannot provide for the well-being of the church in this place." He could retain him, however, only six months, when Viret returned to his charge at Lausanne. With these two worthy individuals Calvin continued in the closest intercourse of friendship; so that Beza remarks, " It was beautiful to observe the union and yet diversity of these three great men in the service of their common master. Farel excelled in boldness and grandeur of mind. The thunders of his preaching could hardly be heard without trembling, or his ardent prayers without the soul being lifted to heaven. Viret, on the other hand, was distinguished by a sweet persuasive eloquence, which made his hearers hang upon his lips, almost whether they would or not. While Calvin filled the mind with nearly as many weighty sentiments as he uttered words. Hence it often appeared to me that the union of the three would have formed a perfect preacher."

Calvin, at this time, was very active in providing for the wants, both temporal and spiritual, of those refugees who had been driven to Geneva by the persecutions which raged in France and Italy. He also wrote several letters to those who were unable to escape from their enemies, that they might be comforted and confirmed in the faith. The doctors of the Sorbonne, being instigated by P. Liset, first President of the Parliament of Paris, this year published articles of faith, which many were induced to subscribe. Calvin soon sent forth an Antidote, in which he united keen irony with solid reasoning.

In 1543, he published his "Defence of the sound and orthodox doctrine concerning the bondage and liberation of the Will," in answer to Pighius, a Dutch divine of some eminence. This work is dedicated to Melancthon, whom Calvin extols as "a distinguished and valiant defender of sound doctrine," as a writer "of great clearness and simplicity," and one whose judgment "should suffice him for that of all beside." In 1544, Calvin published a piece on the "Relics of the Saints;" in which he says that he knew that the Papists "pretend to have the manger, cradle, swaddling-clothes, foreskin, and blood of Christ; the water-pots that were at the marriage of Cana; the wine into which Christ turned the water; the utensils and furniture that were used at the last supper; the manna of the children of Israel; the Cross, cave, nails, spunge, lance, crown of thorns, coat, handkerchief, and tears of Christ; the milk, smock hair, girdle, slipper, comb, and ring of the Virgin Mary; the dagger and buckler of Michael, the Archangel; the skull, jawbone, brains, and finger of John the Baptist; the chair, crozier, mass-attire, and brain of St. Peter; besides the bodies of saints which were to be seen in several places, and yet one and the same." Calvin shows with how great veneration the people adored these things when the priests for money exhibited them at a distance; but which, when viewed near at hand, were trifles of no value—were cheats and impostures.

Calvin having made some severe remarks on Castellio's translation of the New Testament into Latin, the latter asked permission of the Council to dispute publicly with Calvin on the descent of Christ into Hell: this they refused, but allowed the subject to be discussed before the assembly of ministers. The disputation lasted a long while, but without success: Castellio at length became so highly irritated that he attacked Calvin in a sermon, in consequence of which he was condemned to be banished from the city. He retired to Basle, where he died in 1552.

Calvin now republished, with a commentary, the "admonition" of Pope Paul III. to Charles V., who had presumed to promise the two great religious parties in Germany the early convocation of a council, and to grant them, in the mean time, the enjoyment of equal rights. To the Emperor himself, and the diet assembled at Spire, the Reformer also addressed a "suppliant exhortation on the necessity of reforming the church." He was next engaged in refuting the errors of the *Libertines*, who had revived some of the most dangerous heresies of antiquity. The Queen of Navarre, who countenanced this sect, having the highest regard for Quintin and Pocquet, two of their leaders, was offended with Calvin at having written against them; he therefore wrote her a letter, in which, while he treated her with all the respect due to her dignity, he yet asserted his own greater competence to judge in such matters, and urged her to withdraw from them her patronage.

He also at this time wrote against the *Nicodemites;* persons who obtained this name, because they were ashamed openly to confess Jesus Christ. They had embraced the Protestant faith, and yet, through dread of persecution, thought it no sin to remain in the communion of the Romish Church, provided they inwardly approved of the principles of the Reformation.

Calvin wrote to Melancthon for advice, and says, " I do esteem your judgment, as it is fit I should, that it would be very painful to me to find myself differing from you. I know that the tenderness of your nature leads you to concede many things to others which you would not allow to yourself: but we must take care not to loose when God binds." He also sent the following letter to Luther: " To the truly excellent doctor of the Christian church, Martin Luther. My highly honoured father in Jesus Christ,—Finding those Frenchmen, who had been restored from the darkness of Popery to the light of the true doctrine, made no alteration in their confession of faith, but that they continued to sully themselves with the profanations of the Papists, as if they had no relish for the true doctrine, I could not refrain from reproving such extreme stupidity with that vehemence and asperity which I believed they deserved. For can we call that faith, which, buried at the bottom of the soul, never discovers itself by any confession ? Or ought we to call that religion which disguises itself under the mask of idolatry ? I do not here undertake a thorough discussion of the question ; I have already explained myself sufficiently in two small works which I have composed on that topic. And if you will take the trouble to glance at them, you will better understand my opinion on that question, and upon what reasons it is founded. Some persons who have previously slept in great security, buried in profound slumbers, being roused by the perusal of them, have begun to consider what they ought to do. But because it is very hard to the flesh, either to neglect its own interests, so far as to endanger life; or so to irritate the minds of others as to become the object of public hatred; or to abandon our property and our country, and thus to condemn ourselves to a voluntary banishment; it happens but too frequently that these difficulties prevent a constant and firm resolution. They allege, also, other reasons which indeed appear plausible, but which, however, prove sufficiently that their sole design is only to seek pretexts to conceal the irresolution which agitates their minds. They desire to have your judgment for which they entertain a just veneration, and which will have great weight to deliver them from these uncertainties, and to confirm them in their duty. They have therefore entreated me to send you an express which may bring back your conclusion on this subject. This office I could by no means refuse to their solicitation, both because I thought it important for them to be upheld by your authority, that they might not ever float in these uncertainties, and that I myself felt disposed to solicit this help. Thus, my highly honoured father in the Lord, I conjure you by Jesus Christ to bear with this importunity, both for their sakes and mine, and to read for your entertainment in your leisure hours, the letter addressed to you in their name, and my two small books, or to employ some body to read them who shall report the principal particulars to you; and to take the trouble, in the second place, to explain to us in an answer of three words your opinion on this subject. It is contrary to my inclination to divert you from those great and various affairs which occupy you, and to give you this trouble. But I am firmly persuaded, that according to your uniform equity, seeing that necessity urges me to make this request, you will easily forgive the liberty I take and the trouble which I give you. Would to God that I were permitted to fly hence, that I might enjoy, at least for a few hours, your conversation. I should receive much more pleasure, and it would be much more advantageous to confer with you personally on this and on various other subjects. But, I hope, that what may not be granted to us on earth, will soon be given to us in the kingdom of God. Adieu, most illustrious man ! Most excellent minister of Jesus Christ, and my highly honoured father. I beseech the Lord to govern you by his Spirit unto the end, for the common good and edification of his church. Jan. 20, 1545."

To Bullinger, who had been attacked by Luther rather violently, in the controversy on the sacrament, Calvin gives the following judicious advice :—

"I can now hardly ask you to hold your peace ; but I wish you all to remember, first, how great a man Luther is ; what endowments he possesses, and what fortitude and firmness, what skill and what learning he has employed in routing the powers of Antichrist, and in propagating the true doctrine of salvation. I have often said, that though he should call me a devil, I would yet honour him as an illustrious servant of God. It is true, however, that as he is distinguished by eminent virtues, so he labours under great faults. Oh, that he had studied to restrain that intemperance which is ever ready to boil over in him ! That he had always directed that vehemence, which is inseparable from his nature, against the enemies of the truth, and not sometimes turned it upon the servants of God ! That he had bestowed more pains in discovering his own faults ! He was naturally too prone to indulge the impulses of his own mind ; and flatterers have much injured him by cherishing that propensity. It is our duty, however, even in reprehending his faults to acknowledge his great excellencies. I beg, therefore, of you and your colleagues, in the first place, to remember that he whom you have to encounter is a great and leading servant of Christ, to whom we are all deeply indebted. In the next place, consider that all you will gain by involving yourselves in the controversy will be to afford matter of triumph to the ungodly, who will make it an occasion of insulting over the gospel still more than over us. When we become mutual accusers of each other, they will be only too ready to believe us *both*. Dwell upon these considerations rather than on what the intemperance of Luther may have deserved at your hands. Let us not *bite and devour one another, lest we be consumed.*"

During this year Cardinal de Tournon carried into execution the cruel decree of the Parliament of Provence against the Waldenses of Cabrieres and Merindol, three thousand of whom, without distinction of sex, were inhumanly massacred. With those who had escaped the edge of the sword, Calvin deeply sympathized, and greatly exerted himself to alleviate their sufferings; subscriptions were raised in Geneva, and he obtained a considerable sum from Strasburg, and from the German provinces, towards their relief.

The year 1546 was one also of great trouble. Calvin had to fortify the minds of the people against the apprehensions excited by the Emperor Charles, the emissaries of the Pope, and the Council of Geneva. Ami Perrin having been made, by the suffrages of the people, Captain-General, thought it a favourable opportunity for breaking through the restraints which Calvin and his colleagues had imposed. He objected to the continuance of the Consistory, and contended that all cases should be referred exclusively to the Senate and the Civil Courts, where he and his party hoped to find connivance at their vices and disorders. The opposition which Calvin encountered from these men was so violent, that his life was exposed to danger, at one time from the swords of the contending parties, and at another from persons who were waiting for an opportunity to throw him into the Rhone. The Council, however, objected to the abrogation of the Consistory, condemned Perrin to two months' imprisonment, and suspended two of the pastors who had accused Calvin of teaching false doctrines, while Gruet, one of the chief leaders of the cabal, suffered capital punishment. Amidst all this disturbance, our reformer continued faithfully to expose and condemn the vices of the people, and this raised up many enemies against him. On one occasion, a woman whom he had reproved publicly, openly called him a *wicked man*, and spoke of him with the greatest contempt; for which she was imprisoned by the Council, who would have inflicted on her exemplary punishment, had not Calvin obtained her pardon. He this year translated into French the " Sum of Theology," by Melancthon. In 1547 he published an " Antidote" to the Acts of the Seven Sessions of the Council of Trent ; and in 1548, his Commentaries on St Paul's Epistles to the Galatians, Ephesians, Philippians, and Colossians ; and an Exposure of the German Interim. He also wrote to many of the friends of the Reformation. In a letter to Brentius, who had been driven from Halle, in Suabia, and was now at Basle, he says,—" Amidst all these calamities, one consideration supports and refreshes my mind : I assure myself that God, in commencing the wonderful restoration of his church, which we have witnessed, has not held out a vain and transient hope to us, but has begun a work which he will not fail to accomplish, in spite of the malice of men and opposition of Satan. In the mean time, let us patiently undergo the purification which is necessary for us." In a letter to the Protector Somerset, October 22, 1548, referring to the Reformation in England, he says,—" The Church of God cannot subsist, or your work endure, without catechetical instruction, by which the seed of the future harvest is sown, the people prepared to understand the word preached, and their minds fortified against those who broach novel and strange doctrines."

It was also during this year that the celebrated Theodore Beza settled in Switzerland. He was born at Vezelay, in France, in 1519, and was now, at Calvin's recommendation, appointed professor of Greek, and a preacher at Lausanne.

In 1549 Calvin suffered a severe domestic affliction in the death of his wife. He calls her " the most excellent partner of his life, who stood prepared, if difficulties and dangers arose, to be his voluntary associate, not only in exile and want, but in death itself." She had borne him one son, who died in 1545, when the father thus consoled himself in a letter to Viret. " The Lord has inflicted a heavy and severe wound on us by the death of our little son ; but he is our father, and knows what is expedient for his children." She had, however, other children surviving by her former husband. As she made no mention of them on her deathbed, Calvin remarked to her, that he should regard them as his own ; when she replied, " I have committed them to the Lord, and I know that you will not neglect what you are sensible has been commended to him." She also ejaculated the following expressions, " O glorious resurrection ! God of Abraham, and of all our fathers ; the faithful in all generations have hoped in thee, and not one has been disappointed. I also will hope in thee."

As the churches of Saxony were not agreed respecting the nature and use of things indifferent, they consulted Calvin, who frankly gave his opinion, and admonished Melancthon, who was thought by some to be too yielding, but, " unjustly," says Beza, " as Calvin, better informed, was afterwards aware ; for it was not then known what spirit actuated the evil genius of Flacius and the whole tribe of his followers, by which they afterwards caused such disturbances, and to this day so obstruct the work of the Lord, that they could not have done it more audaciously and furiously had they been hired to it by the gold of the Roman Pontiff!" As these adherents of Flacius affected the name of *genuine Lutherans*, Calvin, some years after, spoke of them in the following severe terms : " They ruin the churches, not merely by vain confidence, but by an absolutely savage pride. The greater part think they reflect the *genuine* image of Luther, if, instead of the greatness of soul which characterised him, they swell with an inflated arrogance. They are the apes of Luther, for he has left few imitators."

This same year he published his Commentaries on the Epistles to Titus, Philemon, and the Hebrews, and also wrote to Lælius Socinus, from whom and his nephew Faustus, the Socinian heresy took its name. Calvin does not touch on any of the anti-trinitarian questions, for Socinus had not yet openly avowed his sentiments; but gives his opinion on intermarrying with Papists, the lawfulness and validity of Popish baptism, and the resurrection of the body.

The year 1550 was remarkable for the rest which the Genevan church enjoyed. There were indeed some who circulated an unfounded report that Calvin, because he was opposed to the general festivals, wished to abrogate the Sabbath. In consequence of which he published a treatise on " Scandal," which he dedicated to his old and faithful friend Lawrence of Normandy. He also published this year his Commentary on the First Epistle to the Thessalonians, which he dedicated to Cordier, who had taught him the Latin language. He says, " I take this opportunity to testify to posterity, that, if they derive any benefit from my writings, they must in a great measure acknowledge it to have flowed from your instructions."

He published his Commentary on the Epistles of James, Peter, John, and Jude, and on the Prophet Isaiah, in 1551. The latter he dedicated to the most noble and renowned Edward the Sixth, King of England, and a true Christian Prince, to whom he thus speaks :—" And here I do expressly summon you, most excellent Kings or rather God, by the mouth of his Prophet Isaiah call, you, namely, to go on employing whatsoever power and

force God has endued you withal; and with new increases
to set forward the restoration of the Church, which is
now so happily begun in your kingdom. First, you
daily hear and read that this charge is committed unto
you in that kingdom over which God hath placed you.
Yea, and Isaiah calling Kings nursing fathers of the
Church, permits not that the help which she in this behalf requires of you in her affliction, should now be wanting unto her. Neither ought your heart to be lightly
touched with that, where the Prophet denounceth a heavy
curse to fall upon all Kings and nations which shall defraud her of their aid." He then, in conclusion, says,
" England shall receive an incomparable fruit for this so
happy a going forward; and we shall have cause too,
with you and your whole kingdom, to rejoice. In the
mean while, I will not cease to further your holy endeavours, as there is good cause, by my poor prayers, in regard they are the best means I am able to afford you.
Farewell, most noble King. The Lord long preserve
your flourishing estate, assist and guide you by his Holy
Spirit, and in all things bless and prosper you. So be it.
From Geneva, this five and twentieth of December,
1551."

A violent storm, however, during this year arose in Geneva, the factious party openly contended that the right
of citizenship ought not to be granted to strangers who
took refuge in Geneva. On one occasion they mocked
and jostled Calvin on his return from preaching, while
Raymond, his colleague, passing over the bridge across
the Rhone, nearly fell headlong into it, in consequence
of their having secretly removed one of the piles. It
was also during this year that Jerome Bolsec publicly
opposed the doctrine of unconditional predestination.
He had been a Carmelite monk at Paris, but had laid
aside the habit some years before. He appeared at Geneva as a physician, and had some private discussions with
Calvin, but on October 16, after St André, minister of

Jussy, had delivered a sermon, Bolsec, obtaining permission to speak, "openly dared to support free-will, and the foreknowledge of works for the purpose of subverting the decree of eternal predestination, which is superior in order to all causes." When he had finished, Calvin came forward and spoke for more than an hour in defence of the doctrine held by the churches of Geneva, adducing from memory not only so many passages of Scripture, but so many testimonies from Augustine, "that it might have been supposed he had employed the whole day in collecting them." A magistrate in the congregation, who was empowered for that purpose, seized Bolsec, dismissed the assembly, and committed the offender to prison. During his imprisonment conferences were held with him by Calvin, and the judgment of the Swiss churches was obtained, but the result was that Bolsec was banished from Geneva, and threatened with corporal punishment if he should ever return. Calvin shortly after published a treatise on Predestination, which did not, however, allay the storm which had been raised; some of the neighbouring churches of Berne charged him with having made God the author of sin, and threatened to enter into a controversy with him, while Castellio and Troillet were active in fanning the flame, and even " Melancthon himself wrote on predestination in such a manner, that it was thought he pointed to the ministers of Geneva as if they were introducing a stoical fate."

Calvin wrote the following letter to Lælius Socinus, January 1, 1552:—" You need not wait for my answer to those monstrous questions which you propose to me. If you are inclined to indulge in such airy speculations, suffer me, I pray you, a humble disciple of Jesus Christ, to employ myself in those meditations which tend to my edification in the faith of the gospel. And I shall certainly obtain by my silence, what I so much wish, that you may not trouble me in this way in future. I am truly grieved to perceive, that the noble talents which God has bestowed on you, are not merely misemployed about objects of no moment, but actually perverted by pernicious fancies. What I formerly declared to you I seriously warn you of again, that unless you restrain in time this inquisitive pruriency of mind, there is reason to fear that you are preparing for yourself grievous punishment in a future world. Were I, under the pretence of indulgence, to encourage you in a fault which I judge so ruinous, I should certainly act toward you a treacherous and cruel part. Wherefore I am willing that you should now for a little be offended by my seeming asperity, rather than that you should not be reclaimed from those curious and alluring speculations, by which you have been already captivated. The time will come, I hope, when you shall rejoice that you have been awakened, even in this violent manner, from your pleasing but fatal dream."

It was amidst these disturbances that Calvin published his Commentary on the Gospel according to John, in the dedication of which to the "right honourable Lords, the Syndics, and Senate of Geneva," he says, "Although all the world doth know how I have instructed this church with many of my writings, yet I thought it would be worth the pains if there should be some monument thereof extant, dedicated unto you. I profess before the world, that I am far from that diligence as a good shepherd which is exacted, and from other virtues which the greatness and excellency of mine office do require, and I do continually, before God, bewail my state, that I am troubled with so many vices which do hinder my course ; yet I dare profess that I want no faithfulness and goodwill. And if, in the mean while, the wicked do not cease to repine and speak against me, as it is my duty by well doing to refute their slanders, so it shall be your part to suppress the same by that holy authority wherein you excel. January 1, 1553."

But that which occasioned the greatest disturbance in the city, brought the most reproach on our reformer, and which, perhaps, has made more noise throughout Christendom than any other example of persecution, was the burning of Servetus. This individual was born 1509, at Villenueva in Spain. He studied medicine and the civil law at the University of Toulouse in France, in the former of which he attained to great eminence, and is said to have anticipated the celebrated Harvey in the important discovery of the circulation of the blood. But theology seems to have been his favourite study ; he thought the church wanted to be reformed ; he therefore commenced, and with some degree of self-confidence, the work of reformation. So early as the year 1531 he published his first work on the " Errors of the Trinity;" and in the following year his " Dialogues concerning the Trinity." But it was not before the year 1553 that he published his large work, under the name of Villanovanus, on the " Restitution of Christianity." It contained the following subjects :—1. Of the divine Trinity, that there is not an illusion of three invisible beings in it ; but the real manifestation of the substance of God, and communication of his spirit.—2. Of the faith of Christ, and the righteousness of his kingdom excelling that of the law ; and of charity.—3. Of regeneration from above, and the reign of antichrist.—4. Thirty epistles to John Calvin, preacher at Geneva.—5. Sixty signs of the reign of antichrist, and his discovery just now at hand.—6. Of the mystery of the Trinity. Calvin had a copy of this book sent to him, and was informed that Servetus was the author, who at that time was residing at Vienne. Shortly after he was cast into prison. On the 5th and 6th of April he was examined by the inquisitor-general, the vicar, and the vice-bailiff. On the 7th he got up at four o'clock in the morning, and asked the key of the prison garden from the jailer, who was going to work in the vineyard ; the latter observing that he had on his nightcap and nightgown, did not suspect that he was dressed, and so gave him the key, and went out shortly after with his workmen. When Servetus thought they were at a proper distance, he left his cap of black velvet and his fur nightgown at the foot of a tree, jumped from the terrace to a hog-sty that was against the wall, and thence to the ground without hurting himself in the least. He then quickly passed through the gate of the bridge of the Rhone, which was not very far from the prison, and so made his escape. On June 17, sentence of death was pronounced against him, and he was burned in effigy by the common hangman, together with five bales of his books. A few weeks after this he came to Geneva. " Perhaps," says Calvin in a letter to Farel, " he meant to pass this way ; for his intention of coming is not known." The annotators on Spon say, that after his arrival in Geneva, " he kept himself concealed for a month, waiting for a convenient opportunity of departing." It appears, however, that on the day he was discovered, he was imprisoned ; and on the following day, August 14, he was brought to the bar to answer to the several charges brought against him. The trial was procrastinated, and on the 22d of August, Servetus, fearing what was likely to be the result, addressed a petition to the magistrates, stating that it was " a practice unknown to the apostles of Christ and to the ancient churches, to institute criminal proceedings against persons for their religious opinions ; that he had published nothing at Geneva or within its dependencies which could give offence ; that while in Germany he had never spoke of these questions but to Œcolampadius, Bucer, and Capito ; that in France he had not mentioned them to any one ; that his writings were not addressed to the people, but to the learned (being in the Latin tongue) ; and that he had nowhere shown himself seditious or a disturber of the peace ; that as he was a stranger, and did not know the customs of the country, he begged to have counsel assigned him to conduct his cause." To the prayer of this petition the following answer was returned :—" That those who broached such impieties as he had done, were not worthy to have an advocate allowed them."

The magistrates requested Calvin to extract the objectionable passages from Servetus's book ; he reduced the whole to thirty-eight propositions, which were declared to be " full of impious blasphemies against God, and of other mad and profane errors, altogether repugnant to the Word of God, and the orthodox agreement of the Genevese Church." These were all answered by Servetus. They were then transmitted to the Helvetic Churches for their judgment as to the heretical character of the opinions contained in the propositions. On the 31st of August, the Syndics and the Council of Geneva received a letter from the Vice-bailiff of Vienne, and the King's Procurator of the same city, thanking them that Servetus had been arrested and imprisoned at Geneva ; and entreating them to remit the prisoner, that the sentence pronounced against him, of being burned alive in a slow fire, be executed. This letter was brought by the captain of the King's palace at Vienne, and Servetus was then asked if he would rather stay at Geneva in the hands of the magistrates, or return to Vienne with the person who was come to demand him. Servetus, in a flood of tears, said that he would rather be judged by the magistrates, and that they might do with him whatever they pleased. The annotators of Spon affirm, that in his examinations " he disowned some of the most atrocious dogmas imputed to him." During the trial, Perrin and others urged that the case should be referred to the Council of Two Hundred, which had the power of suspending or altering the penal laws. This attempt, however, was in vain, and the following sentence was pronounced :—" You, Michael Servetus, are condemned to be bound, and led to Champel (a small eminence a very short distance from the city), and there fastened to a stake and burned alive, with your book written with your hand and printed, until your body shall be reduced to ashes, and your days thus finished as an example to others who might commit the same things; and we command you, our lieutenant, to put this our sentence into execution. Read by the Seigneur Syndic D'Arlord." He was accordingly burned alive, October 27, 1553. On the preceding day, Calvin wrote thus to Farel, at Neuchatel:—" The messenger is returned from Switzerland. The cantons unanimously declare that Servetus has revived the impious errors with which Satan formerly disturbed the Church, and that he is an intolerable monster. Those of Basle are right; those of Zuric are the most vehement, for they express the heinousness of his impiety in very emphatical words, and exhort our magistrates to use him severely. Those of Schaffhausen subscribe to their judgment. The letter of the divines of Berne, which is also to the purpose, is attended with that of the Senate, whereby our magistrates have been very much animated. Cæsar (Perrin), a comical man, pretended to be sick three days, but came to court at last to acquit that profligate fellow; for he was not ashamed to propose that the cause should be removed to the Council of Two Hundred. Nevertheless, he has been condemned without any dispute;—he will be executed to-morrow. We have endeavoured to commute that sort of death; but it was in vain. I will tell you when I see you why the judges have not granted our request."

Calvin informs us that Servetus, two hours before his execution, sent for him, and " begged his pardon." Calvin told him that he had never thought of revenging himself on him for any personal injuries, and exhorted him to ask forgiveness of God; but finding that what he said was unavailing, he, " according to St Paul's command, went away from the heretic, who was condemned by his own conscience." Farel, it seems, had unexpectedly arrived in the city before the execution took place;

for Calvin remarks, " when Servetus arrived at the place
of punishment, the request was with difficulty extorted
from him by the exhortations of our excellent brother
and fellow-labourer, Farel, that the people would unite
with him in prayer. Farel exhorted the people to supplicate for him, particularly that the Lord, taking compassion of the otherwise lost man, would reclaim him
from his execrable errors to a right mind." But Servetus, it seems, in the speech which he delivered, " avowed
his adherence to his former sentiments."

In reviewing the whole of this unfortunate case, the
reader will no doubt be anxious to know what were the
real sentiments of Servetus, as contained in his book on
the " Restitution of Christianity," for publishing of which
he suffered death. So far as I am capable of judging, it
certainly contains many very gross errors. He ought
not to have set himself up for a theologian. His opinion
respecting the sacred Trinity, as given in many parts of
the work, is, without doubt, exceedingly confused, and
even heretical ; and yet he does not hesitate to speak in
the following terms :—" The Father is God, the Son is
God, the Holy Spirit is God. The Father is not the Son,
neither is the Son the Holy Spirit, nor is the Holy Spirit
the Father, according to propriety of person. In the
Son we see the Father, and in the Holy Spirit within us
we see the Son. The Son really differs from the Father, and the Holy Spirit from the Son, but not essen-
tially, because the essence of Deity is one and the
same."—*Christian Restitution,* 274.*

* The Rev. John Scott, in his history of Calvin, has the following
note :—" Mr R. Watson, in his popular life of Mr Wesley, has reprinted a passage from Mr W.'s journals, in which he asserts, from
an apparently very hasty examination of Calvin's account of the case
of Michael Servetus, when he happened to be in the Bodleian
Library, that Servetus often declared in terms, ' I believe the
Father is God, the Son is God, and the Holy Ghost is God '—
leading us to infer that the charges of heresy brought against him

As to the conduct of the *magistrates*, it certainly deserves censure. They had no right, in the first place, to imprison Servetus, who was not a subject of the republic, and who had not been detected in doing any thing contrary to the law. What he had done in another country did not belong to them, and they could not retain a stranger who was passing through their city, and who, while he remained in it, was peaceable, without manifest injustice. Their refusing to grant him counsel to conduct his cause was neither just nor equitable. Their giving information to the judges of Vienne, that they had made him prisoner, displayed no disposition to show any mercy; while their proposing to him to choose whether he would stay at Geneva, or be delivered into the hands of those who had already passed sentence of death upon him, looks something like cruelty. To ask a man if he preferred to go and be burned alive in a slow fire! This was certainly enough to induce him to submit to a jurisdiction that had no right over him;

were Calvin's calumnies. I can only say that I have again examined Calvin's account, for the express purpose of discovering any such declaration, but without finding any thing like it! I must believe, till the contrary is shown, that here, as in other instances, Mr Wesley has been misled by glances far too hasty to warrant the assertions he has founded upon them." Having carefully examined Calvin's work to which the reference is made, I find that Mr Scott is correct in saying that it contains no such passage as the one mentioned. Indeed, it is not likely that Calvin in publishing the " errors" of Servetus would give a sentiment so truly orthodox. The probability then is, that Mr Wesley did not see the declaration in Calvin's " account of the errors of Servetus," but in the work of Servetus from which the above extract is taken, and for which he was put to death. It may also be remarked that Mr Watson introduces the matter, not for the purpose of calumniating Calvin, but simply gives it as a specimen, with several others, of Mr Wesley's laconic notices of books. What the " other instances " are, in which Mr Wesley has been led to make unwarrantable assertions, I am unable to judge.

LIFE OF CALVIN 43

and this was probably what they intended, in order to *legitimate* their proceedings which in its principle was unjust. But the judges of Servetus have been generally forgotten or overlooked, while for nearly three centuries the heaviest reproach has fallen upon *Calvin.* What part then did our Reformer really take in this matter? The assertion that he had nourished through life an implacable hatred to Servetus is certainly contradicted by his long and somewhat friendly correspondence, in which he labours to reclaim him from his errors. Nor is there sufficient evidence that Calvin abused the confidence of Servetus by putting his private letters into the hands of the magistrates of Vienne, and by instigating them to proceed against him. Calvin denies it thus : " A report flies about that I had endeavoured to get Servetus apprehended at Vienne, upon which a great many say that I have not behaved discreetly, in exposing him to the mortal enemies of the faith, as if I had thrown him into the jaws of wolves. But whence this sudden and powerful intimacy with the satellites of the Pope ? It is very credible, indeed, that we should correspond together by letters, and that those who agree with me as well as Belial agrees with Jesus Christ, should enter into a plot with such a mortal enemy as with their own companion." It is, however, true, that the judges of Vienne did obtain Servetus's letters to Calvin, through the medium of William Trie, a citizen of Lyons, then a resident at Geneva, who by his importunity obtained twenty of them from our Reformer, and forwarded them during the trial to a friend of his at Vienne, though for what purpose it is not stated. And that Calvin enticed Servetus to come to Geneva is not correct, for he certainly all along dreaded his arrival. Nor can I allow that he was active in urging forward the condemnation and execution of Servetus after his case had been committed to the public prosecution. " By a recantation," says Calvin, " he might have averted his punishment : I would have it attested that my hostility was not so deadly, but that by humility alone, had he not been deprived of his senses, he might have saved his life; but I know not how to account for his conduct without supposing him to have been seized with a fatal insanity, and to have plunged himself headlong into ruin."

On the other hand, it is undeniable, that shortly after the arrival of Servetus in Geneva, he was informed against by Calvin and committed to prison, who was certainly under no necessity of doing this, for Servetus had not propagated his opinions in that city, nor did he intend to continue there.

The next steps necessary to his prosecution were taken by Nicholas de la Fontaine, Calvin's secretary; but it was by Calvin's direction. This he explicitly acknowledges. " I do not want to deny," says he, " but that it was upon my accusation that he was made prisoner. For as by the laws of the city it is necessary that some person should state himself a party to have the cause opened, I confess that the person who demanded justice against him, did it by my advice. Let malicious and ill-spoken people throw out as much jargon as they please; I declare frankly, that since, according to the law and custom of the city, none can be imprisoned for any crime, without an accuser, or prior information; in order to bring this man to reason, I have made it so, that a party should be found to accuse him, not denying but the action laid against him was drawn up by my advice, in order to commence the process."

He states that after Servetus was convicted of heresy, he did not in the least insist that he should be punished with severity. But he could not be ignorant that the laws which punished heretics with death were in force in Geneva; that the action raised against Servetus in Fontaine's name, was a criminal cause, which clearly shows that those who raised it knew very well, that if he was convicted he would be punished with death. It was

the conviction that they wanted his life, that led Servetus to object to the penal laws, and to request that the
case might be referred to the Council of Two Hundred,
who had the power to suspend or abolish them ; yet Calvin opposed him therein.

But in a letter so early as February, 1546, Calvin declared, that " if Servetus come to Geneva, I will use my
authority in such a manner, as not to suffer him to go
away alive."   On August 20, 1553, shortly after the
trial had commenced, he wrote to Farel thus : " I hope
that a capital sentence will be passed."   To the ministers
at Francfort, he says, " Servetus is detained in prison by
our magistrates, and will, as I hope, speedily suffer punishment."   And in a letter to Sultzer, September 9, he
writes—" I avow that I thought it my duty, as far as in
me lay, to restrain a man who is more than obstinate, and
untameable, in order that the contagion might spread no
farther. We see how violently impiety every where stalks
abroad, whence new errors spring up, and how great is
the remissness of those to whom God has confided the
power of the sword in vindicating the honour of his
name.   While the Papists are so alert and fierce in sup-
porting their superstitions that they riot in innocent
blood, Christian magistrates might be ashamed to show
themselves destitute of all spirit in defending the sure
truth of God's word.   I confess, indeed, that nothing
could be more inconsistent than for us to imitate their
intemperate fury ; but some bounds are to be observed
in our moderation, that the impious may not be allowed
to vomit forth their blasphemies with impunity, where
the power of restraining them exists.   I will only mention one thing farther to you, that the treasurer of our
city, who will bring you this letter, is right minded in
this business, that Servetus may not escape the issue
*which we desire."   It is remarkable that in this very let-
ter he informs his friend, that " the last Sabbath three
pious brethren were burned at Lyons, and a fourth sent

to a neighbouring town to undergo the same punishment. It is scarcely credible with what a perfect understanding of the Gospel those persons, though illiterate men, had been enlightened by the Spirit of God, and with what invincible constancy they were endowed."

The above, I trust, will be found a faithful statement of Calvin's conduct in this unhappy affair. I am conscious that I have not set down " aught in malice " against him, or designedly in any instance misrepresented the case. Still, however, justice will not be done to him unless the circumstances in which he was placed be kept specially in view. His errors were not so much those of the man as of the age; nor is it fair to trace them to his peculiar system of doctrine. It was certainly his deliberate conviction that the corrupters of divine truth deserved the severest punishment; but however censurable and anti-scriptural such an opinion undoubtedly is, it was then entertained by all parties. Bullinger, Farel, Viret, Peter Martyr, Beza, and even Melancthon, all approved of the sentence passed on the unfortunate physician. But it is hoped that no Protestant of the nineteenth century would for one moment attempt to justify it. If Papists, therefore, take occasion from the case of Servetus bitterly to reproach Calvin, and to condemn the principles of the Reformation, they do it without reason. They should remember that this said Servetus was first imprisoned and condemned to be burned alive in a Popish country, and that had he not escaped to Geneva, but been executed in Vienne, he would only have made one of the tens of thousands of victims which have been slain by the cruelty of Popery. The author of the " Memoirs of Literature," justly says, " If the religion of Protestants depended on the doctrine and conduct of the reformers, he should take care how he published the account of Servetus; but as the Protestant religion is entirely founded on the Holy Scripture, so the defaults of the reformers ought not to have any ill influence on the Reformation. The doctrine of non-toleration, which obtained in the sixteenth century among some Protestants, was that pernicious error which they had imbibed in the Church of Rome, and I believe I can say, without doing any injury to that church, that she is in a great measure answerable for the execution of Servetus. If the Roman Catholics had never put any person to death for the sake of religion, I dare say that Servetus had never been condemned to die in any Protestant city. Let us remember, that Calvin and all the magistrates of Geneva, in the year 1553, were born and bred up in the Church of Rome; this is the best apology that can be made for them." And should the Socinians, who are so ready to boast of their liberality, oppugn the orthodox faith because Servetus was executed by its professors, we refer them to the case of Francis David, superintendent of the Socinian churches in Transylvannia, who was persecuted by Faustus Socinus, and died in prison in consequence of his opinion, that Christ, *if* a mere man, was not a proper object of prayer.

In concluding our remarks on this part of Calvin's history, we may express the hope that it will afford some useful lessons to those who, after struggling for the rights of conscience, have, when possessed of power themselves infringed those very rights, and, with equal inconsistency and injustice, have persecuted such as claimed the privilege of private judgment. We regret that our reformer, on any occasion, appeared in the character of a political ruler; but in the sixteenth century, the province of ecclesiastical jurisdiction was not sufficiently marked out, and separated from that of the civil. It was not yet discovered, that " consciences and souls were made, to be the Lord's alone;" and that the intellect can only be affected by argument and evidence. It was left for John Goodwin and other master-spirits of the seventeenth century, openly to advocate the doctrine of religious liberty, and to establish it on Scriptural and rational principles—showing that all descriptions of persons who conduct themselves in a peaceable manner are entitled to the full protection of the civil power, whatever may be the peculiarities of their creed.

At the very time that proceedings were going on against Servetus, Calvin was severely tried from another quarter. Philibert Bertelier, a citizen of Geneva, and registrar of one of the courts, had, on account of his immoral conduct, been forbidden by the consistory the Lord's table. Encouraged by Perrin and others, he petitioned the Senate for an absolution. Calvin boldly protested against its interference in the matter; as, however, there was a general cry that the presbytery had usurped the power of the magistrates, "those twice-sworn men," says our judicious Hooker, "adventured to give their last and hottest assault to the fortress of the same discipline, childishly granting, by common consent of their whole senate, and that under their own seal, a relaxation to Bertelier, whom the eldership had excommunicated: further also decreeing, with strange absurdity, that to the same senate it should belong to give final judgment in matters of excommunication, and to absolve whom it pleased them." This was regarded as a complete triumph by those who were opposed to Calvin. They thought if he resisted he would bring down upon himself the displeasure of the senate ; and that if he yielded, the discipline of the church would be at an end. But Calvin was not to be intimidated. In a sermon before the sacrament, having uttered with uplifted hands and in a solemn tone, many heavy denunciations against those who despised the sacred mysteries, " I will rather," said he, " after the example of Chrysostom, suffer myself to be slain at the table than allow this hand to give the holy things to those who are lawfully condemned as despisers of God." These words had such an effect that Perrin immediately gave secret orders to Bertelier that he must not present himself at the table, and the ordinance was celebrated in the most solemn and edifying manner. In the afternoon of the same day, while explaining Paul's address to the elders of Ephesus, Calvin, after protesting that he was not the man who resisted magistrates or taught others to do so, and exhorting the people to persevere in the doctrine they had heard, concluded by saying, " since affairs are in such a state, permit me, brethren, to say with the Apostle, ' *I commend you to God, and to the word of his grace.*' " These words struck his enemies dumb ; while the pious were confirmed, and admonished of their duty. The next day, Calvin, together with all the members of the presbytery, demanded of the Senate and Council of Two Hundred, that as the code of ecclesiastical laws had been established by the people, they should not be abrogated or altered by any other authority ; it was therefore determined that the decree of the council should be suspended, the four reformed states of Switzerland consulted, and that no alteration, in the mean time, should be made in the existing laws. Calvin immediately wrote to the principal ministers in each place, begging for a favourable reply. The four churches, though they had not established such discipline among themselves, returned the answer : " That they had heard already of those consistorial laws, and did acknowledge them to be godly ordinances, drawing towards the prescript of the word of God ; for which cause they did not think it good for the church of Geneva, by innovation, to change the same, but rather to keep them as they were." The ecclesiastical polity was then confirmed by the common suffrages of the people, to the great mortification of the disaffected party.

About this time Farel, who had been unexpectedly restored from a dangerous illness, came from Neuchatel on a visit to Calvin. While in Geneva, relying on his age, character, and former acquaintance, he, in a sermon, reproved the factious with great keenness. This gave great offence, and after his return home was made a matter of accusation against him. He was cited to Geneva to answer the charge. This he did, but not without considerable danger, for the factious were so incensed against him that they threatened to throw him into the Rhone. As soon as the senate had notice that he was arrived, they let Calvin know that Farel should not be suffered to ascend the pulpit. " I shall proceed no farther," said Calvin ; " let it suffice to give you a taste of their ingratitude, which will raise a just aversion in all men of honour and probity. But because I havemany reasons which hinder me from publicly deploring our calamity, take it briefly thus : unless Satan be chained up by you, he must be let loose." A courageous young man warned Perrin not to allow the venerable minister to be injured ; others joined him, until the seditious were abashed, and Farel obtained an audience and an honourable acquittal. Calvin said of him, " The people owe their ownselves to him. He is to be regarded as the father of their liberties, and the father of this church."

In 1554, he published his book, entitled, " A faithful exposition of the errors of Michael Servetus, and a short refutation of the same ; in which is shown, that heretics ought to be punished with fire and sword." This was answered by Castellio, and vindicated by Beza. He also wrote against Westphal and Heshusius, on the subject of the Sacraments.

The following year, the factious in the city entered into a conspiracy to massacre the refugees, particularly those of the French nation, who, they thought, were appointed to offices, while they themselves were overlooked. A disclosure was made by certain drunkards concerned in it. Some of them suffered capital punishment, and others fled the country. Perrin, Vandal, and Bertelier, were, in their absence, sentenced to lose their heads. Persecution now violently raged in France, while in England, where the government had passed from the mild and pious Edward VI., to the rigorous Mary, the storm drove to heaven, along with innumerable others, those three bishops and martyrs of unrivalled piety, Hooper, Ridley, and Latimer, and at length the great Cranmer. In a letter which Calvin wrote, Jan. 18, 1555, to the English who had fled to Francfort, and written to him for advice, he says, " For my part, as in things indifferent, such as external rites are, I am very easy and accommodating, so I do not hold it useful always to yield to the foolish obstinacy of those who will give up nothing to which they have been accustomed. In the English liturgy, as you describe it, I perceive there have been many tolerable follies, by which words I mean that there has not been that purity in it which was to be desired. As, however, they involved no manifest impiety, and could not be immediately corrected, they might be borne for a time. Proceeding, therefore, from such rudiments, it was fit that grave, and upright, and learned ministers of Christ should press forward, and aspire at somewhat more pure and perfect. If true religion had continued to flourish in England, something might have been improved, and many things withdrawn. But now, when the foundations have there been overthrown, and you had to institute for yourselves a church elsewhere, and were at liberty to adopt a form, such as seemed best adapted to the benefit and edification of the church, I know not what they mean who so much delight themselves with the remains of the Popish dregs. They love what they are accustomed to ; but this is childish and trifling ; and it is to be considered that forming a new institution differs from changing an old one. As I would have you, if the infirmity of some cannot rise to the highest degree of improvement, to avoid excessive rigidity, so I would admonish others not to be too well pleased with their own want of proficiency, and not to obstruct the progress of the church by their obstinacy. Nor let a foolish rivalry hurry them away ; for what cause have they for contention, but a shame of yielding to their betters? But they will probably give no heed to counsel proceeding from me."

On Wednesday, March 20, this year, he commenced a course of Lectures on Deuteronomy, which he finished on Wednesday, July 15, 1556. They are two hundred in number, delivered on the Monday, Tuesday, and Wednesday of each week.

Calvin carried on at this time an extensive correspondence with several respectable individuals in Poland, for the purpose of promoting the establishment of the churches in that country.

The errors of Servetus were now, however, revived by several members of the Italian church at Geneva. John Paul Alciati, a military officer from Milan, George Blandrata, a physician from Piedmont, Matthew Gribaldo, a lawyer, who resided at Fargias, and Valentine Gentilis, were the most active in diffusing the pernicious tenets. An extraordinary assembly was convened, at which, in presence of a certain number of senators chosen for the occasion, and of all the ministers and elders, the reasons adduced in support of their doctrines were refuted by Calvin. Many of the heretical were therefore banished from Switzerland, and thence went into Moravia, Poland, and Transylvania. Gentilis, in 1667, proposed a public disputation with the orthodox on the following terms:—" That the party who could not prove their doctrines from the Word of God should be put to death as impostors." He was seized, and, on conviction, was beheaded at Berne, for having obstinately, and contrary to his oath, which he took in 1558, impugned the doctrine of the sacred Trinity.

Bolsec and Castellio revived this year also the predestinarian controversy, and being supported by some ministers in the neighbourhood, they brought a charge against Calvin of having made God the author of sin. He, therefore, accompanied with envoys from Geneva, repaired to Berne, to defend his doctrine, where he ac-

quitted himself in such a manner as led to the banishment of both his opponents. Shortly after his return
from Berne, he was attacked with a tertian fever, which
seized him while preaching, and obliged him to leave the
pulpit. A report of his death was now spread, which was
so acceptable to the Papists, that those at Noyon made
a solemn procession, and the canons of the cathedral
returned public thanks. In the month of August Calvin
was able to take a journey to Francfort, for the purpose
of terminating some disturbances which had arisen in
the French church there. On his return to Geneva,
though much indisposed, he so diligently prosecuted his
studies, as to publish in the following year his Commentary on the Psalms. He also succeeded in urging the
German Princes to intercede with the King of France,
which tended greatly to allay the storm of persecution
in that country ; while a perpetual alliance was now
contracted between Geneva and Berne, which was considered advantageous to the reformed religion.

In 1558, our author was seized with a quartan ague,
which gave a great shock to his constitution, already
worn out with incessant labour and study, and from
which he did not recover for eight months. During this
period he continued to dictate and write numberless letters, to revise and republish his Institutes, and correct
his commentary on Isaiah ; which, in the beginning of
1559, he dedicated "to the most high and renowned Prin-
cess Elizabeth, Queen of England, a most gracious defender of the true Christian faith." After speaking of
the persecution that had recently prevailed, and of the
banishment of the first edition of this work from England, he proceeds : " Although, I confess, my meaning
is not so much to obtain your favour, only in respect of
my labours, as humbly to beseech, yea, and by the sacred
name of Christ, to adjure you, that not only all good books
may find entertainment, and be freely used in your kingdom under your allowance : but also that you be careful,

in the first place, of that true religion which has been so shamefully corrupted. If Jesus Christ, the only Son of God, doth justly challenge this, of all the kings of the earth, then hath he bound you, most noble queen, with a more holy band to put your hand to such a work. For, in that time, wherein yourself, the daughter of a king, was not free from that dreadful tempest rushing down so furiously upon the heads of all the faithful; (this Lord Jesus, I say) plucking you safe thereout, albeit you had your part with them in the fear of this danger ; he hath obliged you to bow yourself and all your designs to his service. Moreover, your duty to religion, most excellent Queen, should the rather provoke you ; seeing our Isaiah requires, that queens should be no less nursing mothers to his Church, than kings nursing fathers thereof. Neither are you only bound to purge out the filth of Popery again, and that the flock, lately affrighted and dispersed, be again gathered together and fostered ; but that you also call home the banished exiles, who chose rather to lose the present profits of their native country, than there to continue, whilst piety was chased thence. The Lord guide and govern you, most noble Queen, by his spirit of wisdom ; strengthen you with invincible fortitude ; defend and enrich your Highness with all sorts of blessings. From Geneva, January 15, 1559, which, as they say, is appointed for the day of your coronation ; for which cause I did the more willingly set pen to paper, having obtained some release from a quartan ague."

The same month, he wrote to Cecil, Elizabeth's Minister, urging him to zeal and decision in promoting the reformed faith. It was at this time that the celebrated Scottish Reformer, John Knox, took his final departure from Geneva. He had resided there for two or three years, and formed an intimate acquaintance with Calvin. " They were nearly," says M'Crie, " of the same age, and there was a striking similarity in their sentiments, and in the principal parts of their character. The Genevan reformer was highly pleased with the piety and talents of Knox, who, in his turn, entertained a greater esteem for Calvin than for any of the other reformers." The freedom of the city was conferred on Knox when he quitted it to return to his own country,—though it is remarkable that Calvin was not so honoured till the close of the same year. Shortly after his return to Scotland, Knox, in a letter to Calvin, proposed the following questions ;—1. Whether the children of excommunicated persons and idolaters (Papists) ought to be admitted to baptism, before their parents professed repentance, and were thus reconciled unto the church. 2. Whether monks and mass-priests, who, though they now acknowledged their errors, neither served nor were capable of serving the church, should be allowed a maintenance from the funds which had been set apart for religious purposes. To the first of these questions, Calvin, in his reply, said, "The promise extended not only to the children of believers in the first generation, but to a *thousand generations*. Hence that interruption of true religion which had prevailed under the Papacy did not take away the power and efficacy of baptism. We ought not to doubt that the descendants of pious ancestors, though their immediate fathers and grandfathers were apostates, yet belonged to the body of the church. The practice of the Papists, indeed, in stealing the children of Jews and Turks, in order to baptize them, was a depraved and insane superstition : yet, wherever the profession had not utterly failed and become extinct, infants were deprived of their just privileges if they were excluded from the common symbol, for it was unjust, when God had honoured them with his adoption three hundred years or more before, that the subsequent want of piety in their parents should cut off the current of the Divine favour. Further, as no one is received to baptism merely from respect or favour to his immediate parent alone, but on account of God's uninterrupted covenant, so no reason

would suffer that, for the displeasure borne to one parent, children should be precluded entrance into the
church. Proper sponsors, however, are necessary : for
nothing could be more absurd than to insert into the
body of Christ those who we do not hope will be his disciples. If no relation, therefore appears, who will en-
gage to the church, and undertake the instruction of the
infant, the proceeding is a mockery, and the sacrament
is profaned." As to the monks and priests, though he
contends that they had no claim upon the church for
support, as they rendered her no service, yet he observes,
" it would be hard that they who had devoted themselves to that kind of life, under the influence of ignorance and error, should be deprived of support: and, as
at their death the church would recover the funds which
had been set apart for her service, the present annual
emolument should not be made the subject of contention."

Calvin, in the year 1556, had proposed the establishment of a college at Geneva, for the instruction of youth;
but the danger to which the republic was exposed, especially from Henry II. of France, who was bent upon the
restoration of the Duke of Savoy, prevented the council
from attending to the object before 1559, when the
wishes of our reformer were accomplished. " The se-
minary was dedicated in a solemn manner, before a full
assembly of the people, in the first church of the city to
the most high and holy God, where the laws which related to the object of this most useful and pious institution, and its perpetual confirmation, were for the first
time read and published." There were eight masters
and several professors of Hebrew, and Greek, philosophy
and divinity. Beza was appointed rector, while Calvin
contented himself with the office of professor of theology.
Mosheim says, that " Calvin laid a scheme for sending forth from this little republic the succours and ministers that were to promote and propagate the Protestant
cause through the most distant nations, and aimed at

nothing less than rendering the government, discipline, and doctrine of Geneva, the model and rule of imitation to the reformed churches throughout the world. The undertaking was certainly great, and worthy of the extensive genius and capacity of this eminent man ; and great and arduous as it was, it was executed in part, nay, carried to a very considerable length, by his indefatigable assiduity and inextinguishable zeal." And Butler, in his life of Grotius, remarks, that Calvin, "having prevailed with the senate of Geneva to found an academy, and place it under his superintendence ; and having filled it with men eminent throughout Europe for their learning and talent, it became the favourite resort of all persons who leaned to the new principles and sought religious and literary instruction. From Germany, France, Italy, England, and Scotland, numbers crowded to the new academy, and returned from it to their native countries saturated with the doctrine of Geneva, and burning with zeal to propagate its creed."

It was in the month of May this year, when a siege of the city was apprehended, that Calvin, with the professors and the pastors, undertook to complete one of the bastions of the place. Montesquieu remarks, that " the Genevese ought to bless the moment of the birth of Calvin, and that of his arrival within the walls of Geneva."

Francis Stancari, in the year 1560, propagated the opinion that Christ was our mediator only in his human nature, and accused those of Arianism who contended that Christ was mediator in his divine nature, as if they thereby made the Son inferior to the Father. Calvin refuted the error, but saw at the same time that some writers on his side of the question were in danger, through their inexperience, of running into the opposite error of Tritheism ; he, therefore, wisely cautioned them to guard against " so asserting the mediation of Christ in the divine, as well as human nature, as to *multiply the*

Deity." To two Christian brethren, deputed by the Waldenses of Bohemia, to consult with him on certain points of doctrine and discipline, Calvin, about this time gave important advice, and exhorted them to enter into a close union with the other reformed churches. This year, also, Nicholas Gallar was sent from Geneva to London, to take charge of the French refugees, who in that city had formed themselves into a presbyterian church, with the permission of her Serene Highness Queen Elizabeth.

Shortly after the death of Francis II. King of France, which took place at the conclusion of this year, the new king, Charles IX., sent letters to Geneva, complaining that persons from that city were exciting disturbances in his kingdom. Calvin was summoned with his colleagues before the Senate, and was requested to reply to the complaints. This he did in such a manner that the business proceeded no farther.

In 1561 he published his Sermons on Daniel; wrote short answers to Baldwin, Saconay, Gentilis, Blandrata, and Heshusius; and drew up, for the French Protestants, a Confession of Faith, which was presented by Beza to Charles IX. at the celebrated conference between the Papists and Protestants held at Poissy. The following year he prepared a short Formula to vindicate the French Protestants against the calumnies spread against them in Germany. It was presented to the Diet at Francfort. December 19, Calvin being confined to his bed with the gout, and the north wind being unusually high, he said to some friends present—" I know not indeed what it means; but I have thought during the night that I heard a very loud sound of drums used in war, and I cannot divest myself of the opinion that it was a reality. I entreat you, therefore, let us pray, for some event of very great moment is undoubtedly taking place." This was considered remarkable when the news arrived during the week, that on that day the battle of Dreux was fought between the King's army, and that of the Prince of Condé.

He published his Commentaries on four of the Books of Moses, in the form of a Harmony, in 1563 ; and commenced his Commentary on Joshua, which he finished only a short time before his death. He also left his Annotations on Ezekiel, in an unfinished state. They were published by Beza in 1565, who modestly observed, that " he knew not when any one would arise who might be worthy to finish a picture begun by Apelles."

On the 6th of February, 1564, he delivered his last sermon, but with considerable difficulty, in consequence of asthmatic oppression. His diseases were various and complicated, as he states in a letter to his physician at Montpelier. He was naturally, says Beza, of a spare and feeble frame, tending to consumption ; during ten years, the only food he took was in the evening. His sleep was very unsound, and to a headache he was very subject, the only remedy for which was fasting ; so that he has often refrained from food for thirty-six hours together. Five years before his death he was attacked with a spitting of blood, and successively with the asthma, gout, cholic, an hemorrhoidal affection, and the stone. But though he was tormented with so many violent diseases, he uttered no unbecoming expressions. In his greatest agonies, he would lift up his eyes to Heaven, and say,—" How long, O Lord ? " a phrase which he had constantly used in health, when hearing of the calamities of his brethren. Sometimes he would repeat the words of David,—" I held my peace, because thou didst it ; " or, those of Isaiah, —" I did mourn as a dove." And on another occasion he said,—" Thou bruisest me, O Lord ! but it amply sufficeth me that it is thy hand." His friends entreated him to forbear dictating and writing during his sickness, but he replied,—" What ! would you have my Lord find me idle when he cometh."

On the 10th March, Beza and the other ministers

visiting him, found him sitting at the little table at which he was accustomed to study. For some time he was silent, resting his forehead on his hand, as he frequently did, while in study, and then, with a voice occasionally interrupted, but with a kind and cheerful countenance, he said, " I return you, dearest brethren, my most hearty thanks for all your solicitude on my account, and hope in a fortnight I shall be present for the last time at your consistory, for I think the Lord will then manifest his pleasure with respect to me, and take me to himself." He did attend the consistory on the 24th of March, and when the business was finished, he observed that he thought some further continuance was granted him by the Lord.   He then took up a French Testament, read some of the annotations, and requested the opinion of his brethren concerning them.   This exertion, however, was too great, and he was worse on the following day ; but on the 27th, he was carried to the door of the Senate house, and being supported by two of his attendants, walked into the hall, and after proposing a new rector, he uncovered his head and returned them thanks for the favours conferred upon him, and especially for the kindness they had shown him in his last illness.   " For," said he, " I think I have entered this house for the last time."   These words he uttered with a faltering voice, and then took his last farewell of the Senate, overwhelmed with sorrow, and bathed in tears.   On the second of April, which was Easter day, he was carried to church in a chair, and received the Lord's Supper, which was administered by Beza, and with a trembling voice, but with joy shining in his countenance, joined in singing.   On the 25th, he sent for a notary and dictated his will, which he signed ; and the next day caused to be read to Beza, Raymond Chauvet, Michael Cops, Louis Enoch, Nicholas Colladon, James de Bordes, ministers of the gospel, and Henry Scringer, professor of arts ; and attested by them in his presence.   The following extract will be interesting to the reader,—" In the name of the Lord, Amen. I, John Calvin, minister of the word of God in the Church of Geneva, finding myself so much oppressed and afflicted with various diseases, that I think the Lord God has determined speedily to remove me out of this world, have ordered to be made and written, my testament and declaration of my last will, in form and manner following. First, I give thanks to God that taking compassion on me whom he had created, and placed in this world, he not only delivered me by his power out of the deep darkness of idolatry, into which I was plunged, that he might bring me into the light of his gospel, and make me a partaker of the doctrine of salvation, of which I was most unworthy; but with the same goodness and mercy he has graciously and kindly borne with my multiplied transgressions and sins, for which I deserved to be rejected and cut off by him; and has also exercised towards me such great compassion and clemency, that he has condescended to use my labour in preaching and publishing the truth of his gospel. I also testify and declare, that it is my full intention to pass the remainder of my life in the same faith and religion, which he has delivered to me by his gospel; having no other defence or refuge of salvation than his gratuitous adoption, on which alone my safety depends. I also embrace with my whole heart the mercy which he exercises towards me for the sake of Jesus Christ, atoning for my crimes by the merits of his death and passion, that in this way satisfaction may be made for all my transgressions and offences, and the remembrance of them blotted out. I farther testify and declare that, as a suppliant, I humbly implore of him to grant me to be so washed and purified by the blood of that Sovereign Redeemer, shed for the sins of the human race, that I may be permitted to stand before his tribunal in the image of the Redeemer himself. . . . Further, I will, after my departure out of this life, that my body be committed to the earth in that manner, and with those funeral rites, which are usual in this city and church, until the day of the blessed resurrection shall come. As for the same patrimony which God has bestowed upon me, and which I have determined to dispose of in this will, I appoint Anthony Calvin, my very dearly beloved brother my heir, but only as a mark of respect. Let him take charge of, and keep as his own, my silver goblet, which was given me as a present by Mr Varanne : and I desire he will be content with it. As for the residue of my property, I commit it to his care with this request, that he restore it to his children at his death. I bequeath also to the school for boys, ten golden crowns, and to poor strangers the same sum; furthermore, I wish my heir to give, on his death, to Samuel and John, sons of my said brother, my nephews, out of my estate, each forty crowns; and to my nieces Ann, Susan, and Dorothy, each thirty golden crowns. To my nephew David, as a proof of his light and trifling conduct, I bequeath only twenty-five golden crowns."

Having thus made his will, he sent to inform the four syndics, and all the senators, that he wished once more to address them in their hall, whither he hoped to be carried the following day. They, however, begged him to regard his health, and promised to attend him at his own house. They accordingly came, and he addressed them thus : —" I return you my warmest thanks, honoured lords, for conferring such great honours upon me, who had done nothing to merit them, and for manifesting such forbearance towards my numerous infirmities, which I always considered the strongest proof of your uncommon kindness. Though, in the discharge of my ministerial duty, I have been engaged in various disputes, and have endured numerous insults, a necessary part of the trials, even of the best characters, yet I know and acknowledge that none of these have befallen me from any fault of yours. I earnestly entreat you also, if I have not performed my duty in any instance as I ought, to ascribe it rather to want of ability, than to want of will to serve you. For I can testify with sincerity, that I have felt a deep and lively interest in the welfare of your republic ; and, if I have not fully discharged all the duties of my station, I have certainly exerted myself to the utmost in promoting the public welfare. I certainly grant, that I am very much indebted to you, on account of your patience in enduring that vehemence of mine, which has sometimes been immoderate. I trust God himself has pardoned all these, my sins. I admonish the aged not to envy such young persons as are endowed by God with particular gifts. I warn younger persons to conduct themselves with modesty, and to avoid all presumption. Let there be no interruption of one another in the performance of your duties. Shun animosities, and all that acrimony which has diverted so many from a proper line of conduct in the discharge of their office. You will avoid these evils if each of you confines himself within his proper sphere, and all perform with fidelity the part intrusted to them by the state. In civil trials, I beseech you to avoid all favour, or enmity ; use no crooked arts to pervert justice ; let none, by any plausible address of his own, prevent the laws from having their due effect, nor depart from equity and goodness. If the evil passions excite temptation in any one, let him resist them with firmness, and look to him by whom he has been placed on the seat of judgment, and ask the same God for the guidance of his holy Spirit. Finally, I beseech you to pardon all my infirmities, which I acknowledge and confess before God, and his Angels, and in your presence also, my honourable lords."

On the 28th, the ministers under the jurisdiction of Geneva, at his request, assembled in his chamber, and he addressed them in the following terms :—" Stand fast, my brethren, after my decease, in the work which you have begun, and be not discouraged, for the Lord will preserve this church and republic against the threats of its enemies. Let all divisions be removed far from you, and embrace one another with mutual charity. Consider on all occasions what you owe to the church in which the Lord hath stationed you, and let nothing draw you from it. It will, indeed, be easy for such as are wearied of their flocks to find means for escaping from their duty by intrigue, but they will learn by experience that the Lord cannot be deceived. On my first arrival in this city, the gospel was indeed preached, but every thing was in the greatest confusion, as if Christianity consisted in nothing else than the overturning of images. Not a few wicked men arose in the church, from whom I suffered many great indignities, but the Lord our God so strengthened me, and banished all fear even from me, who am by nature far from bold (I state the real fact), that I was enabled to resist all their attempts. I returned hither from Strasburg in obedience to a call, against my inclination, because I thought it would not be productive of any advantage. I knew not what the Lord had determined, and the situation was full of very great difficulties. But I perceived at length that the Lord had indeed blessed my labours. Do you, therefore, also persist in your vocation, preserve the established order, and see that the people be at the same time retained in obedience to the doctrine delivered to them, for there are yet among you some wicked and stubborn characters. Affairs, as you see, are not now in an unsettled state; you will therefore be the more guilty before God, if they are subverted in consequence of your inactivity. I declare, my brethren, that I have lived united with you in the bonds of true and sincere affection, and I take my leave of you with the same feelings. If, at any time, you have found me too harsh or peevish under my disease, I entreat your forgiveness, and I return you my warmest thanks, for having taken upon you the burden of my duties during my confinement." He, then, says Beza, reached out his right hand to each of us, and we took leave of him with hearts overwhelmed with sorrow, and eyes flowing with tears.

On having been informed by a letter from Farel, who was now seventy-five years of age, and very infirm, that he was determined to come and see him from Neuchatel, Calvin replied thus:—" Farewell, my best and most faithful brother; and since God is pleased you should survive me in this world, live mindful of our friendship, which has been of service to the church of God, and the fruits of which we shall enjoy in Heaven. Do not expose yourself to fatigue on my account. I respire with difficulty, and continually expect to draw my last breath. It is sufficient happiness to me that I live and die in Christ, who is gain to his people in life and death. Again, farewell with the brethren.—Geneva, May 2, 1564." The good old man, however, came, and after an interview with his afflicted friend, he returned the next day, to Neuchatel.

The remainder of his days, Calvin spent in almost constant prayer. His voice, indeed, was interrupted by the difficulty of respiration, but his eyes, which retained their brilliancy to the last, uplifted to Heaven, and the expression of his countenance, showed the fervour of his supplications. " His doors," Beza remarks, " must have stood open day and night, if all had been admitted, who, from sentiments of duty, were desirous to see him ; but as he could not speak to them, he requested they would rather pray for him, than be solicitous about visiting him. Often also, though I always found him glad to receive me, he was very scrupulous respecting the least interruptions thus given to the duties of my office, so sparing was he of the time which he thought ought to be spent in the service of the church." On the 19th of May the meeting of the ministers, previous to the celebration of the Lord's supper at Whitsuntide, was held, by his request, in Calvin's own house. He was carried from his bed to the adjoining room where they were to take supper, and then said to them—" I am come to see you, my brethren, for the last time, never more to sit with you at table." He then offered up a short prayer, took a small portion of food, and conversed, as his weakness permitted. Before supper was finished, he ordered himself to be carried back to his chamber, observing with a smiling countenance, on leaving the company, " This wall will not prevent my being with you in spirit." He never again left his bed. On May 27, the day of his death, he appeared stronger, and spoke with less difficulty ; but it was the last effort of nature. About eight o'clock in the evening the symptoms of dissolution were suddenly manifested. Beza, who had but just left him, was sent for, but on entering the house, he found he had expired, having lived fifty-four years, ten months, and seventeen days.

His death was no sooner known throughout the city than the greatest lamentation prevailed. A great number of individuals came to see his corpse, and among them, the English ambassador to the French court. At first, all who came were freely admitted ; but as the curiosity became excessive, and to prevent the calumnies of foes, the coffin was closed ; and on Sunday, the 29th of May, at two o'clock in the afternoon, he was taken to the common burying-place, called Plein-Palais, without any monument or inscription to distinguish the spot. His funeral, however, was attended by the members of the senate, the pastors, all the professors of the College, and a great many of the citizens, who, by the abundance of the tears which they shed, showed their deep sense of the great loss they had sustained. Beza wrote the following epitaph ;—

" Why in this humble and unnoticed tomb
Is Calvin laid—the dread of falling Rome ?
Mourned by the good, and by the wicked fear'd,
By all who knew his excellence, revered ;

From whom even Virtue's self might virtue learn,
And young and old its value may discern ?
'Twas modesty, his constant friend on earth,
That laid this stone, unsculptured with a name ;
Oh! happy turf, enriched with Calvin's worth,
More lasting far than marble is thy fame ! "

Alexander Morus, a popular preacher in the seventeenth century, in an address which he delivered as rector of the academy at Geneva, speaks of him in the following glowing language :—" I conjure you, my illustrious hearers, with all the ardour which I possess, and to the full extent which religion will permit, to venerate the name of the great Calvin; let him live in your remembrance ; let him inflame your hearts ; let him be revered in the senate ; let him be honoured in the church ; let your academy and your schools crown him daily with fresh praises and applauses ; let your citizens have his triumphs continually in their mouths ; let your youth respect him ; let his memory, victorious over calumny, be venerated by the whole earth ; let him descend from our children to their children's children, to the most remote posterity, that future ages may celebrate with immortal praises, the precious recollection of the greatest man whom Providence ever raised up to relieve the church of Geneva."

But we must now proceed to give a brief description of his person, and an analysis of his character. Beza, who for sixteen years was intimately acquainted with him, informs us, that his stature was of a middle size, his complexion dark and pallid, his eyes brilliant even till death. His dress was plain and neat, while in food his moderation was known unto all. The portrait is expressive of gravity, acuteness, and decision.— But his intellectual and moral endowments were not exhibited to advantage by his external appearance. To have a correct view of these we must look at his writings. His mind, perhaps, was not of the very first order; he had not much genius, and his imagination was neither powerful, sublime, nor beautiful. His element was not the lofty and the vast; his conceptions never rose into sublimity, nor expanded into grandeur. But, if in originality, elegance, loftiness, and comprehensiveness of mind, and in splendour of imagination, he was inferior to some of his contemporaries, and to many of the mighty men of the following age; in perspicuity of understanding, solidity of judgment, acuteness in reasoning, he has been surpassed but by few. The tendency of his mind was to the abstract and subtle in the department of reason, which enabled him to unravel with facility the tangled web of sophistry, and to construct from the confused materials, a system of his own. The freedom of his writings from the various errors of Popery in which he was educated, is truly astonishing. If asked, therefore, what we consider the peculiar individuality by which he was marked, we should unhesitatingly answer, a sound and discriminating judgment. In confirmation of this, we may observe, that in the numerous volumes which he sent into the world, he seldom or never contradicts in one part, what he had asserted in another. And, if we except what he has said on the doctrine of unconditional predestination, there is a remarkable exemption in his writings, from bold and unhallowed speculation. The times in which he lived, and the scenes in which he moved, must also be taken into the account. Theology was by no means of such easy acquirement then, as it might be at present. He and the other reformers had to grope their way; their lights were few and obscure; the intellectual eye had long been shut; divine truth was laid under a load of ceremonies and imposture; and the doctrines which are so clearly revealed in the Holy Scriptures were in those days almost unknown throughout Christendom.

The learned Joseph Scaliger mentioned among other

things, as a proof of Calvin's good sense, his not having ventured to write a Commentary on the Revelations.

His memory was quick and tenacious. It is said that he easily remembered persons he had seen but once, many years after ; that when he was dictating any matter, and happened to be interrupted for some hours, he renewed the thread of the discourse without having to be reminded where it was he left off; and, indeed, that he seldom forgot any thing that was entrusted to his memory.

Calvin possessed, in an eminent degree, those qualities which fit an individual for being the head of a party. In addition to a clear and penetrating judgment, which we have already noticed, he had a cautious hand and a commanding power, together with a firmness and inflexibility of purpose, which bound him to the cause he had espoused, with a devotedness which no opposition could overcome, and which no vicissitude could shake. It has been justly observed, that his faults primarily resulted from those very energies which gave him pre-eminence. Indomitable firmness imparts a certain sternness to the deportment, and not unfrequently degenerates into a spirit of persecution. Bayle says that our reformer, " was frighted at nothing."

He was naturally of an irritable temper, and this was no doubt increased, by his sedentary habits, and his numerous bodily maladies. His language is occasionally bitter, and he employs epithets, when speaking of his opponents, such as " knave, dog, Satan, liar, impostor, serpent-plague, hangman, buffoon," &c.—expressions which, though too common at that period, would not be tolerated in the present day. Mr Scott, when speaking of the temper of Calvin, says, " he is not (like Melancthon) one of those characters whose exquisite loveliness continually holds out a bribe to our better judgment, in deciding upon their tenets and their conduct. The sentiment he excites is rather that of veneration for a superior intelligence, than of affection for a captivating fellow mortal."

Many writers have represented him as a very great wit; I can only say, that I have not been able to discover this in any of his writings, and from the notices of him that have come down to us, I should conclude that this was not the case. His manners were grave and serious, yet, in the intercourse of social life, he is said to have shown great suavity. He exercised much forbearance towards all such infirmities in others, as are consistent with integrity; but towards flattery, and every species of insincerity, especially where religion was concerned, he was severe and indignant.

He also excelled more in pure intellect, than in warmth of feeling. He dwelt chiefly in a frigid zone, where his affections were congealed; and yet from expressions which he uttered on the loss of his son, and of his wife, he showed, that if not a person of the warmest sensibility, he was not altogether destitute of fine feeling.

He is also generally thought to have been too fond of power. This, however, does not appear to me to have been a leading feature in our author. He does indeed acknowledge, that "it gave him some pain to see others differ from him;" but from the great confidence placed in him by the members of the senate, and from the manner in which his colleagues speak of his talents as President of their Ecclesiastical Court, as well as of his general deportment, it would appear that the power which he possessed was not an assumption of his own, but a talent with which he was invested by them. Or, at least, if the love to have the pre-eminence, had occupancy of his soul, it cannot be shown to have been the ruling passion. "He is charged," says Beza, "with ambition, yea, with aspiring at a new Popedom—an extraordinary accusation against a man who preferred this kind of life, this republic, this church, which I may truly call the very seat of poverty, to all other honours."

His *disinterestedness* will not be disputed. The regular stipend which he received was very moderate, and yet so far from being dissatisfied with it, he refused an increase when it was offered him, as well as a present of twenty-five crowns, which the council wished to present to him, during his sickness. In the preface to his Commentary on the Psalms, which he wrote in 1557, he said, "that I am not a lover of money, if I fail of persuading men while I live, my death will demonstrate."* And it was a fact that all his effects, though his library sold high, scarcely amounted to three hundred guilders.

The following is a beautiful exemplification of his own sentiments on this subject. Eckius, the Pope's legate, one day knocked at his door, which was opened by Calvin himself; Eckius, enquiring for M. Calvin, he was told that he was the person. They soon entered into conversation on the subject of religion, when Eckius enquired of him, why he left the Romish church, and offered some arguments to induce him to return; but they had no influence on the mind of Calvin. At last, Eckius told him that he would put his life in his hand; and then said, that he was Eckius, the Pope's legate. At this Calvin was not a little surprised, and begged pardon that he had not treated him with the respect due to his quality. Eckius returned the compliment; and told him that if he would come back to the Roman church, he would certainly procure for him a cardinal's cap. But Calvin was still immovable. Eckius then asked him what revenue he had; he told the Cardinal that he had that house and garden, and fifty livres per annum, beside an annual present of some wine and corn. Eckius promised him a better stipend if he would come over to them. But Calvin assured him that he was quite contented with what he had. After dinner, Eckius wished to see the church; and, coming out of Calvin's house, he drew out a purse, with about a hundred pistoles,

* John Wesley said, "if I die worth ten pounds independent of my books, and the arrears of my fellowship, I will give the world leave to call me, a thief and a robber."

and presented it to Calvin ; but Calvin desired to be excused. Eckius told him he gave it to buy books, as well as to express his respect for him. As they were quitting the church, Calvin took out the purse of gold, and said to the syndics and officers who were present, that he had received it from this worthy stranger, and that now he gave it to the poor, and he put it all into the poor-box that was kept there. The syndics thanked the stranger, and Eckius admired the charity and modesty of Calvin. Our reformer then walked a mile with him out of the territories of Geneva, where, in the most friendly manner, they took a farewell of each other.

Calvin chose, with great propriety, those expressive words, which formed his device—*Sincerely and promptly*. Many who have differed from him have acknowledged, that in his principles he was devoutly sincere, while his amazing promptitude and indefatigable industry, have been the wonder of all. He lived in continual action, and almost constantly with his pen in his hand. His labours were so important and numerous, as to leave him scarcely any time for repose, though his pale, worn, and meagre body, pleaded loudly for relaxation. His works, both in number and size, almost exceed those of any other man. The lectures and sermons he delivered annually were above three hundred. Weekly he was present in the consistory, and very frequently was consulted by the Senate. His visitors were numerous, his correspondence extensive. In one of his letters to Farel, he says,—" When the messenger called for my book (his Commentary on the Romans), I had twenty sheets to revise—to preach—to read to the congregation—to write forty-two letters—to attend to some controversies, and to return answers to more than ten persons, who interrupted me in the midst of my labours, for advice." The annotators on Spon's History of Geneva remark, that " affairs public and private, ecclesiastical and civil, occupied him in succession, and often altogether. Consulted from all quarters, both at home and abroad; carrying on a correspondence with all the churches and all the learned men of Europe, with the princes and other persons of high distinction, who had embraced the reformed religion; it seems almost inconceivable how one man could be capable of so many things, and how he should not sink under the weight of the business which pressed upon him." Thus,—"in the midst of life, he consumed away like incense upon the altar, burning bright, and diffusing fragrance, till not a residue can be seen."*

It would be altogether foreign to our object to attempt to give any thing like a review or an analysis of his works. D'Alembert says,—"Calvin justly enjoyed a distinguished reputation, and was a scholar of the first order. He wrote with as much elegance in Latin as a dead language admits; and the extraordinary purity of his French style is now admired by our skilful critics, and gives his writings a decided superiority over the greatest part of his contemporaries." His reading was accurate, his knowledge various, and his learning extensive. With the works of the early Christian fathers he appears to have been familiarly acquainted. In his Commentaries, however, he very seldom quotes them, nor did he entertain any special reverence for their authority. He frankly acknowledges, that on the subjects of predestination and free agency, they were against him.

The pure intellect of our author gives to his writings an aspect of cold severity, so that the reader must not expect to meet with any bursts of impassioned feeling, or with any singularly splendid passages. But, if his object be to have his understanding enlightened, and his heart improved, he will not be disappointed. His Commentaries on the Holy Scriptures are inferior to many

* This was said by Montgomery, of the lamented Richard Watson, who died January 8, 1833, in the fifty-second year of his age. Between whom, and Calvin, it is not difficult to discover several points of resemblance.

similar works which have since made their appearance, in biblical criticism, clear statement of doctrine, and in rich evangelical sentiment; but they are written in a style of elegant simplicity, without any parade of learning, and are remarkably practical. Dr Watts observes, " That the most narrow and rigid limitations of grace to men are to be found chiefly in his Institutions, which were written in his youth. But his comments on Scripture were the labour of his riper years, and maturer judgment."

It is clearly established that the peculiar doctrines contained in Calvin's writings were held by Zuingle and others of the early reformers, before they were advocated by our author; but, as he formed them into a system, especially in the Confession of Faith, which he prepared for the French reformed churches; and, as this greatly differed from the Augsburg Confession, on predestination and redemption; the doctrines of the one were denominated Lutheran, and of the other Calvinistic, which names have continued to be used to the present day. It should, perhaps, here be added, that the churches which adhered to the doctrinal sentiments of Luther and Melancthon, differed also from the other reformed churches respecting ecclesiastical discipline and government.

Such was the accuracy of Calvin's mind, and his long practice of dictating to an amanuensis, that he attained to speak very nearly as he would have written. As a preacher, he is said, to have been particularly eloquent; but after having read some hundreds of his sermons, I certainly should not be led to the conclusion, that he greatly excelled as a public speaker. He addressed the understanding of his hearers, more than their affections, and convinced them by the force of his reasoning, rather than by the graces of persuasion. The most conspicuous feature in his preaching, was *faithfulness*. He was not a " son of thunder," yet with the most inflexible severity he repressed licentiousness, and made the " lewd fellows of the baser sort," who occasionally sat under his ministry, to tremble beneath his cutting rebukes. The Laodicean professors, he endeavoured to rouse from their dangerous apathy, by such language as the following :—" There are some who go on securely in sin, alleging that if they are of the number of the elect, their vices will not hinder them from going to heaven. Such abominable language as this is not the holy bleating of Christ's sheep, but the impure grunting of swine."

It now only remains that we speak of the *piety* of this great man. It was this that presided over the various talents with which he was gifted, and determined them to their appropriate objects. He was strongly impressed with a sense of his responsibility to the author of all good, and felt that the unreserved presentation of himself as a living sacrifice, holy and acceptable to God, was but a reasonable service. Though deeply meditative and devotional, his piety was not tinged with asceticism or enthusiasm, but was scriptural and practical. His views of the evil of sin, the spirituality of the law, and of the holiness and justice of God, were strong and impressive. He appears to have habitually preserved on his mind a devout sense of the presence of his Maker, and to have thought and spoke of him with the deepest veneration. He assiduously laboured to promote the glory of God and the welfare of man. He was found at his post, as a faithful and wise servant, when his master came, and said,—" *It is enough : come up hither. Enter thou into the joy of thy Lord.*"

To conclude—while we are unable to approve of every thing that he spoke and did, we would not forget, that to him and his noble coadjutors in the glorious cause of the reformation from Popery, we owe the dawn of that Scriptural light and liberty which we now enjoy, and which shall continue to spread, until there be heard a voice as the sound of many waters, saying, " BABYLON THE GREAT, THE MOTHER OF HARLOTS AND ABOMINATIONS OF THE EARTH, IS FALLEN, IS FALLEN ! "

EXTRACTS

FROM THE

REGISTERS OF THE COUNCIL OF STATE OF GENEVA

Feb. 13, 1537.—Six crowns were awarded to Cauvin, or Calvin, because he has hitherto received scarcely any thing.

March 11, 12, 1538.—The preachers, particularly Farel and Calvin, are forbidden to meddle with politics.

April.—A decree was made to exclude Calvin from the pulpit, if he should refuse to administer the Lord's Supper as they do at Berne.

April 23.—Farel and Calvin are ordered to leave the city in three days, since they will not obey the magistrates : and they answer, " Be it so ; we must obey God rather than man."

Oct. 20, 1540.—In order to the furtherance and progress of the word of God, it has been resolved to send to Strasburg for Master John Calvin, who is a very learned man, to be our minister in this city.

Sep. 13, 20, 1541.—Calvin is entreated to remain always here, and a cloth gown is given to him.

Oct. 4.—A large salary is given to M. Calvin, on account of his great learning, and because the journeys cost him a great deal. He was desired, by the 21st of November, with three counsellors, to compile laws for the government of the people.

Jan. 19, 1542. — The commissioners named in the Basle matter are ordered to confer with Calvin and Doctor Fabri, whom the city is accustomed to consult on important occasions.

May 15.—Messrs Claude, Boset, Calvin, and Doctor Fabri d'Evian are ordered to draw out the political edicts.

Nov. 17.—A cask of old wine awarded to Calvin for the trouble which he takes for the city.

June 1, 1543.—The minister, Peter Blanchet, having died at the fever hospital, the ministers are directed to send another ; but they are forbidden to choose Calvin, because of the great need which the church and state have of him.

Nov. 26.—M. W. Farel having come into the city with very shabby clothes, new ones were given him.

Dec. 19, 1544.—Christmas-day will be celebrated as usual, although Calvin has represented to the Council that we might very well get rid of this festival, as well as of the other three.

June 8, 1545.—A collection for the poor, made upon the remonstrances of Calvin, which produced 76 fl. Calvin declares that he has very strong reasons for never consenting to the reception of De Troilet into the ministry.

August 31.—Calvin being rather unwell, the Council has granted him a secretary at the public expense.

Dec. 12.—M. Calvin caused a woman to be liberated who had been imprisoned for having spoken of him as a bad man.

Jan. 25, 1546.—The Council having learnt that M. Calvin had fallen ill, and that he needed assistance, sent him ten crowns, which he hesitated to receive.

Dec. 29, 1547.—They presented him with all the furniture of his house, which belonged to the public. He refused, on the 5th June, 1553, two crowns of gold sol., which the council wished to give him on account of his labours for the state at Berne. The Council having sent him some firewood, the 28th December, he brought the money for it, which they would not accept. The Council sent him, on the 14th of May, 1560, a hogshead of the best wine they could procure, because that he had none good. He made great difficulties in receiving twenty-five crowns to discharge the expenses of his illness, and earnestly entreated the Council to take back again, the 22d June, 1563.

Jan. 27.—Peter Ameaulx was accused of having said that M. Calvin preached false doctrine, was a very wicked man, and that he was only a Picard.

March 17.—All the ministers and elders assembled in Council, on account of the accusations of Ameaulx against Calvin, bear their unanimous testimony to the piety of Calvin (who was not present), to his charity, to his pure and Christian conduct, and to his doctrine, in every respect conformable to the word of God, and in the profession of which they were determined to live and die,—not having any sect among them.

August 3.—Ant. Calvin received the freedom of the city gratuitously, in consideration of the services of J. Calvin, his brother.

Oct. 11.—M. Calvin complains of the licentiousness of the youth : nothing being more common than licentiousness and adultery.

July 9, 1548.—Calvin having denounced from the pulpit certain disorders with too great warmth ; and another minister having said that the youth of Geneva wished to overturn religion, the Council directed them to inform it of the abuses which they observed, but not to exclaim against them from the pulpit in that manner.

July 12.—They reply that it is a case of conscience, and that this is to deprive their ministry of its liberty.

October 15.—Farel has represented how much Calvin, Viret, and he have always been attached to the interests of the city ; and has entreated the Council to look upon Viret the same as formerly, and to show the same esteem and regard as formerly for Calvin, whose merit was so exalted that there was not another man on earth who had opposed Antichrist with so great success, from Jesus

Christ, as he; and that he perceived, with grief, that they did not pay the deference to this servant of God which was due to him.

October 18.—J. Calvin having been summoned before the Council to answer for his conduct, he was told that he must another time attend better to his duty towards the magistrates. William Farel, who was present at this examination, thought that the Council paid but little respect for the character and merit of Calvin, who was so much distinguished, that it might justly be said no man equalled him in learning; that they should not be so very scrupulous as to what he might have said, since he had reproved, with much boldness, the greatest of men, such as Luther, Melancthon, &c.; and that they should not so easily credit what a mob of insignificant people, supporters of an alehouse, might say against so great a man. Upon which it was resolved that thanks should be given to the said Farel.

Dec. 18.—The Council and ministers sup together, to lay aside all hatred and animosity.

Feb. 1, 1549.—It appears that Calvin presented a remonstrance, in Council, on account of the nomination of the Syndics.

May 3.—Eight French gentlemen, among whom is Theodore Beza, have arrived here, and obtained permission to remain.

Dec. 23.—At the suggestion of Calvin, men and women are forbidden to bathe together in the same baths, which is a shameful practice.

June 3, 1550.—The Duke of Wirtemberg has shown many civilities to our deputies at Basle, and desired them to present his compliments to Calvin.

Nov. 3.—Calvin complains, as of a mockery of God, that it has been inserted in the sentence of a criminal executed for coining false money, that he retired hither on account of his religion, and went every day to hear preaching.

March 27, 1551.—Philibert Bertelier complains to the Council, because the Consistory has refused him the Lord's Supper, because he would not confess that he had done wrong in maintaining that he was as good a man as Calvin.

Jan. 5, 1552.—M. Calvin makes a present of a copy of his Commentaries, with a fine Preface, addressed to the Magistracy.

Feb. 27.—Some persons having thought it wrong that the ministers should be present at the Geneva Council, since the priests did not attend it before the Reformation, Calvin answered, that the former feel themselves bound by their oath, as citizens; and that the comparison is not just, since the latter acknowledge no temporal authority.

Nov. 13.—Calvin and his colleagues have represented that they have heard with sorrow that some young persons had urged a complaint against the minister, William Farel, which could not but bring dishonour and great scandal upon the Church. Those who brought forward this complaint having been sent for, as well as Farel, there was much noise on both sides. After which Farel declared that he did not intend to blame the community; that he has for Geneva a sincere affection. This so much affected those who were present (many of the people having entered the Council-Chamber), and in particular those who had complained of the said Farel, that they all considered Farel as a faithful minister of the holy gospel, and their Spiritual Father. Upon which the Council decreed that they should all shake him by the hand, and that there should be a feast of reconciliation.

Jan. 31, 1554.—All the lesser Council, the magistrates, M. Calvin, and many of the chief men of the city, dined together, to confirm the peace made yesterday; and it is decided that if any one should break it, all the others shall join against him.

July 19.—The physician, Beljaquet, is ordered to examine a book which Calvin wished to have printed.

April 28, 1556.—Seeing the great trouble which Messrs Viret and Farel take on our account, a present is made them of sweetmeats.

October 12.—M. John Calvin thanked the council for the attendant which had been given him to accompany him to Francfort.

February 4, 1558.—M. Calvin exhorts the councillors to elect for Syndics worthy men, and to recollect in how great danger the Republic had been of late years, from having been governed by bad magistrates ; also to recollect our weakness, and not to be elated with pride. It was judged right, that in future we should not support, as has been too much the case formerly, those who are puffed up with pride, and who despise the laws.

June 19, 1559.—A prodigious number of persons were present at the sermons of Messrs Calvin and Viret.

December 25.—Many ministers and professors having asked for and obtained the right of citizens, it has been urged that M. Calvin ought to be entreated to accept it also. He was very thankful for the honour, saying, that if he had not solicited it sooner, it was in order not to give rise to suspicions, to which too many persons are inclined.

July 3, 1561.—A minister is granted to the Duchess of Ferrara, on condition that it shall be neither M. Calvin nor M. de Beza.

January 3, 1564.—The secret committee to which M. Calvin was called, has agreed that if we were to ask a garrison from any but the authorities of Berne, we should show by this that we distrust them, from whom we are obliged to receive one in time of need : whereas, if we were to send for one from France, it would cost us a great deal ; and it would seem as if this town were in a state of weakness which would not do it credit.

March 10.—Decreed that every one should pray for the health of M. Calvin, who has been for some time indisposed, and even in danger of death.

March 13.—He refuses twenty-five crowns, which the Council had sent to his brother, saying, that not performing his duties his conscience would not allow him to receive his salary.

June 8.—All the ministers and professors came to the Council on account of the death of Calvin, and called to mind that that holy man made to them excellent exhortations to union, both among themselves, and with the Magistracy, and that this was the only way to prevent them feeling sensibly the loss of this true servant of God. The council replied, that it regretted very much this great man upon whom God had bestowed such great gifts, and upon whom he had impressed a character of so much dignity.

July 8.—Resolved to purchase for the Public Library such of M. Calvin's books as M. de Beza shall think proper.

CHRONOLOGICAL LIST OF CALVIN'S WORKS

1. Commentary on Seneca's Treatise Concerning Clemency. 1532.
2. Psychopannychia, 1534. Translated by T. Stocker. London, 1581, 8vo.
3. Institutes of the Christian Religion, 1536. French edition, 1560, fol. Spanish edition, per Cypriano de Valera, 1597, 4to. Italian edition, per Givlio Cesare, 1557, 4to. Latin edition, by A. Tholuck, Berlin, 1834, 2 vols. 8vo. Translated into English, by Thomas Norton, 1561, 1562, 1574, 1580, 8vo; 1582, 1583, 1587, 4to; 1599, 1611, 1634, fol. By John Allen, London, 1813, 3 vols. 8vo. Edinburgh, Beumie's Abridgment of the Insti-

tutes, 1576, 8vo. Translated by Edward May, London, 1680, 8vo.

4. An Epistle on attending Mass, 1537. Translated by T. Brooke. London, 1548, 8vo.

5. The Life and Conversation of a Christian Man, 1537. Translated by T. Brooke. London, 1549, 8vo.

6. Answer to Cardinal Sadolet's Letter, 1539.

7. Commentary on the Romans, 1539. Translated by Chr. Rosdell. London, 1577, 1583, 4to. By F. Sibson, 1834, 12mo.

8. Treatise on the Lord's Supper, 1540. Translated, 1545, 4to.

9. Song of Victory to Christ, 1541.

10. Antidote to the Articles of the Sorbonne, 1542.

11. Answer to Pighius, 1543.

12. Remarks on the Admonition of Paul III. to the Emperor Charles V. 1544.

13. The Necessity of Reforming the Church, 1544.

14. The Errors of the Anabaptists and Libertines, 1544. London, 1549, 8vo.

15. The Relics of Saints, 1544. Translated by S. Wythers. London, 1561, 12mo.

16. A Catechism, 1545. London, 1563, 12mo; 1582, 8vo. Middleburg, 1594, 12mo. Edinburgh, 1596, 1611, 8vo. In French. London, 1552, 8vo.

17. On Superstitions, 1545.

18. Answer to the Nicodemites, 1545.

19. Antidote against the Council of Trent, 1547.

20. Form of Administering the Sacraments, Public Prayers, Form of Marriage, 1547.

21. The true way of securing the peace of the Church and its Reformation, 1547.

22. An Answer to a Franciscan Libertine, 1547.

23. Commentary on Galatians, Ephesians, Philippians, and Colossians, 1548. Translation of Galatians, by A. Golding. London, 1574, 4to. Of Ephesians, by A. Golding. London, 1577, 4to. Of Philippians, by W. Becket. London, 1584, 4to.

24. Commentary on Titus, 1549.

25. Commentary on Philemon, 1549.

26. Commentary on Hebrews, 1549.   Translated by Clement Cotton, 1605, 4to.

27. Against Judicial Astrology, 1549.   Englished by Goddres Gulby.   London, W. D. 12mo.

28. Treatise on Scandals, 1550.   Translated by A. Golding.   London, 1567, 8vo.

29. Commentary on the Thessalonians, 1550.

30. Commentary on Isaiah, 1551.   Translated by Clement Cotton.   London, 1609, fol.

31. Commentary on James, Peter, John, Jude, 1551. Translation of the First Epistle of John and Jude, by W. H., without date, probably 1580, 8vo. Translation of James.   Aberdeen, 1797, 8vo.

32. On Predestination and the Providence of God, 1551.

33. Commentary on John, 1553.   Translated by C. Fetherstone.   London, 1585, 1610, 4to.

34. Harmony of the Sacraments, 1554.

35. Exposure of the Errors of Servetus, 1554.

36. Three Exhortations to Westphal, 1554, 1556, 1557.

37. Commentary on Genesis, 1555.   Translated by T. Tymme.   London, 1578, 4to.

38. Commentary on Matthew, Mark, and Luke, in the form of a Harmony, 1555.   Translated by E. Paget.   London, 1584, 4to.

39. Commentary on 1 and 2 Corinthians. 1556. Translated by T. Tymme.   Lond. 1577, 4to.

40. Commentary on 1 and 2 Timothy. 1556.

41. Commentary on the Psalms. 1557.   Translated by A. Golding.   Lond. 1571, 4to.

42. Commentary on the twelve minor Prophets. 1559.

43. Commentary on the Acts. 1560. Translated by C. Fetherstone.   Lond. 1585, 4to.

44. Against Heshusius and Stancar. 1560. Against Baldwin. 1561.

45. Four Sermons against Idolatry.   Translated into

English by divers godly and learned men. Lond.
1561. 12mo.

46. Answer to Gentilis, Blandrata, and Castellio. 1561.

47. Commentary on Jeremiah. 1561.

48. Confession of Faith for the French Reformed
Churches. 1562.

49. Two Epistles to the Faithful in Poland. 1563.

50. Commentary on Exodus, Leviticus, Numbers, and
Deuteronomy, in the form of a Harmony. 1563.

51. Commentary on Daniel. 1563. Translated by A.
Golding. Lond. 1570. 4to.

52. Commentary on Joshua. 1564. Translated by W.
F. Lond. 1578. 4to.

53. Commentary on the first twenty chapters of Ezekiel.
1565. Prayers and collects. Translated by E.
Murray, Lond. 12mo. without date.

54. Three Propositions or Speeches. Translated by T.
W. Lond. 1580, 8vo.

55. Prayers used after reading Hosea. Translated by
John Field. Lond. 1583, 12mo.

56. Against Extreme Unction. Translated by W. B.
Without date, place, or printer's name.

SERMONS WHICH WERE TAKEN DOWN WHEN DELIVER-
ED, AND PUBLISHED SINCE CALVIN'S DEATH

1. Sermons (3) on Melchisedec ; Abraham's courage in
rescuing Lot, and his godliness in paying Tythes.
Four on Abraham's Faith, and three on his Obedience. Translated by T. Stocker, gent. Lond.
1592, 8vo.

2. Sermons (16) on the Decalogue. Translated by J.
Harmar. Lond. 1579, 1581, 4to.

3. Sermons (200) on Deuteronomy. Translated by
A. Golding. Lond. 1583, folio.

4. Sermons on Samuel. Geneva. 1604. folio.

5. Sermons (159) on Job. Translated by A. Golding. Lond. 1574, 1580, 1584, folio.

6. Sermons (3) on the 46th Psalm. Translated by W. Warde. Lond. 1562, 12mo.

7. Sermons (22) on the 119th Psalm. Translated by T. Stocker. Lond. 1580, 4to.

8. Sermons on Hezekiah's Song. Translated by A. L. Lond. 1569, 8vo.

9. Sermons (22) on the first five chapters of Jeremiah. Translated. Lond. 1578, 1620, 4to.

10. Sermons on the last eight chapters of Daniel. Translated by A. Golding. Roch. 1565, folio.

11. Sermons on Jonah. Translated by N. Baxter. Lond. 1578, 4to.

12. Sermons on the beginning of the Harmony of the three Gospels.

13. Sermons on the 10th and 11th chapters of 1 Corinthians.

14. Sermons (43) on Galatians. Translated by A. Golding. Lond. 1574. 4to. By R. N. 1581, 4to.

15. Sermons on Ephesians. Translated by A. Golding. Lond. 1577, 4to.

16. Sermons on Timothy and Titus. Translated by L. T. (Leonard Tomson). Lond. 1579, 4to.

17. Sermons (27) on the Divinity, Humanity, &c. of Christ. Translated by T. Stocker. Lond. 1581, 4to.

18. Sermons on Election and Reprobation. Translated by J. Field. Lond. 1579, 4to.

19. Sermons (4) on Matters very Profitable for our Time. Translated by J. Field. Lond. 1579, 4to.

20. Sermons (2) on Patience and Assurance. Translated. Lond. Without date. 8vo.

21. Sermons (2) on Psalm, xvi. 3., and Heb. xiii. 13. Lond. 1584, 4to.

CHRISTIAN THEOLOGY

I — THE SCRIPTURES

IT is needful to say somewhat of the authority of the Scripture, not only to prepare men's minds to reverence it, but also to take away all doubt thereof. Now, when it is a matter confessed that it is the word of God that is there set forth, there is no man of so desperate boldness, unless he be void of all common sense and natural wit of man, that dare derogate the credit of him that speaks it. But because there are not daily oracles given from heaven, and the only Scriptures remain, wherein it has pleased him to preserve his truth to perpetual memory; the same Scripture by no other means is of full credit among the faithful, but in that they do believe that it is as verily come from heaven, as if they heard the lively-voice of God to speak therein. This matter, indeed, is right worthy, both to be largely entreated of and diligently weighed. But the reader shall pardon me if herein I rather regard what the proportion of the work which I have begun may bear, than what the largeness of the matter requires. There is grown up among the most part of men a most hurtful error, that the Scripture has only so much authority as by common consent of the church is given unto it : as if the eternal and inviolable truth of God did rest upon the pleasure of men. For so, to the great scorn of the Holy Ghost, they ask of us who can assure us that these Scriptures came from God ; or who can ascertain us that they have continued unto our age safe and uncorrupted ; who can persuade us, that this one book ought to be reverently received, and that other to be struck out of the number of Scripture, unless the church did appoint a certain rule of all these things? It hangs therefore, say they, upon the determination of the church, both what reverence is due to the Scripture, and what books are to be reckoned in the canon thereof. So these robbers of God's honour, while they seek under colour of the church to bring in an unbridled tyranny, care nothing with what absurdities they snare both themselves and others, so that they may enforce this one thing to be believed among the simple, that the church can do all things. But if it be so, what shall become of the poor consciences that seek stedfast assurance of eternal life, if all the promises that remain thereof stand and be stayed only upon the judgment of men? When they receive such answer, shall they cease to waver and tremble? Again, to what scorns of the ungodly is our faith made subject? Into how great suspicion with all men is it brought, if this be believed, that it hath but as it were a borrowed credit by the favour of men?

It is a vain forged device, that the church has power to judge the Scripture, so as the certainty of the Scripture should be thought to hang upon the will of the church. Wherefore when the church doth receive the Scripture, and seals it with her consenting testimony, she doth not of a thing doubtful, and that otherwise should be in controversy, make it authentic and of credit; but because she acknowledges it to be the truth of her God, according to her duty of godliness, without delay she does honour it. Whereas they demand, how shall we be persuaded it came from God, unless we resort to the decree of the church? This is all one as if a man should ask, how shall we learn to know light from darkness, white from black, or sweet from sour? For the Scripture shows in itself no less apparent sense of her truth, than white and black things do of their colour, or sweet and sour things of their taste.

The principal proof of the Scripture is commonly

taken of the person of God the speaker of it. The Prophets and Apostles boast not of their own sharp wit, or any such things as procure credit to men that speak, neither stand they upon proofs by reason, but they bring forth the holy name of God, thereby to compel the whole world to obedience. Now we have to see how not only by probable opinion, but by apparent truth it is evident, that in this behalf the name of God is not without cause, nor deceitfully pretended. If then we will provide well for consciences, that they be not continually carried about with unstedfast doubting, nor may waver, nor stay at every small stop, this manner of persuasion must be fetched deeper than from either the reasons, judgments, or the conjectures of men, even from the secret testimony of the Holy Ghost. True indeed it is, that if we listed to work by way of arguments, many things might be alleged that may easily prove, if there be any God in heaven, that the law, the prophecies, and the gospel, came from him. Yea, although men, learned and of deep judgment, would stand up to the contrary, and would employ and show forth the whole force of their wits in this disputation ; yet if they be not so hardened as to become desperately shameless, they would be compelled to confess that there are seen in the Scripture manifest tokens that it is God that speaks therein ; whereby it may appear that the doctrine thereof is from heaven. And shortly, hereafter, we shall see that all the books of the Holy Scriptures do far excel all other writings whatsoever they be. Yea, if we bring thither pure eyes and uncorrupted senses, we shall forthwith find there the majesty of God, which shall subdue all hardness of gainsaying, and enforce us to obey him. But yet they do disorderly, that by disputation travail to establish the perfect credit of the Scripture. And truly, although I am not furnished with great dexterity nor eloquence, yet if I were to contend with the most subtle despisers of God, that have a desire to show themselves witty and pleasant in feebling the authority of the Scripture, I trust it should not be hard for me to put to silence their babblings.

It is marvellous how great establishment grows thereof, when, with earnest study, we consider how orderly and well framed a disposition of the divine wisdom appears therein, how heavenly a doctrine in every place of it, and nothing savouring of earthliness, how beautiful an agreement of all the parts among themselves, and such other things as avail to procure a majesty to writings. But more perfectly are our hearts confirmed, when we consider how we are even violently carried to an admiration of it, rather with dignity of matter, than with grace of words. For this also was not done without the singular providence of God, that the high mysteries of the heavenly kingdom should for the most part be uttered under a contemptible baseness of words, lest if it had been beautified with more glorious speech, the wicked should call that the only force of eloquence doth reign therein. But when that rough, and in a manner rude, simplicity doth raise up a greater reverence of itself than any rhetorician's eloquence, what may we judge but that there is a more mighty strength of truth in the Holy Scripture, than that it needs any art of words? Read Demosthenes or Cicero, read Plato, Aristotle, or any other of all that sort, I grant they shall marvellously allure, delight, move, and ravish thee. But, if from them thou come to this holy reading of Scriptures, wilt thou or not, it shall so lively move thy affections, it shall so pierce thy heart, it shall so settle within thy bones, that in comparison of the efficacy of this feeling, all that force of rhetoricians and philosophers shall in a manner vanish away, so that it is easy to perceive that the Scriptures, which do far excel all gifts and graces of man's industry, do indeed breathe out a certain divinity.

We see what is happened in the Popedom, under colour of being simple. Men say there, O, we must walk in simplicity. It is true ; but their meaning is, that men should suffer themselves to be led like brute beasts, without discerning between white and black. But it is not for nothing that our Lord promises his faithful ones the spirit of discretion. It is to the intent they should not be led here and there to dance at every man's pipe, nor be led about like poor blind men. What is to be done then ? We must be taught, and we must have the knowledge and certainty of God's truth, to follow and obey the same ; and when any man shall have showed us our faults, we must take warning aright thereby to follow the good, and eschew the evil.

The Holy Scripture, saith St Paul, is fit to teach, to encourage, to warn, to reprove, and to redress. Yea, but it must be considered what manner of one the party is that must be applied unto. If we see a poor sinner that is cast down and mourneth for his sins, and desireth nothing but to return unto God, let it be shown him that God is ready to accept him and receive him. You see then how we ought to deal in that behalf. Contrariwise, if we see one that is proud and stately, we knock upon his hard pate with a beetle, to make him meek in himself before God. And if we see a slothful person, he must be pricked forward like an ass. Thus ye see how the Holy Scripture may be profitable to us. But in the mean season we must also keep the same manner of proceeding on our own behalf ; for we must be the same to our neighbours that we be to ourselves. We see that when their conscience is cumbered, and themselves are disquieted in mind, they feed their own humour. For they take God's threatenings so rigorously, as they think they should never come soon enough to despair. Let us keep us from such dealing ; and when we spy Satan's wiliness in making us believe that we be utterly past recovery, and that there is no help to comfort us, let us resist it, and apply the remedy thereunto. It is Satan that works, and therefore we, on the contrary, must seek some assuagement to bring us back unto God; we must enter into his promises, we must give heedful ear unto them, and we must set all our wits upon them. Moreover, when we see there is too much slothfulness in ourselves, so as we have need to be pricked and spurred, let us take us to the exhortations that are in the Holy Scripture. Thus you see how we may be good physicians both towards ourselves and towards our neighbours, by considering what is meet and convenient for us.

This is worthy to be noted, that Christ uses the Scripture for his shield. For this is the right manner of fighting, if we desire to obtain the victory. For Paul does not in vain call the Word of God the spiritual sword, and arms us with the shield of faith; whereby we also gather, that the Papists, as if they had made a covenant with Satan, gave our souls to be destroyed at his pleasure, when they maliciously suppressing the Scripture, spoiled the people of God of their weapons, by the which they could only defend their salvation. They that willingly cast from them this armour, and do not daily exercise themselves in the school of God, are worthy every moment to be slain of Satan, to whom they betray themselves unarmed. And truly there is no other cause why Satan is so weakly withstood, and that every where he taketh away so many, but because that God revenges their slothfulness and contempt of his word.

The oracles of God contain nothing vain or unprofitable; and the assiduous study and perusal of these records of unchanging wisdom contribute to advance our piety and holiness of life. Let us, therefore, labour most assiduously in learning the contents of the Book of God, and never forget it is the only writing in which the Creator and Preserver of heaven and earth condescends to converse with man. It would be a reproach on the Holy Spirit of truth to imagine he had taught us any thing whose knowledge might not be of use to us; and let us ever remember that his instructions tend invariably to the advancement of our piety.

THOUGH in times past there have been some, and at this day there arise up many that deny that there is any God, yet whether they will or no, they oftentimes feel that which they are desirous not to know. We read of none that ever did break forth into more presumptuous and unbridled despising of God than Caius Caligula ; yet none more miserably trembled when any token of God's wrath appeared. And so against his will he quaked for fear of him whom, of wilful purpose, he endeavoured to despise. And the same may a man commonly see to happen to such as he was. For the bolder despiser of God that any man is, the more is he troubled at the very noise of the falling of a leaf. And whence comes that, but from the revengement of God's majesty, which doth so much the more vehemently strike their consciences as they more labour to flee away from it. They do indeed look about for all the starting holes that may be, to hide themselves from the presence of the Lord; but whether they will or no, they are still holden fast tied. For howsoever some time it seems to vanish away for a moment, yet it often returns again, and with new assault doth run upon them, so that the rest which they have, if they have any at all, from torment of conscience, is much like to the sleep of drunkards or frantic men, which, even while they sleep, do not quietly rest, because they are at every moment vexed with horrible and dreadful dreams. Therefore, the very ungodly themselves serve for an example to prove that there always lives in all men's minds some knowledge of God.

God in the law, after he had once challenged the glory of his deity to himself alone, meaning to teach us what manner of worshipping him he alloweth or refuseth, addeth immediately, " Thou shalt make thee no graven image, nor any similitude," in which words he restrains our liberty, that we attempt not to represent him with any invisible image. And there he shortly reckons up all the forms wherewith of long time before, superstition had begun to turn his truth into lying. For we know that the Persians worshipped the Sun, yea, and so many stars as the foolish nations saw in the sky, so many gods they feigned them. And scarce was there any living creature which was not among the Egyptians a figure of God; but the Grecians were thought to be wiser than the rest, because they worshipped God in the shape of a man. But God compareth not images one with another, as though one were more and another less meet to be used, but without any exception he rejects all images, pictures, and other signs, whereby the superstitious thought to have God near unto them.

It is true that God hath no hands, for he hath no body, but his speaking so is by similitude. As if he should say, do ye think me to be like any creature? No, for all the world is nothing in comparison of me. It is but as a grain of dust in a man's hand, and you yourselves are here beneath as a sort of frogs or grasshoppers. So then, if ye will needs make some puppet to represent me, is it not as good as a defacing of my glory and a spiting of me to the uttermost of your power? We see that God is a spirit as the Scripture declareth, and shall we then go about to make him a body? It is he that giveth life to all things, and shall we go take a dead thing to represent him thereby, and say, there is God? When we have shaped out a stone or piece of wood, and made it a nose, ears, and all the rest of man's limbs, yet hath it no feeling at all, and shall we nevertheless say, Behold there is God? What a dealing were that? For the same cause is it said in the Psalm, are idols remembrances of God? Indeed men make them mouths, and they have feet, hands, noses, and ears, but yet have they no power to go, nor any other ability, they be but corruptible and dead things. And is there any remembrance of God in them; serve they not rather to lead men into error and beastliness, so as they should make more account of God? The very heathen men themselves could skill to say it, not that they did practise it indeed, but God wrested such words out of their mouths to the intent they might all be convicted.

His substance, indeed, is incomprehensible, so that his Divine Majesty far surmounts all men's senses; but he hath in all his works graven certain marks of his glory, and those so plain and notably discernible, that the excuse of ignorance is taken away from men, be they never so gross and dull witted. Therefore the prophet rightly crieth out, That he is clothed with light as with a garment; as if he should have said, that then he first began to come forth to be seen in visible apparel, since the time that he first displayed his ensign in the creation of the world, by which even now what way soever we turn our eyes, he appears glorious unto us. In the same place, also, the same prophet aptly compares the heavens as they be displayed abroad to his royal pavilions; he saith that he hath framed his parlours in the waters, that the clouds are his chariots, that he rideth upon the wings of the winds, that the winds and lightnings are his swift messengers. And because the glory of his power and wisdom doth more fully shine above, therefore commonly the heaven is called his palace. And first of all, what way soever thou turn thy eyes, there is no peace of the world, be it never so small, wherein are not seen at least some sparkles of his glory to shine. But as for this most large and beautiful frame, thou canst not with one view peruse the wide compass of it, but that thou must needs be on every side overwhelmed with the infinite force of the brightness thereof.

As God hath once created this world, so by his infinite power he sustains it, by his wisdom he governs it, by his goodness he preserves it, and specially mankind he rules by his righteousness and judgment, suffers by his mercy and safeguards by his defence; but also because there can no where be found any one drop either of wisdom, or of light, or of righteousness, or of power, or of uprightness, or of sincere truth, which flows not from him, or whereof he is not the cause; to this end verily, that we should learn to look for and crave all these things at his hand, and with thanksgiving account them received of him.

What is the cause that men are so saucy with God as to hold plea against him, and specially as to make themselves his judges? It is because they have not considered how great and incomprehensible his works are. But if the works of God be incomprehensible, have we a measure that is great enough to declare what is in them? What is our wit? When we have stretched it out to the uttermost length and breadth that may be, is it able to comprehend the hundredth part of God's works, and of his determination, which is so high as all of it is hidden from us? We must go out of ourselves, if we mind but only to taste the wonderful and infinite wisdom that appears in God's works. Now, if we must mount above all our own wits to get but a little taste of them, what shall become of us when we will enclose all, and when we will know all that is in them to the uttermost? I pray you, can we attain thereunto? We see then how men are worse than mad when they be so presumptuous as to desire to determine of God's works, which are incomprehensible. For true it is that we cannot gage the bottom of God's works to comprehend the reason of them; but yet God keeps a good way to give us such a knowledge of them as he knows to be for our behoof. And so we note that God's works are incomprehensible in themselves; that is to say, that if we will search out all that ever is in them by piecemeal we shall never be able to attain to the depth of them. Therefore we must be, as it were, whelmed under the said greatness, assuring ourselves, that if we take upon us to be judges of God's works, we shall find wherewith to stop our eyes, because we cannot attain to the secrets that are in them. Furthermore, when we shall have proceeded in such humility, knowing that we be not competent judges to know the thing that is too high and too deep for us, let us pray God to give us the spirit of wisdom, that we may judge aright of his works; and then will he grant us the grace to perceive so much as is for our behoof. Not that we may discover and decipher all that is in them, so as nothing should be unknown to us, and all should fall out after our imagination. No, God will hold us short of that, so as we shall not know but in part; but in the mean season, the said knowledge must suffice us, forasmuch as nothing shall be hidden from us that is good and convenient for our welfare.

Whereas God's works are called wonderful, or secret; it is to bring us to the reverencing of them. For God's meaning is not that our knowing of such greatness in his works should be to astonish us, and to drive us farther off from him, but, contrariwise, to draw us to such a reverence as we should honour him, saying, Lord, how mighty art thou? Lord, how great is thy power, thy goodness, thy justice, and thy wisdom? Undoubtedly, David knew well the infinite greatness of God's works; and yet, notwithstanding, he ceaseth not to say,—" Lord, thy works are full of wisdom and righteousness." He knew well what we have to consider of God's works, and yet he honoured them nevertheless. Let us learn, then, not to conceive such a greatness in God's works as might make us dull, like brute beasts, so as we should not know where to become, nor take any instruction of good learning by them; but so to conceive of it as the same may serve to repress us, that our wits be not overwandering, and that we play not like horses that are broken loose, and so take liberty to say, I will know how this and this cometh to pass. Not so; but let us be modest. For our true wisdom is to be ignorant in the things that God will have hidden from us. Thus we see·how we must prepare ourselves to lowliness and modesty; and further-more, let us understand therewithal, that we must reve-rence the works of God. And how? To comprehend the infinite wisdom, righteousness, and power that is contained in them, according to our small capacity, assu-ring ourselves that God doth not any thing without rea-son, no, not although the same be not known unto us at the first dash. For God doth not always utter a present reason in his works, so as men may perceive them; and again, the said wisdom is so deep, as it is named a bot-tomless pit. Therefore let us learn to reverence God's works, although we perceive not evermore the cause why he worketh so. We see well then in what ways God's works are wonderful; and he saith expressly, " that they have no end," whereby men are yet better humbled. For if we chance to come to the full understanding of some one thing—O, it seemeth to us that nothing can go beyond us—we be so cunning, that all questions which can be propounded unto us shall be assoiled out of hand. But put the case, we be able to judge of God's works as of two or three, or of a hundred. What is that? It is right nought. And why so? For they are without number. But the least of God's works is enough to overwhelm us; and what then shall become of us, when we come to the said bottomless depth, whereof there is no end? Lo, how it behoveth us to weigh well that which is spoken here generally in way of preface, to make us enter into better consideration of all God's works than we are wont to do, that we may yield the honour unto his Majesty which is due to him.

All things are present with him. Howbeit, for as much as we understand not that, it is for our behoof to have some such manner of speeches as we are better acquainted with, and that God should not show himself such a one as he is in his own infinite being, for then should we be swallowed up; but such as we may conceive him, and such as we may bear. And herein we see his great goodness towards us, in that whereas we be not able to come up unto him, he cometh down unto us here, to the end we might know him, at least-wise so far forth as is for our profit. For if we should presume to enter into his great Majesty, we should be overwhelmed. If we be not able to look upon the sun, but our eyes shall be dazzled, I pray you, how shall we behold the glory of God in full perfectness? It is impossible for us to do it till we be made new again; according as St John saith, that we shall see him as he is when we become like unto him. In the mean while, let us be contented to be his children, and to have the grace of his adoption sealed in our hearts by the Holy Ghost; and consequently let us know him in the image wherein he shows himself unto us.

No conception can be formed of God without his eternity, power, wisdom, goodness, truth, justice, and mercy. His eternity appears from his being the author of all. His power, because he holds all things in his hand, and makes all things to consist in himself. His wisdom is evident by the most well-ordered disposition of every thing. His goodness, because no other cause can be assigned why he should create all things, nor could any other reason than this induce him to preserve what was created. His justice appears in the administration of the world, because he punishes the guilty and defends the innocent. His mercy, because he endures, with so much patience, the perverseness of men. His truth, because he is immutable. Whoever, therefore, has formed a proper notion of God, owes him praise for his eternity, his wisdom, his goodness, and his justice.

If the Creator and Maker of the whole world is the God of all mankind, he will manifest his kindness and benignity to all, by whom he has been invoked and acknowledged as the Supreme Being. For, since his mercy is immense, it must necessarily diffuse itself among all those by whom it has been desired and sought. " Rich" is here taken in an active sense, and means kind and beneficient. Is the riches of our heavenly Father diminished by his liberality? Are our divine blessings lessened, because others are enriched by the abundant affluence of his grace? There is, therefore, no occasion why some should envy the blessings of others, as if they were, on this account, deprived of any boon they themselves enjoyed.

If the grace of God had been simply denied to Jerusalem, their unthankfulness might so much the less have been excused; but since God tried by lovingness and gentleness to allure the Jews unto him, and prevailed nothing by so great gentleness, the offence of their proud contempt was so much the greater. Here is also to be added their untamed frowardness; for God went not about to gather them once or twice, but continually time after time he sent unto them divers Prophets, all which almost were refused for the most part. Now we understand why Christ in the person of God compareth himself to a hen; namely, that he might lay so much the more shame upon this wicked nation, which had refused his sweet and more than motherly allurements. And certainly this was a wonderful and incomparable token of love, that he disdained not to humble himself even to entreat them, that he might so by that means bring those rebels to obey him.

If God be the author of all good, it would be absurd to account him the author of evil. It is his peculiar and natural property, from whom all good things come, to do good; and to do any thing evil is altogether unnatural to him. But as it sometimes happens that a person who behaves generally well through life, may occasionally fail in some part, he anticipates the surmise, and declares it not applicable concerning God; he assures us that God is not changeable like man. Now if in all

things, and at all times, he is like himself, from this
steady and consistent course of conduct it follows, that
his beneficence is perpetual and uninterrupted.

There is shown in the Scriptures a certain distinction
of the Father from the Word, and of the Word from
the Spirit. In discussing whereof, how great religiousness and sobriety we ought to use, the greatness of the
mystery itself doth admonish us. And I very well like
that saying of Gregory Nazianzen,—I cannot think upon
the one but by and by I am compassed about with
the brightness of the three; and I cannot severally discern the three, but I am suddenly driven back to one.
Wherefore let it not come in our minds once to imagine such a Trinity of persons as may hold our thought
withdrawn into severalities, and doth not forthwith
bring us again to that unity. The names of Father,
Son, and Holy Ghost, do prove a true distinction, that
no man should think them to be bare names of addition,
whereby God according to his works is diversely entitled,
but yet it is a distinction, not a division. The places
that we have already cited do show that the Son hath a
property distinct from the Father, because the Word had
not been with God, if he had not been another thing
than the Father; neither had he had his glory with the
Father, but being distinct from him. Likewise he doth
distinguish himself from the Father when he says that
there is another which beareth him witness. And for
this purpose makes that which in another place is said,
that the Father created all things by the Word, which
he could not, but being after a certain manner distinct
from him. Moreover, the Father came not down into
the earth, but he that came out from the Father. The
Father died not, nor rose again, but he that was sent by
him. Neither yet did this distinction begin at the
taking of the flesh; but it is manifest that he was also
before, the only begotten in the bosom of the Father.
For who can abide to say, that then the Son entered

into the bosom of the Father, when he descended from heaven to take manhood upon him? He was therefore before in the bosom of the Father, and enjoyed his glory with the Father. As for the distinction of the Holy Ghost from the Father, Christ speaketh of it when he says, that it proceedeth from the Father. And how oft doth he show it to be another beside himself? as when he promises that he will send another Comforter, and often in other places.

III — MAN

WE will make man. Although this be spoken in the future tense, all men, notwithstanding, will confess, that this is a speech of one taking as it were deliberation. Hitherto he has set God before us commanding simply: and now when he comes to the most excellent work of all the rest, he takes consultation. God might have commanded here also by his bare word whatsoever he would have done: but his purpose was to give this to the excellency of man, that he would after a sort deliberate about his creation. This is great honour which he vouchsafes to give unto us: to the consideration whereof, Moses, by this speech, went about to provoke us. For God doth not now begin to bethink him, what form he were best give unto man, and what gifts were meetest to adorn him: neither doth he stay upon it, as upon a hard matter: but even as we admonished before, that the creation of the world was distributed into six days for our sake, to the end our minds may be the better retained in the meditation of God's works; even so now, to commend unto us the worthiness of our nature, he takes consultation about the creation of man, declares that he takes some great and singular thing in hand. There are many things in this corrupt nature which may bring contempt: but if thou weigh all things rightly, man of all other things, is a certain notable pattern of the wisdom, righteousness, and goodness of God. Insomuch that he is rightly called of the ancient fathers, A little World. Moreover, seeing the Lord needs not any other counsellor, there is no doubt but that he himself, did deliberate with himself. And the Jews are very fond in feigning that God communicated his word with the earth or with angels. As though the earth were a convenient counsellor. And to ascribe the least part of so notable a work to angels is abominable sacrilege. Where will they find they were created after the image of the earth or of angels? Doth not Moses utterly exclude all creatures, when he reported that Adam was made after the image of God? Others which think themselves more wise, being twice more foolish, say that God spake after the manner of princes, of himself in the plural number. As if that barbarousness which hath crept in but a short time, reigned then in the world. But it is well that their doggish wickedness is joined with so great blockish dullness, that they may betray their foolishness even to children. Therefore, Christians do very aptly affirm upon this testimony that there are more persons in God, and that God calleth unto him no foreign person. Hereof we gather that he findeth within him somewhat which is distinct: that his eternal wisdom and power may rest in him. " In our image." By this speech the whole integrity of nature is noted, when Adam was endued with a right understanding, when all his affections were ordered by reason, when all his senses were uncorrupted, and when he truly excelled in all graces. So that the chief seat of God's image was in the mind and in the heart, where it had the pre-eminence : notwithstanding there was no part wherein some sparks did not appear. For there was a temperature in all parts of the soul, which consisted of equality. In the mind, the light of true understanding reigned : and to this was joined, as a companion, the sincerity of the mind. All the senses were prompt and framed to the obedience of reason. In the body there was a certain equal proportion to that order. Now, although certain obscure lineaments and marks of that image remain in us; yet, notwithstanding, they are so corrupted and lame, that we may truly say that it is blotted out. For beside the deformity which appears in every part to be foul, this mischief shows forth itself, that there is no part which is not infected with the pollution of sin.

Apostasy is not a small offence, but a detestable wickedness, whereby man refuses to be subject unto his Maker; nay, whereby he doth resist and deny him. Moreover, it was not apostasy alone; but other heinous contumelies and reproaches against God were joined therewith. Satan accuses God of a lie, of envy, and of maliciousness: to the which foul and execrable slander they subscribe; at length they, not regarding the commandment of God, do not only give place to their lusts, but do also make themselves servants of the devil. To speak more briefly: infidelity opened the gate to ambition, and ambition was the mother of rebellion, that our parents, setting the fear of God aside, did cast off the yoke of obedience. In consideration hereof, Paul teacheth, that through disobedience of Adam sin entered into the world. Let us imagine that there is nothing worse than the transgression of the commandment; yet, notwithstanding, we shall thereby profit little to extenuate or diminish Adam's sin. God appointing him to be free in all things, and the king of the world, would try his obedience in abstaining from one tree only. This condition pleased not him. Let perverse rhetoricians make excuse that the woman was enticed with the beautifulness of the tree, and that the man was enticed with the flatteries of Eve: yet, notwithstanding, the more sufferable and easy the commandment of God was, the less tolerable was their crookedness in refusing to obey. For they durst never to have rebelled against God, except they had first refused to give credit to his word. And nothing enticed them to desire the fruit but mad ambition. So long as they, believing the word of God, suffered themselves to be governed by him, their affections were rightly ordered and framed. For this cogitation, that God is just, which was graven in their minds, was a notable bridle; and that nothing is better than to obey his commandments; also, that it is the sum of a happy life to be loved by him. But after that they gave place to the blasphemy of Satan, they began, as if they had been bewitched, to want reason and judgment; and seeing they were the bond slaves of Satan, he had their senses also captive. Moreover we know that sins are not esteemed before God, according to the outward show, but after the inward affection.

Consider well how Moses says, that when Satan came to beguile Eve, and consequently her husband, after that they had given ear unto him, and been corrupted with desirousness to be like unto God, they looked upon the tree of the knowledge of good and evil, and saw it was to be liked for the obtaining of knowledge. And how looked they upon it? had not Adam and Eve seen it already before? for God had said unto them, eat not of the fruit that I have forbidden you; for in what hour soever you eat thereof, I tell you plainly you are separated from me, and condemned to death. So, then, you see that Adam and Eve had looked upon the tree before; and why then doth Moses lay it now to their charge as a sin? because they did behold it with a liking of it, that is to say, with an ungracious and untoward lust, in that they thought it good to eat of. And whereof came that? even of their heart, which being corrupted, did immediately mar their eyesight. And like as when a man has his eyesight marred with overmuch drinking, there is some inward disease and some burning, or some other income going before the loss of his eyes; or like as when a man becomes blind, there went commonly some rheum or some other like thing before, which in process of time takes away his sight; even so is it with all the wicked looks which are to be condemned. For if the heart were not already infected and corrupted with some lewd liking, the eye should be pure and clean of itself, so as we might behold God's creatures, and not be tempted to any wickedness.

Since the woman was with the deceit of the serpent led away by infidelity, it appears that disobedience was the beginning of the fall, which thing Paul confirms, teaching that all men were lost by one man's disobedience. But it is withal to be noted, that the first man fell from the subjection of God, for that he not only was taken with the enticements of Satan, but also despising the truth, did turn out of the way to lying. And surely God's word being once despised, all reverence of God is shaken off. Because his Majesty doth no other ways abide in honour among us, nor the worship of him remain inviolate, but while we hang upon his mouth. Therefore, infidelity was the root of that falling away. But thereupon arose ambition and pride, to which was adjoined unthankfulness, for that Adam, in coveting more than was granted, did irreverently despise the so great liberality of God wherewith he was enriched. And this was a monstrous wickedness, that the son of the earth thought it a small thing that he was made after the likeness of God, unless he might also be made equal with God. If apostasy be a filthy and detestable offence, whereby man draws himself from the allegiance of his Creator, yea, outrageously shakes off his yoke, then it is but vain to extenuate the sin of Adam. Albeit it was no simple apostasy, but joined with shameful reproaches against God, while they assented to the slanders of Satan, wherein he accused God of lying, envy, and niggardly grudging. Finally, infidelity opened the gate to ambition, ambition was the mother of obstinate rebellion, to make men cast away the fear of God, and throw themselves whither their lust carried them.

As the spiritual life of Adam was to abide joined and bound to his Creator, so his alienation from him was the death of his soul. Neither is it marvellous if he, by his falling away, destroyed all his own posterity, which perverted the whole order of nature in heaven and earth. "All the creatures do groan," saith Paul, "being made subject to corruption against their will." If one should ask the cause ; no doubt it is for that they bear part of that punishment that man deserved, for whose use they were created. Since then the curse that goeth throughout all the coasts of the world, proceeded from his fault both upward and downward, it is nothing against reason, if it spread abroad into all his issue. Therefore, after that the heavenly image in him was defaced, he did not alone suffer this punishment, that in place of wisdom, strength, holiness, truth, and justice, with which ornaments he had been clothed, there came in the most horrible pestilences, blindness, weakness, filthiness, falsehood, and injustice, but also he entangled and drowned his whole offspring in the same misery. This is the corruption that comes by inheritance, which the old writers called original sin, meaning by this word sin, the corruption of nature, which before was good and pure.

Surely it is not doubtfully spoken that David confesses that he was begotten in iniquities, and by his mother conceived in sin. He does not there accuse the sins of his father or mother, but the better to set forth the goodness of God toward him, he begins the confession of his own wickedness at his very begetting. Forasmuch as it is evident that that was not peculiar to David alone, it follows that the common estate of all mankind is noted under his example. All we, therefore, that descend of unclean seed, are born infected with the contagion of sin, yea, before that we see the light of this life, we be in the sight of God filthy and spotted.

We hear that the uncleanness of the parents so passes into the children, that all without any exception at their beginning are defiled. But of this defiling we shall not find the beginning unless we go up to the first parent of all of us, to the well head. Thus it is, therefore, that Adam was not only the progenitor, but also the root of man's nature, and, therefore, in his corruption was all mankind worthily corrupted; which the Apostle makes plain by comparing of him and Christ. As by one man sin entered into the whole world, and death by sin, and so death went over all men, forasmuch as all have sinned, so by the grace of Christ, righteousness and life is restored unto us.

There are two vices that reign and have always reigned in the world; the one is contempt of God, that men care not at all for him, but trample him under their feet, as much as in them lies. True it is, that they be not able to impeach his majesty. Nevertheless there is such a devilish pride to be seen in men, that instead of worshipping God, and of submitting themselves unto him, they could find in their heart to throw him under foot, and to triumph over him, and not suffer him to have any kind of authority over them. Thus see we a malady that is overgreat and outrageous, and yet it has been in all times; that is to say, that men are so over-heathenish, as they know not the reverence which they owe unto God. The other vice is superstition, which is, that under the shadow of devotion, men gad here and there to seek after foolish inventions. And whereof comes this mischief; even because God is not known rightly with that which is properly belonging unto him; for, were it well understood what his mightiness, justice, and goodness are, it is certain that men would not be carried so away. For men forge to themselves under-gods; that is to say, they forge idols in their own heads, and assign offices to them, as though they would deal out the virtues that pertain unto God, and are in him

alone, or as though they would put him to the spoil, and
every one have his share and booty of him.

If God's image were the same in us that it was in our
father Adam at the beginning, undoubtedly all our sense
should be pure and clean without any infection, and all
our looks should tend to God. So soon as we should
look upon any creature, the glory of God would utter
itself in it, and we should be led by it to honour him,
and to be wholly inflamed with his love. There would
be no vanity nor disorder, and much less would there be
any wicked rebelliousness; insomuch that we should not
see any thing, but it would further us to goodness. All
unchaste looks and all other temptations which we conceive by means of our eyes, do spring out of the said
fountain of original sin; that is to say, out of the corruption which we draw from our father Adam, and from
the frowardness of our nature inasmuch as we be alienated from God.

The natural depravity which we bring from our mother's womb, though it does not so soon produce its
effects, is still, however, sin in the presence of the Lord,
and deserves his punishment. This is what divines call
original sin. For as Adam, at his first creation, had
received the gifts of divine grace for his posterity, as
well as himself, so on departing from the Lord he corrupted, vitiated, depraved, ruined our nature in himself;
for being deprived of the image of God, he could only
produce a seed resembling himself. We have, therefore,
all sinned, because we are all imbued with natural corruption ; on which account we are wicked and perverse.

Such is the pride that is naturally planted in us, we
always think ourselves righteous, innocent, wise, and
holy, until that with manifest proofs we be convinced of
our unrighteousness, filthiness, folly, and uncleanness.
But we are not convinced thereof, if we look upon ourselves only, and not upon God also, who is the only rule

whereby this judgment ought to be tried. For because we are naturally inclined to hypocrisy, therefore a certain vain resemblance of righteousness does abundantly content us instead of righteousness indeed. And because there appears nothing among us, nor about us, that is not defiled with much filthiness, therefore that which is somewhat less filthy pleases us, as though it were most pure, so long as we hold ourselves within the bounds of man's uncleanness. Like as the eye which is used to see nothing but black, thinks that to be pure white, which yet is but darkish white or brown. Yea, we may yet more plainly discern by our bodily sense how much we are blinded in considering the powers of the soul. For if at mid-day we either look down upon the ground, or behold those things that round about lie open before our eyes, then we think ourselves to have very assured and piercing force of sight; but when we look up to the sun, and behold it with fixed eyes, then that same sharpness that was of great force upon the ground is with so great brightness by and by dazzled and confounded, that we are compelled to confess, that the same sharp sight which we had in considering earthly things, when it comes to the sun, is but mere dulness. Even so comes it to pass in weighing our spiritual good things. For while we look no farther than the earth, so long being contented with our own righteousness, wisdom, and strength, we do sweetly flatter ourselves, and think us in manner half gods. But if we once begin to raise up our thoughts unto God, and to weigh what a one he is, and how exact is the perfection of his righteousness, wisdom, and power, after the rule whereof we ought to be framed; then that which before did please us in ourselves with false pretence of righteousness, shall become loathsome to us as greatest wickedness; then that which did marvellously deceive us under colour of wisdom, shall stink before us as extreme folly; then that which did bear the face of strength shall be proved to be most miserable weakness. So slender does that which in us seems even most perfect, answer in proportion to the pureness of God.

No easier is the condemnation of the heart, when it is called guileful and perverse above all things; but because I study to be short, I will be content with one place alone, but such a one as shall be like a most bright looking-glass, wherein we may behold the whole image of our nature. For the Apostle, when he goeth about to throw down the arrogancy of mankind, doth it by these testimonies:—That there is not one righteous man, there is not one man that understands or that seeks God. All are gone out of the way, they are made unprofitable together, there is none that doeth good, no not one; their throat is an open sepulchre, with their tongues they work deceitfully, the poison of serpents is under their lips, whose mouth is full of cursing and bitterness; whose feet are swift to shed blood, in whose ways is sorrow and unhappiness, which have not the fear of God before their eyes. With these thunderbolts he inveighs, not against certain men, but against the whole nation of the sons of Adam. Neither declaims he against the corrupt manners of one or two ages, but accuses the continual corruption of nature. For his purpose is, in that place, not simply to chide men, to make them amend, but to teach rather that all men are oppressed with calamity, impossible to be overcome, from which they cannot get up again, unless they be plucked out by the mercy of God. And because that could not be proved unless it had been by the overthrow and destruction of nature, he brought forth these testimonies whereby is proved that our nature is more than destroyed. Let this, therefore, remain agreed, that men are such as they be here described, not only by fault of evil custom, but also by corruptness of nature. For otherwise the Apostle's argument cannot stand, that there is no salvation for man but by the mercy of God, because he is in himself utterly lost and past hope. I will not here busy myself in proving the applying of these testimonies that no man should think them unfitly used; I will so take them as if they had been first spoken by Paul, and not taken out of the prophets. First he takes away from man righteousness, that is integrity and pureness, and then understanding. The want of understanding, he proves by apostasy or departing from God, whom to seek is the first degree of wisdom. But that want must needs happen to them that are fallen away from God. He says farther, that all are gone out of the way and become as it were rotten, that there is none that does good, and then he adjoins the heinous faults wherewith they defile their members that are once let loose into wickedness. Last of all he testifies that they are void of the fear of God, after whose rule our steps should have been directed. If these be the inheritable gifts of mankind, it is in vain to seek for any good thing in our nature. Indeed, I grant that not all these faults do appear in every man; yet can it not be denied that this hydra lurks in the hearts of all men.

There is nothing in us but sin; there is nothing in us but corruption; God must needs reject us and hate us; he must needs become our deadly enemy, and utter his vengeance upon us. To be short, we are in the dungeons of hell until God have reached us his hand, and had pity upon us. It is not for any man to exempt himself from this confusion, for from the greatest to the least of us we are all plunged into it. Nor let us boast of the things which we have by nature. For God finds us void of all goodness; we have not one drop of virtue, wisdom, or righteousness, but contrariwise, we are full of corruption; we are ready to burst for filth and uncleanness; we are bond slaves to Satan, under the tyranny and bondage of death; and at a word we are plunged in hell.

We are so froward and full of corruption that the law can serve us to no other purpose but to curse us, and to make us perceive how loathsome we are in the sight of

God, inasmuch as we are his deadly enemies ; and so we have double cause to be abashed and ashamed of ourselves when we see that the good is so turned to our harm, and it is more than if the nature of the sun were changed by our infection. Would it not make us to loathe ourselves, if we should find such foul and vile smoke in us as should darken and quench the light of the sun ? Yes, verily. Now we see that God's law is the light of our life, and yet we not only dim it, but also turn it into the darkness of death, and it is impossible that it should stand us in any stead, until our Lord Jesus Christ have wrought in us and reformed us by his Holy Spirit, and by writing his law new again in our hearts. For as much as we see, then, that men turn life into death, light into darkness, and benefit into bane, alas, ought we not to be exceedingly abashed ? Yes, but yet must not that put us out of conceit with the doctrines of the law, so as that we should not lose it, howbeit we cannot perform it until God have changed our hearts to cause us to submit ourselves unto him, and have made us new creatures in our Lord Jesus Christ.

While the devil holds us in his cords and nets, is it not a horrible matter, and enough to make our hairs to stare upon our heads ? If we consider our first beginning, God made us as his children ; he caused his glory to shine in us, and placed us in this world, to the end we should be as lively images of him. And, therefore, we must needs say, that sin makes a horrible breach, when the devil takes possession of us, and when so noble, so worthy, so excellent a creature as man is cast down so far, that the devil holds him in his cords.

We see what negligence and little regard there is in man, and how drunk they are with vain pride, insomuch that they know not what it is to come to a reckoning before God ; and though they hear every day that God takes them for his deadly enemies, and that he is armed, and that his vengeance is ready against them, they pass not one pin : and this is not only a drunkenness, but they are bewitched, they are choked up with their filthiness, so that they cannot feel a whit of this wrath of God which is ready for them, and wherewith the Scripture threatens them.

As often as men are led away to sinning by the concupiscence of their flesh, in the beginning thereof they consult in themselves, and feel some bridle which restrains them, and which, doubtless, would hinder them from committing of evil, if they were not overcarried by a contrary tempest, which shakes off and puts away all remorse of conscience. When any man is enticed or stirred up to evil, his conscience, by a secret instinct, asks him, What doest thou ? And sin never creeps thus upon us but we feel some remorse. And God hath thus indeed prevented men, to the end all should not give over themselves with an unbridled licentiousness to commit evil. Whence comes it, then, that men are so obstinate in their naughtiness ? To say the truth, they suffer themselves to be beguiled by allurements, and do so drench their minds with delighting themselves therein, that they despise the judgments of God, and all to pursue their sins with greediness. They flatter themselves in believing that which is sin to be no sin ; or else they mince them, making them less than they are ; or excuse themselves in them under one pretence or other.

The wicked think that God takes his ease in heaven, and cares not for men's matters, as certain epicures, who placed God's chiefest happiness in this, that he had nothing to do. And although they imagine that there is some God, yet they acknowledge him not in his judgments, but in the mean while they make good cheer, and never pine away themselves with such thoughts. Let the prophets and ministers cry, and that with open mouth, let them threaten and terrify us while they list, we will securely lie still, waiting till that which they threaten come to pass, and in the whilst we will make merry.

The similitude of the sea is elegant and very fit to express the disquietness of the wicked. For the sea troubles itself, and is tossed with hideous tempests, though the winds be calm; the waves jostle one against another with great violence, and break with a very terrible noise; and so the wicked are vexed with a secret worm, which cleaves fast to their consciences; for they are in continual terrors, by reason of the gnawing and stings thereof, which is a torment that surmounts all the rest, and the most cruel hangman that is to be found in the whole world. The furies of hell harry and pursue the wicked, not with burning torches, as the poets feign; but through anguishes of conscience, and the torment of their wilful rebellion; for every one of them is affrighted, and extremely tortured by his own iniquity; their wicked cogitations amaze them, and cause them to rage, and the guilt and scruples of their consciences astonish them.

IV—CHRIST

As OUR own iniquities had cast a cloud between God and us, and utterly excluded us from the kingdom of heaven, no man could be the interpreter for restoring of our peace but he that could attain unto God. But who could have attained unto him? Could any of the sons of Adam? but all they did with their fathers shun the sight of God for fear. Could any of the angels? but they also had need of a head, by whose knitting together they might perfectly and unseverably cleave unto God. What then? It was past all hope, unless the very majesty of God would descend unto us, for we could not ascend unto it. So it behoved that the Son of God should become for us Immanuel, that is, God with us; and that in this sort, that by mutual joining, his Godhead and the nature of man might grow into one together. Otherwise neither could the nearness be near enough, nor the alliance strong enough for us to hope by, that God dwelleth with us ; so great was the disagreement between our filthiness and the most pure cleanness of God. Although man had stood undefiled without any spot, yet was his estate too base to attain to God without a Mediator. What could he then do, being plunged down into death and hell with deadly fall, defiled with so many spots, stinking with his own corruption, and overwhelmed with all accursedness ? Therefore, not without cause, Paul, meaning to set forth Christ for the Mediator, doth expressly recite that he is man. Our Mediator of God and man, the Man Jesus Christ. He might have said God ; or at the least he might have left the name of man as well as of God. But because the Holy Ghost, speaking by his mouth, knew our weakness ; therefore to provide for it in time, he used a most fit remedy, setting among us the Son of God familiarly as one of us. Therefore, lest any man should trouble himself to know where the Mediator is to be sought, or which way to come unto him, in naming man he puts us in mind that he is near unto us, yea, so near that he touches us, for as much as he is our own flesh. Truly he means there even the same thing that in another place is set out with more words ; that we have not a bishop that cannot have compassion of our infirmities, for as much as he was in all things tempted as we are, only sin excepted.

Moreover, it was for the same cause very profitable, that he which should be our Redeemer, should be both very God and very man. It was his office to swallow up death ; who could do that but life itself ? It was his office to overcome sin ; who could do that but righteousness itself ? It was his office to vanquish the powers of the world and of the air ; who could do that but a power above both world and air ? Now in whose possession is life, or righteousness, or the empire and power of heaven, but in God's alone? Therefore the most merciful God, in the person of his only begotten Son, made himself our Redeemer, when his will was to have us redeemed.

Now where it is said that the word was made flesh, that is not so to be understood as though it were either turned into flesh, or confusedly mangled with flesh, but because he chose him a temple of the Virgin's womb to dwell in, he that was the Son of God became also the son of man, not by confusion of substance, but by unity of person. For we so affirm the Godhead joined and united to the manhood, that each of them has its whole property remaining, and yet of them both is made one Christ. If any thing in all worldly things may be found like to so great a mystery, the similitude of man is most fit, whom we see to consist of two substances, whereof yet neither is so mingled with the other, but that each keeps the property of its own nature. For neither is the soul the body, nor the body the soul. Wherefore both that thing may be severally spoken of the soul, which can no way agree with the body; and likewise of the body that thing may be said which can by no means agree with the soul; and that may be said of the whole man, which can be but unfitly taken neither of the soul nor of the body severally. Finally, the properties of the soul are sometimes attributed to the body, and the properties of the body sometimes to the soul; and yet he that consists of them is but one man and not many. But such forms of speech do signify both that there is one person in man compounded of two natures knit together, and that there are two diverse natures which do make the same person. And so do the Scriptures speak of Christ; sometime they give unto him those things that ought singularly to be referred to his manhood, and sometime those things that do peculiarly belong to his Godhead, and sometime those things that do comprehend both natures, and do agree with neither of them severally. And this conjoining of the two natures that are in Christ, they do with such religiousness express, that sometime they do put them in common together; which figure is among the old authors called communicating of properties.

Paul affirms that Christ is the first begotten of all creatures, which was before all things, and by whom all things keep their being; and he himself reports that he was in glory with the Father before the creation of the world, and that he works together with the Father; these things do in nothing agree with the nature of men. It is therefore certain, that these and such like are peculiarly ascribed to the Godhead. But whereas he is called the servant of the Father; and whereas it is said, that he grew in age, wisdom, and favour with God and men; that he seeks not his own glory; that he knows not the last day; that he speaks not of himself; that he does not his own will: where it is said, that he was seen and felt; this wholly belongs to his own manhood. For in respect that he is God, neither can he increase in any thing, and he works all things for his own sake, neither is any thing hidden from him, he does all things according to the free choice of his own will, and can neither be seen nor felt. And yet he does not severally ascribe these things to his nature of man only, but takes them upon himself, as if they did agree with the person of the Mediator. But the communicating of properties is in this, that Paul says, that God did by his own blood purchase unto him a church, and that the Lord of glory was crucified. Again, where John says, that the word of life was felt. Truly God neither hath blood, nor suffers, nor can be touched with hands. But because he which was both very God and man, Christ being crucified, did shed his blood for us; those things that were done in his nature of man, are unproperly, and yet not without reason given to his Godhead. A like example is, where John teaches that God gave his soul for us; therefore there also the property of the manhood is communicate with the other nature. Again, when Christ said, being yet conversant in earth, that no man has ascended into heaven, but the son of man that was in heaven; truly according to his manhood, and in the flesh that he had put on, he was not then in heaven; but because himself was both God and man, by the reason of the unity of both natures, he gave to the one that which belonged to the other.

What is there more unlikely, than to believe that he should be king of all the people, who was not account-ed worthy of a mean place among the common people? and to hope for the restitution and salvation of the kingdom from him, who for his want and poverty was thrown out into a stable? Yet Luke writes, that none of these things hindered the Shepherds, but that with great admiration they praised God; namely, because that the glory of God was throughly fixed in their eyes, and the reverence of his word printed in their minds, that whatsoever they met with either infamous or con-temptible in Christ, they with the height of their faith do easily pass over the same. Neither is there any other cause why every of those small offences do either hinder or turn our faith from the right course; but because that we taking small hold upon God, are easily drawn hither and thither. For if this one cogitation possessed all our senses, that we have a certain and a faithful witness from heaven, it were a defence strong and stable enough against all kinds of temptations, and it should well enough fortify us against all offences.

God fetched wise men out of Chaldee or Persia, which should come into Judea to worship Christ, where he lay without honour and contemned. Truly a wonderful counsel of God, that God would his Son should come forth into the world under this obscure humility; yet he excellently adorned him, as with phrases, so with other tokens, lest any thing for the trial of our faith had been wanting from his divine majesty: yet here is to be noted a notable harmony of things seeming to be repugnant. The star from heaven declares him to be a king, whose throne is the beast's stall, because that he is denied a place even among the common sort of men. His majesty shines in the East, which not only appears not in Judea, but is also defiled with many reproaches. To what purpose is this ; namely, the heavenly Father's will was to appoint that the star and the wise men should lead us the right way to his Son ; but yet he stripped him naked of all earthly honour, that we might know his kingdom to be spiritual. Wherefore this story is not only profitable, because that God brought these wise men to his Son, as the first-fruits of the Gentiles, but also because he would set forth the kingdom of his Son, as with the praise of them, so of the star for the help of our faith, lest the wicked and malicious despite of his own nation should cause him to be despised of us.

Now it is to be noted, that the title of commendation of Christ belongs to these three offices. For we know that in the time of the law, as well the prophets as priests and kings were anointed with holy oil. For which cause the renowned name of Messias was given to the promised mediator. But though, indeed, I confess that he was called Messias, by peculiar consideration and respect of his kingdom ; yet the anointings in respect of the office of prophet and of priest, have their place, and are not to be neglected of us. Of the first of these two is express mention made in Isaiah, in these words, the "Spirit of the Lord Jehovah is upon me. Therefore the Lord hath anointed me, that I should preach to the meek, should bring health to the contrite in heart, should declare deliverance to captives, should publish the year of good-will," &c. We see that he was anointed with the spirit, to be the publisher and witness of the grace of the Father. And that not after the common manner, for he is severed from other teachers that had the like office.

And here again is to be noted, that he took not the anointing for himself alone, that he might execute the office of teaching, but for his whole body, that in his continual preaching of the gospel, the virtue of the Spirit should join withal. But in the mean time this remains certain, that by this perfection of doctrine which he has brought, an end is made of all prophecies, so that they do diminish his authority, that being not content with the Gospel, do patch any foreign thing unto it. For that voice which thundered from heaven, saying, this is my beloved Son, hear him, has advanced him by singular privilege above the degrees of all others.

So often as we hear that Christ is armed with eternal power, let us remember that the everlasting continuance of the church is upholden by this support, to remain still safe among the troublesome tossings wherewith it is continually vexed, and among the grievous and terrible motions that threaten innumerable destructions. So when David scorns the boldness of his enemies, that go about to break the yoke of God and of Christ, and says that the kings and people raged in vain, because he that dwells in heaven is strong enough to break their violent assaults ; he assures the godly of the continual preservation of the church, and encourages them to hope well so often as it happens to be oppressed. So in another place when he says, in the person of God, sit at my right hand, till I make thine enemies thy footstool ; he warns us, that how many and strong enemies soever do conspire to besiege the church, yet they have not strength enough to prevail against that unchangeable decree of God, whereby he has appointed his Son an eternal king, whereupon it follows, that it is impossible that the Devil with all the preparation of the world, may be able at any time to destroy the church, which is grounded upon the eternal seat of Christ. Now for so much as concerns the special use of every one, the very same eternal continuance ought to raise us up to hope of immortality. For we see that whatsoever is earthly and of the world, endures but for a time, yea, and is very frail. Therefore Christ, to lift up our hope unto heaven, pronounces that his kingdom is not of this world. Finally, when any of us hears that the kingdom of Christ is spiritual, let him be raised up with this saying, and let him pierce to the hope of a better life; and whereas he is now defended by the hand of Christ, let him look for the full fruit of this grace in the world to come.

The miracles which Christ wrought amongst a few, and which he would not should be much boasted of, were able to shake the heaven and the earth. Therefore he doth plainly show how far he was from the vain glory and pomp of the world. Yet it is convenient to sift the purpose of Matthew more narrowly; for he would declare by this circumstance that the glory of the Godhead of Christ ought not to be the less esteemed because it appeared not in a glorious show. And certainly the Holy Ghost directed the eyes of the Prophet to this purpose. For as flesh does always desire an outward glorious show, lest the faithful should seek for it in the Messiah, the Spirit of God does declare that he shall be far unlike to earthly kings, who make great stirs and noises, and fill the cities and towns with tumult, that they may be had in admiration wheresoever they come. Now we see how aptly Matthew applies the saying of the Prophet to the present cause; for because God has laid so humble and so abject a person upon his Son, lest the simple should take offence at his so contemptible and obscure estate, as well the Prophet as Matthew do meet in one, and they say that it was not done without consideration, but by a celestial decree that he should come in that estate. Whereof it follows that all they do wickedly which despise Christ because his outward condition answers not their fleshly affections. Neither is it lawful for us to devise a Christ, which shall be like to our imagination; but it is simply necessary for us to embrace him as he is offered unto us by the Father. Therefore he is unworthy of salvation in whose eyes the humility of Christ seems vile, in the which the Lord declares that he is delighted.

Because the just curse possesses the entry, and God, according to his office of Judge, is bent against us, it is necessary that some expiation be used, that he being a priest may procure favour for us, to appease the wrath of God. Wherefore, that Christ might fulfil this office, it behoved that he should come forth with a sacrifice. For in the law it was not lawful for the priest to enter into the sanctuary without blood, that the faithful might know, that though there were a priest become means for us to make intercession, yet God could not be made favourable to us before that our sins were purged. Upon which point the Apostle discourses largely in the Epistle to the Hebrews, from the seventh chapter almost to the end of the tenth. But the sum of all comes to this effect, that the honour of priesthood can be applied to none but to Christ, which by the sacrifice of his death hath wiped away our guiltiness, and satisfied for our sins. But how weighty a matter it is, we are informed by that solemn oath of God, which was spoken without repentance. Thou art a priest for ever according to the order of Melchisedec. For without doubt his will was to establish that principal point which he knew to be the chief joint whereupon our salvation hung, for as it is said, there is no way open for us or for our prayers to God, unless our filthiness being purged, the priests do sanctify us, and obtain grace for us, from which the uncleanness of our wicked doings and sins do debar us. So do we see, that we must begin at the death of Christ, that the efficacy and profit of his priesthood may come unto us. Of this it follows, that he is an eternal intercessor, by whose mediation we obtain favour, whereupon again arises, not only affiance to pray, but also quietness to godly consciences, while they safely lean upon the fatherly tenderness of God, and are certainly persuaded that it pleases him whatsoever is dedicated to him by the Meditator. But, whereas, in the time of the law, God commanded sacrifices of beasts to be offered to him; there was another and a new order in Christ, that one should be both the sacrificed host, and the priest; because there neither could be found any other satisfaction for sins, nor any was worthy so great honour to offer up to God his only begotten son. Now, Christ beareth the person of a priest, not only by eternal mean of reconciliation to make the Father favourable and merciful unto us, but also to bring us into the fellowship of so great an honour.

The Son of God did willingly submit himself to death that he might reconcile the world unto the Father, for there was no other means whereby either the guiltiness of sins could be washed away, or the righteousness obtained for us ; then, that he died not as one oppressed so with violence which he could not escape, but because that he offered himself willingly to death. Therefore he says, that he comes purposely to Jerusalem to die there. For when as he was at liberty to go back again, and to pass away that time in some safe and secret place, wittingly and willingly, he goes forth amongst them even in the appointed time. And though the disciples profited nothing at that time by the warning that was given them of the obedience which he yielded to the Father, yet afterwards their faith was much strengthened by this doctrine. As also at this day we receive no small profit thereby ; for it sets before us as in a lively glass that free-will offering and sacrifice, whereby all the transgressions of the world are blotted out, and we behold the Son of God gladly and boldly going forward to death, and now a conqueror of death.

The thief, who not only had never been a scholar in Christ's school, but by thrusting himself into bloody murders, had endeavoured to quench all sense of righteousness, does of a sudden pierce deeper than all the Apostles and the rest of the disciples, in teaching of whom the Lord himself had bestowed so much labour; and not that only, but Christ, being upon the tree of execution, he worships as a king; he celebrates his kingdom in that horrible and more than deformed baseness; he calls him, who is about to die, the author of life. Truly, if he had been instructed in the true faith, had heard many things before of the office of Christ, and had also been confirmed in the same by miracles; yet that knowledge being covered with the cloud of a reproachful death, might vanish away. Now it was more than wonderful that he being rude and a youngling, yea, his mind altogether corrupted, should presently at the first instructions upon the cursed cross, apprehend salvation and the celestial glory. For with what marks or ensigns did he see Christ adorned, that he might lift up his mind to that kingdom? And certainly this was as if he should climb out of the deepest hells above the heavens. But to the flesh this was but as a fable, and to be laughed at, to attribute to a man cast away and condemned (whom the world could not abide) a kingdom far more noble than all earthly empires. Hereby we do gather how quick the eyes of his mind were, wherewith he beheld life in death, height in ruin, glory in reproach, victory in destruction, and a kingdom in slavery. If that the thief extolled by his faith Christ now hanging upon the cross, and as it were overwhelmed with cursing, into a heavenly throne, wo be to our slothfulness if we do not reverence him now sitting at the right hand of God, if we do not fasten the hope of life in his resurrection, if we go not into heaven whither he is entered. Now, if on the other part we do consider what state he was in, when he besought Christ of his mercy, his faith shall grow to further admiration; with a torn body now almost without life he waits for the last blow of the slaughter-men, and yet he reposes himself in the only grace of Christ. First, whence has he this hope of forgiveness, but because that in the death of Christ, which seems detestable to all other, he conceives the sacrifice of a good savour, to be effectual to wash away the sins of the world? And where he with courage regards not his torments, nay, as it were forgetting himself, is carried to a hope and desire of a better life, it does far pass the understanding of man. Wherefore let us not be ashamed to learn both mortification of the flesh, and patience, and excellency of faith, and constancy of hope, and zeal of godliness of this master, whom the Lord set over us to humble the pride of the flesh. For the readier that any man follows him, the nearer he shall so come to Christ.

Though in the death of Christ the infirmity of the flesh for a while covered the glory of the Godhead; yea the Son of God himself lay without form under reproach and contempt, and he was made of no reputation, yet the heavenly Father ceased not to adorn him with some marks, and when he was at the lowest cast he erected some tokens of the glory to come, which might strengthen the minds of the godly against the offence of the cross. So the majesty of Christ was royally set forth by the darkening of the sun, the earthquake, cleaving of rocks, and rending of the vail, even as if heaven and earth should yield the worship due to their maker and framer. But first it is demanded for what purpose the sun was eclipsed. For where the old poets in their tragedies do feign that the light of the sun is withdrawn from the earth where any notable offence is committed, tends to note the greatness of the wrath of God, and this fantasy was gathered of the common sense of nature. Therefore some interpreters do think that God sent darkness in sign of detestation; as if God by darkening the sun should hide his face from the most filthy wickedness of all. Others do say that by the darkness of the

visible sun was the death of the Sun of Righteousness
declared. Others had rather to apply it to the making
of that nation blind, which followed shortly after. For
the Jews rejecting Christ, after he was taken from
amongst them, were deprived of the light of the heavenly doctrine, neither was there any thing left them besides
the darkness of desperation. But I do rather think that
this people, because they would not see the light they
were so blockish, were stirred up by darkness to consider the wonderful counsel of God in the death of
Christ. For the unwonted alteration of the order of
nature, if they had not been altogether hardened, should
have earnestly moved their senses to attend to that renewing of the world to come. In the mean while a
sight full of terror was showed them, that they might
fear before the judgment of God. And truly this was
an incomparable testimony of the wrath of God, that
spared not his only begotten Son, neither could he
otherwise be appeased than by the price of that sacrifice.
But where the scribes and priests, and a great part of
the people carelessly neglected, and as it were with
closed eyes passed by the darkening of the sun, their
wonderful madness should make us afraid. For they
must of necessity be more blockish than the brute beasts,
who, being warned by such a wonder of the rigour of
the heavenly judgment, ceased not their scoffing.

Though there appeared more than the force of a man
in the crying of Christ, yet it is certain that the vehemency of grief wrested it out of him. And certainly
this was the chief conflict, and sharper than all other
torments, because that in his sorrows he was not so
comforted with the aid and favour of his father, that he
thought himself in some sort forsaken. For he not only
offered his body for the price of our reconciliation with
God, but in soul he also bore the punishments due to
us, and so he rightly became a man full of sorrows.
And truly they are too foolish who, passing by this part

of the redemption, do only rest upon the outward punishment of the flesh. For to the end that Christ might make satisfaction for us, it was behoveful for him to stand as guilty before the judgment seat of God. And there is nothing more horrible than to feel God a judge, whose wrath exceedeth all deaths. Therefore when this kind of temptation is laid upon Christ as if, God being his enemy, he should now be given over to destruction, he is taken with horror wherein all mortal men had been swallowed up a hundred times; but he by the marvellous power of the Spirit escaped with the victory. And he makes not this complaint dissemblingly, or after the manner of a player, that he was forsaken of his Father. And where many do pretend that he spake thus according to the opinion of the common people, it is but a fond cavil; for the inward sorrow of the mind compelled him forcibly and earnestly to break out into this cry. And it was not only a redemption to serve the eye which he wrought; but as he had offered himself a pledge for us, his will was to bear in deed the judgment of God in our place. But it seems to be absurd that this desperate speech should pass from Christ. The answer is easy,—though the sense of the flesh beheld destruction, yet his faith was fast settled in his heart, wherein he beheld God present, of whose absence he complains.

The rending of the vail was not only the abrogation of the ceremonies which were of force under the law, but also an opening of the heavens, so that now God doth familiarly call the members of his Son unto him. In the mean while the Jews were admonished that the outward sacrifices were ended, and that afterward there should be no use of the old priesthood; although the building of the temple should stand, God was no more to be worshipped after the accustomed order; but because the substance and truth of the shadows were now fulfilled, the figures of the law are turned into the spirit. For though Christ offered a visible sacrifice, yet it must be spiritually esteemed, that the price and fruit of the same may appear. But the outward sanctuary profited nothing to miserable men when the vail being broken it was left naked; for the inward vail of their infidelity took from them the sight of the light of their salvation.

By the very token of the curse we do more plainly learn that the burden wherewith we were oppressed was laid upon him. And yet it is not so to be understood, that he took upon him such a curse, wherewith himself was overladen, but rather that in taking it upon him, he did tread down, break, and destroy the whole force of it. And so faith conceives acquittal in the condemnation of Christ, and blessing in his being accursed. Wherefore Paul does not, without a cause, honourably report the triumph that Christ obtained to himself on the cross, as if the cross, which was full of shame, had been turned into a chariot of triumph. For he says, that the hand-writing which was against us, was fastened to the cross, and the princely powers were spoiled and led openly. And no marvel, because Christ offered up himself by the eternal Spirit. And thereupon proceeded that turning of the nature of things. But that these things may take stedfast root, and be thoroughly settled in our hearts, let us always think upon his sacrifice and washing. For we could not certainly believe that Christ was the ransom, redemption, and satisfaction, unless he had been a sacrificed host. And therefore there is so often mention made of blood, where the Scripture shows the manner of our redeeming. Albeit the blood of Christ, that was shed, served not only for sacrifice, but also instead of washing to cleanse away our filthiness.

It follows in the creed, that he was dead and buried: Where again it is to be seen, how he did every where put himself in our stead, to pay the price of our redemption. Death held us bound under his yoke. Christ, in our stead, did yield himself into the power of death, to deliver us from it. This the Apostle means where he writes that he tasted of death for all men. For he by dying brought to pass that we should not die, or which is all one, by his death he did redeem life for us. But in this he differed from us, that he gave himself to death, as it were to be devoured, not that he should be swallowed up with the gulfs of it, but rather that he should swallow up it, of which we should have been presently swallowed; that he gave himself to death to be subdued, not that he should be oppressed with the power thereof, but rather that he should overthrow death which approached near us, yea, and had already beaten us down, and triumphed upon us. Finally, that by death he might destroy him that had the power of death, that is the Devil, and might deliver them that by fear of death were all their life long subject to bondage.

Though he manifested his resurrection in other order than our fleshly wisdom would desire, yet this means which pleased him must also seem best to us. He came out of the grave no man seeing it, that the empty place might be the first token; next, his will was that the angels should tell the women that he was alive; shortly after he appeared unto them, and at length to the apostles, and that ofttimes. So by little and little he led his, according to their capacity, to further knowledge. But that he first began with the women, and not only showed himself to be seen of them, but also enjoined them to preach the gospel to his apostles, that they might be as it were their schoolmistresses. In this was the slothfulness of the apostles first chastised, who through fear lay almost without life, when as the women hasted busily to the sepulchre, who also were thoroughly rewarded for the same. For though their purpose to anoint Christ was not without a fault, as if he should have still remained dead, yet he, pardoning their infirmity, bestowed upon them this singular honour, by resigning to them the office of the apostleship for a while, which was taken from men.

Now follows his resurrection from the dead, without which all that we have hitherto were but imperfect. For since there appeareth in the cross, death, and burial of Christ, nothing but weakness; faith must pass beyond all those things, that it may be furnished with full strength. Therefore, although we have in his death a full accomplishment of salvation, because by it both we are reconciled to God, and his just judgment is satisfied, and the curse taken away, and the penalty fully paid; yet we are said to be regenerate into a living hope, not by his death, but by his rising again. For as he in rising again rose up the vanquisher of death, so the victory of our faith consists in the very resurrection: but how this is, is better expressed in the words of Paul. For he says, that Christ died for our sins, and was raised up again for our justification: as if he should have said, that by his death sin was taken away, and by his rising again, righteousness was renewed and restored. For how could he by dying deliver us from death, if he himself had lain still overcome by death? How could he have gotten victory for us, if he himself had been vanquished in fight? wherefore we do so part the matter of our salvation between the death and resurrection of Christ, that by his death we say sin was taken away and death destroyed, and by his resurrection righteousness was repaired, and life raised up again: but so that by mean of his resurrection, his death does show forth her force and effect in us. Therefore, Paul affirms, that in his very resurrection he was declared the Son of God, because then at last he uttered his heavenly power, which is both a clear glass of his godhead, and a stedfast stay of our faith. As also in another place he teaches, that Christ suffered after the weakness of the flesh, and rose again by the power of the Spirit. And in the same meaning in another, where he entreats of perfection, he says: that I may

know him and the power of his resurrection. Yet, by
and by, after he adjoins the fellowship with death. Wherewith most aptly agrees that saying of Peter: that
God raised him up from the dead and gave him glory,
that our faith and hope might be in God: not that our
faith, being upholden by his death, should waver, but that
the power of God which keeps us under faith, doth principally show itself in the resurrection. Therefore, let
us remember, that so oft as mention is made of his death
only, there is also comprehended that which properly
belongs to his resurrection, and like figure of compre-
hension is there in the word resurrection, as oft as it is
used severally without speaking of his death, so that it
draws with it that which peculiarly pertains to his death.
But forasmuch as by rising again he obtains the crown
of conquest, so there should be both resurrection and
life; therefore, Paul doth for good cause affirm that faith
is destroyed, and the gospel is become vain and deceitful, if the resurrection of Christ be not fastened in our
hearts.   Therefore, in another place, after he had gloried
in the death of Christ against all the terrors of damnation, to amplify the same, he says further: Yea, the
same, he which died, is risen up again, and now stands a
mediator for us in the presence of God.   Furthermore,
as we have before declared, that upon the partaking of
his cross hangs the mortification of our flesh; so is it
to be understood, that by his resurrection we obtain
another commodity which answers that mortification.
For we are therefore grafted into the likeness of his death,
that being partakers of his resurrection, we may walk in
newness of life. Therefore, in another place: as he gathers
an argument of this, that we are dead together with
Christ, to prove that we ought to mortify our members
upon earth; likewise, also, because we are risen up with
Christ, he gathers thereupon that we ought to seek for
those things that are above, and not those that are upon
the earth.   By which words we are not only exhorted

to be raised up after the example of Christ, to follow a newness of life; but we are taught that it is wrought by his power, that we are regenerate into righteousness. We obtain also a third fruit of his resurrection, that we are, as by an earnest delivered us, assured of our own resurrection, of which we know that his resurrection is a most certain argument.

To his resurrection is not unfitly adjoined his ascending into heaven. For although Christ began more fully to set forth his glory and power by rising again, for that he had now laid away that base and unnoble state of mortal life, and the shame of the cross: yet by his ascending up into heaven only he truly began his kingdom. Which the Apostle shows, where he teaches that Christ ascended to fulfil all things. Where, in seeming of repugnancy, he shows that there is a goodly agreement; because he so departed from us that yet his presence might be more profitable to us, which had been penned in a base lodging of the flesh while he was conversant in earth. And therefore John, after that he had rehearsed that notable calling,—"if any thirst, let him come to me," &c.—by and by says that the Holy Ghost was not yet given to the faithful, because Jesus was not yet glorified. Which the Lord himself also did testify to the disciples, saying,—it is expedient for you that I go away, for if I do not go away the Holy Ghost shall not come: but he gives them a comfort for his corporal absence, that he will not leave them as parentless, but will come again to them after a certain manner; indeed invisible, but yet more to be desired, because they were then taught by a more assured experience that the authority which he enjoins and the power which he uses, are sufficient for the faithful, not only to make them live blessedly, but also to die happily. And truly we see how much greater abundance of his spirit he then poured out; how much more royally he then advanced his kingdom; how much greater power he then showed both in helping his, and in overthrowing his enemies. Being, therefore, taken up into heaven, he took away the presence of his body out of our sight; not to cease to be present with the faithful that yet wandered in the earth, but with more present power to govern both heaven and earth.

Wherefore, it by and by follows, that he is set down at the right hand of his Father; which is spoken by way of similitude, taken of princes that have their sitters by, to whom they commit their office to rule and govern in their stead. So it is said that Christ, in whom the Father will be exalted and reign by his hand, was received to sit at his right hand; as if it had been said that he was invested in the dominion of heaven and earth, solemnly entered upon the possession of the government committed unto him, and that he not only entered upon it, but also continues in it, till he comes down to judgment. For so does the Apostle expound it, when he says thus:—"The Father has set him at his right hand, above all principality, and power, and strength, and dominion, and every name that is named, not only in this world but in the world to come." "He has put all things under his feet, and has given him to be head of the Church above all things." Now you see to what purpose belongs that sitting; that is, that all creatures, both heavenly and earthly, may with admiration look upon his majesty, be governed with his hand, behold his countenance, and be subject to his power. And the Apostles mean nothing else when they so oft rehearse it, but to teach that all things are left to his will.

Hereupon does faith gather manifold fruit; for it learns that the Lord by his ascending into heaven has opened the entry of the heavenly kingdom, which before had been stopped up by Adam. For when he entered into it in our flesh as in our name, thereupon follows that which the Apostle says, that we do already in him, after a certain manner, sit in heaven; for that we do not with bare hope look for heaven, but already in our head we possess it. Moreover, faith perceives that he sits with his Father to our great benefit; for he is entered into a sanctuary not made with hands, and there appears before the face of the Father a continual advocate and intercessor for us: he so turns the Father's eyes to his righteousness, that he turns them away from our sins ; he so reconciles his mind unto us, that by his intercession he prepares us a way and passage to his throne, filling it with grace and mercifulness, which, otherwise, would have been full of horror to wretched sinners. Thirdly, faith conceives his power, wherein consists our strength, might, wealth, and glorying against the hells; for, ascending into heaven, he led captivity captive, and spoiling his enemies he enriched his people and daily fills them with heaps of spiritual riches. He sits, therefore, on high, that from thence pouring out his power unto us, he may quicken us to a spiritual life, sanctify with his spirit, and garnish his church with the divers gifts of his grace, preserve it safe against all hurts by his protection, restrain with the strength of his hand the raging enemies of his cross and of our salvation ; finally, hold all power both in heaven and in earth till he has overthrown all his enemies, which are also our enemies, and made perfect the building up of his Church.

Christ is now seated at the right hand of the Father; by which is signified that he obtains the dominion of heaven and earth, and the full rule and authority of all things. Christ, finally, is so seated, according to Paul, as to be a constant advocate and intercessor in defence of our salvation ; and it hence follows, every accuser, desirous to condemn us, not only makes Christ's death to be vain, but wages war with his incomparable power, which was bestowed upon him as an ornament by the Father, who committed to the Messiah, with such distinguished might, the most absolute dominion. This security, so great as to dare triumphantly to vaunt over the devil, death, and sin, and the very gates of hell, ought to be seated in all pious breasts; for we have no faith unless we are certainly assured that Christ is ours, and the Father reconciled to us in our loving Redeemer. No imagination, therefore, can be conceived more ruinous, pernicious, or destructive, than the opinion of the school-men concerning the uncertainty of faith. " Who inter-cedes"—It was necessary to make this express addition, lest the divine majesty of the Saviour should make us tremble. Paul clothes Christ, who from his lofty throne holds all things under his feet and subject to his autho-rity, with his mediatorial character ; on which account it is absurd to tremble at his presence, since he not only kindly and courteously invites us to himself, but appears as intercessor on our account in the presence of his Father. We must not, therefore, measure this intercession by our carnal sense and judgment; we must not consider Jesus to be interceding with the Father in a suppliant posture on his bended knees, and with stretched out hands. Christ is justly said to intercede, since he constantly appears with his death and resurrection, which act instead of an eternal intercession, and possess the power and efficacy of the most lively pleading, and thus reconcile the Father to us, and make the God of love ready to listen to our entreaties.

The Papists shall never be able to show one syllable in all holy writ, that God allows that which they do, but that it is but their foolish opinion, which they have con-ceived in their own brain without all reason. In like sort is that which they say, " O I am not worthy to go to God ; therefore the saints must be my advocates and patrons." But who gave you this office to appoint advocates in paradise ? It is true that we are not worthy to go to God, and we must needs have a mediator to bring us to him, and to open to us the way ; but Jesus Christ is appointed to this purpose. In an earthly court, if there be any ad-vocates and preachers, the judge must appoint them, else they should not be admitted and received. And when we come to the kingdom of God, must we presume to set and appoint states there ? have we to establish advocates and proctors at our pleasure ?

Christ shall in visible form come down from heaven, even such as he was seen to go up : and he shall appear to all men with unspeakable majesty of his kingdom, with bright glittering of immortality, with infinite power of Godhead, with a guard of angels. From thence, therefore, we are bidden to look for him to come as our Redeemer at that day ; when he shall sever the lambs from the goats, the chosen from the forsaken : and there shall be none of all either the quick or the dead, that shall escape his judgment. For from the farthest corners of the world shall be heard the sound of the trumpet, wherewith all shall be called to his judgment-seat, both they that shall be found alive at that day, and they whom death hath before taken out of the company of the quick.

Forasmuch as we do see that the whole sum of our salvation, and all the parts thereof are comprehended in Christ, we must beware, that we do not draw away from him any part thereof, be it never so little. If we seek for salvation, we are taught by the very name of Jesus, that it is in him : if we seek for any other gifts of the spirit, they are to be found in his anointing : if we seek for strength, it is in his dominion : if we seek for cleanness, it is in his conception : if we seek for tender kindness, it shows itself in his birth, whereby he was made in all things like unto us, that he might learn to sorrow with us : if we seek for redemption, it is in his passion : if we seek for absolution, it is in his condemnation : if we seek for release of the curse, it is in his cross : if we seek for satisfaction, it is in his sacrifice : if we seek for cleansing, it is in his blood : if we seek for reconciliation, it is in his going down to the hells : if we seek for mortification of the flesh, it is in his burial : if we seek for new-

ness of life, it is in his resurrection: if we seek for immortality, it is in the same: if we seek for the inheritance of the kingdom of heaven, it is in his entrance into
heaven: if we seek for defence, for assuredness, for plenty
and store of all good things, it is in his kingdom: if we
seek for a dreadless looking for the judgment, it is in
the power given to him to judge. Finally, since the
treasures of all sorts of good things are in him, let us
draw thence and from no where else, even till we be full
with all. For they which being not content with him
alone, are carried hither and thither into diverse hopes,
although they have principal regard to him, yet even in
this they are out of the right way, that they turn any
part of their knowledge to any other where. Albeit,
such distrust cannot creep in where the abundance of his
good gifts hath once been well known.

V — REPENTANCE.

" HAVE I any pleasure at all that the wicked should
die ? says the Lord God ; and not that he should turn
from his ways and live ? " It is here declared that God
desires nothing but that whosoever are perishing and
rushing towards death, should return into the way of
salvation. And thus, not only is the Gospel now preached in the world, but in all ages God has sought to testify his desire of showing mercy. For, although the
Gentiles had neither the law nor the prophets, yet they
were always, in some degree, conscious of this doctrine.
It was, indeed, overlaid by many errors ; but we shall
find that they were always led by some secret impulse
to seek for pardon, because this feeling was, as it were,
borne within them, that God is merciful to all who seek
him. Moreover, God has in the law and the prophets
still more clearly declared the same thing. And we

know how kindly he addresses us in the Gospel when he promises us pardon. And this is the knowledge of salvation; to embrace his mercy which is offered to us in Christ. It therefore follows that the prophet most truly says that God desires not the death of a sinner; because he goes forth to meet him, and is not only ready to receive all those who fly unto his mercy, but with a loud voice recals them unto him, when he sees them, as it were, alienated from every hope of salvation. And we must observe the manner in which God wills that all should be saved; namely, when they turn themselves from their ways. God, therefore, does not so will the salvation of all, as to take away all distinction between good and evil; but penitence goes before pardon, as is here declared. How, then, does God desire that all should be saved? Because now his Spirit, by the Gospel, as formerly by the prophets, " reproves the world of sin, and of righteousness, and of judgment." God plainly, therefore, lays open unto men their misery, that so he may receive them unto himself. He wounds, that he may heal; he kills, that he may make alive again. Now, therefore, we see that God wills not the death of a sinner; because he calls all indifferently to repentance, and promises that he will be ready to receive them if they will but repent.

The light of the Lord alone can open our eyes to be able to behold the foulness concealed and lurking in our flesh. Whoever, therefore, has been taught to be dissatisfied with himself in real earnest, and to be confounded with shame and bashfulness on account of his own wretchedness, has been then only imbued and furnished with the first elements of Christian philosophy.

The law is nothing else but a preparation unto the Gospel. The faithful cannot profit in the Gospel until they shall be first humbled, which cannot be until they come to a knowledge of their sins. It is the proper function of the law to call the consciences into God's judgment, and to wound them with fear. Christ is promised only to those who are humbled, and confounded with the sense of their own sins.

True repentance is a disliking of sin, conceived of a fear and reverence of God, which, withal, brings forth of it a love and desire of righteousness. The ungodly are far from this affection ; for they would desire never to make an end of sinning : yea, they strive as much as lies in them to delude both themselves and God ; but their conscience torments them with a blind horror against their wills, and they striving against the same : so, although they hate not their sin, yet they feel the same with sorrow and doubtfulness grievous and troublesome unto them. Hereof it comes to pass, that their sorrow is unprofitable to them ; because they do not freely turn unto God, neither yet seek to be better, but fast settle to their own wicked desire, they pine away in that torment which they cannot escape. If Judas had given ear to the admonition of Christ, there had been yet place to repentance ; but because that he had despised so loving a calling to salvation, he is delivered over to serve Satan, who should cast him headlong into desperation.

True repentance requires not only an acknowledgment of our faults, but also that we should be sorry for them ; and that upon the feeling of our own evil, we should go unto God, referring ourselves wholly unto him, and seeking nothing but to be governed thenceforth by him, forasmuch as we have nothing but frowardness in ourselves.

If we will have our repentance to be allowed of God, let us not give back, as is the common use; neither let us make light of our sins, but with a free confession let us testify before all the world what we have deserved.

Herein a man may see what a mockery is in those that think themselves to have done very much, when they have granted that they have done amiss, that they

have committed a great offence against God, and that
they have cast a stumblingblock into the Church; and
yet, peradventure, if a man grate upon them but a little
further, and would make them to understand their faults,
it would make them to say, O, that were too much; and
it would seem unto them that God were oversharp and
rigorous against them. But in any wise we must not
think that God receives us as repentant persons, except
we bring him the sacrifice that is spoke of in the fifty-
first Psalm. And what manner of sacrifice is that? That
we have our hearts and minds so distressed as we can no
more; and that we be so ashamed of the committing of
the sins whereof our conscience hath remorse and accuses
us, as we know not where to become, until we have
found favour in our God. Thus much then as concerning this point, that repentance consists not in ceremonies, but hath her seat in the heart of man, howbeit
that if she must show herself by signs, and that if we
have a mind well-disposed, she must so appear before
men, as we may not only have this word in our mouth,
to say we have offended; but also our heart must speak
it before our tongue.

Grant, O Almighty God! seeing that daily thou dost
solicit us to repentance, and every of us also is pricked
with the guiltiness of his own wickedness; grant that
we securely sleep not in our iniquities, neither deceive
ourselves with vain flatteries; but rather that every one
of us diligently examine himself, and then that with one
mouth and heart we may confess all of us to be guilty,
not of a small fault only, but even of eternal death; and
that no other remedy remains for us but thine immeasurable mercy; and so, also, that we may seek and embrace that grace which by the Son was offered unto all
men, and daily, through his Gospel, is offered, that we,
having him our mediator, may not cease to hope well,
even in the midst of a thousand deaths, until we be
gathered together into that blessed life which is purchased unto us by the blood of the same thy Son.

THOUGH Christ be ready to reveal his Father to all, yet the most part neglect to come, because they are not touched with the feeling of their wants. Hypocrites care not for Christ, because they being drunk with their own righteousness, neither hunger nor thirst for his grace. They that are given to the world make no account of the heavenly life; therefore Christ should call those two sorts of people to him in vain; he turns therefore himself to the miserable and to the afflicted. Also he calls them that labour and mourn under the burden; neither does he generally mean all them that are oppressed with sorrow and grief, but them who, being confounded in their own sins, and stricken with the fear of God's wrath, are ready to fall down under so great a burden. Christ means by men weary and laden them that have their consciences afflicted with the guiltiness of eternal death, and are pricked so inwardly with their own miseries that they faint; for this feebleness makes us apt to receive his grace. For it is as if he should have said that his grace is therefore contemned of the most part, because few do feel their own want; yet there is no cause why their pride or obstinacy should hinder afflicted consciences which sigh for remedy. Wherefore let us leave all them which are bewitched with the sleights of Satan, and do either persuade themselves to have righteousness without Christ, or else do imagine themselves to be blessed in this world. Our miseries drive us to seek after Christ. And because Christ admits none to the enjoying of his rest but them that faint under the burden, let us learn that there is not a more deadly poison than that sluggishness which plants in us a false and deceitful opinion, either of an earthly felicity or of righteousness and virtue;

therefore let every one of us daily stir up ourselves, and first let us busy ourselves to shake off the delights of the world, then let us empty ourselves of all vain trust in ourselves.

Though our salvation be always hid with God, yet Christ is the conduit pipe whereby it cometh to us, and is by faith received of us, that it may be confirmed and ratified in our hearts. Wherefore it is not lawful to shrink from Christ, except we will refuse the salvation prepared for us.

He doth again cast in their teeth that nothing hindered them but malice, to take the life offered in the Scriptures. For when he says that they will not, he ascribes the cause of ignorance and blindness unto frowardness and stubbornness. And truly, seeing that he offered himself so courteously unto them, they must needs be wilfully blind. And since that they fled from the light of set purpose, yea, seeing that they did covet to overwhelm the Sun with their darkness, Christ does sharply chide them for good causes.

The Apostle, that he may prevent men's minds from going astray in circuitous paths, and being led off from salvation, prescribes the limits of the word of God, within whose precincts they are to confine all their thoughts, wills, and affections. He orders believers to be satisfied with the word of truth, and admonishes them to contemplate in this mirror the secrets of heaven, which are calculated to dazzle the sight with their splendour, to surprise and delight the ears with the melody and harmony of sounds, and to overwhelm the mind itself in wonder and astonishment. The minds of believers derive, from this passage, great consolation concerning the certainty of the word of God, for they can truly lean and assent unto it with no less confidence and security than they can depend on the most realizing and present sight and appearance of terrestrial objects.

The seat of faith, it deserves to be observed, is not

placed in the brain, but the heart; not that I wish to enter into any dispute concerning the part of the body which is the seat of faith, but since the word *heart* generally means a serious, sincere, and ardent affection, I am desirous to show the confidence of faith to be a firm, efficacious, and operative principle in all the emotions and feelings of the soul, not a mere naked notion of the head.

Faith, therefore, ought not to look to our weakness, our wretchedness, and our defects, but attend with our undivided care and zeal to the alone power of God.

Unless our faith flies upwards on heavenly wings, and looks down at a distance on all carnal feelings, it will always stick in the mire of the world.

Hereby we be warned to receive simply the promises that God offers us. And although they seem at the first blush that they shall never be accomplished, and that there are a number of impediments to hinder them; yet must we do him the honour to believe that he is faithful, and to abide patiently for the convenient time of his performance of the thing that he has said. For if we gainsay his truth, and murmur, and fall to questioning and disputing with, How can this be? Is it possible? God seems to mock us if we go that way to work. Well may he perform his promise for all that, but it shall be to our shame, so as we shall always be found liars. We may well triumph for a time, as we see the unbelievers do, who malapertly despise God, spewing out their blasphemies against him; but yet in the end God shall continue faithful, and his trueness shall be known, spite of our truth, and therewithal we shall be put to shame.

The doctrine that is set forth in the name of God, ought to be of as much authority in the mouth of man as if all the angels of Heaven came down to us, or as if God showed his majesty presently before our eyes; yea, and it is the thing wherein he will try the obedience of our faith. True it is that we ought to use good discretion when men speak; for if we should receive all that is put to us, there would be no difference between the liars and false prophets that seduce our souls, and the true ministers of God. But if we have sure warrant that the thing which is brought us proceeds from God, as if it should be shown us by the Holy Scripture that men should not invent any thing of their own heads, but hold themselves to the pure simplicity of the law and gospel, it is certain that whosoever makes any resistance in that case, does not make war against the creature, but manifestly withstands God, who will be heard when he speaks so by men, and serves his turn by them as by his instruments.

For the same cause does our Lord Jesus Christ avow, that if men refuse to hear the ministers of the gospel, he will take that wrong to be done to himself; therefore, let not man make a jest of it. When God causes his word to be preached nowadays, and stirs up men to publish it abroad, if any man think to escape by saying they are but men with whom they have to do, and de-spise his doctrine therewithal, they shall know in the end that it came from Heaven, and that they set them-selves against God, and not against mortal creatures, for he will have his majesty to be known there ; that, if men take him for their sovereign Lord, they must stoop unto him, and do him homage in his doctrine ; for he has printed his mark in such wise there, that if any man en-counter the things contained therein, it is all one as if he should put his truth under foot ; wherein he has shown himself openly as in his lively image ; look that we bear that point well in mind. For if earthly princes revenge the despite that is done to their coat-armours, and think themselves to be misused therein, I pray you, is it not more rightful reason that God should do so, when men make no reckoning of his word ? Yes, verily ; for this case concerns not some painted picture, or blazing of arms, but it is the image of God which appears to us in substance ;

yea, even with such power as we ought to be trans-figured into it.

Men are inwardly as full of poison as toads, and that they are stuffed with pride, which makes them to mouth up in such wise, as in effect they refuse to obey God, forasmuch as they vouchsafe not to yield all superiority to him. That is the cause why pride or presumption is matched in this place with unbelief; and it is the same thing which I have declared before, that the true hardi-ness must be grounded in God, so as men must not attempt any thing upon opinion of their own power, nor persuade themselves that they have this or that; but only stand upon that which God promises us. If it is not so with us, then will our hardiness be turned into presumptuousness. And in this respect ought we to condemn men's rashness, when they advance themselves too much; and to commend their invincible constancy when they submit themselves out of hand to God's word, so that having his promise, they rest upon it as upon a rock, despising all stumblingblocks, and keep on their pace still, notwithstanding any trouble or storm that can be stirred up against them, or any threatening or mena-cing of them?

When we call to mind the death and passion of our Lord Jesus Christ, we must needs be delivered from all anguish and distress of mind. For he tells us that it is not for us to allege any more. Who shall go down into hell, as we have been wont to do? How, now! If all sinners must be condemned before God, seeing that we are sinners, surely we are all undone. And who is he that can assure me that hell shall have no power over me? I feel the sin which doth accuse me, and that is all one as if I should behold the gulf open, ready to swallow me up; Satan has got the mastery over me. See how men are dismayed and plunged in continual grief and trouble of mind, until they have received knowledge of the benefit that comes by the death and passion of our Lord Jesus Christ. But we know that our Lord Jesus suffered the sorrows of hell, and yet was not held prisoner of the same; whereby we are well assured that the bands of death are broken, and that hell has no more power to swallow us. And why? Because the Lord Jesus has purchased us freedom; but how know we that? By the Gospel. But if I still stand in doubt whether I am delivered from the curse of God, it is as much as if I should draw Christ again from death; for he is not dead in vain. To what end is it? Let us consider a little, wherefore the only Son of God yielded himself to such shame as to be hanged on a tree; and to be as it were accursed before God his father, and to be beaten by the hand of God until he seemed as vile as a leper, as the prophet Isaiah saith, — That he bare the burden of all our offences as if he had been a miserable sinner, and was environed with such extreme sorrow, that he wist not what to say, but to cry out,—" My God, my God, why hast thou forsaken me?" And think we that the Son of God dallied when he was so humbled, yea, and not only was made utterly of no reputation, as St Paul says, but also fought with the pangs and sorrows of death? He offered himself in the person of us as a wretched sinner, to bear that vengeance of God that was due unto us, so as he knew that God was bent against him, to thunder down upon him for our sakes. Forasmuch, then, as we know that Jesus Christ abode such encounters for our redemption, stand we yet still scanning and replying, as who would say:—O! I cannot tell, and how can I be sure of it? Surely, that were even as much as to deny the death and passion of our Lord Jesus Christ. For it is a plain scorning of all, that he ever endured and suffered for our salvation, when we acknowledge not the fruit that doth grow unto us thereby. So then, the first point is, that having the Gospel, we have whereupon to rest, so as we need not allege, What is he that shall go down to hell ? For Jesus Christ has been there, to the end that we should not come there at all, and at this day he gives us witness of the same by the Gospel, to the intent we should know that his death has always present power and operation for all such as fly unto it for refuge.

Also there is on the other side, that we have no more cause to reply, Who is he that shall mount up unto the heavens ? Why ? That is as much as to pluck down Christ from the heavenly glory whereunto he is exalted. We say, in an article of our faith, that Christ descended into hell. In so saying, we ought to assure ourselves that we are now out of danger, for he entered thither to the end that we should be free from it. We add thereunto that he also ascended into heaven. And why ? To the end that we might know that the gate thereof stands open for us. We hear also how he told his disciples, " In my Father's house are many mansions," signifying thereby that heaven was not only for himself, but that it is the common heritage for all the faithful, and that he has taken possession thereof, as it were, in our behalf. Now then, we protest, in the article of our belief, that the heavens at this time stand open for us, and that we ought to assure ourselves to come hither, because our Lord Jesus Christ, our head, is gone up hither, and will not be separated from the members of his body. Notwithstanding that we have confessed this, yet we stand scanning still, and are full of wavering fancies. Ah ! say we, I know not for all that what shall become of me. I cannot tell whether God doth reckon me to be one of his children ; who is he that has been in heaven ? who is he that has come hence again to bring us news ? See these devilish blasphemies. This is not only to stand in doubt of the truth of the Gospel, but also to tear Christ Jesus in pieces as much as we can. O, horrible outrage against the Son of God ! For he that doubts of his salvation, shows himself to believe no whit of that which we confess, namely, that Jesus Christ has sovereign dominion both in heaven and in earth ; that God governs the world by him ; that he makes all creatures to kneel down to do him homage. To be short, we acknowledge not that the Lord Jesus Christ is risen again from the dead, but, to the uttermost of our power, we go about to deface and to abolish the power of the Holy Ghost, which showed itself in his resurrection. See now in what case we are, if we receive not the testimony of the Gospel, to be assured that we are, as it were, wrapped up into heaven, even to enter directly into the possession of all those goods which lie hidden from us, and are not visible, as the prophet Isaiah says, — such as the heart of man is not able to conceive ; if we see not an open gap even into hell, to spite Satan, to defy death, and to triumph over all things that may impeach our salvation. Well, let us, on the other side, consider how St Paul says, — That when we have received the gospel through faith, we be forthwith set down in the heavenly places ; we are, as we would say, enthroned with the angels of Paradise, as already raised up thither by God. It is true, that here beneath we are as wretched worms creeping upon the ground ; but when we have once the doctrine of faith, we have the earnest-penny of our salvation, according as St Peter says, That through faith we may put ourselves into the hands of God in such manner, that, lifting up our eyes and minds into heaven, we be brought in thither, because that Jesus Christ, our head, is there before on our behalf, and hath prepared the heritage which he will hold in common with us. Thus you see how we must practise this, following the exhortation of St Paul. Moreover, we must likewise mark how he says,—That we must believe with the heart to justification, and confess with the mouth to salvation. I have therefore shown you briefly, the substance of our faith, how it must rest wholly upon the death and resurrection of our Lord Jesus Christ. I say upon his death, because that he, by his obedience, hath put away all our iniquities and transgressions; he has suffered the punishment that was due to us; to discharge us of the same, he has also despatched away the curse that lay upon us.

Truly it were to small purpose if we did but talk of the graces and blessings which our Lord Jesus Christ has brought unto us, as we see a great number of babblers do; they talk much thereof, but what are they the better of it, saving that it increases their condemnation? It is no great matter, then, to have the Confession of Faith on the tip of the tongue before men, for it must be rooted in the heart; we must have the virtue of the death and resurrection of our Lord Jesus Christ imprinted within us.

To have faith with God signifies as much as to promise himself certainly, and to look for from God whatsoever is needful. But because that faith, if there be any in us, does presently break out into prayer, and pierces into those treasures of the grace of God which are shown in the word, that it might enjoy the same; therefore Christ adds prayer to faith, for if he had only said that we should have whatsoever we shall desire, faith to some might seem to be too imperious or too secure. Wherefore Christ declares that they do then believe aright who, trusting in his goodness and promises, do humbly flee unto him. This is a notable place to express the force and nature of faith, namely, that it is a certain assurance resting in the goodness of God without any doubtfulness. For Christ does not acknowledge any others to believe but them which do undoubtedly account God to be merciful to them, and doubt not but that he will give what they do ask. Whereby we see with what a devilish imagination the Papists are bewitched, who do mix faith and doubting together; nay, they charge us with foolish presumption, if we, being persuaded of the fatherly favour of God towards us, dare be so bold as to present ourselves before him. And

Paul does especially commend this benefit of Christ, that by faith in him we have boldness and entrance to God with confidence. Furthermore, this place does teach that the true examination of faith is contained in prayers. If any man do object that these prayers were never heard, that mountains should cast themselves into the sea; the answer is easy:—Christ does not slack the reins to men's prayers, that they should desire what they lust, while he makes their prayers subject to the rule of faith. For so is it necessary that the spirit should bridle all our affections, and bring them into obedience to the word of God. Christ requires a certain and assured confidence in prayer without doubting. And whence shall the mind of man conceive this, but out of the word of God? Now then we do see that Christ promised nothing to his disciples, except they keep themselves within the bounds of the good will of God.

How may we be sure that God will take us up into his heavenly kingdom? We must have recourse to this word that was spoken to the poor thief,—" This day shalt thou be with me in paradise." Seeing it is so that our Lord died, and that he entered into such gulfs of sorrow that he was pinched so far as to abide the torments that were due to us, and not only endured the reproach and grief of bodily death, but also felt the justice of God, and became as a wretched offender to bear all the sins of the world; let us not doubt but he has delivered us from the pains and anguish which we should have felt, and will lift us up to himself; and therefore now let us not be afraid of death. But, first of all, it behoves us to follow the poor thief. What had he in him to bring him to the kingdom of heaven? He was fastened to a cross; he had his arms and legs broken; he seemed to be but a wretched carcass; there was nothing but reproach in him. Thus, then, you see how he was an ugly mirror to look upon; and yet, nevertheless, Jesus Christ promises him to make him his partner, and companion of his heavenly glory. And what had he been all the time of his life? So lewd and wicked both before God and man, that he was worse than condemned and accursed. Will we then be the heirs of God? we must follow this thief, who had the pre-eminence to go before us into the heritage of heaven. And how must we follow him? We must acknowledge that naturally there is nothing in us but utter wicked-ness, and that God might justly hold us accursed, al-though we must think ourselves to be as folk that have their arms and legs broken, yea, and as men utterly dis-membered, so as we have not one whit of strength in us, at least as in respect of ourselves. And yet for all that, therewithal, we must not doubt but that God accepts us to himself, when we link in with our Lord Jesus Christ by right faith and pure affection, acknowledging him to be our King, and having our eyes fastened upon the in-visible kingdom. For if the wretched thief, who saw death before his eyes, who was in as great torment as was possible, and saw himself, as it were, hated of all the world, did put his trust in Jesus Christ, what ought we to do? Again, in what state was our Lord Jesus Christ at the same time? He hung upon a cross, full of reproach and shame; all men did spit at him; all men did spite him. And yet, notwithstanding that reproachful state, the poor wretch ceased not to be-hold life in death, and to say,—" Lord, remember me, when thou comest into thy kingdom!" But now we know that Jesus Christ is exalted to the right hand of God his Father, and hath sovereign power over all crea-tures, so that if we yield him not his due honour, now that he is entered into his glory, we shall have no excuse at all. True it is that he was once hanged upon a gib-bet, full of reproach and shame, but yet we see there-withal that the same was turned into glory and triumph, so that the victory he obtained was more royal than all the triumphs of all the princes in the world. Seeing,

then, that we do see that Jesus Christ hath rid away all
the slander of his cross by the power of his resurrection,
ought we not to look up to the kingdom where he dwells,
whereunto he calls us, and which he has purchased so
dearly?

If faith were nothing but a wandering knowledge, or
some imagination of God, or else some certain and resolved doctrine; yet, such as had no seat in the heart,
St Peter would not say that the hearts are cleansed
by faith. For be it that I am very well learned, and
a great clerk, and can prate of the mysteries of God, it
is not to say that my heart is pure. And is it so that
whoso hath this cleanness that St Peter speaketh of?
Let us conclude, then, that it is no simple and bare
knowledge, but it is an assurance that we have of the
goodness of our God.

If we have not this key of faith, Jesus Christ shall be
strange to us, and all that he has suffered, shall not profit us one whit, as, indeed, it belongs not to us. This
is a very profitable doctrine; for there is no man but
confesses that it is the greatest benefit that man can
desire in this world to be a partaker of that salvation
that Jesus Christ has brought us, but there are very
few that take the right way. For we see how the gospel is despised, we see that all men are deaf, or else stop
their ears against this voice, which God will have to be
published throughout all the world.

True faith, where it prevails, is also productive of true
charity. It cannot rest satisfied with saying to the needy,
" be ye warmed, and be ye filled," without giving them
the things which are needful for the body: but, while
it feels for their wants, it is also forward to relieve
them. The words of Solomon are often in remembrance:
" He that giveth unto the poor, lendeth unto the Lord."
True faith, as it were, figures unto itself the judgment
to come, the judge seated, the books opened, all mankind
standing at the bar, and Him who once shed his blood on

the cross, speaking unto those on his right hand, and saying, "Inasmuch as ye did it unto these my needy disciples, ye did it unto me." Lord, what can our substance do, though it were all bestowed in charity for thy sake, to bring from thy lips such a declaration!

While we know by the doctrine of one apostle, " that we are justified by grace, through faith, which is the gift of God;" let us give good heed, also, to what is so plainly taught by another; " that faith, without works, is dead." What God has joined together, let no man put asunder. While we magnify the riches of that grace, by which we hope to be saved, let us, at the same time, remember, that this grace, which bringeth to us salvation, teacheth and prevaileth with all its happy subjects; all who are actually saved by it, to deny ungodliness and worldly lust, and to live soberly, and righteously, and godly in this present world.

St Paul says, that they which turn away from a good conscience, and uprightness, are sunk by tempests, as if a ship should be sunk in the midst of the sea. Let us take good heed, therefore, that we keep faith: for that it is that holds us up, it is the prop of our salvation: if we be not well-grounded therein, we are straightway sunk in the bottomless pit of hell. Thus we see that St Paul's meaning is to confirm the exhortation, which he made to Timothy, touching this uprightness and roundness, and his duty, and the duty of all the ministers of the word. This is very notable: for it is as much as if St Paul should show us, that faith is so great a treasure, that it is well worthy to be kept. If a man have a piece of money, he will not cast it away he careth not whither: but if he have a coffer, or cupboard, there will he keep it fast locked, and have his eye always upon it, that no man may steal it away. But gold and silver are but corruptible metals, and such as quickly pass away: faith is a thing far more precious, as St Peter says. Seeing it is so, it deserves to be much the more diligently kept.

And what is the coffer or closet to keep it in? It is a good conscience, says St Paul. For they that play with God, and make but a jesting matter of it, when they once know the gospel they are always talking of it, and yet are given still to all their vanities, and are profane persons, and shall at last be sunk and drowned. And why so? for they have not kept the faith, which was so singular and excellent a gift, and deserved to be kept fast, and held sure: because they made no account of it, God has reason to make them perish from the faith, and to be drowned. We shall better understand this, if we consider the state of men during this mortal life. We are here, as it were, in a sea. What is the life of man and all the race of it? It is a saying—We are not only passengers, as the Scripture terms us, but we have no steadfastness. They that travel on foot or on horseback upon the land are yet in good case, for they have a certain and sure way: but we must not only march in this world, as on foot, or on horseback, but we must be as it were in the sea, and have no sure nor steadfast way: we are as men in a boat, which are always, as it were, within half a foot of their death, and the boat is, as it were, a grave unto them; for they see the water round about them ready to swallow them up. Such is our case while we live here; for behold on the one side the fragility that is in us, which is more floating than the water, we do nothing but run away with the stream: and again, all that is about us, is but as a water that runneth on the one side, and on the other, and yet, in the mean while, the winds, the storms, the tempests, rise and rage at every turning of a hand. Let us learn, then, that our life is but a kind of navigation and sailing, which we make by water, so that, in the mean season, we are subject to many storms and tempests. Seeing it is so, what will become of us, if we have not a good boat, and be not well guided? We must needs sink, the tempests must needs drown us at every instant. And this is it that St

Paul meant, showing that all such as think to play with
God, shall in the end feel a horrible vengeance, for that
they have not kept this inestimable treasure of faith : but
when God hath lightened them, and shown himself unto
them, and gave them hope of salvation, they cast it into
the winds, they played with it as with a counter, whereas
they should have hid this treasure in a good conscience,
and withdrawn themselves, and be not carried away by
vanities of the world, to be tossed this way and that way
with every wind.   Seeing, then, that they have not kept
themselves so well locked up, God punishes them for
being so light.   And why so?   For they drown themselves, they are as it were in the midst of the sea, and
God suffers a tempest to rise, and swallow them up suddenly, as indeed they well deserved.

VII —JUSTIFICATION

By CHRIST is forgiveness of sins preached unto you, and
every one that believes in him is justified from all those
things, from which you could not be justified in the law
of Moses.   You see that after forgiveness of sins, justification is added in place of an exposition.   You see
plainly that it is taken for absolution ; you see that it is
taken away from the works of the law ; you see that it is
the mere beneficial gift of Christ ; you see that it is received by faith.   Finally, you see that there is a satisfaction spoken of, where he says that we are justified
from sins by Christ.   So when it is said that the publi-
can came justified out of the temple, we cannot say that
he obtained righteousness by any deserving of works.
This, therefore, is said, that after pardon of his sins obtained, he was counted for righteous before God.   He
was therefore righteous, not by approving of works, but
by God's free absolution.

If we look upon the thing itself, as it is described unto us, there shall remain no more doubt. For truly Paul does express justification by the name of acceptation, when he says we are appointed unto adoption by Christ, according to the good pleasure of God, unto the praise of his glorious favour, whereby he hath accounted us acceptable or in favour. For the same is meant by it that is said in another place, that God does freely justify. In the Romans, he first calls it an imputation of righteousness, and sticks not to say that it consists in forgiveness of sins. That man, said he, is called of David a blessed man, to whom God accounts or imputes righteousness without works, as it is written; blessed are they whose iniquities are forgiven, &c. Truly he there does entreat not of one part of justification, but of all justification wholly. And he testifies that David in that place makes a definition of justification, when he pronounces that they are blessed to whom is given free forgiveness of sins. Whereby appears that this righteousness whereof he speaks, is in comparison simply set as contrary to guiltiness. But for this purpose, that is the best place where he teaches that this is the sum of the message of the gospel, that we should be reconciled to God; because it is his will to receive us into favour through Christ, in not imputing sins unto us. Let the readers diligently weigh all the whole process of the text. For by and by after, where he adds, by way of exposition, that Christ which was without sin was made sin for us, to express the manner of reconciliation, doubtless he means nothing else by the word reconciling but justifying. And that which he said in another place, that we are made righteous by the obedience of Christ, could not stand together, unless we are accounted righteous before God, in him, and without ourselves.

Forasmuch as a great part of men imagine righteousness to be made of faith and works, let us first show this also, that the righteousness of faith and works do so differ, that when the one is established, the other must needs be overthrown. The Apostle says, that he esteemed all things as dung, that he might win Christ, and find in him the righteousness that is of God by faith, counting not his righteousness that which is by the law, but that which is by the faith of Jesus Christ. You see that here is also a comparison of contraries, and that here is declared that he which will obtain the righteousness of Christ, must forsake his own righteousness. Therefore, in another place, he says, that this was the cause of fall to the Jews, that going about to establish their own righteousness, they were not subject to the righteousness of God. If in establishing our own righteousness, we shake away the righteousness of God, therefore, to obtain God's righteousness, our own must be utterly abolished. And he shows the same thing, when he says, that our glorying is not excluded by the law, but by faith. Whereupon follows, that so long as there remains any righteousness of works, how little soever it be, there still remains to us some matter to glory upon. Now if faith exclude all glorying, then the righteousness of works can no wise be coupled with the righteousness of faith. To this effect he speaks so plainly in the fourth chapter to the Romans, that he leaves no room for cavilations or shifts; if, says he, Abraham was justified by works, he has glory. And immediately he adds, but he has no glory in the sight of God. It follows, therefore, that he was not justified by works. Then he brings another argument by contraries, when reward is rendered to works, that is done of debt and not of grace. Therefore it is not of the deservings of works. Wherefore farewell their dream, that imagine a righteousness made of faith and works mingled together.

The Scripture, when it speaks of the righteousness of faith, teaches us, that turning away from the looking upon our own works, we should only look unto the mercy of God and perfection of Christ. For it teaches this order of justification, that first God vouchsafes to embrace man being a sinner, with his mere and free goodness, considering nothing in him but misery, whereby he may be moved to mercy, forasmuch as he sees him altogether naked and void of good works, fetching from himself the cause to do him good; then, that he moves the sinner himself with feeling of his goodness, which despairing upon his own works casts all the sum of his salvation upon God's mercy. This is the feeling of faith, by which feeling the sinner comes into possession of his salvation, when he acknowledges by the doctrine of the Gospel that he is reconciled to God; that obtaining forgiveness of sins, by means of the righteousness of Christ, he is justified.

It is manifest that no man is justified by the law before God; because the righteous man shall live by faith. But the law is not of faith; but the man that does these things shall live in them. How could this argument otherwise stand together, unless we agree upon this point, that works come not into the account of faith, but are utterly to be severed from it? The law differs from faith. Why so? because works are required to the righteousness thereof. Therefore it follows that works are not required to the righteousness of faith. By this relation it appears that they which are justified by faith, are justified beside the deserving of works, yea, without the deserving of works, because faith receives that righteousness which the Gospel gives. And the Gospel differs from the law in this point, that it binds not righteousness to works, but sets it in the only mercy of God. Like hereunto is that which he affirms, that Abraham had nothing to glory upon, because faith was imputed to him unto righteousness, and he adds a confirmation, because then there is place for the righteousness of faith, when there are no works to which a reward is due. Where works are due, reward is rendered unto them; that which is given to faith is freely given

For the very meaning of the words that he uses in that place serve to prove the same. Whereas he adjoins within a little after, that therefore we obtain the inheritance by faith as according to grace; hereupon he gathered that the inheritance is of free gift, because it is received by faith; and how comes that, but because faith, without any help of works, leans wholly upon the mercy of God?

How true that is, that the righteousness of faith is the reconciliation with God, which consists upon the only forgiveness of sins. We must always return to this principle, that the wrath of God rests upon all men, so long as they continue to be sinners. That hath Isaiah excellently well set out in these words: The hand of the Lord is not shortened, that he is not able to save; nor his ear dulled that he cannot hear; but your iniquities have made disagreement between you and your God, and your sins have hidden his face from you that he hears you not. We hear that sin is the division between man and God, and the turning away of God's face from the sinner. Neither can it otherwise be. For it is disagreeing from his righteousness to have any fellowship with sin. Wherefore the Apostle teaches that man is an enemy to God till he be restored into favour by Christ. Whom therefore the Lord receives into joining with him, him he is said to justify; because he can neither receive him into favour, nor join him with himself, but he must of a sinner make him righteous. And we further say, that this is done by the forgiveness of sins.

The Spirit of God affords us such a testimony that our spirit can determine the adoption of God to be firm and unshaken, when he is our leader and master. For our mind would not, of its own accord, dictate this faith to us, unless the testimony of the Spirit preceded it. This is also an explanation of the following sentence, for while the Spirit testifies to us that we are the children of God, he, at the same time, infuses this confidence into our minds, that we dare invoke God the Father. And certainly, since the confidence of the heart alone can open our mouth, unless the Spirit bears testimony to our hearts concerning the fatherly love of God, our tongues will continue mute in conceiving and uttering praises. For this must always be maintained as a principle, that we can no otherwise properly pray to God but by invoking the Father with our mouth, and we must be certainly persuaded and assured in our minds that he stands related to us in his fatherly character. The other position, that our faith can be proved only by invoking God, corresponds with this principle.

An inheritance is destined for sons ; when, therefore, God has adopted us for his children, he has also destined an inheritance for us. He then hints what such an inheritance this is, namely, a heavenly ; and, on this account, incorruptible and eternal, and such as has been manifested in Christ. All uncertainty is removed by this manifestation ; the excellence of the inheritance, which we partake with the only-begotten Son of God, is also increased.

VIII —REGENERATION

BELIEVERS are never reconciled to God without the gift of regeneration ; nay, we are justified for this very end and design, that we may afterwards worship God in purity of life. Nor does Christ in any other manner wash us by his blood, and render God propitious to us by his expiation and atonement, than while he makes us partakers of his own Spirit, which renews us into a holy life. It would, therefore, be the most preposterous inversion of the work of God, if sin should acquire strength by means of that grace which is offered to us in Christ. We might, with as much truth, consider medicine to be the fomenter of that disease which it destroys.

Paul applies the simile to the case immediately before him, by admonishing the believers in Rome, that they were not the slaves of sin ; and he adds also thanksgiving, for the purpose of showing them, in the first place, that their deliverance from the power of sin does not arise from their own proper merit, but the peculiar mercy of God ; and, in the second place, their gratitude to God shows how great a blessing the Giver of all good had bestowed upon them, while their detestation of sin was thus more powerfully excited in their minds. He returns thanks on account of their deliverance from sin, which had resulted from ceasing to follow the course of their former iniquity, and has no respect to the period when they were the slaves of sin. By tacitly comparing the former state of believers with their present, Paul emphatically attacks the calumniators of the grace of Christ, since he shows the whole human race to be led captive by sin, when grace ceases to reign, and the dominion of sin to be destroyed by the active operation of divine grace.

Are we not all damned and forlorn by nature ? hath not the devil a tyrannical dominion over us, from whence no man can deliver himself by his own power ! Even so, if we consider where God seeks us when he calls us to him, we shall find that the wilderness through which the Jews passed, is not so dreadful and terrible as is the damnation wherein we were. For we are in bondage of it, we are under the thraldom of death. Satan reigns over us, and is king and prince of the whole world. Seeing, then, that God rids us out of so miserable slavery, and sets us at liberty by his holy spirit : is it not all one as if he should make us way through the gulfs of hell ? Yes ; for we are there in very deed, and we cannot come at Jesus Christ, except we are brought through the dungeons of death.

Is it in any man's power to create himself ? No. But God fashions us new again, and, therefore, that praise is to be given unto him. Again, our wits are utterly dull, or rather stark blind, God must be fain to enlighten them. And is that in our power? Whereas there is nothing but corruption in our hearts; whereas there is nothing but secret rebelliousness and malice; God must be fain to rid and cleanse away every whit of it.

We must also seek the remedy by praying unto God to play the physician in curing all our diseases. And forasmuch as he does now send us to our Lord Jesus Christ, unto whom he has given this charge and office, let us commend ourselves unto him. It is said in the Prophet Isaiah that Christ at his coming into the world, should make the blind to see, the deaf to hear, the lame to go upright, and that he should raise the dead. All these things has he done visibly, as is to be seen throughout all the history of the gospel. But St Matthew tells us that the same tends to a higher purpose, for in healing the bodily diseases, he shows himself to be the spiritual physician of our souls, and says that the same was done to the end that the saying which was spoken by the prophet Isaiah should be accomplished, namely, that he did bear our infirmities. Now, it is certain that the prophet spake not there neither of the fever, nor of the burning ague, nor of any other disease that appertains to the body; he speaks of the diseases of our souls. Seeing it is so, let us then conclude that it is the peculiar office of Jesus Christ to give sight to the blind, and to give hearing to the deaf. And forasmuch as he has the spirit of wisdom and discretion in all fulness, we must come directly to him to be instructed. Wherefore, let us not doubt but that God is forward and ready to receive us. In consideration whereof, let us give this honour to Jesus Christ, to acknowledge him to be the light of the world, and the physician of all our spiritual diseases, and that he will work towards us according as his father has charged him.

As he made us, so he fashioned us anew to his image,

to imprint the mark of his adoption in us, to the end we may be his children and heirs. We are of nature strangers to God, we are utterly cast away and condemned; but he pities our misery, and being not willing that we should perish, draws us unto him: for, because he is the fountain of life, when he calls us to him, our life stands therein. And how so? When he lightens us by his word and by his Holy Ghost; and frames our hearts anew, to the end that we may serve him in all pureness; and when he gives us virtue, and strength to continue, and holds us by the hand to fight with us against Satan, and against all assaults that are made against us. We see, therefore, that all our salvation comes from God: he begins it, he continues it, he brings it to perfection: a man may ascribe nothing to himself herein, no not so much as one drop.

Conversion, is as it were a resurrection from eternal death; for we are but dead all the while we remain unconverted; but being once converted, we enter into favour with God, and are delivered from hell. Not that we merit this grace by our repentance; but because by this means the Lord raises us as it were from death to life. To this repentance there is a promise added. Whence we gather, that our requests are not in vain, when we crave pardon for our sins: provided that our repentance be not hypocritical.

To beget us spiritually is God's own work; for, although it seems sometimes to be ascribed to the ministers of the gospel, it is to be understood only in this sense, that God acts by means of these; and although he act by them as means, he is, nevertheless, still the sole agent. The word begat signifies that we become new men, that we put off our former nature when we are effectually called by God. He adds, how God begat us anew; namely, "with the word of his truth;" to teach us, that we cannot, by any other door, enter into the kingdom of God.

If the heart were wholly given unto God, the performance of things would follow out of hand. It follows, then, that when we be so hindered we obey God but in part. But as I have already declared, this hinders not, but that we may serve God in singleness of heart. When there is no feignedness in us, but that our chief desire and seeking is, that he should quietly possess us, and govern us by his Holy Spirit, and that our life may be conformable in all points to his word. Therefore, when we have this desire in us, although we are held back and hindered by the infirmities of our flesh, yet God imputes not that evil unto us.

IX —SANCTIFICATION

CHRIST came furnished with the Holy Spirit after a certain peculiar manner, to the end that he might sever us from the world, and gather us together into the hope of an eternal inheritance. For this cause he is called the Spirit of sanctification ; because he does not only quicken and nourish us with that general power which appears as well in mankind as in all other living creatures, but also is in us the root and seed of heavenly life. Therefore the prophets do principally commend the kingdom of Christ by this title of prerogative, that then should flourish the more plentiful abundance of the Spirit. And notable above all the rest is that place of Joel : In that day I will pour out my Spirit upon all flesh. For though the prophet there seems to restrain the gifts of the Spirit to the office of a prophesying, yet, under a figure, he means that God by the enlightening of his Spirit will make those his scholars which before were unskilful and void of all heavenly doctrine. Now, forasmuch as God the Father does for his Son's sake give us his Holy Spirit, and yet has left with him the whole fulness thereof, to the end that he should be a minister and distributor of his liberality ; he is sometimes called the Spirit of the Father, and sometimes the Spirit of the Son. Ye are not in the flesh, but in the Spirit ; for the Spirit of God dwells in you. But if any have not the Spirit of Christ, he is not his. And hereupon he puts us in hope of full renewing ; for that he who raised up Christ from the dead shall quicken our mortal bodies, because of his Spirit dwelling in us. For it is no absurdity, that to the Father he ascribed the praise of his own gifts, whereof he is the author ; and yet that the same be ascribed to Christ, with whom the gifts of the Spirit are left, that he may give them to those that are his. Therefore he calls all them that thirst to come to him to drink. And Paul teaches that the Spirit is distributed to every one, according to the measure of the gift of Christ. And it is to be known that he is called the Spirit of Christ, not only in respect that the eternal word of God is with the same Spirit joined with the Father, but also according to his person of Mediator ; because if he had not had that power he had come to us in vain. After which meaning he is called the second Adam, given from heaven to be a quickening Spirit ; whereby Paul compares the singular life that the Son of God breathes into them that are his, that they may be all one with him, with the natural life that is also common to the reprobate. Likewise, where he wishes to the faithful the favour of Christ and the love of God, he joined with all the common partaking of the Spirit, without which no man can taste either of the fatherly favour of God, or of the bountifulness of Christ. As also he says, in another place, the love of God is poured out into our hearts by the Holy Spirit that is given us.

He is called the Spirit of adoption, because he is a witness unto us of the free good will of God wherewith God the Father has embraced us in his beloved only begotten Son, that he might be a father unto us, and does encourage us to pray boldly, yea, and does minister us words to cry without fear, Abba, Father: by the same reason he is called the earnest pledge and seal of our inheritance, because he so gives life from heaven to us wandering in the world, and being like to dead men, that we may be assured that our soul is in safeguard under the faithful keeping of God; for which cause he is also called life, by reason of righteousness. And forasmuch as by his secret watering he makes us fruitful to bring forth the buds of righteousness, he is oftentimes called water, as in Isaiah, All ye that thirst, come to the waters. Again, I will pour out my Spirit upon the thirsty, and floods upon the dry land; wherewith agrees that saying of Christ, If any thirst, let him come to me. Albeit sometimes he is so called by reason of his power to purge and cleanse, as in Ezekiel, where the Lord promises clean waters wherewith he will wash his people from filthiness; and forasmuch as he restores and nourishes into lively quickness them upon whom he has poured the liquor of his grace, he is therefore called by the name of oil and ointment. Again, because in continually seeking out and burning up the vices of our lust, he sets our hearts on fire with the love of God and zeal of godliness; he is also, for this effect, worthily called fire. Finally, he is described unto us as a fountain from whence do flow unto us all heavenly riches; or the hand of God wherewith he uses his power, because by the breath of his power he so breathes Divine life into us, that we are not now stirred by ourselves, but ruled by his stirring and moving; so that if there be any good things in us, they be the fruits of his grace; but our own gifts without him, be darkness of mind and perverseness of heart.

To what end the whole law tends, it shall not be hard to judge: that is, to the fulfilling of righteousness, that it might frame the life of man after the example of the pureness of God. For God has therein so painted out his own nature, as if a man do perform in deeds, that which is there commanded, he shall in a manner express an image of God in his life. Therefore, when Moses meant to bring the sum thereof into the minds of the Israelites, he said,—And now, Israel, what doth the Lord thy God ask of thee, but that thou fear the Lord, and walk in his ways ? love him and serve him in all thy heart, and in all thy soul, and keep his commandments ? And he ceased not still to sing the same song again unto them, so oft as he purposed to show the end of the law. The doctrine of the law hath such respect hereunto, that it joins man, or as Moses in another place terms it, makes man to stick fast to his God in holiness of life. Now, the perfection of that holiness consists in the two principal points already rehearsed : That we love the Lord God with all our heart, all our soul, and all our strength, and our neighbours as ourselves. And the first indeed is, that our souls be in all parts filled with the love of God. From that by and by of itself forth flows the love of our neighbour. Which thing the Apostle shows when he writes, that the end of the law is love out of a pure conscience, and a faith not feigned. You see how, as it were in the head is set conscience and faith unfeigned, that is to say, in one word, true godliness, and that from thence is charity derived. Therefore he is deceived, whosoever thinks that in the law are taught only certain rudiments and first introductions of righteousness, wherewith men became to be taught their first schooling, but not yet directed to the true mark of good works ; whereas, beyond that sentence of Moses, and this of Paul, you can desire nothing as wanting of the highest perfection. For how far, I pray you, will he proceed that will not be contented with this institution, whereby man is instructed to the fear of God, to spiritual worshipping, to obeying of the commandments, to follow the uprightness of the way of the Lord ; finally to pureness of conscience, sincere faith and love ? Whereby is confirmed that exposition of the law which searches for and finds out in the commandments thereof all the duties of godliness and love. For they that follow only the dry and bare principles, as if it taught but the one half of God's will, know not the end thereof, as the Apostle witnesses.

To what purpose was it that we should be drawn out of the wickedness and filthiness of the world, if we give ourselves leave all our lives long to wallow in them still? Moreover, it also admonishes us that to the end we may be reckoned among the people of God, we must dwell in the holy city Jerusalem. Which, as he has hallowed to himself, so is it unlawful that it be unholily profaned by the uncleanness of the inhabitants. From hence came these sayings, that they shall have a place in the tabernacle of God that walk without spot, and study to follow righteousness, &c. Because it is not meet that the sanctuary wherein he dwells should be like a stable full of filthiness.

And the better to awake us, it shows that God the Father, as he has joined us to himself in Christ, so has printed an image for us in him, after which he would have us to be fashioned. Now let them find me a better order among the philosophers, that think that the philosophy concerning manners is in them only orderly framed. They, when they will excellently well exhort us to virtue, bring nothing else but that we should live agreeably unto nature. But the Scripture brings her exhortation from the true wellspring, when it not only teaches us to refer our life to God, the author of it to whom it is bound; but also when she hath taught that we are swerved out of kind from the true original and state of our creation, she immediately adds, that Christ, by whom we came again into favour with God, is set before us for an example, that we should express the form thereof in our life. What may a man require more effectual than this one thing? Yea, what may a man require more than this only thing? For if the Lord has by adoption made us children with this condition, that our life should resemble Christ, the bond of our adoption ; if we do not give and avow ourselves to righteousness, we do not only, with most wicked breach of allegiance, depart from our Creator, but also we forswear him to be our Saviour.

And here is a fit place to speak unto them, that having nothing but the title and badge of Christ, yet would be named Christians. But with what face do they boast of his holy name, since none have any fellowship with Christ but they that have received a true knowledge of him out of the word of the Gospel ? But the Apostle says, that all they have not rightly learned Christ that are not taught that they must cast away the old man that is corrupted according to the desire of error, and have not put on Christ. Therefore it is proved that they falsely, yea, and wrongfully pretend the knowledge of Christ, although they can eloquently and roundly talk of the Gospel. For it is not a doctrine of tongue, but of life ; and is not conceived, as other learnings are, with only understanding and memory, but is then only received when it possesses the whole soul, and finds a seat and place to hold it in the most inward affection of the heart. Therefore either let them cease, to the slander of God, to boast of that which they are not, or let them show themselves not unworthy scholars for Christ their master.

This is a great thing, that we are consecrated and dedicated to God ; that we should from henceforth think, speak, imagine, or do nothing but to his glory. For the thing that is consecrate cannot be applied to unholy uses without great wrong done unto him. If we are not our own but the Lord's, it appears what error is to be avoided, and whereunto all the doings of our life are to be directed. We are not our own : therefore let neither our own reason nor our own will bear rule in our counsels and doings. We are not our own : therefore let us not make this the end for us to tend unto, to seek that which may be expedient for us according to the flesh.

We are not our own : therefore so much as we may, let us forget ourselves and all things that are our own. On the other side, we are God's, therefore let us live and die to him. We are God's : therefore let his wisdom and will govern all our doings. We are God's : therefore let all the parts of our life tend toward him as their only lawful end. Oh, how much has he profited, that having learned that himself is not his own, has taken from himself the rule and government of himself to give it to God ! For as this is the most strong working pestilence to destroy men, that they obey themselves ; so it is the only haven of safety, neither to know nor will any thing by himself, but only to follow God going before him. Let this, therefore, be the first step, that man depart from himself, that he may apply all the force of his wit to the obeying of the Lord. Obeying, I call not only that which stands in obedience of the word, but that whereby the mind of man, void from his own sensuality of flesh, binds itself wholly to the will of God's spirit. Of this transformation, which Paul calls renewing of the mind, whereas it is the first entry into life, all the philosophers were ignorant. For they make only reason the governess of man ; they think she only ought to be heard ; finally, to her only they give and assign the rule of manners. But the Christian philosophy bids her to give place, and to yield and be subject to the Holy Ghost ; so that man now may not live himself, but bear Christ living and reigning in him.

Truly a Christian man must be so fashioned and disposed, to think throughout all his life that he has to do with God. In this sort, as he shall examine all his doings by God's will and judgment, so he shall reverently direct unto him all the earnestly bent diligence of his mind. For he that has learned to look upon God in all things, that he has to do, is therewithal turned away from all vain thoughts. This is that forsaking of ourselves which Christ, even from the first beginning of

instruction, so earnestly gave in charge to his disciples ;
which, when it once has got possession in the heart,
leaves no place at all, first neither for pride, nor dis-
dainfulness, nor vain-glorious boasting, then neither for
covetous, nor filthy lust, nor riotousness, nor daintiness,
nor for other evils that are engendered of the love of
ourselves. Contrariwise, wheresoever it reigneth not,
there either most filthy vices do rage without shame, or
if there be any spice of virtue it is corrupted with perverse desire of glory. For show me a man, if thou
canst, that unless he have forsaken himself according to
the commandment of the Lord, will of his own free will
use goodness among men. For all they that have not
been possessed with this feeling, if they have followed
virtue, they have done it at the least for praise sake.
And as the philosophers that ever most of all affirmed
that virtue was to be desired for its own sake, were puffed
up with so great pride, that it appeared that they desired
virtue for no other thing but that they might have matter to be proud upon. But God is so nothing at all delighted, neither with those gapers for the people's breath,
nor with these swelling beasts, that he pronounces that
they have already received their reward in the world, and
makes harlots and publicans nearer to the kingdom of
Heaven than they. And yet we have not thoroughly
declared with how many and how great stops man is
hindered from that which is right, so long as he hath
not forsaken himself. For it was truly said in times
past that there is a world of vices hid in the soul
of man. And thou canst find no other remedies but
denying thyself, and leaving regard of thyself, to bend
thy mind to seek those things that the Lord requires
of thee, and to seek them therefore only because they
please him.

All confess that cleanness of heart is mother of all
virtues, but yet it is scarce the hundredth man that does
not account subtlety as a most notable virtue. Hereof

it comes to pass that they are commonly thought blessed, who are most subtle in crafty conveyances, who by evil means do craftily circumvent them with whom they have to do.   Therefore Christ agrees not with the judgment of the flesh, while he calls them blessed who are not delighted with craftiness, but walk sincerely among men, and in words and countenance pretend no other thing than they think in heart.

Because many do abuse the grace of Christ, while they turn it to serve the wantonness of the flesh, therefore after Christ has promised joyful rest to the miserable afflicted consciences, he also warns them that he is a deliverer upon this condition, that they should take his yoke on them ; as if he should have said that he did not therefore free them from sins, that they having God merciful to them should thereby take a liberty to sin ; but that they being comforted by his grace, should take on them a yoke, and that they being freed in conscience, they might keep in bondage the wantonness of the flesh.   And hereof is gathered a definition of that rest whereof he spake ; that is, it frees not the disciples of Christ from the warfare of the cross, that they should live pleasantly, but it exercises them under the burden of discipline, and contains them under the yoke.

This work of God is not perfected on the first day when it commences its operations in us, but gradually increases ; and, making daily advancement, is brought by little and little to its completion.   To sum up all, if you are a Christian, you must exhibit in yourself a sign of your communion with the death of Christ, and, as a fruit of this, your flesh will be crucified with all its desires. You must not, however, conclude that you have made no progress in this communion, if you find the remains of sin still continuing to live in you, but you must never cease to meditate on the best plans for increasing your participation of Christ's death, until you shall have reached the goal.   It is well with the believer, if his flesh is continually mortified; and he has made great progress when the Holy Spirit has taken possession of the kingdom which has been acquired from the flesh.

No liberty is allowed for our going back in this mortification; since, if we again return to our wallowing in the mire, we deny Christ, for we can only become partakers of him by newness of life, as he now enjoys a state of incorruptible existence.

The Apostle adduces our perpetual deliverance from the yoke of death by the example of Christ, which he had already mentioned, as well suited to support his opinion that we are indeed no more subject to the tyranny of sin; and this truth is demonstrated by the final cause of the death of Christ, for he indeed died to accomplish the utter destruction of sin. The very form of expression, as applied to Christ, shows that he did not, like us, die to sin for the purpose of ceasing to commit it, but he died as a ransom for sin, thus annihilating its power and authority. The Apostle says, Christ died unto sin once, not only because he sanctified believers for ever by the eternal redemption which he procured by his one oblation, and by the cleansing of sin accomplished by the shedding of his blood, but for the purpose of establishing a mutual resemblance between us and our Redeemer.

As Christ died once for the destruction of sin, so you are indeed once dead, that you may cease to sin for the future; nay, you must daily advance in the mortification of your flesh, which has been commenced, until sin shall be completely extinguished. As Christ was raised to an incorruptible life, so you are renewed by the grace of God, that you may spend the whole of your life in holiness and righteousness, since the power of the Holy Spirit, by which you are renewed, is eternal, and will always flourish in strength and vigour.

The Apostle, in calling our members instruments, or arms, derives the simile from a military life; for as a soldier has his armour always in a state of readiness, that he may be prepared to use it whenever his commander shall issue his orders, and never girds on his arms except at the nod of his general; so Christians ought to regard all their members as arms for a spiritual combat; and if any of them are abused in gratifying depraved inclinations, they are in the service of sin. Believers have also devoted themselves, by their military oath, to Christ and God, and are held bound to pay them obedience, and it becomes the pious to keep at a distance from all intercourse with the camp of sin. We may hence see what right those have to call themselves Christians, with all the pomp of pride, whose every member is in a state of readiness, as if sold to the service of Satan, to commit all uncleanness with greediness. Paul now orders us, on the other hand, to stand entirely ready for the service of God, that, restraining our mind and inclination from wandering after any of those vices into which the desires of the flesh might lead us, we should keep our attention fixed on the will of God alone, be always ready to obey his commands, and in a state of preparation to observe his orders. Our members also should be prepared and consecrated to his will, so that all the faculties, both of our mind and body, should breathe after nothing but his glory. The reason is also added,—because the Lord, having destroyed our former life, has created us for another, with which our actions ought to correspond.

There is so great a dissension between the yoke of Christ and of sin, that no one can endure both at the same time. If we sin, we give ourselves up to the bondage of sin; but, on the contrary, believers are redeemed from the tyranny of sin, to become the servants of Christ; and, on this account, it is impossible for them to remain the slaves of sin.

Paul opposes the secret power of the Spirit to the external letter of the law; as if he had said, Christ forms our hearts in a more complete manner internally by his love, than the law can compel us by its threatenings and

terrors. This removes the calumny of those who maintain the licentiousness of sinning to be introduced by
Christ freeing us from obedience to the law, since he
does not send forth his followers to indulge in unbridled
wantonness, and to exult, without moderation and sobriety, as horses, when set at liberty, gallop across the
plains, but conducts them to a lawful course and manner
of life.

It is absurd for any one to remain in bondage after he
has gained his liberty, for he ought to maintain the
state of freedom bestowed upon him; nor is it consistent
with the character of believers to be brought under the
power of sin, from which they have been emancipated
by Christ. This argument is taken from the efficient
cause, and the following from the final; you are delivered from the bondage of sin, that you may enter the
kingdom of righteousness, on which account it is your
bounden duty to forget all sin, and to turn your whole
heart and soul to righteousness, under whose obedience
you are now brought. It must be observed that none
can devote himself to the service of righteousness, unless he has first been delivered by the power, kindness,
and favour of God, from the tyranny of sin, as Christ
himself testifies, "If the Son, therefore, shall make you
free, ye shall be free indeed." What preparations then
for divine grace shall we derive from the power of the
freedom of the will, if the commencement of our goodness arises from that emancipation which the grace of
God alone performs?

The Apostle more fully proves the great wickedness
and grossness of the calumny, which pretends and ima-
gines a licentiousness to be granted for sinning by the
liberty that Christ hath procured for his people. He, at
the same time, also instructs believers, that there is no
greater absurdity, or rather dishonour and shame, than
for the spiritual grace of Christ to be inferior to an
earthly emancipation in its power over their conduct-

As if the Apostle had said, I could show, by instituting a comparison between righteousness and sin, with how much greater vehemence and zeal you ought, with all speed, to enter the service of the former than to obey the latter; but I spare your infirmity, and omit the adopting of such a plan. I may, however, showing you the utmost indulgence, justly demand of you not to practise righteousness, on any consideration, in a more cold or negligent manner than you have subjected yourselves to the dominion of sin. He means more than meets the ear, for he exhorts them to obey righteousness with so much greater earnestness, as its dignity is much superior to that of sin, though his expressions do not seem to warrant the full extent of this sense. " For as you have yielded "—Your wretched bondage and devotedness to the affections of your flesh was clearly apparent from the readiness with which all your limbs and members paid obedience to the power of sin: let your alacrity and promptitude be equally striking in performing the commands of God; nor let your activity in doing good actions be inferior to your former conduct in sinning.

" For when ye were the servants "—He repeats the disagreement already mentioned between the yoke of righteousness and sin, which are so contrary in their character, that whoever devotes himself to one must necessarily forsake the other. His object is, that by examining them separately we may more clearly see what is to be expected from both, for a just distinction gives greater light in investigating the character of any thing. After carefully considering the difference between sin and righteousness, he points to the consequences which may be expected to result from each. The Apostle, it must be remembered, argues from contraries in the following manner: While you were the servants of sin, you were free from righteousness; but now, on the other hand, it is your duty to be the servants of righteousness, because you are delivered from the yoke of sin. He calls those free from righteousness, who are under no restraint or check of obedience for the purpose of practising it, since the licentiousness of the flesh so emancipates us from obedience to God, that we become the slaves of the devil. Wretched, therefore, and cursed is that liberty which, with an unbridled, or rather furious violence, exults even to our ruin.

We must take these foxes (I mean these lusts) betimes, and kill them whilst they are cubs, lest, if we nourish them over long in our breasts, they grow wild and impregnable. We are evermore to watch over our own hearts, that a wicked lust no sooner creeps in to carry us away to the love of idols, but we forthwith root it out, for fear of falling into these deep gulfs ; because even the best of us all bear about with us some seeds of this brutishness, which by no means can be weeded out ; nay, they will bud and sprout up in us without ceasing, unless we are purged of them by the power of the Holy Ghost.

A dirty and torn garment disgraces its wearer, while a clean and beautiful one secures him additional regard and esteem. To put on Christ, means our being surrounded and protected in every part by the virtue of his Spirit, and thus rendered fit for the performance of every duty of holiness. For the image of God, which is the only ornament of the soul, is thus renewed in us.

As ancient sacrifices were dedicated to God by certain sanctifications, purifications, and washings, so believers in Christ are consecrated as victims to the Lord by the Spirit of consolation, truth, and peace ; and are separated from the world lying in the wicked one by the inward operations and power of the Holy Ghost. For, although purity of mind arises from faith in God's word, yet, because the voice of man can of itself accomplish nothing, and is dead, the office of purifying the believer belongs truly, really, and properly, to the Spirit of grace and love.

Since the rays of heavenly light have now begun to

shine upon us towards the dawn of day, we ought to imitate the conduct of those, who are employed in the midst of light, and in the presence of their fellow-men. For they take diligent care not to perpetrate any base or dishonourable action, since they are assured, by committing any kind of offence, they will be exposed to the observation of too great a number of witnesses. But it much more becomes us, who always stand in the presence of God and of angels, and are invited by Christ, the true Sun of Righteousness, to behold himself, to avoid every kind of shameful conduct.

The servant of Christ, who obeys his Redeemer with a calm and placid conscience by means of the righteousness which is by faith, commends himself both to God and man. The kingdom of God is complete and entire in all its parts, where righteousness, peace, and spiritual joy exist, and it therefore does not consist in things of a mere bodily nature. The obeyer of the will of the Most High must be necessarily acceptable to the God of love. Men cannot fail to approve of the conduct of those who exhibit in their lives and conversation a clear evidence of their being guided by virtue. The wicked, it must be granted, do not always spare the children of the King of glory ; nay, the enemies of divine truth pour forth, without the least cause or occasion, the most opprobrious language against believers ; and defame, by calumnies of their own invention, men of the most blameless characters. Even the good actions of the pious are perverted by malignant interpretations into vices. Paul is speaking concerning the judgment of sincerity and truth, without any admixture of moroseness — without the least spark of hatred, and without the perverse statements of superstition.

True holiness begins within us, insomuch that if we show all the fairest countenances in the world before men, and that our life be so well guided that every man shall commend us ; yet if we have not this plainness and soundness before God, all is right nought. For it behoves that the fountain be first pure, and afterwards that the streams that run out of it be pure also. Otherwise the water may well be clear; and yet nevertheless be bitter, or else have some other filthy corruption in it. True it is that we may well withhold ourselves from ill-doing, and that we may well have a fair show before men ; but that shall be nothing, if there be any hypocrisy or covert dissimulation before God, when it comes to the root that is within the heart. What must we do then ? We must begin at the foresaid point, and then to have perfect soundness, it behoves that our eyes, our hands, our feet, our arms, and our legs be answering thereunto ; so as in our whole life we may show that our will is to serve God, and how that it is not in vain that we pretend a meaning to keep the same soundness within. And here you may see why Saint Paul also exhorts the Galatians to walk after the Spirit, if they live after the Spirit, as if he should say—Verily, it behoves that the Spirit of God dwell in us and govern us. For it is to no purpose to have a gay life that pleases men, and is had in great estimation, unless we are renewed by the grace of God. But what ? It behoves us to walk, that is to say, it behoves us to show in effect, and by our work, how the Spirit of God reigns in our minds. For if our hands be stained with robbery, with cruelty, or with other annoyances ; if the eyes be carried with lewd and unchaste looks, with coveting other men's goods, with pride, or with vanity ; or if the feet be swift to do evil, thereby we well declare that our heart is full of naughtiness and corruption. For it is neither the feet nor the hands, nor the eyes that guide themselves ; the guiding of them comes of the mind and of the heart.

Ye see the reason why God proves whether we serve him faithfully or not. It is not for that he has need of our service, or of any thing that we can do ; but because that when we deal well with our neighbours, so as we keep our faithfulness towards all men, according as nature itself teaches us; in so doing we yield assurance that we fear God. We see many which bear the face of very zealous Christians, so long as it is but to dispute, and to hold long talk, and to bear men in hand that they study to serve God, and to honour him; and yet for all that, as soon as they have to do with their neighbours, a man shall perceive what they have in their hearts. For they seek their own advantage, and make no conscience to rake to themselves, and to beguile folk when they have them in their danger, by what means soever it be. Now then there is no doubt but that those which seek their own advantage and profit, are hypocrites, and that their heart is corrupt; and how earnest Christians soever they seem outwardly, God bewrays that they have nothing but dung and poison in their hearts. And why so ? For look where soundness is, there must needs be uprightness also; that is to say, if the affection be pure within, then will it follow, that when we have to deal with men, we shall procure the welfare of every man, in such ways as we shall not be given to ourselves and to our private commodity, but shall have that indifference which Jesus Christ avouches to be the rule of life, and the whole sum of the law and the prophets, namely, that we do not that thing to any other man, which we would not have done to ourselves.

Under the law and before the law, when men offered sacrifices, it behoved the offerers to be cleansed before hand; and that was to do them to wit, how we be not worthy to approach unto God, by reason of our uncleanness and filthiness. If we come unto God such as we be of ourselves, we deserve to be shaken off, and to be taken at his hand for stinking carrions. Therefore it stands us in hand to make ourselves clean. And how may that be done ? The men of old time had certain ceremonies, according as it was needful that they should have such helps before the coming of our Lord Jesus Christ, by reason of the rawness of the time. But now, in these days, we know how we ought to have recourse to the precious blood of God's Son, which was shed to wash us withal. Therefore, if we mean to be received for clean before God, it behoves us to repair to the blood of our Lord Jesus Christ. And furthermore, we must also sigh for our sins. For by this means are we to be cleansed, namely, by acknowledging the evil that is in us, which by and by causes a sorriness, and hatred of ourselves, for that we have been so unhappy as to displease God. And thus we see why we have no more the figures that were before the coming of our Lord Jesus Christ, and yet do keep still the truth and substance of them. What is to be done then at all times and as oft as we call upon God? Every one of us must have an eye to his own poorness and uncleanness, and be displeased with himself for it, and therewithal also desire our Lord Jesus Christ to wash us and make us clean with his blood, so that we may appear as if we were pure and clean, in the presence of God his Father. And this is to be done not only one day in the week, nor for some certain time, but continually all our life long; and we must bear in mind how St Paul says, that our Lord Jesus Christ was sacrificed as the true Easter Lamb, to the end that we should still be copartners of that sacrifice, specially in all pureness. He says not that Christians ought to sanctify themselves unto God once a-year, but that they ought to continue their holiness all their life throughout.

Let us take heed of ourselves, and of our wicked affections, which serve to turn us aside from God. Then afterwards let us beware of lewd persons, who are, as it were, firebrands to set the mischief more on fire; and these are mortal plagues. Now, then, when we see so much iniquity, so much looseness, and so much outrage in the world, that vices have their full scope; what is to be done? Let us withdraw ourselves, and let us shun occasion, according also as Saint Paul alleges the same re-

cord, saying: withdraw yourselves, and flee far from
Babylon, you that carry the Lord's vessels. Hereby
Paul means, that after we be once baptized in the name
of our Lord Jesus Christ, it behoves us to be holy both
in body and mind, and to be given wholly unto God,
and dedicated to his service; which thing cannot be done,
but by withdrawing ourselves from the defilements that
may corrupt us. So then let us eschew occasions of
evil. And when we see the world so overflowed with
all vice, let us advisedly withdraw ourselves, and fasten
our eyes upon God, who makes us holy.

The service which the angels do unto God is perfect,
according to the perfection that can be in creatures;
likewise as in that respect, when in praying we desire
God, that his will may be done on earth as it'is in
heaven, we witness that there is no untowardness in the
obedience which the angels yield unto him, but that he
reigns in them after such a peaceable manner, as they
are wholly conformable to his will. But we must always bear in mind that which I have touched, that as
long as we go no further but to the degree and state of
creatures, there shall be a perfection in the angels, verily
such perfection as may in creatures. But come we once
unto God, the said perfection is as it were swallowed
up, like as the stars appear not any more when the sun
gives his light.

Let us come to Job's words, " I have made a league
or covenant with mine eyes." I have told you that this
is a token of great perfection. And why? For if a
man can withhold his sight, so as he conceive not any
thing that might draw him unto evil by looking about
him, and show that there is true chastity and honesty in
him, it must needs be said that he is clear as an angel
from all corruption. And Job's protesting hereof is not
in vain; wherefore let us consider that he lived in this
world as an angel of God. True it is that of nature he

was not so ; and also whereas he says that he made a co-venant, that was done after he had so profited in the fear of God, as he had thrust his unruly lusts under foot, and so overmastered his affections, as he was able to bridle them and keep them under, to say, I will not lust any evil, to covet it or wish it ; I will have no vein in me that shall tend to the displeasure of God, but I will bridle myself both in mine eyes, and in my mouth, and in mine ears. Thus you see in what wise Job made his covenant. It was not by having such a soundness in his nature, for he was a man subject to affections as we are ; and no doubt but he had many temptations in his life. Howbeit, he walked in such wise, as he was so inured with the fear of God, as not to admit any wicked lusts. Then was it become a habit ; that is to say, he was so inured unto it, as he was no more wavering to start out on the one side or the other, or to provoke himself to this or that. To be short, we see here how Job meant to de-clare, that he not only endeavoured to serve God, but also had enforced himself in such wise to it, as he had tamed and subdued all the affections of his flesh ; insomuch that it was no more pain to him to serve God, because he had not the battles which we have in us by reason of our frailty, yea, and by reason of the corruption that is in our nature. But let us mark that this came not of his own power, neither could he of himself have purchased such perfection ; but it behoved God to reform him in such wise by his Holy Spirit, as he was after a sort se-parated from the common range of men. For it is not without cause that David makes this request unto God : Lord turn away mine eyes that they may see no vanity. If Job had of himself had the things which he protests here, no doubt but David might have obtained such a steadfastness as well as he, so as he should not have con-ceived any vanity, nor had his eyes misled and carried away by any means.

It is said, that thou shalt love the Lord thy God with all thy heart, and with all thy strength. What is meant by mind and strength? God has not limited the love that we owe unto him, that it should be only in our hearts and minds, but he said, that our wit, reason, and understanding, and all our strength, that is to say, all the abilities and powers that are in our nature, must also be thoroughly applied thereunto. Now then if a man conceive any evil, although he consent not to it nor yield his affection fully thereunto, I pray you, does he love God with all his mind? No—if a man have never so little a piece of himself inclining to corruption, although with all the rest he endeavour himself to acccomplish the law, does he love God as he ought to do? No, undoubtedly—for sin is nothing else but a transgressing of God's law.

God is not contented with goodly countenance and fair disguisings of outward shows and other likelihoods; he looks on the heart, he searches the thoughts, and discovers all that is hidden in darkness. Seeing it is so, let us bridle ourselves to walk soundly and uprightly. But on the contrary part we are drawn here and there, we are given to devising of shifts and fair deckings to colour our doings withal, and when we have no better stuff, it is enough for us to cover ourselves with leaves as our father Adam did. Wherefore let us mark well the lesson that is shown here to all the faithful: which is, that when we intend to walk as it becomes us, we must not behave ourselves as it were before men, neither must we rest our eyes upon them; but we must behold the heavenly judge, and understand that it is he to whom we must make our answer, and yield our account.

It is not enough for a man to have abstained from whoredom, except he be also clear from theft, guile, and extortion; for God will not have the things sundered which he hath set together. He has given his whole law to rule our life, and as he has forbidden whoredom, so has he also condemned stealing, lying, extortion, and such other things. Therefore if a man intend to serve God, it is not enough for him to be clear from one sin, but he must frame his whole life after the law.

X—LOVE

As OUR best bond for mutual union with each other, is found in the knowledge of God, since, in the character of a common Father to all, he reconciles us in the best manner to each other, so out of Him every thing is merely in a scattered and dissipated state ; because want of humanity generally follows our ignorance of God, while each, treating others with contempt, loves and seeks himself.

We are improved by tribulations for performing the duty of patience ; and patience affords us a proof of the divine assistance by which we are more emboldened and encouraged to hope ; for much as we may be troubled and seem wearied out, yet we cease not to feel the divine kindness towards us, which is the most abundant consolation, and much greater than if prosperity attended all our undertakings. Since as what appears to be happiness is misery itself, when the wrath and opposition of God are arrayed against us, so our very calamities will undoubtedly terminate in prosperity and joyful success, if our heavenly Father be propitious ; since all things must be subservient to the will of our Creator, who, according to his fatherly favour towards us, orders and tempers all the trials of the cross for our own salvation. This knowledge of the divine love towards us is instilled into our hearts by the Spirit of God: for neither eye has seen, nor ear heard, nor has it entered into the heart of man to conceive, the blessings God has prepared for such as worship him ; the Spirit alone can reveal these things. The participle, " shed abroad," is very emphatic ; for it signifies that the revelation of divine love to us is so abundant as to fill our hearts. And this being poured forth upon every part of our character and feelings, not only mitigates our sorrow in adversity, but sweetly seasons and gives a loveliness even to our tribulations.

The real genuine fountain of all charity is the persuasion, which the faithful experience, of the love entertained by God for them ; nor are they merely tinctured in a slight degree, but have their minds completely replenished and anointed with this conviction.

That love keeps within due and constant bounds, which never goes beyond the altar; if we love in God, and not out of the fountain of all love, the ardour of our most intense affection will never be excessive.

It is difficult to give a view of the ingenuity with which a large portion of mankind assume the appearance of that love which they really do not possess. For they not only deceive others, but impose upon themselves, while they endeavour to believe that they entertain a very considerable share of love, even for those whom they not only treat with neglect, but in reality renounce and despise. Paul declares that only to be genuine love which is free from all dissimulation and guile ; and every person can best judge for himself whether he entertains any feeling in the innermost recesses of his heart opposed to this noble and lasting affection.

As nothing is more opposed to brotherly concord than contempt arising from pride, by which a person exalts his own character, and treats others with indifference, neglect, or disdain ; so modesty, by which due honour is paid to every one, nourishes and supports love with the longest continuance and greatest power.

Since those are generally most treated with contempt, who are more oppressed with the load of poverty than others, and on this account require greater and more immediate assistance, because benefits conferred upon such indigence are considered to be entirely thrown away, the God of mercy commends these applicants to our care in a peculiar manner. For then, finally, we prove the sincerity of our love, when we assist our brethren, without having any other view than the exercise of our kindness. Now hospitality, namely, the benevolence and liberality which are shown to strangers, may justly be considered not the last kind of charity, because these objects of mercy are the most destitute of all, on account of their distance from relatives ; and Paul, therefore, expressly recommends to us so important a duty. We see, therefore, that we ought to watch over every person with greater care, in proportion as he is generally more neglected by the rest of our fellow-men.

Paul requires a train of conduct yet more difficult, not to pray for evil and curses to light on the heads of our enemies, but to wish them every kind of prosperity, and supplicate God to grant them every blessing, however much they may harass, and treat us with the most barbarous inhumanity. We ought to labour after the attainment of this mildness with the more intense diligence, in proportion to the difficulty of its attainment. For our heavenly Father gives no command, which he does not require us to obey. Nor is any excuse to be admitted, if we do not attain that feeling and disposition, by which God wishes us to be distinguished from wicked and worldly characters. I grant it is difficult, and entirely contrary to human nature ; but there is no duty, however arduous, which cannot be performed by the powerful aid of God ; nor will he ever withhold his divine grace, provided we do not neglect to pray for it with ardent and incessant supplication. And though you can scarcely find one, who has made such distinguished advancement in the divine law as fully to perform that commandment, yet none can boast himself to be a son of God, or glory in the name of a Christian, who has not in part put on this mind, which was in the Lord Jesus, and does not daily wrestle against and oppose the feeling of enmity and hatred. Prayer for our enemies is more difficult than to refrain from the active revenging of an injury which we have suffered. For there are some characters, who, notwithstanding they hold their hands from violence, and are not driven on by a desire of injuring their enemies, would still be glad to find destruction or loss befall them from another quarter. Even if the injured are so much appeased as to wish no evil to their foes, yet scarce one in a hundred desires the safety and prosperity of the injurer ; a large portion of mankind has immediate recourse, without feeling any shame, to horrid imprecations. But God, by his word, not only restrains our hands from any act of violence and injury, but also subdues all bitter feelings in our minds. Nay, he even desires us to be solicitous for the eternal salvation of those, who bring ruin on themselves by cruelly harassing us·in an unjust manner.

Such is the nature of true and genuine Christian love, that it would rather grieve with a brother, when weighed down with the load of poverty and affliction, than turn aside from the wailings of sorrow, or disregard, in the midst of its own delicacies, its own ease, or its own security, the moanings of distress. It is, in fine, our duty to accommodate each other as far as we possibly can, and in every circumstance of life to cultivate a reciprocal fellow-feeling, whether we have to condole with our brother in the cold blasts of adversity, or rejoice with him when basking in the sunshine of prosperity. Envy alone prevents us from rejoicing with a brother in his happiness, and the most barbarous inhumanity from sorrowing with him in his distress. Let us, therefore, cultivate that sympathy with each other, which may make us at the same time mutually harmonize in all our affections.

" Dearly beloved, avenge not yourselves."—The evil here corrected, as hinted above, is greater than the former already stated ; yet both spring from the same source, namely, an immoderate love of ourselves, and innate pride, which make us indulgent to our own vices, while we are inexorable to those of others. Since, therefore, this disease generally produces in all a furious desire for vengeance, when we are in the least touched, Paul here commands us not to attempt to revenge ourselves, but to give it into the hands of the Lord. And because such as have been once seized with this unruly passion cannot easily be curbed, he uses a kind expression to retain us in the performance of our duty by calling us beloved. The precept is, neither to avenge nor to desire to avenge any injuries which we have received ; and the reason is added, because we must give place unto wrath. We mean, by giving place unto wrath, to grant the Lord the power of judging, and he is deprived of this by all self-avengers. If, therefore, it is criminal to usurp the place of God, we are not allowed to revenge ourselves, because we anticipate the judgment of the Most Holy, who has expressed it to be his will to preserve for himself the execution of this office. At the same time it is intimated that God will avenge those who patiently wait for his assistance ; and, such as pre-occupy this office, leave no room for his aid and succour.

We ought not to supplicate God to avenge our enemies, but should pray for their conversion, that they may become our friends ; and if they pursue their wicked career, they will experience the same judgment, which other despisers of God may expect. Nor does Paul cite this testimony, as if we might indulge in anger immediately after we have been injured, and, according to the natural desire of the flesh, to pray to God to avenge our injuries. But, in the first place, he teaches us that it is not our duty to demand vengeance, unless we wish to arrogate to ourselves the part belonging to the fountain of all justice. He secondly intimates that we have no cause to fear the insulting ferocity of the wicked, if they see us bearing their treatment with patience, because God does not assume to himself, without effect, the office of revenging our cause.

We have to contend with the most perverse dispositions : if we endeavour to retaliate, we confess ourselves to be conquered ; if, on the contrary, we render good for evil, we display by such conduct an invincible constancy of mind ; and this is truly the most beautiful and glorious kind of victory ; and its advantage is not only imagined, but in reality felt, since the Lord grants the most desirable success, that can be conceived, to their patience. On the contrary, whoever shall endeavour to overcome evil by evil, will perhaps by his wickedness overcome his enemy, but it will be to his own ruin ; for by pursuing such a line of conduct, he is fighting under the banners of Satan.

Every conspiracy, combination, and union, out of God, is misery : and whatever alienates our affections from the truth is out of God. And to make our union in Christ still more desirable, Paul points out its great necessity, since we cannot glorify God truly, unless the hearts of all believers unite to celebrate his praise, and their tongues also sing one joyful hallelujah to his glory. Let none dare to boast that he will glorify God in his own way ; for the fountain of love sets so high a value upon the unity of his servants, that he will not suffer his glory to be sounded in the midst of the din of discord and contention. This one thought, " our harmony in praising God," ought to silence for ever the madness and wantonness with which dispute and controversy are carried on by too many at the present period.

The world accounts them happy who are careless of the miseries of other men, and provide for their own ease ; but Christ here calls them blessed who are not only ready to bear their own harms, but do also take other men's upon themselves, that they may help them that are in misery, and willingly join themselves to them that are troubled, and put on the same affections, that thereby they may the more willingly employ themselves to help them.

When he expressly says that no man can be otherwise the child of God, except he love them that hate him, who now dare say that we are not bound to observe this doctrine? For it is as much as if he should have said, whosoever will be accounted a Christian, let him love his enemies; surely it is a horrible monster that the world in three or four ages should be so overwhelmed with thick darkness, that it could not see that to be expressly commanded which whosoever neglects, he is wiped out from among the number of the children of God. Further, it is to be noted that he proposes not the example of God to be followed, as though that whatsoever he did became us. For he punishes the unthankful, and often driveth the wicked out of the world, in which respect he proposes not himself for us to follow; for the judgment of the world belongs not to us, but is proper to him; but he would that we should be followers of his fatherly goodness and liberality. And not only the profane philosophers did see that, but some of the most wicked contemners of godliness could make this confession, we are in nothing more like to God than in being liberal. In sum, Christ witnesses that this is a note of our adoption, if we do good to the evil and to them that are unworthy. Yet you must not understand that we by this liberality are made the children of God, but because the same Spirit (which is the witness, earnest, and seal of our free adoption) does reform the wicked affections of the flesh which strive against charity. Christ proves of the effect that none else are the children of God, but they which show it in gentleness and clemency.

Men flatter and spare themselves, and every man is a severe censor against others. And there is a certain sweetness in this sin, so that there is almost no man that itches not with a desire to enquire out other men's faults. All men do confess that it is a mischief intolerable, that they who spare themselves in their own sins should be so malicious against their brethren. And in times past profane men did also condemn it by many proverbs; yet it continued in all ages, and also remains at this day; nay, there is added to it another plague worse than that, that the most part, by condemning others, seek to get themselves further liberty of sinning. This wicked delight in biting, carping, and slandering, does Christ refrain when he says "judge not." Neither ought the faithful to be so blind that they should discern nothing; but only that they should bridle themselves, that they be no more desirous to judge than is meet. For it cannot be otherwise but that whosoever desires to be judge of his brethren should be too extreme and rigorous.

Christ does not command to forgive but when the sinner does turn to us and shall testify his repentance; for by this means he seems to grant his liberty to deny mercy and forgiveness to the wicked. I answer, offences are forgiven two ways. If any man do me an injury, and I, laying aside the desire of revenge, do not cease to love him, but instead of injury I bestow a benefit upon him, though I think hardly of him as he deserves, yet am I said and accounted to forgive him. For when God commands us to do well to our enemies, he does not therefore presently require that we should allow those things in them which he condemns; but he would only have our minds free from all hatred. In this kind of forgiveness it is not to be looked for that he who has offended should come of his own accord to appease us; so that it behoves us to love them who of set purpose exasperate us, who refuse favour, and heap old offences and new together. The second manner of forgiving is, when we so receive a brother into favour that we think well of him, and are persuaded that the remembrance of his sin is blotted out before God. And this is that I gave warning of before, that Christ does not here speak only of injuries done to us, but of all kind of offences. For he would have them that are fallen to be helped by our compassion, which doctrine is therefore very necessary, for that by nature we are almost all froward beyond measure ; and Satan, under pretence of severity, drives us to extreme rigour, so that those miserable men that are not forgiven are swallowed up of sorrow and despair.

Christ sets forth sometimes the greatness of his love towards us, to the end he may the better establish the hope of our salvation ; and now he goes farther, that he may inflame us to love our brethren by his own example. Yet he couples both things together ; for he will have us to receive by faith the infinite sweetness of his goodness, and secondly, he allures us by this means unto the study of love.

If a man endure adversity, and it happens that others come to serve him or to do what they can for him ; if he be of opinion that they which do him good have no care of him, nor are touched with compassion of his misery, it will be but as a doubling of his grief. True it is that he shall receive the good that is done unto him, but he regards it not in comparison of their compassion, insomuch that whereas other men succour him not at all, nor give him any aid, yet if he perceive in himself that those poor folk have a feeling of his misery as if they were his own members, he will make more account of that than of all the succour that a man can give him without it. So then, when we mind to discharge ourselves of our duty towards those that are in adversity, let us begin at this point, that is to wit, to pity their miseries, and to feel some part of them as near as we can. For this is the true trial of love. And herewithal it is true that we must also show this compassion of ours by our doings. There are that will be sorry enough when they see their neighbours in adversity, but yet

therewithal they fare as blocks, so as a man can get no
succour of them, they are so dismayed. But we must
follow the fashion that is set down here, namely, to be
pitiful and tender-hearted after such a sort when we see
any man endure adversity, as we always have our hands
at liberty to succour him after the ability that God has
given us. Then must we not have our minds so over-
set with sorrow as our hearts should be dismayed and
our wits utterly amazed; but rather this pitifulness of
ours must extend yet farther, and quicken us up to seek
how we may salve the sores that we see in our neighbours.

If we be not too cruel, the very necessities themselves
ought to move us to succour our neighbours. And,
truly, though we had neither law written, nor the prophets, nor aught else, is not nature herself a sufficient
good mistress to bow us, and to soften our hearts when
we see men in any necessity? Behold, one man is blind,
another lame, and the third lacks the goods of the world,
and another wants defence, and another has need of
counsel, in this case we see our own flesh, as Isaiah says,
we cannot renounce our own nature. Therefore, when we
see men, who are made after our own likeness in necessity,
if we succour them not are we not as ill or worse than
brute beasts? So then let us bethink ourselves, for we
may perchance allege this and that, but no ignorance
can excuse us. For although we had not one word of
teaching, yet does very kind itself show us that we are
blameworthy, if we endeavour not to help such as are so
in extremity. And the very heathen men bear sufficient
witness that the very nature of man teaches us in this
behalf as much as is needful, yea, and every one of us is
sufficiently convinced by experience. For when we see
any man in adversity, it is certain that we have then an
instinct and motion within us, so as if it be possible we
must needs run thither. But what? Every one of us stops
his eyes, we turn our back at it, and we pluck our heads

out of the collar by some vain and trifling shift or other. Nevertheless, the said inward motion of ours shall be as a process against us before God, for that we have not endeavoured to help the necessity of our neighbours. For we must not think that mens' wanting of aid after that sort comes by casual chance. God has appointed it after that fashion, to the end that our charity might be tried, or else that we might be convinced to have been too cruel.

It is not enough for us to bear our enemies no evil will; we must also have a mind to seek their benefit and welfare. And this is well worthy to be noted. For divers have thought they should be discharged before God, so they ran not with naked sword against those that have offended them or done them any wrong. As for me I will seek no revenge, but I pray God avenge me of them, and it would do me good at the heart if I might see a mischief light upon them. Yea? Nay, here is another manner of practising of this doctrine, when Jesus Christ declares unto us that we must pray for them that curse us, speak well of them that backbite us, and do good to them that seek to hurt us. But, contrariwise, we are so full of poison that we desire nothing but that God should overwhelm them. And on what side soever any mishap befalls them, we are glad of it. Can this be done without the overthrow of all that is contained in the doctrine of our Lord Jesus Christ? There are others also to be found who have not so malicious a heart as to suffer their wicked lusts to have open liberty; but they will say, as for me I am ready to forgive him, and I wish him no more harm than to myself; and yet, in the mean season, they cannot wish the welfare and profit of such as have displeased them, or with whom they are offended. But let us mark that it is not enough for us to abstain from all revenging with our hands and our tongues, neither is it enough for us to put away evil-will, so as we would not wish any harm or adversity to such as are our enemies; but it behoveth us to go one degree farther. And how is that? It is that we must love them.

As touching this brotherhood, God will have it to move us, and to be as a certain bond to knit us together, so as nature may persuade us to be kind-hearted one to another, and restrain us from doing harm or wrong to any man. True it is that there is not fleshly kindred between all men, to make them so near of blood as they might call one another cousins, and name themselves by any lineage whereof either other were descended; but yet is there a certain common kindred in general, which is, that all men ought to think how they are fashioned after God's image, and that there is one nature common among them all. Even the heathens knew that very well; so then we have some discretion to maintain peace and concord, and to yield every man his right, without taking away of any man's goods, and without committing of any extortion or outrage; and we pervert the order of nature, and are worse than the wild beasts, which make countenance one to another when they are all of one kind; for the wolves are not at such variance among themselves as men are. And therefore let us learn, that although there are not any near kindred among us, yet, notwithstanding inasmuch as we are men, there ought to be some common bond between us, and a certain brotherly love. But there is yet another consideration among Christians, for God has adopted them to be of his household, and that ought to avail more than all the kindred of the earth; for, seeing that God has told us that he intends to take us to himself, because that being of his church, we are as it were his own children, and call upon him as with one mouth, saying—our Father; if we nevertheless agree as cats and dogs among ourselves, may it in anywise be borne withal, especially considering that we cannot claim him for our Father, unless we be governed by his holy spirit? No, surely, for either his spirit must cry in our hearts, or else we shall have our mouths shut; again, on the other hand, by what title can we claim so great a benefit and honour as to be the children of God, if we are not members of Jesus Christ? But we are not of his body, but upon condition aforesaid. Whosoever then hurts his neighbour; whosoever is void of loving-kindness and pity; whosoever lies to catching and snatching on all sides as much as in him is, rends Jesus Christ in pieces. And therefore let us mark well, that when God alleges kindred, we are warned to consider in what degree God has put us, and every one of us to discharge ourselves faithfully thereof, to the intent that whereas God has set us together to maintain us in good agreement and love, we make not a confused disorder.

As touching worldly conversation, let us live in such wise with men, that, as we receive good by them, so we also on our side may look to do good to them, so as there may be a mutual answerableness on both sides, now it is certain that none of us can forbear his neighbours. Let a man be of as good ability as he can wish, and yet nevertheless he must stand in need of other men's service in many things. Now, when he knows that he has such need and necessity of other men's help, should he draw back from his neighbours, or be so nice that he will bear no burden, but be loath to take any pain for the common weal? It is no reason; for if they that serve him should be at the same point, and be as peevish and proud as he, must it not needs be that all should go to wreck? Yes; and therefore let us learn, that inasmuch as even in the church we have this bond of serving our neighbours, it behoves likewise, in respect of this present life, and all worldly affairs, to consider with ourselves, that, inasmuch as God makes others to do us good, and to profit us divers ways, so as we be succoured by them, we also ought to render the like again on our side.

Seeing, then, that God calls us so one with another, and will have all to agree in one accord, like good me-

lody, it is not for us to separate ourselves any more asunder. Wherefore let us consider, that, to advance the
kingdom of our Lord Jesus Christ, and the salvation of
all his, to build up his church, and to made his gospel to
prosper and flourish, every man must not only work alone
by himself, but we must also agree all in one, and draw
all by one line, and every one of us strain himself to
serve such as have need of his help. And so we see that
all such as will needs build so alone by themselves, do
but work confusion ; of which sort there are that think
themselves very able men, and that they could work
wonders to their own seeming, insomuch that they despise their neighbours, and would even bear down all
other men before them, to show themselves valiant fellows, and that they do a hundredfold more than all the
rest. And what comes of such pride but overthrow and
confusion ? Let us mark well, therefore, that we shall
never serve God by furthering of the glad tidings of our
salvation, unless we have the said concord that we are
ready and well-disposed to help every man his neighbour.

We see how God would not bind men, but left them
at liberty, to the intent they should serve him of a more
frank and free good-will. St Paul says, that God loves
him that gives with a cheerful affection ; that is to say,
with a mind void of constraint, and of a pure devotion, as
men call it. For if we offer any thing to God of necessity, as if we do an alms, being constrained thereto, or full
sore against our wills, it is ejected of him as a man shall
see these miserable pinch-pennies do who, when they
give an alms, gnash their teeth at it, and would, if it were
possible, withhold themselves from bestowing any ; and
when they open one hand, would hold fast with the
other whatever escapes them. May such offerings be
acceptable unto God ? Doubtless, not. You see, then,
the reason why we say how that God would not tie men
in any strait bond, but rather leave them free unto them-

selves, to the intent he might be served with a tender free-hearted affection.

Here the case stands, to know whether we serve God truly or hypocritically ; for if I love God, doubtless I will declare this love of mine towards those who bear his image. And we must have recourse unto that which St John says, That if when we dwell with men, and live together with them, we bear them no love—is it not plain mockery to protest that we love God, whom we see not ? Therefore, all such as vaunt themselves that they love God, and are yet so full of cruelty that they will spoil poor folks of whatsoever they can possibly catch from them, without all pity or compassion, are no better than hypocrites and shameless liars. And so we see the reason of this sentence, and how God, albeit he prizes his honour greatly, has said, notwithstanding, that he will not esteem, so much of all the sacrifices which men make unto him, as he will do of the mercy which men show one unto another ; for indeed our alms-deeds are those sweet-smelling sacrifices which God accepts.

Although a poor man become unthankful, yet shall not we therefore fail to be blessed of God. For the heat which he shall have received by us, when we have given him his coat or his covering, shall bless us. And if he be so wicked as to forget it, as too many are, with whom it is grown, as it were into a common custom, that, when they are relieved, they will not vouchsafe to acknowledge the good which is done unto them ; but rather there is nowadays such pride in some of them, that they will think a man is the more bounden unto them, for that he hath done them all the pleasure in the world; insomuch that some will say, What hath he done unto me, but he was bound to do more ? And what is this in respect of all that which he owes me ? Such is the unthankfulness which you shall see some poor folk to use ; but, as I have said, although they are dumb and speak not a word, yet shall

the good turn which we have done them serve us for a
blessing with God.

Some, when they ask alms, think they require nothing
but their own, insomuch that to their seeming they have
wrong if they are made to wait for it, and that men prevent not their necessity; they would that a man should
put off his cap, and desire them to receive an alms; there
are some which are full of this presumption. But God
contrarily declares, that he will have him which receives
a good turn to acknowledge it, and to bless him by whom
he is relieved. And in very deed, if a man is helped in
his need, and he forget, and seeks not at leastwise God
to requite it—when himself according to the world has
no means to do it, he is a thief, and pretend he never so
fairly that a man gave him such a thing, yet because he
abused the liberality which was used towards him, he is
a thief. A man helped me, and on what condition?
God binds me to pray for the prosperity of him which
has in such wise succoured me, and to protest at least
that I am bound unto him, and when I am able to recompense him I must do it. But if I cannot, I must have
God for my witness, that I acknowledge myself bound
unto him for his courtesy; if I do not, verily it is theft
as I told you. So then as the rich are taught in this
place, and as God shows them that they ought to be contented when they whom they have helped do bless them,
so, on the other side, the poor are taught to know, that
if they borrow or have any thing given them, it is to the
intent they should be moved to pray for their neighbours,
forasmuch as they have succoured and relieved them that
charity may by that means be maintained. For the true
bond thereof is, that they which have of themselves no
ability, should know that God calls them unto himself,
and that they ought to do that which belongs them to do,
namely, resort unto prayer, because they are able to do
no other thing.

If without all vanity and show, we have pity on them

which seek for refuge at our hands, and help them without grieving them at all, it shall be reckoned unto us for righteousness, and before whom ? Before the Lord our God. We are in this place summoned before the heavenly throne, to the intent that we seek not our reward before men. For that also is another thing whereunto our Lord Jesus leads us, when he says, that we must not blow with the trumpet when we give an alms, but that we must rather hide ourselves, and not let our left hand know what our right hand doeth, nor be desirous of many witnesses by whom we may vaunt ourselves. And in very deed, if it suffice us not that God likes of us, and that he accepts the service which we do unto him in bestowing of our alms, we seek for our payment here below, and therefore we are then recompensed, when men praise us and say, O, he discharges his duty faithfully in this respect. If we have once gotten such a report, and that the same do please us, verily we have our reward. Let us not think that God will set it any more in his book of account, for so should we be twice paid, I say if we seek through ambition to be seen of all men. For although when we give our alms we may sometimes make it known, yet nevertheless we must take heed that we are not led away with a vain desire to be esteemed of in this world, but whatsoever we give, let us conceive it as it were into the bosom of God. And forasmuch as the good which we have done, shall be received and esteemed of him, let us seek no other thing but that every one be edified thereby, and that every one for his part enforce himself to relieve the necessity of his neighbours. But however the world go, seeing it is God unto whom we ought to lend the alms which we bestow upon a poor man, and that he receives it, this consideration ought so to ravish us, that we should not desire to lean unto the world, nor to any of the fair praises which we may receive, nor to the reputation which we may get by it. God says that when we give unto a poor man we lend unto himself. Behold here a manner of speech that might seem strange at the first sight, that we lend unto God; but yet nevertheless he uses this manner of speech, and that not without cause, and says that he is well able to pay us usury and gain for our money, so as we need not fear that we shall lose any thing by our long waiting for it, for he will recompense us to the utmost. Seeing that God has once declared that he becomes debtor unto us, and that he puts all these items into his book of accounts, as though he had borrowed them at our hands, I pray you, are we not over blockish if we for all that seek for praise here below, and hang upon it wholly?

You are of opinion that all is lost which you give unto a poor man, and that because he has not wherewith to recompense you, or because he is unthankful, as we see many are. But hold yourselves contented with this, that before God it shall be accounted unto you for righteousness; fear you not, seeing God accepts that which you offer unto him. Cease to regard men; this ought to suffice you. Yea, put the case that one render unto you evil for the good which you have done, yet notwithstanding your God will not reject your prayers and requests, but will acknowledge that wherein you have served him. And because he makes a trial of your charity by this means, and will know how you love him by your helping of those which he offered to you in his own name, if you receive them which fly unto you for succour, let it suffice you that God accepts both of you and of that which you have bestowed on him which sought unto you.

XI —PEACE

PEACE, a singular fruit of the righteousness of faith. For every desire to seek for security of conscience by works, as is apparent in profane and ignorant characters,

will be unsuccessful. For the breast is either lulled to
rest by the contempt or oblivion of the divine judgment,
or is full of fear and trembling until it has leaned on
Christ, for he alone is peace. Serenity of conscience,
therefore, is peace ; which arises from feeling God to be
reconciled to us in Christ. Neither the Pharisee, inflated by a false confidence in his works, nor the stupid sinner, inebriated by the sweetness of his vices, enjoys this
tranquillity of mind. For though neither of these seems
to be at open war with the Lord, as a person struck with
a sense of sin feels himself to be, yet, because they do not
truly assent to the judgment of God, they experience no
harmony and union with him ; for a stupid state of conscience implies in itself an undoubted departure, as it
were, from God. Peace, therefore, towards God is opposed to the drunken security of the flesh, since the rous-
ing of themselves to give an account of their mode of
living, is the first point to which their attention ought
to be directed. No one indeed can stand before God
without fear, unless he relies, with confidence, on gratuitous reconciliation ; because, while a Being of infinite
holiness is considered to be our Judge, all men must be
affected with terror and dismay.

We know that we are born the children of wrath, and
by nature that we are enemies to God; so that it is then
necessary that we should be vexed with horrible disquietness so long as we find God offended with us ;
therefore a short and an evident definition of peace is to
be gathered of the contraries, that is of the wrath of God,
and the terror of death, and so there is a double relation
to be had ; the one to God, the other to men ; because
that we have then peace with God, and he blotting out
our guiltiness and not imputing our sins, begins to be
merciful unto us ; and we, resting in his fatherly love,
do call upon him with a sure faith, and without fear we
rejoice in that salvation promised us. And although in
Job the life of man upon earth is called a continual war-

fare, and the thing itself declares that there is nothing more troublesome than our estate while we remain here in the world, yet the angels expressly place peace on the earth, that we might know that no troubles can hinder us, but that we, enjoying the grace of Christ, might have settled and quiet minds. Therefore let us remember that there is a seat of peace placed even in the midst of the storms of temptations, amongst divers dangers, amongst violent tempests, in the midst of battles and fears, lest our faith, being driven back with any of these engines, should waver or wax faint.

The hatred of godliness does oft reconcile the ungodly together, that they who before could agree in nothing should conspire together to extinguish the name of God. And when the ungodly do on every side deliver the children of God to death, they do not purchase mutual friendship as with a great reward, but that which they think the most vile they do not hardly stick at, even as if a man should cast a crust of bread to a dog. But Christ by abolishing discord should conclude another peace amongst us, namely, that we being first reconciled to God, might with a godly and holy consent partly help each other to maintain righteousness, partly that we might strive in brotherly duties and mutual humanity.

Peace is a singular gift of God : and how is that ? when we shall have called upon God with a true assurance that he will hear us, and that he requires nothing else but that we should come unto him : it is an inestimable benefit, and such a treasure as can never be sufficiently valued : neither can we obtain the same but by the means of faith, when we know that God is our father in our Saviour Jesus Christ. Now this is not understood only of the eternal salvation of our souls ; but also for that in this world we have the privilege to run unto God, and to commend our lives into his hands, and to seek him in all our needs and necessities. When we shall have got this peace, that we can stay ourselves upon the providence of God, and cast all our carks and cares upon him, it is a singular benefit that God has bestowed upon us. Contrariwise, when we are troubled, it is said it is an extreme curse. And why? Is not the state and condition of man most miserable when he is in such fear and astonishment, as he sees nothing but dangers on every side of him, and yet cannot come unto God for to find rest and assurance in him? When man is in such fear, is he not already, as it were, in hell? Yes, surely. And, therefore, let us assure ourselves, that although all things come to pass as we would wish; yet if we have not peace, it is nothing. Howbeit, let us note also, that we must not seek our peace in this world, as the wicked do, for so long as they are not troubled nor molested, they persuade marvellous things to themselves, they triumph thereupon, and do all things to spite God withal. We must not have a peace that proceeds of recklessness and blockishness. And why? For they which so triumph in this world, have never any peace, but while they forget God, and that is a cursed peace. It were better for us to be in trouble that we might come unto our God, and seek means to be reconciled unto him, than to be so past feeling. Let us note, then, that our peace may not be only while we live at ease: But it must be grounded in God, and have respect unto him. In the mean season, let us know that when we are in trouble, it is God that visits us for our sins; yea, and also by this means he calls us unto him, to the end we should seek such peace as he has promised us from him.

Lo, what two similitudes are here, to show how God loves peace and amity among men, and above all things among brethren. They make us to understand, that when men embrace one another with hearty love, it is all one as when the fields and herbs receive nourishment by the dew of heaven: and also that it is a thing that yields a very sweet savour before God, as a good and acceptable

sacrifice unto him, even like the scent of the holy oil that
was poured upon Aaron's head. Nevertheless, this is
spoken of such as embrace one another after a godly
manner. For it may well be, that wicked men shall
bear an affection of love one towards another, and they
may, peradventure, link themselves together to accomplish their appointments: but all this is nought, friendship must come from God, and go to God. And mark
here how the name of brotherhood is set down, to the
end we should be taught to lift up our eyes unto God,
and to look unto him as often as there is any question of
loving one another.

Many will say they desire nothing but peace, howbeit, that is but to their profit, and to their neighbour's
loss. And that is no mean of peace indeed. Desire we
then to be at peace? Desire we to have agreement with
them that dwell with us? Let us on our side deal uprightly. Let us abstain from all wrong doing. Let us
grieve no man. Let us draw no man's goods to ourselves. Let us yield every man that which is his due.
Lo, what peace is. And, herein, we see that all the fair
protestations which they make that are given to ruin
and extortion are but lies. For the Holy Ghost hath
told us here that there is no word of peace, but where
just dealing and uprightness are observed, so as no man
is vexed in any way. And like as we must endeavour
to be reasonable toward our neighbours, to maintain
friendship with them, so, if they offer us reason, we
must look that we refuse it not. For if we are immeasurably hard to be contented, the thing must needs be performed in us which is written in the Psalm. He refused
blessedness, and it is far off from him, therefore cursedness shall cover him as a cloak, and it shall stick fast to
his flesh and to his skin. Would we then that God
should bless us, and cause men also to bring us favour
and friendship? Let us on our behalf seek blessedness
to the utmost of our power, and when words of peace

are offered us, let us not go seek occasion of controversy, to stir up strife and debate.

Will we then, that God be merciful to us? We must lay down all enmity one against another. God will also cast us off, for he will receive none but such as are members of his Son; and we cannot be members of Jesus Christ, unless his Spirit do govern us, which is the Spirit of peace and unity, as we have shown. Let us learn, therefore, to be in good friendship and brotherhood one with another, if we wish God to receive us to him, and have his bosom open to receive us when we come to him.

Let it be your constant care, O Christian, to govern your tongue aright, knowing from experience that the tongue is un unruly member; set a watch upon your lips, and let no corrupt communication proceed out of your mouth. Let the declaration of your Saviour be always in remembrance; that, "for every idle word which men shall speak, God will bring them into judgment." It is much to be lamented, that multitudes, even of those that think they have received the truth as it is in Jesus, and are sound in the principles of their faith, are yet grossly addicted to calumny and detraction, and judge too lightly of this abominable practice. Do you not perceive that this sin is often mentioned in Scripture, in conjunction with murder and adultery, and the blackest crimes? Be not you, then, of their number, who make detraction necessary to their profession of the faith, for, "this wisdom descends not from above, but is earthly, sensual, and devilish." It was an ancient saying among the heathens, and greatly to the honour of the primitive Christians, "Behold how these people love one another!" Shall the adversaries of the Gospel have it in their power to reverse this maxim, and to say, "See how the disciples of Jesus —of him who once loved them unto the death—now tear and devour each other!" You pretend that you have the truth, but if this is your practice, you lie, and the truth is not with you; " for the wisdom that is from above, is first pure, then peaceable, and easy to be entreated, full of mercy, and of good fruits, without partiality, and without hypocrisy." Lord, who shall abide in thy tabernacle? Who shall dwell in thy holy hill? He that backbites not with his tongue, nor takes up a reproach against his neighbour.

The Spirit of Christianity is a Spirit of peace, of humility, of love, of brotherly kindness, and charity, and were it not owing to our perverse dispositions, under the influence of this Spirit, society would be happy. See, then, O Christians, that ye cultivate the true spirit of your religion, and, as much as in you lies, live peaceably with all men, use no unlawful means to promote your temporal interest. While you look up to God, and solicit his blessing to crown your honest industry with success, guard your affections and desires, and wish for nothing that you may consume it on your lusts. Forget not that he who brought you into existence, is the constant preserver of your lives, and that you owe every thing that makes life comfortable unto his bounty. Draw nigh, then, to God, and he will draw nigh to you. With every rising and setting sun let the incense of thy sacrifices, of praise, and of thanksgiving, rise up to heaven. Collect your family around you, and be not ashamed to worship him before whom myriads of angels bow down and adore. Have you any hope through the mercy of thy God? Do you believe that his Son died for you? And yet you forget to call on him by prayer, and to render thanks unto his name—O! base ingratitude. Verily, the day is approaching when you will fly to him for protection, and cry for pity; but he will laugh at your calamity, and mock when your fear comes.

THE Scripture, when it speaks of the fear of God, sometime means outward worship, sometime again true piety. Where outward worship is touched, there it is a small thing ; for hypocrites are accustomed to use their ceremonies, and testify that they worship the true God ; but yet because they submit not themselves unto God with a sincere affection, neither bring forth faith nor repentance, therefore do they nothing else but mock and counterfeit. But the fear of God is oftentimes taken for godliness itself; and then is it called the beginning and head of wisdom, and also wisdom itself. The fear of God, therefore, that is, that reverence whereby the faithful willingly submit themselves to God, is the beginning or head of wisdom. But oftentimes also, it comes to pass that men are touched with a servile fear, so that they desire to obey God in the mean time; yet they rather desire that he were plucked from the throne. This servile fear is full of contumacy, because they which cannot exempt themselves from his power, yet do gnaw the bridle.

If we mind to keep his law duly, and to have our life acceptable unto him, we must begin at this point of yielding him such reverence as to be desirous to be under his hand and government, and to do him homage as our sovereign Lord, and to give over ourselves to him as to our maker, and to honour him as our father. If we be thus minded, it is the beginning of all the law and of all the righteousness ; and that is the cause why it is said, that the true wisdom is to fear God. And if we will know whether we have profited in God's law or no, we must always sift and search ourselves whether we have such desire and zeal that God should be honoured and glorified by us. For if there be that fear in our hearts, the fruits thereof will show themselves both in our feet and in our hands, that is to say, in all our members, according to the rule which he has set down in publishing his law. And as for them that boast of the fear of God, and nevertheless behave themselves lewdly in their conversation, they belie themselves with their own mouths, and betray that they are shameless in bragging so of the fear of God.

Why is the fear of God the beginning of wisdom ? Because it is the thing that we must begin at ; like as men will not at the first dash set a young child to the high and profound sciences, but must first teach him his entrances or principles. But they which take Solomon's words in that sense, do ground themselves upon that which is said in the canonical Epistle of St John, where it is said, that true and perfect love doth drive away fear. But in that place St John speaks of the fear that the infidels have when they shun God, trembling at his Majesty, because they know not in what case they be. For whosoever has not caught hold of God's goodness to come unto him and to trust in him, of which number all those are which know not that God intended to be at one with us in our Lord Jesus Christ, and therewithal that forasmuch as he has adopted us, we must not doubt but that he will always show himself loving toward us, and receive us to mercy, all they that have not tasted of this, are afraid and astonished when men speak to them of God, and are like a wretched offender that could find in his heart that all justice were abolished. You see, then, what the state of all unbelievers is, how they be half beside themselves, and eschew God as much as is possible. But when we are once persuaded of God's mercy, we are drawn to him by that gracious goodness to join with him, and we come unto him, as it were, with our heads upright. Not that we do at any time omit our reverence and humility, but because we are fully resolved that God likes well of us. And so we are no longer in the doubt and unquietness wherewith the wretched unbelievers are tormented. St John speaks of the said fear; but when it is said in Solomon that the fear of God is the chief or beginning of wisdom, it is to show that it is the chief point. And, to be short, the very meaning of all the things that are taught us here by Job is, that if men will be wise, they must learn to walk in the fear of God, and be edified to rule their life accordingly, and not give themselves to speculations which hold them in a wavering without any certainty.

This fear imports that we must be fully minded to suffer ourselves to be governed by God's hand, and above all things know what his goodness and mercy is, and yield him such reverence as we may be truly joined unto him. And, undoubtedly, when he speaks of the honour that belongs unto him, he not only alleges his majesty, nor only says that he is Master and Lord, but therewithal also says that he is a father. For he cries out by his prophet Malachi, "If I be your master, where is your fear? And if I be your father, where is your love?" True it is that in that place he puts a difference between love and fear. But afterward he shows that those two words come both to one end; that is to wit, that forasmuch as we ought to acknowledge him both as a father and a master, we ought to love him, howbeit with such reverence as in all our life we desire nothing, nor seek nothing but to obey him.

God cannot be rightly served but with quiet settled minds; for they who are not persuaded but are in doubt with themselves whether they shall find him merciful or offended, whether he accepts their obedience or refuses the same; to be short, they which uncertainly waver between hope and fear, it may be that sometimes they carefully busy themselves in serving him, but they never submit themselves sincerely and from the heart unto him; for fear and doubtfulness cause them to abhor him; so that, if it were possible, they would rather wish

that his Godhead were extinguished. But we know
that no sacrifice is acceptable to God, but that which
comes of a free will, and which is offered with a glad
heart. Wherefore, that men may worship aright, it
is necessary that their consciences be first quieted.
Mercy is with you that you may be feared. For God,
having given peace to men, does call them lovingly to
him, and causes them to come gladly, and with a free
and bold affection to worship him.

We have to understand, that it is not a slavish fear, as
men term it, but is so termed in respect of the honour which
we owe him, for that he is our Father and Master. Do we
fear God? Then is it certain that we desire nothing but to
honour him and to be wholly his. Do we know him?
That must be in such a way as he has uttered himself,
that is to wit, that he is our Maker, our maintainer, and
one that has shown such fatherly goodness towards us,
that we of duty ought to be as children towards him, if
we will not be utterly unthankful. Also, it behoves us
to acknowledge his dominion and superiority over us, to
the end that every one of us yielding him his due honour,
may learn to please him in all respects. Thus you see,
that, under this fearing of God, here is comprehended all
religion, that is to wit, all the service and honour which
the creatures owe unto their God. And surely it was a
right excellent virtue in Job to fear God after that manner, considering how the whole world was turned aside
from the right way. When we hear this, we perceive
that although we live among the veriest naughty packs
in the whole world, we shall be utterly inexcusable, if
we are not given to the serving of God as we ought to
be. And this is well to be marked, because many men
are of opinion, that when they are among the thorns,
God will hold them acquit and excused; and that if afterwards they corrupt themselves, or, as the proverb says,
hold with the hare and hunt with the hound, which
is all one, God will pardon them. But, contrariwise,

look upon Job, who is called a man that feared God. In what country ? It was not in Jewry, it was not in the city of Jerusalem, it was not in the Temple, but it was in a defiled place, in the midst of such as were utterly perverted. Albeit, then, that he were among such people, yet had he such stay of himself, and lived in such a manner that he walked purely among his neighbours, notwithstanding that at that time all was full of cruelty, of outrage, of robbery, and of such other like enormities in that place. Whereupon we have to consider, that it shall turn so much to our greater shame, if we on our behalf have not a care to keep ourselves pure in the service of God, and of our neighbours, seeing he gives us such occasion as we have, that is to wit, that God's word is continually preached unto us that we may be exhorted unto it, and that he reforms us when we have done amiss.

God's protection is a brazen wall to us ; and we may rest safe, without fear or care, in the midst of all dangers when our heavenly Father shows us his kindness. Paul does not mean that we shall experience no adversity, but promises victory against every assault, and every description of enemies. If God be for us—This is the chief, and, therefore, the only prop that can support us in every temptation. For, if God is not propitious, although every thing besides should smile upon us, yet we can form no conception of certainty, and of confidence. On the other hand, his favour alone is a sufficiently great consolation for all our sorrow, a sufficiently powerful protection against all the storms and tempests of evils and misfortunes. The numerous testimonies of Scripture afford light and evidence to this truth, where the saints of God, relying on the power of Omnipotence alone, dare despise every adversity they meet with in the world. " If I walk in the midst of the shadow of death, I shall fear no evil." " In the Lord put I my trust : how say ye to my soul, Flee as a bird to the mountain ?" " I will not be afraid of ten thousands of people, that have set themselves against me round about." For there is no power, either under or above heaven, which can resist the arm of the Most High. We need not, therefore, tremble at any mischief that might befall us while he is our defence. True confidence, therefore, in God, is at last manifested by the believer, who, content with his protection, dreads nothing so much as despondency. The saints are, indeed, often shaken, but never entirely cast down. The Apostle's advice may be summed up in the following sentence : " The pious soul ought to stand firm and unshaken, relying on the internal testimony of the Spirit, and cast off all dependence on external things."

Although we are armed and fenced with God's promises, so as we ought to be sufficiently resolved, that he will guide us unto the end ; yet shall we have many occasions to make us grudge and repine, so as we might swerve aside from the right way, or utterly forsake it, if we had not constancy to overcome all the stops and hinderances that the devil thrusts in our ways ; for of nature we are fearful. True it is that in many things we are but too hardy, when any fond thing is to be attempted foolishly : in that case men need not to be heartened, for they are but too bold already to attempt this and that, and to mount above the clouds, as they say. But when God should be followed whithersoever he calls us, our eyes run here and there, up and down, we are at our wit's end ; yea, and if a fly do but whisk before our eyes, or a straw stir at our feet, by and by we are at a stop.

Now, seeing we have this vice in our nature, let us determine to fight on all sides against this fearfulness, to the end we are not held back from following God whithersoever he commands us ; but that we may overcome all the temptations of Satan, though he be never so wily in forging and framing of innumerable occasions in that behalf, to turn us away from our calling.

Good reason it is, that when we will not believe God's single word, we should pay very dear for our experience, and be made to know, in spite of our teeth, that he will be steadfast in his purpose, and bring the thing to pass that he has spoken. And hereby we are warned not to provoke God's wrath, nor to tempt him: so soon, then, as he speaks, let us stand in awe; for it is a part of faith, as is shown by the example of Noah. He beheld the flood at such time as men made great cheer in the world. How so? for God had told him that the world should perish, and he contented himself therewith. And, therefore, let us not tarry till God arm himself and utter his power against us; but as soon as he has spoken, let us be afraid, that we may prevent his wrath; and then shall we be taught, as we ought to be, to our welfare. But if we are hardheaded, and think that whatever is said is but a mockery, we shall find, to our confusion, that God has an effectual word, and that his hand and his word go together, so as all that ever comes from him shall be found to be certain and infallible.

We know that when bees are angry they sting men, and they regard not whether men be too strong for them, but they fly upon them with such choler and fury, as they cannot but be astonished. They seek to sting their eyes, so as there is not the hardiest of them but he is put to his shifts, and is fain to run away from those little pretty fowls. Moses, then, has used this similitude to show that the enemies had lions' hearts, because God had encouraged them; for it belongs to him only to strengthen men. When it pleases him to defend us, though our enemies were as mad as might be, yet should they shrink away, and be dismayed at a thing of nothing. But else, if there were but little children against us, God would so strengthen them as we should not know where to become, but be discomfited before them. Therefore, let us not have an eye to the strength of men, nor to their furniture; for our God will stir up folk against us that could do nothing before, and in whom there was no likelihood at all, and we shall be so cumbered to withstand them, that, to our seeming, all the world is against us; and, moreover, we shall be so dismayed, and God shall so bereave us of all sense and reason, that even a visor shall be enough to scare us out of our wits.

If we were cumbered with any perplexity or anguish, and knew not whether God would leave us in the mire or no, we might well be afraid; and if we would not be afraid, we should be too blockish. But when God says unto us,—my children, it is true that you are weak, you can do nothing of yourselves, and you have too strong an enemy, by means whereof you could by no means withstand him if you were not helped and upheld by me; but I tell you your temptations shall not be greater than you shall be able to bear: I know what your power is; I will give you strength and courage at your need; I will mitigate the temptations that might overthrow you; and although the world and the devil be stark mad against you, yet will I bridle them, so that, although you be roughly assailed, yet shall you overcome them;—trust thereunto. Has God spoken as this man tells us? Let us never doubt of it. Not that we can be utterly exempt from all fear, so long as we live in this world; insomuch that although we have God's promises, whereby we are assured that he will never leave us, but that we shall ever feel his help at our need; yet must we not think that we shall be utterly void of care and doubt, or that we should not beware of the dangers that environ us round about. No; but yet must not this fear so over-awe us as we should not take heart to call upon God, and to rest upon him, and to go on still forward.

Let us mark here, that in such cases we must weigh well the power of God, not doubting but that when he shall have suffered men to advance themselves, and all things to be fully furnished according to their desire, he

will dash it all under foot ; mark that for one point.
True it is, that when we fall to the considering of our
own estate and condition, we must not imagine that
God is not merciful towards us, so we have our recourse to him ; yet, notwithstanding, now and then to
give the greater gloss to his own goodness and power, he
will suffer us to be in some distress, insomuch that when
we look about us, we shall cry out, alas ! how shall I do,
what will become of me ?   We shall not know to whom
we may betake ourselves ; and when we have made all
the shifts we can, we shall be as folk half vanquished
beforehand. But our God has wherewith to supply all
our wants, only let us tarry his leisure, and say with
Jehosaphat,—It is as easy for our God to give victory
to a small number against an infinite number, as to give
victory to a great army against a few folk: all is one with
him.   So, then, let us trust in him, let us stay ourselves
upon his strength, and let us not doubt but he will give
us wherewith to withstand all temptations that shall be
laid before us.   And specially when Satan goes about
to weaken our courage and to cast us into despair, let us
resist that.

All the experiences which God has given us before
must assure us the better of our salvation, and make us
to trust the more unto him, for his former succouring of
us.   And let us gather thereupon that he can well find
other means which we never thought of, and, moreover,
that his goodness diminishes not, and that he is always
alike strong.   Let us conclude that he is able to save
us, so we resort unto him ; and therefore let us bethink
us of the gracious goodness that God has extended toward us aforetimes, and of the succour that he has given us.
And in considering those things, let us not only give
him thanks for his showing of himself to be our preserver
heretofore ; but also let us take further matter and occasion to trust to him afterward, and to resort boldly unto
him, and not to doubt but that he will continue as he began,

until he has brought our salvation to full perfection. Now, if this be spoken concerning our bodily enemies, much more reason have we to apply the same to Satan, to sin, and to all other things that fight against the endless salvation of our souls.

Let every one of us consider his own infirmities thoroughly, and we shall find that if our Lord had not a care of us, and fought not mightily for our defence, we should perish every minute of an hour. How is it, then, that we are assured of our salvation? Surely because our Lord who watches over us is strong enough; and, therefore, albeit that all the armies of hell were banded against us, yet shall they not prevail any thing at all, if God be on our side; insomuch that we shall not only be preserved from the hand of our enemies, but also have the victory over them, and bring them under our feet, because God dwells among us. You see, then, on the one side, how men ought to feel what need they have that God should help them, seeing they are themselves over weak, and have no help to defend themselves, and also how, for all that, they may boldly boast. And why? Because God has received them unto himself, and will preserve them and be their safeguard. Behold what the glory of the faithful is, which notwithstanding, proceeds of humbleness. For we can never be safeguarded by our God until we have learnt to distrust ourselves, and feel ourselves forlorn, considering the weakness which is in us.

As soon as we begin once but to call God's promises into question, our minds are distracted with many passions, we stand amazed at the greatness and diversity of the dangers, we are daily assaulted with vexations of spirit; at last we grow sottish, and cannot be brought to taste how gracious our God is. Our minds, therefore, being thus possessed with despite, have we not need that this voice should again and again ring in our ears, I am with thee, fear not? that so this fear may either be wholly rooted up out of our hearts, or at least so corrected by little and little, that we may not be overcome of it : for I can tell you, if it take never so little rooting there, it is not so easily displanted. Hence we observe, that we ought to place our hope in nothing but in God's being present with us : for if he be absent, we must needs tremble for fear, or wax dull and dead-hearted, or stagger to and fro like a drunken man. And yet the Lord would not have us be so void of fear, as that we should thereby grow careless or idle ; but when we hear that he is near, and that he will assist us, faith must then overcome all difficulties in the midst of imminent dangers.

XIII — JOY

The true and only way to obtain gladness is to feel that God is reconciled unto us, whose favour alone is sufficient to yield us perfect felicity ; yea, so far, as to make us rejoice in tribulation. Contrariwise, what can comfort or glad us if God bereave us of his reconciliation ? Hence we gather a sure doctrine, to wit, the faithful cannot be said to rejoice as they ought unless they join praises unto God therewith ; this spiritual joy must therefore be distinguished from carnal and profane joy and delights, into which the wicked plunge themselves ; for they rejoice indeed, but the issue shows how dangerous the lasciviousness of the flesh is, when we flatter ourselves in the contempt of God. It is not without good cause, therefore, that St Paul calls this joy spiritual, for it consists not in the enjoying of earthly things, as in riches, honours, treasures, which perish and come to nothing in a moment ; but this joy is secret, it hath its seat in the heart, and out of it can it not be removed nor taken away by any means whatsoever, though Satan indeed endeavours with might and main upon all occasions to disturb and afflict us.

Nor is it to be wondered at that as our diseases are various, so the remedies applied for their cure should also be various. And hence, because the vices of ambition, of avarice, of envy, of gluttony, of the immoderate love of this world, and the innumerable other lusts with which we abound, cannot be cured by one and the same medicines, the Lord visits us with manifold and various afflictions. When he requires them " to count it all joy," &c., it is as if he had said, that such temptations were so far to be accounted profitable, as to be really the subject matter of rejoicing; in fine, it signifies that there is nothing in afflictions that ought to disturb our joy, and thus he not only enjoins to bear adversity with quietness and equanimity, but teaches that there is reason why the faithful should rejoice, even when hard pressed by calamities. There is no doubt but the constitution of our nature is such, that any trial or affliction will affect us with pain and sorrow ; nor can any of us so far divest ourselves of our natural feelings as, when we sensibly experience evil, not to grieve and be sad. But this is no reason why the children of God, under the direction of the Spirit, may not rise above all the pains of the flesh ; and hence it is, that even in the midst of sorrow, they need not cease to rejoice.

It might be objected—how is it possible we should account that joyous or pleasant which to our natural senses is grievous and bitter ? In answer to this, he shows that it is on account of the effect of afflictions, we ought to rejoice in them, because they produce patience, which is a fruit of high price. Since God, then, by these provides for our future welfare and salvation, he certainly furnishes us with just ground of rejoicing.

Certainly it is on this account that we dread diseases,

poverty, banishment, imprisonment, disgrace, and death, because we account them to be evils; but when we come to understand that by the goodness of God they are converted into the means of our salvation, it would be ungrateful in us to repine when visited with them; or rather, not voluntarily to present ourselves as the subjects of such fatherly treatment.

XIV —HOPE

WHAT shall become of us, if we know not that we are created to a better life? It were better for us that we were asses and oxen. For the brute beasts enjoy the present life; they feed, they take their rest, and they travel without any great feeling of it. But men eat not one morsel of bread without care; in the midst of their pleasure they have a number of heart-bitings of their own, besides that they want not annoyances at other men's hands, for every man for himself becomes his own hangman. Therefore if we have no hope of the second life, what shall become of us? And truly our Lord's will is, that the same should abide printed in the hearts of all men, according as we see that although the heathen men were become brutish, yet notwithstanding they retained still some knowledge of the second life, and of the immortality of the soul. And as for those who knew it not, God has left some mark or other, whereby to make them inexcusable; yea, and it were but even the tombs that they have made to bury dead folks in.

The hope of a future life manifests itself, and dares to exult and glory, because the foundations on which we stand rest on the glory of God. For, according to the Apostle, though the faithful are now wanderers and pilgrims on earth, yet their confidence raises them so far above the heavens as to make them cherish in their bosoms, with calmness and tranquillity, the hope of their future inheritance.

"Hope maketh not ashamed"—Has a most certain effect upon our salvation. Hence we are evidently tried with afflictions by the Lord, for the very purpose of using these as steps to promote the advancement of our salvation. Those troubles, therefore, cannot render us wretched, which in their own way are the supports of our happiness.

The true constancy of the faithful is hope; for hope is the nourisher of faith. What difference is there between faith and hope? By faith we embrace God's promises, not doubting but he will perform them; nevertheless it is not enough to have believed God after this fashion, for once and away, but we must continue in it steadfastly throughout, and that is done by hoping. And so is hope nothing else but the conceiver or leader of faith, that it vanish not away, nor be a temporal or transitory thing, but that it may hold out and continue to the end. True it is, that we shall have many encounters to abide; we must fight if we intend to hope, and not faint or fall away from our hope.

XV—PATIENCE

No MAN has rightly forsaken himself, but he has so resigned himself wholly up to the Lord, that he suffers all the parts of his life to be governed by his will. He that is so framed in mind, whatsoever happen, will neither think himself miserable, nor will, with enviousness against God, complain of his fortune. How necessary this affection is, shall hereby appear, if you consider to how many chances we are subject. Divers kinds of diseases do trouble us; sometimes the pestilence cruelly reigns, sometimes we are sharply vexed with calamities of war, sometimes

frost or hail devouring the hope of the year, brings barrenness, that drives us to dearth ; sometimes our wife, parents, children, or kinsfolk, are taken away by death, our
house is consumed with fire: these be the things, at
chancing whereof men curse their life, detest the day of
their birth, have heaven and light in execration, murmur
against God, and, as they be eloquent in blasphemies, accuse him of injustice and cruelty ; but a faithful man must
even in these chances behold the merciful kindness and
fatherly tenderness of God. Therefore, whether he see
his house destroyed, his kinsfolk slain, yet he will not
cease to praise God, but rather will turn himself to this
thought—Yet the grace of the Lord that dwells in my
house will not leave it desolate. Or if, when his corn is
blasted or bitten, or consumed with frosts, or beaten down
with hail, he see famine at hand, yet he will not despair,
nor speak hatefully of God, but will remain in his confidence. We are yet in the Lord's protection, and sheep
brought up in his pastures, he therefore will find us food
even in the extremest barrenness. Or if he be troubled
with sickness, even then he will not be discouraged with
bitterness of sorrow to burst out into impatience and
quarrel thus with God; but considering the righteousness and lenity in God's correction, he will call himself
back to patience. Finally, whatsoever shall happen, because he knows it ordained by the hand of God, he will
take it with a well pleased and thankful mind, lest he
should stubbornly resist his authority, into whose power
he has yielded himself and all his. Therefore let that
foolish and most miserable comfort of the heathen be far
from a Christian man's heart, which, to strengthen their
minds against adversities, did impute the same to fortune,
with whom they counted it foolish to be angry, because
she was blind and unadvised, that blindly wounded both
the deserving and undeserving. For contrary ways this
is the rule of godliness, that the only hand of God is the
judge and governess of both fortunes, and that it runs

not forward with unadvised sudden rage, but with most
orderly justice deals among us both good things and evil.

Such as are patient, are sure of some grief, so as they
feel great sorrow and anguish of heart: for were we as a
block of wood, or as a stone, it were no virtue at all in
us. Is that man worthy to be praised, who has no
feeling at all of his adversity? We see sometimes a poor
madman laugh and scorn the whole world, yea, even
when he is at death's door: but that is because he has
no feeling of his misery. This, therefore, deserves not to
be taken and esteemed for a virtue, for it is rather a
blockishness. The brute beasts have some time no feeling, yet are they not patient for all that. So then let us
mark, that this word patient, or patientness betokens not
that men should become blockish, so as they should have
no heaviness at all, nor be cumbered with any grief
when they feel adversities: but the virtue is, when they
can moderate themselves, and hold such a measure, as
they cease not to glorify God in the midst of all their
miseries: nor be so overcumbered and swallowed up with
sorrow and anguish, as to quail altogether: but fight
against their own passions, until they may be able to
frame themselves to the good will of God, and to conclude as Job doth here, and finally to say, that he is
righteous in all respects.

To the intent we may have patience in all our adversities, we must have a taste of God's goodness, we must
rejoice of his grace, and we must assure ourselves that
his scourging of us is for our welfare. And this is the
thing that is showed us in this strain: when it is said,
Refuse not the correction of the Almighty. For it is
he that is the surgeon of all your sores, it is he that will
send you health of all your diseases. God then showed
us here, how his meaning is not that men's submitting
of themselves unto him should be to say, Seeing we can
no otherwise do, needs must God have the mastery of us,
for we cannot exempt ourselves from his jurisdiction.

The case stands not upon coming to him so, but our Lord says, No, but be ye patient, humble yourselves unto me, and take warning by my judgments that ye murmur not against me, nor stomach the matter; or otherwise, ye shall be fain to be beaten down by my hand, yea, even in such wise as ye shall be utterly overwhelmed. But if ye humbly acknowledge your faults, and come to me to crave pardon, ye shall feel assuagement of your miseries, in such sort as ye shall have cause to yield me thanks, even in the midst of your greatest troubles. Behold, what we have to muse upon, that we may have the true patience. Seeing, then, that of our own nature we be stubborn against God, and are angry with him if he do but touch us with his little finger: seeing, also, that we have such a proudness in us, as we think that God doth us wrong if he chastise us: Seeing that we have these two so great vices, it is a very hard matter to purge us of them. So much the more, therefore, must we mind the lesson that is shown us here: that is to wit, that God, by scourging us, means to bring us back to himself, yea, even to our benefit and welfare.

Behold, also, wherefore our Lord Jesus Christ likens his children to lambs or to sheep which follow the voice of their shepherd, and hearken unto him as soon as he calls them. Therefore, let us learn to be reproved, and to receive correction whensoever it is brought us: and generally, let us learn to yield ourselves to all things that we know to be good and of God. Are we taught? Then must we follow. And as I have touched already, as for those that are so wedded to their own opinion, it is certain that God sets them forth to be a mockery and reproach, so as he suffers them not to have any more shamefacedness and modesty, but lets them be as wild beasts, and so revenges himself of such stiffneckedness when men cannot find in their hearts to yield and to bow their necks in agreeing to his will.

Let us learn to hold us always to the word of righteousness, assuring ourselves that God will evermore be
on our side, and that his truth will be so mighty, that in
the end it will get the upper hand. True it is, that for
so much as men are fugitive, and run on so headily, the
truth has not always its full scope, and it will seem
erewhile to be utterly overthrown; but let us have patience until the day of the Lord do appear, as says St
Paul. For that is it whereunto he calls them, mocking
at the overweening of such as judge so awkwardly, over-
thwartly, and confusedly, in charging him with those reproaches. But I will wait for the day of the Lord, till
God at length discover the false slanders wherewith I
have been charged. For when tha begins to appear,
then must righteousness come abroad, then must slanderers be convicted, and then must all things turn to
their confusion. Now if God, even in our whole life,
grants us the grace to get the upper hand of all malicious
persons that go about to trample us under foot, when we
shall have walked unfeignedly in truth, much more shall
we have that pre-eminence when the case concerns faith
and the service of God, and the doctrine of salvation:
that is to wit, God will give us such and so stedfast a
constancy, that when the devil shall have bent all his
force against us, he shall gain nothing at our hands, according also as we have a promise thereof.

Sometimes they that speak not at all cease not to displease God more grievously through their impatience,
than they that blaspheme with full mouth. Doubtless
it is a very heinous crime when men dare open their
mouths to blaspheme God. But yet there are many also
that will not utter one word, and yet are they full of rancour against God, yea, they are much fuller of pride and
bitterness than those that speak. Ye shall see some man
that will chafe upon the bridle like a mule, and yet not
speak one word. But if you examine his heart, you shall
find him ready to burst for spite, and that there is, as it

were, a fiery rage in him ; and if it were possible that he
might fight with God, he would do it.   Another unloads
himself at the first dash, and many wicked words slip
from him ; but yet he has not so much bitterness in his
heart.   But howsoever the world go, both of them are
naught.   What is to be done then ?   If our sorrows
oppress us too sore, let us settle ourselves to pray unto
God, that it may please him to aid us in the midst of
them, so as we may not conceive any moodiness against
him, at leastwise, which should hinder the honouring of
him.   And herewithal we must also labour and fight ;
for whereas men are wont to harden themselves when
they have once conceived any wilfulness and stomaching,
and to nourish themselves therein, it behoves us to know
that we must withstand it.   Then let us restrain our
affections, and let them be tied up like wild beasts.   And
when we have so done our endeavour to repress our passions and to hold them in awe, then let us assure ourselves that we can also discern and say, How now ? Shall
a mortal man have leave to give himself the bridle, so as
he shall stand in contention with God, as if he would
pick a quarrel to him? Then let us keep us from such licentiousness of murmuring against God, as to have our tongue
unbridled to say, How now ?   Is this of God's doing ?
Wherefore handles he me after this manner ?   No, let us
not do so.   But let us make our moan in such sort as God
may always be honoured at our hands, and let us confess
that he is righteous and impartial howsoever he deal with
us. Mark here a special point. And, moreover, therewithal
let all our complaints be made unto him.   For you see
wherein men overshoot themselves oftentimes ; that is, in
shrinking away from God as much as they can when they
would make their complaints, or else in discoursing with
their neighbours.   And how ?   I have a misfortune, say
they, and there is no man that endureth so much as I ;
it should seem that God minds to torment me without
end or ceasing.   Lo ! how men do always grunt.   And

although they utter no such murmurings with their mouth, yet is it sure that they keep ever some store of such stuff behind in their hearts, and lay it not open before God as he requires.

Let us also mark, that when the case stands upon the framing of ourselves unto patience, if we endure any adversity, we must comfort ourselves in God ; and if we be tried, so as the devil tempts and thrusts us forward to despair, there is nothing so good as to gather our wits home.   And why so ?   For so long as we gaze at men, we shall nothing avail, but which more is, we shall do ourselves harm.   If I be troubled that I can no more, well, if I comfort myself with fair shows only, and make great protestations before men, God will laugh my fondness to scorn, in so much that when I come to myself again, and am alone, my conscience will pinch me, and then shall I feel how all that ever I pretended was but smoke.   And why?   Because I have had more regard of men than of God.   So then, when a man intends to frame himself unto patience, it is good for him to withdraw into himself, as if he were separated from the whole world, and to refer himself wholly unto God, and suffer himself to be governed by him.   And truly, seeing we are in such necessities, we have good cause to call upon God ; but how shall we call upon him, if we be not as it were cut off from men ?   For so long as I am fastened to this or that, so long am I turned aside from God.   We see, then, that we must cut off all these cords that hold us back, and present ourselves before the majesty of God as the only party whom we have regard of.   True it is that we must regard our neighbours also, both to edify them and to receive comfort at their hands.   But in the meanwhile we must begin at this point ; that is to wit, at the laying open of our hearts before God, that we disburden all our matters, sorrows, and cares unto him. .

Let us bear in mind that when our Lord sends us any diseases, so as one is stricken with poverty, another is smitten after another fashion, and every man has his grief; if we pray unto him, and the misery is as though it were tied to our shoulders, and he makes no countenance to hear us, it is not to be said, therefore, that God lets us alone therein, to drive us to despair. But if we bear the adversity patiently which he sends, let us look to be delivered of it in the end; and, in the mean while, let it suffice us to be comforted by his Holy Spirit, and let us hope that he will not suffer us to be tempted above that which we are able to bear.

Let us learn to bear all temporal corrections patiently which God sends unto us. Although our condition wax worse and worse to the worldward; although we have a heavy burden to bear; although we have many hard and grievous things to endure, yet, notwithstanding, we must come to this point, that forasmuch as they are but temporal chastisements, we may hold ourselves quiet, for our salvation abides still unimpaired. And although we obtain not something which we ask, yet must we not think ourselves utterly barred from it, until our Lord show us by some evident sign. As how? When a man is in trouble, he repairs unto God and craves mercy, and yet he finds no relief; but instead of easement he finds himself tormented double. All that he gains by his calling upon God is, that his misery is increased; but yet for all this he must not be discouraged, but continue still in praying unto God; and therewithal we must consider this—God knows to what end he does it. And his delaying to grant us our request is to show us that although he suffers us to languish in our adversities, yet does he not forget us, nor disdain to be our Father still, but only teaches us to obey him, and to be subject to him. After that manner, then, must we behave ourselves in praying. When it shall seem that we have lost our time in calling upon God, yet must we still come back to this comfort, saying—No, God shows me that it is not meet for me to ask whatsoever I think good, but that I must come and put myself into his hands with all humbleness, to receive what he thinks good, and to hold all my desires in obedience unto him. Seeing that he shows me this, it behoves me to frame myself thereunto, and to take that to be best for me which he shall vouchsafe to send me.

James uses a word in an active sense, and says— " The trying of your faith worketh patience;" because, if the Lord were not to try and examine us, but to leave us altogether at our ease and in comfort, there would be no need of patience or of fortitude of mind in enduring calamities. Paul, on the other hand, uses the word in a passive sense, and means, when he says, " patience worketh experience," that while through patience we overcome evils, we experience the happy effects of God's power and assistance in our struggle with these calamities; for then the truth is more immediately displayed, that he is a present help in time of need, and hence our confidence and hope in him for the future are increased; for our faith in the divine truth becomes more firm the more we have experienced it. Paul's doctrine then is, that from such an experience of divine grace, hope springs up; not that it then has its first commencement, but that it is thus increased and confirmed; both, however, mean that adversity furnishes ground and opportunity for the exercise of patience. Our minds, however, are not naturally so constituted that affliction should work in them patience; but Paul and James do not so much point at what the nature of man is in this respect, as they do at the providence of God which so orders it; that the faithful learn patience from afflictions, although the ungodly by them are more and more incited to outrage and fury, as the case of Pharoah witnesses.

" Tribulation worketh patience."—This does not proceed from the nature of tribulation, by which we see a large portion of mankind excited to rail against, and even to curse God. But when inward meekness, infused by the Spirit of God, and comfort, suggested by the same, have succeeded in the place of stubbornness and obstinacy, tribulations, which in the obstinate and refractory can only excite indignation and fretting, become the instruments of generating patience in believers.

The first and chief consolation of the pious in adversity is the sure persuasion of God's fatherly kindness : hence our certainty of salvation, our calm security of mind, by which adversity is sweetened, or the bitterness of grief at least mitigated. A more fit exhortation, therefore, to patience cannot be supplied us than a clear understanding of our enjoying God's favour.

Every believer, who has the sure confidence of enjoying the divine favour, can remain unmoved in the midst of the most grievous afflictions, which usually torment mankind to such an extent, because they either do not consider these to happen by the providence of God, or interpret them as signs and marks of the divine wrath, or judge themselves to be deserted and forsaken of the Maker of all things, or expect no termination and issue to their distresses, or do not meditate on a better life, or perplex themselves by reasons of a similar nature. Paul is desirous that the knowledge and lively sense of the love manifested by our Father, should flourish with so much vigour in our hearts, as always to shine forth and display itself in the midst of the greatest darkness in which we are involved by our afflictions. For as clouds, though they obscure the clear sight of the sun, yet do not entirely deprive us of his brightness ; so God sends forth the rays of his grace, through the deepest gloom of our adversity, to prevent the most violent temptation from overwhelming us with despair. Nay, our faith, supported as it were on wings by the promises of God, should ascend upwards, and penetrate heaven itself through all intervening obstacles. Adversity, considered simply by itself, is undoubtedly a sign of God's wrath ; but when preceded by pardon and reconciliation, we must lay it down as a fixed principle, that God, even when his chastening hand is upon us, never forgets his mercy.

We always escape with struggling, and swim out of the waters of affliction and persecution in which we were plunged. It sometimes indeed happens that believers seem to have been overcome by their afflictions, and to lie as if nearly worn out and destroyed, so great is the trial, or rather humiliation with which they are afflicted by the Lord. But an issue is always so granted them in this case that they come off conquerors.

A persuasion of this, firmly fixed in our hearts, will always pluck us out of the depths of hell, raise us to the light of life, and possess sufficient strength to afford us protection.

No child of Adam will submit to bear the cross with a placid and quiet mind, who has not learned to seek his happiness from a source wholly independent of the world, that he may mitigate and alleviate the bitterness of the cross, by the consolations which are inspired by the sure hope of an immortal crown. But since a patient enduring of the cross, and steady hopes of our heavenly crown, very much surpass our own strength, we ought to be instant in prayer, and unceasingly supplicate God not to suffer our minds to faint, be dejected, or broken down, by any events in Providence, even the most disagreeable and disastrous. Paul, also, not only excites us to prayer, but expressly requires perseverance; because our warfare is unceasing, and we are daily attacked by various assaults, which champions, even of the greatest bravery, are unable to support, without an occasional supply of new vigour. Unceasing continuance in prayer is the best remedy against fatigue.

We are not only forbidden to attempt any thing hastily without a command from God; but patience is commanded us in all our troubles and inconveniences. If the flesh, therefore, at any time starts back from adversity, let us remember that a man, who is not free, and master of himself, perverts all law and order, if he does not depend upon the will, nod, and pleasure of his God. A rule of life and death is thus afforded us; for if the Lord lengthens our life in the midst of continued troubles, uneasiness, and weariness, we ought not to desire to depart before our time; and should he suddenly recal us in the very flower of our age, we ought to be invariably ready and equipped for our departure.

The patience of believers is not that unfeeling apathy commanded by the stoics and philosophers in the heathen world, but that meekness and quietness of spirit, by which we willingly and cheerfully submit ourselves to God, while all things are rendered sweet and pleasant to us by the taste and sense of his fatherly goodness, kindness, condescension, and love. This patience so cherishes and sustains peace in our hearts, as to prevent us from fainting.

XVI—CONTENTMENT

The Lord, who gave the life itself, will not suffer that those things should be wanting, which appertain to the sustaining of the same. And certainly we do God no small injury, so often as we distrust that God will not give us food and clothing, as though that he had cast us out upon the earth by fortune. For whosoever is certainly persuaded, that he knows what the estate and condition of our life is, let not the same man doubt, but that he will very well provide for his necessities. Therefore, as often as any fear or carefulness for provision shall assault us, let us remember that God has a care of our life which he has given us.

People do commonly judge, that the more a man possesses, the happier his life is, and they imagine riches to be the cause of a blessed life. Hence comes that intemperate desire of having, which as a burning furnace sends out its heat, and yet ceases not to burn within. If that we were persuaded that riches and all abundance of goods are helps of this present life, which the Lord gives unto us with his own hand, and blesses the use thereof, this one thought would easily appease all wicked desires; and that do the faithful find true by their own experience. For whereof comes it to pass, that with stayed minds they should depend on God alone; but because they bind not their life, nor make it subject to abundance of riches, but they rest in the Providence of God, who only both sustains us by his power, and gives us as much as is meet.

Since, under the type of the land of Canaan, not only the hope of a heavenly life was offered to Abraham, but the full and solid blessing of God, the Apostle teaches us that the dominion of the world was justly promised the father of the faithful. The pious enjoy a certain taste of this in the present life, for however frequently they may be pinched by the straits of want, yet, because they partake of the creatures formed by God for their use with a calm conscience, and enjoy earthly blessings from the hands of a propitious, willing, and kind Father, as pledges and earnests of eternal life, their poverty does not prevent them from acknowledging heaven, earth, and sea, to be their right. The wicked, though they swallow up the riches of the world, can call nothing their own; nay, they rather snatch them by stealth, for they usurp them with the curse of God. The pious feel it a great solace in the midst of their destitution, that while they live sparingly, nothing is stolen from others; but they receive their lawful allowance at the hand of their heavenly Father, until they shall discern the full possession of their inheritance, while all creatures will be subservient to their glory.

If we wish to read the sacred historians with purity and piety, let us remember we ought to handle them in such a manner as to receive from them the advantage of solid learning. They instruct us how to form our life and conversation, how to confirm and strengthen our faith, and how to excite the fear of the Lord. The imitation of the saints will be useful to form our life and manners, if we learn from them sobriety, chastity, love, patience, modesty, contempt of the world, and other virtues. The assistance which God was always ready to afford his saints in former ages, will contribute to confirm our faith; and his unceasing protection, and fatherly care of them, will supply us with consolation in the trials of adversity. The judgments of God, and his punishments of the wicked, if they excite a reverential awe and deep sense of piety in our hearts, will afford us much assistance in our present pilgrimage.

Paul anticipates the objection, which some might deridingly propose, that Christians, notwithstanding all their glory, are in this world harassed and wearied in a surprising manner, which is a condition the very reverse of bliss; and in answer, he declares, that the calamities of the pious, so far from impeding their enjoyment of happiness, contribute to promote the advancement of their glory. He reasons in establishing this proof from the effect, and uses an elegant climax with which he finally concludes, to show that all the afflictions we at present suffer tend to our salvation and happiness. And we must not understand his expression of the saints glorying in their tribulations, as if they did not fear and fly from affliction, or were not sore pressed with its keen blasts when they are overtaken by the howling tempest of adversity; for no patience would result from such trials, if they did not feel a bitterness; but they are properly said to glory, because, in the midst of their grief and sorrows, they experience great consolation, which they consider to be dispensed by the hand of their most indulgent Parent for good, during all their sufferings. For they have always sufficient ground for glorying, where their salvation is promoted and advanced. Hence, therefore, we are taught the design of our tribulations, if we are desirous to be considered as the sons of God. For they ought to accustom us to patience ; and, if this is not accomplished, our vileness renders the work of God again ineffectual. For whence does he prove adversity not to be opposed to the glory of the pious, but because by their patience in enduring they feel the assistance of God, which supports and confirms their hope ? It is certain, therefore, that all persons who do not learn patience are making a bad progress in the divine life.

All events befalling the righteous are so ordered and governed by the special appointment of God, that the final issue proves what was considered by the world to be injurious to believers, contributes to promote their advantage.

XVII —MEEKNESS

There are some that if any heart grief happen to them, so as they be troubled, or if a man do but stir their choler, you shall see them tear God's name to pieces, and they think that it ought to serve them for excuse if they can say, Why then did he chafe me ? If a man happen to do them a little displeasure, or if a fly chance to cross before their eyes, Jesus Christ, and his death, and his blood, and his flesh, and all that ever he hath, shall be torn all to pieces. As who would say that our Lord Jesus Christ had taken man's flesh upon him, to be made a railing stock, at those monsters' hands which are not

worthy to live upon the earth. And yet, notwithstanding, they will take it for their excuse to say, such a man
did anger me. You suppose that you bend yourself against
man, and yet, notwithstanding, when you bend yourself
against him that had grieved you, the case is so that
God is offended by it. But when they come to advance
themselves in that way against God, seem they not monsters contrary to nature? Therefore let us take heed that
we so bridle our affections, as God's name be not blas-
phemed by us, whereas it ought to be praised and blessed.
Mark this for one special point. Furthermore, we see
that in blaspheming of God, men have a certain natural
rhetoric, and are so cunning in the art, that there is no
lack in them. God has given us speech, to the intent we
should confess him to be good, righteous, and full of
equity in all respects and cases, and to the end that in
all our talk, our endeavour should be to speak of him
with all reverence. But when it comes to the point that
God should be honoured above all things, we speak so
faintly of him, that scarcely can a man wring a little word
out of us that shall be well set. But if men will go to
blaspheming, then you shall see them as eloquent as may
be devised, and there is not the man that may not seem
to have been at school to learn fine rhetoric.

Although men trouble and vex us, yet it is not for us
to run upon those that have persecuted us wrongfully.
For God sends them unto us to meeken us, and it behoves us to know that they are rods which come from his
hand. Nevertheless, when men come to trouble us without cause, why, we may well, after the example of Job,
tell them that we could do the like to them. And why?
for a man shall never know his fault well until he is
told it to his face. But when a man perceives that the
mischief may return upon his own head, then he restrains
himself, and falls to saying, How now? what do I? Behold, God, to bring us to upright indifference, says, You
shall do no otherwise to your neighbour than you would be

done unto yourself. Truly he could have said, When you have to do with your neighbours, see that you deal indifferently and uprightly with them ; and that you be not given to wicked covetousness, to spoil other men of their goods, look that you desire not to enrich yourselves by the loss of any man.

Does God keep us ignorant of the thing which is hidden from us, because he envies us ? No : but he means to learn us humbleness thereby. And the principal point of our wisdom, is to be modest and sober, yea, and to feel our own infirmity, that we exalt not ourselves. You see then that God hideth many things from us, to the end we should learn to be lowly ; which thing we would not be, if nothing were unknown to us. Again, he discerns what is good for us ? and that is the thing wherein he intends to occupy us and to hold us wholly. For we find not in the Scripture, that our Lord is minded to feed our curiosity, and to let us know what we would desire. Our ears are always itching and tickling in our desires, and would fain know what is this and what is that. But all these are fond things that can do no good, and God, to redress this vanity and foolish longing that is in us, shows us only those things that are for our behoof. And so let us remember well this sentence, where it is said, that God disposes wisdom, yea, and keeps it to himself ; and yet, notwithstanding, has said unto men, fear you me and you shall be wise.

Let us mark well, that it is not enough for us to bear a sweet and amiable countenance, and to pretend a mild behaviour towards men, but we must look that our heart be not led away in secret, and that we have no pride hidden within. For although it appear not to men, yet shall it not fail to be condemned of God. And therewithal, let us mark, that if covert pride is to be condemned, then shall they not escape which spread out their wings, and vaunt themselves openly. And let us understand, that our Lord sets them here as it were upon a scaffold, to the

end we should know the vice whereunto we are all inclined, and which reigns in us till God correct it.

Let us pray to the Lord, that he would keep us in with
the bridle of his spirit, lest that we going out of our
calling, should presently be punished. We must also
pray unto him so often as we do enterprise to do any
thing, that he would not suffer us to faint in the midst
of our labours, or in the beginning of our work, but that
he would strengthen us from heaven unto the end. The
feeling of our infirmity should be no cause to make us
slothful; but it should restrain our rashness, from attempt-
ing any thing above our calling, and also to stir us up
to prayers, that God, who has given the gift to begin
well, would also give the grace of perseverance.

XVIII —HUMILITY

WE shall never learn true humility, until we are made
to understand, that it is to God to whom we must answer, that we are cited to appear at his throne, to feel him
our judge, and moreover, also, that we cannot escape his
hand, but that all our life must be known and examined
there. When we be brought to this point that we must
be fain to look unto God, we begin after a sort to rouse
up ourselves, so as we be no more so careless and drowsy
as we were; there is no more of this loftiness and fond
overweening, to soothe and flatter ourselves withal: we
come to have some feeling and perceiving of our miseries ;
but above all, when God's majesty is set before our eyes,
it is to make us feel how dreadful it is ; and when his
greatness is set before us, it makes us to tremble yet the
more. We see it is no sporting matter, here is no sleep-
ing for us, nor no bearing of ourselves in hand with this
or that. Wherefore ? For there is no more room for
flatteries, when God, who is a consuming fire, appears,

and makes us to come near unto him, so as we perceive how it is he that makes the mountains to melt, and is able to make clean riddance of all things. Therefore when we know this greatness of God, needs must we sink under it, and forget all pride.

Humble yourselves under the mighty hand of God. For whosoever stoops down with his head, whosoever bows his knee before God to honour him, shall feel his hand ready to relieve him if he fall. But he that lifts himself up against God, shall be sure to feel God's hand against him. Desire we to feel God's hand under us to aid us ? Then let us humble ourselves. But whosoever advances himself, he must needs rush against the hand of God, and feel the thunderclap that shall utterly overwhelm him. And so let us bear well in mind this lesson when it is said, " refuse not the correction of the Almighty." When we shall have caught hold of God's goodness, so as we know his fatherly love, it will serve to sweeten the afflictions, which otherwise will seem harsh and sharp to us. But in the mean while every one of us must apply this lesson to his own use. For it will be an easy matter for us to say, blessed be God for chastising men so ; and yet in the mean season, when we ourselves are chastised, we do not praise him, but rather grudge against him. Truly we must not deal so with him. But whensoever we ourselves are scourged, let us receive the corrections patiently, and let us ourselves take those things for encouragements, which we can skill to give for comforts unto others.

A man cannot have a worse tormentor than himself, by punishing himself with his own inordinate passions. If a man be given to vain-glory, behold such a fire is kindled in him as he shall think with himself that he can never come soon enough to credit and estimation : insomuch that if some man happen not to honour him, you shall see him nettled. And if some other hinder his advancement, straightway he envies him.

Let us keep us well from pampering ourselves with fatness: that is to say, let us keep us from being pampered with pride, that we presume not to make ourselves this or that, but let us walk in all mildness, knowing that we depend upon the hand of God, and that when he has lifted us up, he can also soon cast us down again. Therefore let us be moved so much the more to serve and honour him, and let us not be so ungracious as to give him occasion to overthrow that which he has built, and to destroy it quite because we would make another Tower of Babylon, and presume to lift up ourselves against him.

When God has once pulled down our pride and taught us to bear his yoke, we can stoop to obey him, and make no great ado about it. But until that, our neck is so stiff as we can no skill to yield to any right or reason.

God shows himself an enemy to all the proud; and, therefore, this day of assignation is as much as if God had said, I can no longer endure that men should thus wickedly exalt themselves against me; and, therefore, all such as lift up themselves above measure, shall be broken in pieces by my hand. Now, if this were well rooted in our hearts, who is it that would not abhor and detest pride, by which we thus provoke the wrath of God against us?

Isaiah speaks against sumptuous apparel and superfluous ornaments, which were evident signs of vain ostentation. For where there is this excess in apparel and ornaments, there is always ambition joined with it; and so by consequence many other vices for the most part do go hand in hand with it. For, from whence comes the superfluity both of men and women but from pride? First, then, he justly taxes this vice as the wellspring of all the abuse, and shows it by the sign thereof, to wit, by their going, because the women walked with stretched out necks. Now, as it is an evident sign of modesty to bow down the head, as also profane authors do witness, so to lift it up too much, is a sign of arrogance. And for a woman's head lifted up, what can it show else but pride? The prophet, therefore, did wisely, in beginning at the fountain itself, for if he had begun at the outward signs, as at the garments, walking, and such like things, they would have had their replies at hand, to wit, that their hearts were upright and innocent enough for all that; and that there was no such great necessity to cry out so bitterly against them, and to summon them before the judgment-seat of God for putting on a little brave or light apparel. To the end, therefore, that he may meet with their vain objections, he first discovers the inward disease, which shows itself every way in all outward attire. That which he adds of wandering eyes, shows a shameless lust, which is oftenest seen and espied, as certain witnesses thereof, in the eyes; for bold and audacious eyes are the true messengers of a dishonest heart. On the contrary, chaste women have their eyes steadfast and drawn in as it were, rather than roving and wandering abroad. Tinkling: this gesture suits well with an immodest and lascivious countenance. It is uncertain whether the women had little bells to their pantofles, which tinkled as they went; or rather, whether in keeping measure they carried their countenances as women dancers do, because the manner of attire is much changed since that time.

He begins with the head, where the principal decking is, and afterwards descends to the other parts. Now we are to observe that the prophet reproves not the excessive pomp of these women with this sharpness and vehemency without cause; for above all other vices, wherewith they are stained, they naturally burn with a fond desire to deck and trim themselves bravely. And, although they are prone enough by nature to covetousness, yet will they spare no cost to make themselves fine; yea, they will pinch their bellies, and offer violence to nature itself, that they may have wherewith to attire themselves the more costly and sumptuously; so greatly are they corrupted with this vice, that it surmounts all others. History does show what uproars women have raised at Rome, by reason of the law called Oppie, which was ordained concerning apparel, because one side would establish it, and the other part would have it abolished, so that there could be no conclusion made hereabout by any grave and moderate course because of their riots. But we need not go so far to seek examples, for we may find infinite numbers almost throughout all nations, so as it is a vice too common in all ages.

It is not without cause that the ancients in times past called a woman's cabinet, or chest,—a world. For if all the pieces which are here mentioned should be gathered together, and laid upon a heap, a man should find as many fashions as there are parts in the world. And, therefore, it seems the prophet here rifles the chests of women to bring forth their paltry pack of jewels, which were laid up therein; to the end, that by how much the more they gloried in them and took pleasure therein, by so much the more every one might be the better acquainted with their follies.

Let us be admonished, then, to pray for the spirit of counsel and understanding of the Lord; and when we have obtained it, let us carefully use it in uprightness with all modesty. For God resists men's wisdom when they attribute more to themselves than is meet; and such as too proudly advance themselves, do well deserve to be punished for their folly. He, therefore, ofttimes makes them stand confounded, to the end men may know that their wisdom is nought else but a vanishing smoke.

Let us beware how we brag of our ancestors, as if we were born to it by inheritance; no, let us go to heaven to find wisdom, and let us ask it of him that is author of it. As for antiquity, it is a sottish and vain brag, and yet princes are so hampered with this vice that they could find in their hearts to go and seek their race and beginning beyond the moon, as they say; yea, they can very hardly be dissuaded from this vanity; flatterers, also, help to augment this folly, who, as we see, have found out many pleasant things touching the genealogies of kings and princes. For no music sounds more delectable in their ears, than when they are separated from the common people, as if they were petty gods. But it often comes to pass, that while they be so busy in seeking too curiously their grandfathers and great-grandfathers, that they make themselves ridiculous by it, that they find themselves descended from some handicraftsman or tradesman.

This ambition is exceedingly odious unto God when men are not content with the honours wherewith they were glutted whilst they lived, but they must build them perpetual monuments of their name in the world when they are gone. For they covet to be exalted after their death, and to live again, as it were, in the mouths of men; and albeit things by death are abolished, yet they are besotted, notwithstanding, with this foolish hope that their memory shall endure for ever. But the Lord avenges himself of their pride and presumption, causing that which they erected for a witness and remembrance of their glory to turn to their dishonour and ignominy. For their very name is so accursed that men can neither hear nor see any mention thereof, but it is with detestation. Nay, it sometimes falls out that the Lord suffers them not to be buried in their tombs, but sends them to the gallows, and to the ravens; of which we have many examples in the histories; neither want we some spectacles hereof even in our own times. But as often as I read this place, a like example unto this comes to my mind, and is the nearest in affinity to it of all others: of one Thomas Moore, who had such an office as this Shebna had, for, as it is well known, he was Chancellor to the King of England; he was a sworn enemy of the Gospel, and persecuted the faithful with fire and faggot. This man also meant to get himself a name, and to set up a monument of his cruelty and impiety. To which end he caused the praises of his virtues to be engraven in a fair sepulchre, which was built in a most stately manner. Then he sent his epitaph, which himself had made, to Erasmus, to Basle, to get it printed ; and withal, sent him a palfrey for a present. So covetous was he of glory, that he meant to taste the renown and the praises in his lifetime, which he thought should have lasted when he was dead. Amongst other praises, this was the chiefest—that he had been a great persecutor of the Lutherans, that is to say, of God's children. But what became of him ? He is first of all accused of treason, then condemned, and, lastly, beheaded ; and thus, instead of a tomb, he had a scaffold. Would we desire a more manifest judgment of God than this, by which he punishes the pride of the wicked, their insatiable desire of vainglory, their brags that are so full of blasphemies ?

Now, this vice which God has so sharply punished in one people, is almost common to all ; for who is he that builds such stately houses, but the price thereof is wrung out of the poor ? Sometimes by violence and extortion, sometimes by continual molestations, so as the very mortar, stones, and wood, are replenished with blood, in God's sight. Therefore, the stones shall cry out of the wall, says Habakkuk, and the beam shall answer unto it, Wo to him that builds a town with blood. And let us not wonder at these strange judgments and horrible changes then, when we see that ambition draws with it these wicked extortions and robberies, but rather let us seriously therein consider God's just revenging hand.

Whosoever deceives himself with vain confidence, it cannot be but that he should lift up himself above the brethren ; neither is it any marvel ; for how should it be that he should not despise his equals, which in his pride lifts up himself against God ? And whosoever is puffed up with a trust of himself, purposely makes battle against God, who is reconciled to us only by denying ourselves, while we being without all hope of our own power, virtue, and righteousness, do repose ourselves in his only mercy.

He is truly humble, who neither challenges any thing unto himself before God, nor contemptuously disdains his brethren, nor desires to be seen higher, but satisfies himself to be accounted one of the members of Christ, desiring no other thing than that the head may be only exalted.

A Christian ought not to aspire in an ambitious manner after those things, by which he may surpass others, nor indulge haughty feelings, but meditate rather upon modesty and meekness; for our excellence, in the presence of God, consists in these virtues, not in pride, or the contempt of our brethren. For nothing breaks the unity mentioned by the Apostle more completely than the exalting of ourselves, and our aspiring to something still more elevated, with a view to attain a higher situation. Every feeling of ambition, therefore, and every elation of mind, which insinuate themselves under the name of magnanimity, are here condemned by Paul; because moderation, or rather submission, is the chief virtue of the faithful, which is distinguished by readily yielding an honour to another, and not depriving him of his proper glory.

Calmness, and hence a composed manner of living, which renders us amiable to all, are no common endowments of a Christian. If we are desirous to pursue this, we ought not only to be endowed with the greatest equity, but the highest courteousness and easiness of manners, which may not only gain the affections of the just and good, but influence the minds of the wicked : for a caution is necessary in this instance, not so to affect the securing of the favour and esteem of men, as to refuse to incur, for the sake of Christ, the hatred of any human being when necessary. Yet we observe some, who, while they are worthy of being loved by all on account of the sweetness of their manners, and the tranquillity of their minds, yet are hated on account of the gospel even by their nearest relations. Easiness of disposition must not degenerate into flattery, lest from our zeal to keep peace, we soothe the vices of our fellowmen. Since, therefore, we cannot invariably expect to secure peace with all, Paul has added two sentences as exceptions, " if it be possible," and " as much as lieth in you." We must resolve that according to the duties required by piety and love, we ought never to violate peace unless compelled by one or other of these two causes: for we ought to endure many things with an earnest desire for peace ; to forgive offences, and kindly to remit the utmost rigour of justice, that we may be always courageous, as often as necessity requires, to carry on our Christian warfare with keenness and vigour; for the friends of Jesus cannot possibly enjoy eternal peace with the world, which is under the dominion of Satan.

XIX —SOBRIETY

THEY which invented so many varieties to feed the fond appetites of men, did questionless offend God, and we ought to detest them, notwithstanding that they have been liked of in their times, and that men have said, O here is an excellent cook, O here is an excellent steward. Although they have gained glory by making so many delicates, and by their compounding of so many things to make their fine and new sauces, and I know not what other conceits, to feed the humours of such as desire to be entertained overdelicately ; yet must we detest such

things, and it were to be wished that such men had had
their mother's womb for their grave. But now, what
have we to do but to repress all superfluity, and all that
ever makes unto vice? Ought we not to endeavour this
with all our might? Yes, verily. But what? Every
one of us is so far from mending of one, that it seems
rather that we intend to plead prescription against God.
Whatsoever is told us, we fare not the better by one
whit. And why? Because we have taken it up of
custom. Yea, but God will in the end show, that there
is no lawful possession, but such as is ruled by his law,
and according unto his will. Nay, doubt we not but
God will punish such superfluities, by cutting our com-
mons shorter. Indeed our nature is inclined to this
wickedness of carelessly confounding of things, which
God had distinguished; but yet must we therefore feel
the tokens of his anger, when he shows not himself so
liberal a father towards us as he was wont to do. And
if we were wise, or but well advised, we would not wait
for the declaration. That which is said here would suffice us, namely, that we ought to mingle the creatures of
God, but always to hold us unto a plain simplicity in our
manner of living. You see then what we are to note,
touching our meat and drink, that men ought so to content themselves with that which they have, that being
nourished of God, they may acknowledge it in this sort;
behold our God has a care to feed us, and we may well
see that he is a father towards us, in that he shows himself to have so great a care of our life. .Let men, therefore, take heed that they be not drunken with their delicacies, and besotted in their varieties, but that they have
an eye always unto God. Now, the like ought also to
be observed in our apparel. It is said that a man shall
not clothe himself with divers sorts. This serves to
teach us, that we ought to keep as great sobriety as we
can keep possibly, as well in our apparel as in our meats
and drinks. For if men deck themselves with divers

sorts, and use in their attire many fond disguisings, whereof proceeds it? Surely nature teacheth them no such thing. For the heathen men had skill to say, that every man would so love nature herein, there needs not such varieties of meats or diversities of apparel. Men of themselves do martyr themselves. Lo what our lusts do lead us to! For they busy us about taking pains about this or that, and make us also to trouble others, and so all the world is disquieted. And why is that? If we would be content we should live more quietly. But we are still given unto superfluities, and that is the cause why we can have no end of our travails; we are become like the damned souls. And where is the fault thereof but in ourselves?

There was a law made, that there should be no dancing among us; and the reason was good, for it serves to no purpose, but to be a provocation to whoredom. Men and women do not always play the whoremongers and whores when they dance, I grant, but if we consider well what the nature of dances is, we shall say that it is but a knack of bawdry; and if dances be licensed, the stews' doors will straightways be open. Not that whoredom is always committed, indeed, at dancings, but dances always bend that way. We have known the time when dances were forbidden, and we made a show as though we would see the law kept, yea, we have seen some punished for them; but nowadays, it is made but a jest, insomuch that it is become a lawful thing and very tolerable. And what are plays? It is so usual and ordinary thing to have plays, that if we go about to take order for them, it is to no purpose, for men are hardened, by reason of this liberty that hath been suffered them, and because they have had the reins of the bridle in their own hand, and as it were laid on their necks, without any restrainment or holding back, they think they may do what they list.

We must beware we shroud not ourselves with this foolish cloak of our forefathers, thinking that God will hold us excused, if we can allege the example of this man or that man. Oh sir! Such a man did so, and is it not then lawful for us to do it? Yea, I wis. As though a man might prejudice the law, and the truth of God. As, for example, God shows us what he allows and what he condemns. There comes a man that does clean contrary, can he by his example break that which God has established? Do we not see that it is against reason? And yet there is not one of us all but is glad of this cloak. And why? May we not well do so? Especially if any excellent personages and great servants of God have done any fault, we think it is no more a sin.

There are many at this day that will take the gospel for a cloak to cover all their villanies withal, and think that when they have the name of God in their mouths, their sins are become hallowed, and they are clear forgiven them. We must take good heed that we do not after this sort profane the word of God, but keep it in a good conscience. And when we do so, let us not doubt but that God will give us a steadiness that shall never be overcome, although all the winds in the world do blow, and all surges and seas rise up against us, insomuch that we may seem to be in danger of drowning a hundred times in a day, yet God will keep us safe ; for our salvation is in his hand, and he has promised that he will be our keeper and faithful guard. Therefore let us not have an evil conscience, let us not despise this treasure of faith, and let us honour God as we ought ; let us withdraw ourselves from all vanities and allurements of this world, that we may be hidden under God's hand.

We may see a great sort nowadays, that make the gospel serve to their covetousness, to their deceits, and wicked practices: yea, their talk is full of sugar, and pleasant to the ear. But what are they? Nothing but nets laid to beguile their neighbours, and deceive them, they will not make dainty of the name of our Lord Jesus

Christ, to work their subtle and mischievous practices. Yea, we see that they use the gospel, but as instead of a bawd : they cloak themselves with this covering, only to colour and hide their villanies and filthiness : insomuch that one New Testament shall serve a great number, as a letter of whoredom. And would to God these things were not known : but all the world sees examples of them. And do we marvel that so few stand fast, when we see the name of God so villanously profaned ? If we would tread his master under our feet, we could not do him more spite than when we do so contemn his word, that we mock at it, and make no account of it. God must needs stretch forth his arm, to be revenged upon such unthankfulness of men, when they willingly cast away such a benefit, and such a treasure as God offers them.

Let us think continually upon the example of Caleb and Joshua ; and forasmuch as God shows that he made more account of them, though they were but two in all, than of all the other huge multitude, which were about seven hundred thousand persons, forasmuch as we see that God gives such sentence of them, let us learn to submit ourselves to him, and to regard nothing but that which he commands. And though the world run gadding here and there, in the mean-while let us follow the way that God has shown us by his pure word.

If it so be, that where feasts and banquets are best ruled, yet there is some fault that God mislikes : How is it with them that drive God out of their company, and from their table, as men are commonly wont to do ? For if we shall speak of feasting, whereat do men begin ? At calling upon the name of God ? Nay, that would be thought too sad a matter. Therefore the name of God must be buried. Has a man well sufficed his appetite ? Then is it no time to say grace. For it behoves them to remember the good cheer that they have made, that is to say, that they are swine. For if a man make mention of God, it will be thought that all the pleasure which they have taken in their feasting, is turned into sorrow. And afterwards all must run riot, in such sort as there shall be no talk but of ribaldry and wantonness, or rather of treachery and malice, so as there shall be none other news but of backbiting their neighbour, and of practising devices against this man and that man. See what banqueting breeds. Now, then, since that men are so inclined to vice, it is not possible but there must be some fault, notwithstanding that they give not themselves the bridle in all points. I pray you, then, must it not needs be as it were a gulf of hell, where they meet together to make compacts of wickedness and treason ?

Therefore, let us wake and keep sure watch, that we be not taken unawares. When we are set at the table to drink and to eat, let us pray unto God, beseeching him of his gracious goodness to keep us in such sobriety, that being nourished by his gifts, we may be the better disposed to serve him : so that our meat may not serve to overcharge us, but to sustain us, and to give us strength, that we may be the better able to occupy ourselves in the service of our God ; and that he will grant us the grace so to pass through these corruptible things as we may always labour for the heavenly life, whereunto he calls us by his word. For God maintains us not in this world to live for a day, or for ten, or for fifty years, but to the intent we should come to the said heavenly glory. Let us, then, consider how we ought to behave ourselves: and when we are at the table, let us feed for our repast in such way as if God himself dieted us. And although we are in this world taking our nourishment of the food that we know, let us look up unto God, who shows himself a father towards us, and has witnessed unto us that we are his children, insomuch as he has a care of these our poor bodies here, and will have his love extend even unto them, notwithstanding that they be but rottenness. Therefore, when we see that God does so nourish and sustain us, we may be the merrier and the better assured of his goodness and fatherly love towards us. And hereby we see why St Paul says, that whether we drink or whether we eat, we must do it altogether in the name of God. There are many which suppose that there should be no thinking upon God when men come to eating and drinking, whereas, in very deed, we should therefore think so much the more of God. Seeing that God gives such virtue unto bread by his word, that we be sustained by it, will he not have us to acknowledge his presence, and how he has his hand stretched out over us? So then, it is rather a cause that we should think the more upon God. For we see that our eating and drinking are sanctified by yielding all honour to his name. And, therefore, when it comes to saying of grace, let us acknowledge that some fault may have escaped us; and then will God surely forgive us all our misdoing, if so be that we repair unto him.

XX — ANGER

As GOD has bound together all mankind with a certain unity, that every man ought to regard the safety of all men as a thing given him in charge; in some, therefore, all violence and wrong, yea, and all harm-doing, whereby our neighbour's body may be hurt, is forbidden us. And therefore we are commanded, if there be any power of succour in our travail to defend the life of our neighbours, that we faithfully employ the same, that we procure those things that may make for their quiet, that we watch to keep them from hurt, and if they be in any danger, that we give them our helping hand. If you consider that it is God the lawmaker that so says, then think withal that his meaning is by this rule also to govern your soul; for it were a fond thing to think that he who espies the thoughts of the heart, and principally rests upon them, should instruct nothing but the body to true righteousness. Therefore the manslaughter of the heart is also forbidden in this law, and an inward affection to preserve our brother's life is here given in commandment. The hand, indeed, brings forth the manslaughter, but the mind conceives it when it is infected with wrath and hatred. Look whether you can be angry with your brother without burning in desire to do him hurt. If you cannot be angry with him, then can you not hate him, forasmuch as hatred is nothing but an old-rooted anger. Although you dissemble, and go about to wind out yourself by vain circumstances, yet where anger or hatred is, there is an affection to hurt. If you will still dally out with shifts to defend it, it is already pronounced by the mouth of the Holy Ghost, that he is a manslayer that hates his brother in his heart. It is pronounced by the mouth of the Lord Christ, that he is guilty of judgment that is angry with his brother ; that he is guilty of the council, that says Raca ; that he is guilty of hell fire, that says unto him Fool.

The Scripture notes two points of equity upon which this commandment is grounded : because man is both the image of God, and our own flesh, wherefore, unless we will defile the image of God, we must have care to touch man no otherwise than as a sacred thing : and unless we will put off all naturalness of man, we must cherish him as our own flesh. That manner of exhortation that is fetched from the redemption and grace of Christ shall be treated of in another place. God willed these two things naturally to be considered in man, that might persuade us to the preservation of him, that we should both reverence the image of God imprinted in him, and embrace our own flesh. He has not, therefore, escaped the crime of manslaughter, that has kept himself from the shedding of blood. If you commit any thing, indeed, if you go about any thing with endeavour, if you conceive any thing in desire and purpose that is against the safety of another, you are holden guilty of manslaughter. And again, if you do not travail to your power and as occasion may serve to defend his life, you do, with like heinousness, offend the law; but if there be so much care taken for the safety of his body, let us hereby gather how much study and travail is due to the safety of his soul, which in the Lord's sight does infinitely excel the body.

As hatred or malice is the wellspring of murder, it is not to be wondered at, or to be thought strange, that God should denounce all them to be murderers who hate men in their hearts, and that he should condemn the rancour, though it lie hidden within; for when a murderer comes to examination, is the hand to blame? Is the sword to blame? Or is the stroke to blame that was given? No. But the blame is in the malice that was conceived before, which led the hand, and provoked the man to commit the murder; therefore, mark it for a point, that it is not without cause that our Lord deems all those to be murderers who do so hate their neighbours. And the same must warn us to prevent all dangers, that the sun go not down upon our malice; for in so doing we give Satan possession of us. Beware, my brethren, says St Paul, that you give not place to Satan. And how do we give him place? It is, says he, by suffering the sun to go down upon our wrath; for when we feed any heartburning within us, and multiply rancour in our minds, although we perceive it not at the first, yet are we caught with so cursed affection, as we cannot overcome it afterwards. Seeing, then, that hatred procures such wickedness, let every man look to himself, and when we are moved to any ill-will, although some displeasure be done unto us, and it may seem that we have just cause of revenge, as in respect of men; yet, notwithstanding, let all such things be laid aside, and let us strive earnestly to overmaster ourselves, that our hearts be not hardened, for fear but the devil do so work in us that the hatred which we have conceived to-day, do make us ready to slay or kill to-morrow, so as the heart being envenomed do carry away the hand with it. You see, then, how it is a thing worthy to be marked.

And, generally, let us learn that to examine our faults well, we must not only have an eye to the things that are done by our hands, feet, eyes, and ears, but we must also go to the inward parts and search our thoughts, our wicked desires, and all the things that do tempt and provoke us; for there lies the right examination of our sins. When a man goes about to justify himself because he has committed no murder, theft, or whoredom in actual deed, and yet is infected with wicked lusts in his heart, his labouring to acquit himself after that sort is in vain before God, and therefore let us bear in mind, that to serve ourselves of all our offences and misdoings, we must enter into our own consciences, and not only condemn our wicked lusts, but also even our thoughts, whereby we were provoked and induced to evil; and we must understand that even that is a damnable sin already before God.

Will we then condemn murder in another man? Let us condemn hatred in ourselves, by abstaining from all malice and revengement, that our hearts may be rid of it. If we deal with such uprightness, then will God dwell with us and make us to prosper.

XXI —DISHONESTY

We are forbidden to gape for other men's goods, and that therefore we are commanded every man to employ his faithful travail to preserve to each man his own goods. For thus we ought to think, that what every man possesses is not happened unto him by chance of fortune, but by distribution of the sovereign Lord of all things ; and therefore no man's goods can be got from him by evil means, but that wrong be done to the disposition of God. But of thefts there are many kinds ; one stands in violence, when the goods of another are by any manner of force and robbing licentiously bereaved. The other kind consists in malicious deceit, where they are guilefully conveyed away. Another sort there is that stands in a more hidden subtlety, when they are wrung from the owner by colour of law. Another sort in flattery, where they are sucked away by pretence of gift. But lest we should tarry too long upon renting of all the several kinds of theft, let us know that all crafty means whereby the possessions and money of our neighbours are conveyed unto us, when they once go by crooked ways, from sincereness of heart to a desire to beguile, or by any mean to do hurt, are to be accounted for thefts. Although by pleading the law, they may prevail, yet God doth not otherwise weigh them. For he sees the long captious subtleties wherewith the guileful man begins to entangle the simpler mind, till at length he draws him into his nets. He sees the hard and ungentle laws wherewith the mightier oppresses and throws down the weaker. He sees the allurements wherewith, as with baited hooks, the craftier takes the unaware. All which things are hidden from the judgment of man, and come not in his knowledge. And this manner of wrong is not only in money, in wares, or in lands, but in every man's right. For we defraud our neighbour of his goods, if we deny him those duties which we are bound to do for him. If any idle factor or bailiff do devour his master's substance, and is not heedful to the care of his thrift, if he either do wrongfully spoil, or do riotously waste the substance committed unto him, if a servant do mock his master, if he disclose his secrets by any means, if he betray his life and his goods ; again, if the Lord do cruelly oppress his household, they are before God guilty of theft. For he both withholds and conveys another man's goods, which performs not that which by the office of his calling he owes to other.

We shall therefore rightly obey this commandment, if, being contented with our own estate, we seek to get no gain but honest and lawful, if we covet not to wax rich with wrong, nor go about to spoil our neighbour of his goods that our own substance may increase ; if we labour not to heap up cruel riches and wrung out of other men's blood ; if we do not immeasurably scrape together every way, by right and by wrong, that either our covetousness may be filled, or our prodigality satisfied. But on the other side, let this be our perpetual mark, to aid all men faithfully by counsel and help to keep their own so far as we may ; but if we have to do with false and deceitful men, let us rather be ready to yield up some of our own than to strive with them. And not that only, but let us communicate to their necessities, and with our store relieve their need, whom we see to be oppressed with hard and poor estate. Finally, let every man look how much he is by duty bound unto other, and let him faithfully pay it. For this reason let the people have in honour all those that are set over them, let them patiently bear their government, obey their laws and commandments, refuse nothing that they may bear, still keeping God favourable unto them. Again, let them take care of their people, preserve common peace, defend the good, restrain the evil, and so order all things as ready to give account of their office to the sovereign Judge. Let the ministers of churches faithfully apply their ministry, and not corrupt the doctrine of salvation, but deliver it pure and sincere to the people of God, and let them instruct them not only with learning but also with example of life ; finally, let them so be over them, as good shepherds are over the sheep. Let the people likewise receive them for the messengers and apostles of God, give them that honour whereof the highest master has vouchsafed them, and minister unto them such things as are necessary for their life. Let parents take on them to feed, rule, and teach their children, as committed to them of God, and grieve not, nor turn away their minds from them with cruelty, but rather cherish and embrace them with such lenity and tenderness, as becomes their person. After which manner we have already said that children owe to their parents their obedience, let young men reverence old age, even as the Lord willed that age be honourable. Let old men also govern the weakness of youth with their wisdom and experience, wherein they excel young men, not rating with rough and loud brawling, but tempering severity with mildness and gentleness. Let servants show themselves diligent and serviceable to obey; and that not to the eye, but from the heart, as serving God himself. Also let masters show themselves not testy and hard to please, nor oppress them with too much sharpness, nor reproachfully use them, but rather acknowledge that they are their brethren and their fellow-servants under the heavenly Lord, whom they ought mutually to love and gently to entreat. After this manner, I say, let every man consider what in his degree and place he owes to his neighbours, and let him pay that he owes. Moreover, our mind ought always to have respect to the law-maker, that we may know that this law is made as well for our minds as for our hands, that men should study to defend and further the commodities and profit of other.

We should use our utmost exertions to edify all by our probity. For, as it is necessary for us to enjoy innocence of conscience before God, so we ought to have a character distinguished for integrity among men. For if God ought to be glorified by our good works, he is deprived of this glory when men behold nothing in us worthy of praise. Nor is the glory of God only obscured, but he is dishonoured ; for all our sins are brought forward by the ignorant to the disgrace of the gospel. But when we are ordered to provide things honest in the sight of all men, we must regard the design and end. Our design is not to secure the regard and praises of our fellow-men; for Christ warns us, with much earnestness, against such a design, when he orders us to exclude men from beholding our good deeds, and to admit God only as a witness. But our object is to make men direct their attention to God, and praise him, that they may be roused by our example to the diligent pursuit of justice, and be allured, by the amiableness and excellence of our life and conversation, to the love of God. If we are defamed on account of the name of Christ, we do not cease to provide things honest among our fellow-men; but the passage of Corinthians, as lying, and yet true, is fulfilled in our case.

Whensoever we make any bargain or covenant, we must not only have an eye to the party with whom we have to do, but we must also, as it were, set God among us, and keep our faith and promise to him that we have bound ourselves, as though God watched us at every step, and that we could not so soon work deceit towards any man, but that by and by God would step between us to withstand it. That is the thing which we have to do, but there are very few of us that think upon it; for although the name of God be called upon, and solemn oaths taken, and promises made authentically enough, yea, and that there are order of law to make us feel his majesty, yet do most men shut their eyes, and in all the promises and oaths that are made commonly, there is nothing sought but to deceive one another. He that is most subtle and full of shifts, is the handsomest man, and such kind of dealing is esteemed a virtue, for every man runs gadding after his own lusts and likings, yea, and that in such wise that they are as blindfoldings to keep us from God. Though we think not upon it now, yet will not God forget any of our deceits, spites, treacheries, and falsehoods which we commit against men; for he has told us, that when an oath is taken between man and man, his glory is defaced, and himself openly mocked, if the promise be broken.

Therefore let us be well assured that he will not put up with such wrong, and that although we be never so blind, yet will not he play the blinkard on his side, but will note and mark every whit of it to bring it to account.

XXII —LYING

Because God which is truth, abhors lying, we ought to observe truth without deceitful colour. The sum, therefore shall be, that we neither hurt any man's name either with slanders or false reports, nor hinder him in his goods by lying; finally, that we offend no man, by lust to speak evil, or to be busy; with which prohibition is joined a commandment, that so far as we may, we employ our faithful endeavour for every man in affirming the truth, to defend the safety both of his name and goods. It seems that the Lord purposed to expound the meaning of his commandment in the twenty-third chapter of Exodus, in these words: Thou shalt not use the voice of lying, nor shalt join thy hand to speak false witness for the wicked. Again, Thou shalt flee lying. Also in another place he does not only call us away from lying in this point, that we be no accusers, or whisperers in the people, but also that no man deceive his brother, for he forbids them both in several commandments. Truly it is no doubt, but that as in the commandments before, he has forbidden cruelty, unchastity, and covetousness; so in this he restrains falsehood. Whereof there are two parts, as we have noted before. For either we offend the good name of our neighbours by maliciousness and froward mind to backbite, or in lying, and sometime in evil speaking we hinder their commodities. There is no difference whether in this place be understood solemn and judicial testimony, or common testimony that is used in private talks. For we must always have recourse to this principle, that of all the general kinds of vices, one special sort is set for an example, whereunto the rest may be referred, and that that is chiefly chosen wherein the filthiness of the fault is most apparent. Albeit, it were convenient to extend it more generally to slanders and sinister backbitings, wherewith our neighbours are wrongfully grieved, for that falsehood of witnessing which is used in judicial courts is never without perjury. But perjuries, insomuch as they do profane and defile the name of God, are already sufficiently met withal in the third commandment. Wherefore the right use of this commandment is, that our tongue in affirming the truth, do serve both the good name and profit of our neighbours. The equity thereof is more than manifest. For if a good name be more precious than any treasures, whatsoever they be, then is it no less hurt to a man to be spoiled of the goodness of his name than of his goods. And in bereaving his substance, sometimes false witness does as much as violence of hands.

And yet it is marvellous with how negligent carelessness men do commonly offend in this point, so that there are found very few that are not notably sick of this disease; we are so much delighted with a certain poisoned sweetness both in searching out and in disclosing the evils of other. And let us not think that it is a sufficient excuse, if oftentimes we lie not. For he that forbids thy brother's name to be defiled with lying, wills also that it be preserved untouched, so far as the truth will suffer. For howsoever he takes heed to himself only, so that he tell no lie, yet in the same he secretly confesses that he has some charge of him. But this ought to suffice us, to keep safe our neighbour's good name, that God has a care of it. Wherefore without doubt all evil speaking is utterly condemned. But we mean not by evil speaking that rebuking which is used for chastisement; nor accusation, or judicial process, whereby remedy is sought for an evil, nor public reprehension, which tends to put other sinners in fear, nor bewraying of faults to them for whose safety it behoves that they should be forewarned, lest they should be in danger by ignorance; but we mean only hateful accusing, which arises of maliciousness, and of a wanton will to backbite. Also this commandment is extended to this point, that we covet not to use a scoffing kind of pleasantness, but mingled with bitter taunts, thereby bitingly to touch other men's faults under pretence of pastime, as many do that seek praise of merry conceits with other men's shame, yea, and grief; also when by such wanton railing many times our neighbours are not a little reproached. Now if we bend our eyes to the lawmaker, which must according to his rightful authority, bear rule no less over the ears and mind than over the tongue; truly we shall find that greediness to hear backbitings, and a hasty readiness to evil judgments are no less forbidden. For it were very fond, if a man should think that God hates the fault of evil speaking in the tongue, and does not disallow the fault of evil maliciousness in the heart. Wherefore, if there be in us a true fear and love of God, let us endeavour, so far as we may and as is expedient, and as charity bears, that we give neither our tongue, nor our ears to evil speakings and bitter jestings, lest we rashly without cause yield our minds to indirect suspicions. But being indifferent expositors of all men's sayings and doings, let us both in judgment, ears, and tongue, gently preserve their honour safe.

XXIII—COVETOUSNESS

BECAUSE the Lord's will is that our soul be wholly possessed with the affection of love; all lust is to be shaken out of our mind that is contrary to charity. The sum, therefore, shall be, that no thought creep into us, which may move our minds with a concupiscence hurtful and turning toward another's loss; wherewith on the other side agrees the commandment, that whatsoever we conceive, purpose, will, or study upon, be joined with the benefit and commodity of our neighbours. But here, as it seems, arises a hard and cumbersome difficulty. For if it be truly said of us before, that under the names of fornication and theft, are contained the lust of fornication, and the purpose to hurt and deceive, it may seem superfluously spoken, that the coveting of other men's goods should afterward be severally forbidden us. But the distinction between purpose and coveting, will easily loose us this knot. For purpose is deliberate consent of will, when lust has subdued the mind; but coveting may be without any such either advisement or assent, when the mind is only pricked and tickled with vain and perverse objects. As therefore the Lord has heretofore commanded, that the rule of charity should govern our wills, studies, and works, so now he commands the conceptions of our mind to be directed to the same rule, that there be none of them crooked and writhen, that may provoke our mind another way. As he has forbidden our mind to be bowed and led into wrath, hatred, fornication, robbery, and lying, so he does now forbid us to be removed thereunto.

And not without cause does he require so great uprightness. For who can deny that it is righteous, that all the powers of the soul be possessed with charity? But if any of them do swerve from the mark of charity,

who can deny that it is diseased ?   Now whence comes
it that so many desires hurtful to your neighbour do enter
in your heart, but of this, that neglecting him you care
only for yourself ?   For if your mind were altogether
thoroughly soaked with charity, no parcel thereof should
be open to such imaginations.   Therefore, it must needs
be void of charity, so far as it receives concupiscence.
But some man will object, that yet it is not meet that
fantasies that are without order tossed in man's wit, and
at length do vanish away, should be condemned for concupiscence, whose place is in the heart.   I answer that
here our question is of that kind of fantasies, which while
they are present before our minds, do together bite and
strike our heart with desire, forasmuch as it never comes
in our mind to wish for any thing, but that our heart
is stirred up and leaps withal.   Therefore, God commands a marvellous ferventness of love, which he wills
not to be entangled with never so small snares of concupiscence.   He requires a marvellously framed mind,
which he suffers not so much as with slight provoca-
tions to be any thing stirred against the law of love.
To this exposition Augustine did first open me the way :
because you should not think that it is without consent
of some grave authority.   And though the Lord's purpose was to forbid us all wrongful coveting : yet in re-
hearsing the same, he has brought forth for example
those things that most commonly do deceive us with a
false image of delight ; because he would leave nothing
to concupiscence when he draws it from these things,
upon the which most of all it rages and triumphs.   Lo,
here is the second table of the law, wherein we are taught
sufficiently what we owe to men for God's sake, upon
consideration whereof hangs the rule of charity.

God tells his people expressly by Moses, that they must not be so blind as to worship the Sun and the Moon. For what is the Sun ? True it is that he has a wonderful light in him, and that we see there some marks of God's glory. In like case is it with the Moon. And that also is the cause why it is said that they preach unto us, and that God speaks unto us, as it were by their mouth, to the end we should be allured to come unto him. But therewithal God says unto them, if you worship the Sun and Moon, you are unthankful. For to what end have I created and fashioned them ? It is to the end you should know me, even me that am the Creator of them. If you do the contrary, your unthankfulness will be doubled. For what is the Sun ? Your servant. What is the Moon ? Your handmaid. Wherefore does the Sun shine, but to give you light, and to make the earth fruitful, according as God gives him that use ? So then, seeing that the creatures, how noble soever they be, are subject unto us, and God has ordained them to do us service, is it not a foul unthankfulness for us to make idols of them ?

We see that these hypocrites who have no affection nor zeal do nevertheless make many windlasses, and martyr themselves, and it should seem there were nothing but fire and flame in them, to get near unto God. Yea, but they do nothing else but turn the pot about. It is not for that they are desirous to come the straight way unto God, but they would fain be quit with him, without coming to him at all. As how ? We see how the hypocrites are very full of devotion, and are busy about this and that. And what pretend they thereby ? When the Papists hear three masses in a day, when they make much bibble-babble, when they take holy water, and when they trot from altar to altar, it is certain that they pretend to serve God; but their pretending of it is in such sort as God beholds them not near at hand, but they withdraw themselves and stray far away from him. And that is the cause why the Prophet Jeremy likens all these braveries, and all these maskings, and all these ceremonies that are among men, unto a thief's cave. For like as a thief retires into covert, to the end he might not be seen and his fault come to light; even so do hypocrites make sundry colours and lurking-holes in this and that, and in every thing which they call the service of God. But what for that? It is to the end that God should demand nothing of them, but let them alone as they are, that they may cover themselves under that mummery. Thus then you see that the hypocrites make countenance of approaching unto God, howbeit that the same are not in truth. Therefore, although they be puffed up with fond misweening, yet are they never the nearer unto God for all that; and although they perk up with their nebs, and be bold to make many protestations, insomuch as it seems that they would even run upon God for haste, yet come they never the nearer unto him; but their doing so is, because they are besotted, and think not upon God, for if they thought upon God they would not be so bold. We see then that when the hypocrites have played the fools in their own fond trifles, and dallied with God as it were with a little baby; they think themselves as righteous as the angels, and that there is no fault to be found with them; and that if God demand any thing more at their hand, he does but press them too much, and that they are so far from being indebted unto him, that to their seeming he is beholden unto them. You see then how the hypocrites flash out fire and flame in such sort, as it should seem they would run upon God. But why is that? Because they think not of him, nor have any lively feeing of him in their consciences. To be short, a man shall never come to God with a good heart, and with a pure and free affection, except he honour him, and in honouring fear him, and in fearing trust in him. All these things must be in a man's heart before he can ever come unto God, and have any acquaintance with him. The first point is to honour God; that is to say, to know what his majesty is, and that it becomes us to yield ourselves wholly thereunto, to do him homage. Until we have conceived this majesty of God, which is above us, we shall never be desirous to come unto him. Fear must also be matched therewithal: that is to say, after we have granted him all sovereignty and dominion, we must be desirous to serve him, and to walk as he commands. But this fear alone is not enough. Therefore we must learn to know God's goodness, that we may put our trust in it, which also is the mean to come unto him.

We know how curious and over bold men are, for they would fain know what God's being or substance is, and search out every whit of him by inch-meal, and that so presumptuously, as if they would push up their horns into heaven. Such is their nature, but God will have us worship him in fear and humility, as good reason is it should be so. And he withdraws himself the farther from us, when we enquire farther of him than he commands us. For otherwise were it not all one as if we would have him our 'underling? What pre-eminence should he have if he were so shut up in man's conceit.

Whereas he forbids us to have other gods, he means thereby that we should not give away elsewhere that which is proper to him. For although the things that we owe unto God be innumerable, yet not unfitly they may be brought unto four principal points: adoration, whereunto as a thing hanging upon it, is adjoined spiritual obedience of conscience; affiance, invocation, and thanksgiving. Adoration I call the reverence and worship which every one of us yields unto him, when he submits himself unto his greatness; wherefore, I do not without cause make this a part thereof, that we yield our consciences in subjection to his law. Affiance is an assuredness of resting in him by acknowledging of his power, when reposing all wisdom, righteousness, power, truth, and goodness in him, we think ourselves blessed with only partaking of him. Invocation is a resorting of our mind to his faith and help as to our only succour, so oft as any necessity presses us. Thanksgiving is a certain thankfulness whereby the praise of all good things is given unto him. Of these, as God suffers nothing to be conveyed away elsewhere, so he commands all to be wholly given to himself.

XXV —PRAYER

It is certain that before we call upon God, he is willing and ready to help us. And for proof hereof, whence comes the affection of praying? Comes it not of the Holy Ghost? For a man would never of his own mind resort unto God. Then is it because God looks unto us with pity, when we think he hath turned his back upon us. Again, if we have stood up any time, it must needs be that it was through the power which he gave us, and that his succouring of us with his hand made us to be patient and lowly in our adversities. And true it is that we may have such a conceit as it may seem to us for a time that God has given no ear to us.

Wherein consists all our welfare? Even in that we may boldly come unto God, and have leave to rest as it were in his lap when we are afflicted, so as we know that he will be merciful to us as he has promised. This is the sovereign welfare of men, so long as they live in this world. For undoubtedly prayer is the thing whereby we come unto God. It behoveth us to walk here by faith, and God is absent from us as in respect of eyesight. And although he dwell in us by his power, and make us to feel his grace, yet, notwithstanding, we are, as it were, separated from him to outward appearance. Nevertheless, by prayer we mount up into heaven, and present ourselves before his majesty, and are joined unto him. Ye see, then, that here is a band of familiarity between God and men, in this liberty which he gives us to call upon him. But yet, can we not pray unto him as we ought to do, except we know his goodness, according as it is said in the fifth Psalm: Lord, I will worship in thy temple, even upon the multitude of thy mercies.

Although we be tormented and overpressed with adversities, yet must we not cease to sigh and groan: yea, and therewithal also continually bless the name of God in our prayers, and submit ourselves unto him. If this be wanting, it is not praying, it is rather a defying of God, as if a man should go summon his enemy and defy him. You see, then, that our prayers are sometimes like unto summonings, according as we make them unto God. And how is that? The greatest honour that God requires at our hands, is that we should call upon him in all our adversities. Now, instead of doing that homage to him, we come to spite him. Therefore, we must not think it strange that he should stop·his ears against our prayers, and make no countenance to help us, when we cry upon him. So then, let us have these two things, that is to wit, let us pray to God with an earnest mind, so as it may not be only with lip-labour, or with casting forth some sighs at adventure: but with beseeching him from the bottom of our heart. And secondly, let there be no pride in us, to be desirous to make God subject to us, so as he should do whatsoever comes in our head, and in our fancy: but let us pray unto him with a lowliness, magnifying him and praising him, although he afflict us.

You see wherein the prayers of the hypocrites differ from the prayers of God's children. For an hypocrite, without examining of his own heart, will well enough do the same thing that God's children do; to outward sight he will pray unto God, yea, and he will acknowledge that he has need to do so. But if the least temptation in the world light upon him, he frets with himself, and meddles no more with calling upon God, but grunts against him, and foams up such rage, as he shows well that he neither depended upon God before, nor trusted in him, nor sought him with a right meaning mind, and that all was but counterfeitness. Thus you see how the hypocrisy of the faithless is discovered, when our Lord handles them not after their own liking, but holds them shut up in some distress; for then they fret and fume against him. But, contrariwise, if God scourge the faithful man that has prayed to him in his prosperity and in the time of his rest, he ceases not to hold out still in beseeching him to play the surgeon in healing of the wounds that he has made. To be short, God's children continue in prayer, and have the said perseverance or holding out, insomuch that although God afflict them, and seem to turn his back to them, and to be deaf to their requests, yet nevertheless they hold on still, and never give over clean.

When we have sighed and sobbed to-day, if we feel no assuagement by it, let us return to the same remedy again to-morrow. In good faith, you see that although a sick person perceive not that his physician has done him good at the first, yet will he not cease to believe his counsel still. And is it meet that we should put more trust in mortal men than in our God? So then let us weigh well this saying that is set down here, for praying continually unto God; and let us think that it is to no purpose for us to go to God at starts, to desire him to have mercy upon us; but that we must do it diligently, and every man stir up and task himself to it both evening and morning, saying—What; wretched creature sleepest thou here? Know you not what need you have that your God should aid you? And again, if we be afflicted and suffer adversity, let us not cease to call upon God, neither let our hearts fail us, assuring ourselves that our afflictions shall turn to our welfare and soul's health. But let us hold on all the days of our life, yea, and let our holding on be such as we may be importunate, according as our Lord Jesus Christ shows us in the parable, where he exhorts us to pray without ceasing, although God shows not by effect at the first that he hears us.

Where the prayer is conceived with earnest affection, the tongue does not run before the mind. Also the favour of God is not obtained with a vain heap of words; but the godly heart does rather send out its affections, which as arrows shall pierce the heavens; yet their superstition is here condemned, who think they please God and do him service with their long murmured prayers, with which error we see Popery so infected, that the greatest force of their prayer is supposed to consist in many words; for the more words any man has muttered, the more effectually he is accounted to have prayed. Also they daily resound out in their churches long and tedious songs, as though they would allure God's ears. "For your father knows." This one remedy is sufficient to purge and take away this superstition which is here condemned; for from whence comes this foolishness, that men should think that they have profited much, whereas they weary God with their much babbling; but because they imagine him to be like a mortal man, which has need to be taught and admonished. But whosoever is persuaded that God has not only a care of us, but knows also our necessities, and notes our desires and cares before he is admonished, he uses not many words, but thinks it sufficient to make his prayers as is expedient for the exercise of his faith. And he acknowledges it to be a thing absurd and to be laughed at, to deal with God rhetorically, as if that he were bowed with copy of words. But if God, before we ask, does know what we have need of, it seems to be in vain to pray; for if of his own accord he be ready to help us, to what purpose is it for us to add our prayers, which break, as it were, the willing course of his providence ? The answer is easy by considering the end of prayer ; for the faithful do not pray as if they admonished God of things that he knew not, or exhorted him to do his duty, or stirred him up as one negligent or slow ; but rather that they might stir up themselves to seek him and exercise their faith in meditating of his promises, and that they might ease themselves by discharging their cares into his bosom ; and lastly, that they might testify as well to themselves as to others, that of him alone they hope and ask whatsoever is good. And that which he freely and unasked determined to give us, he yet does promise to give at our requests. Wherefore both is to be held, he of his own will prevents our prayers, and yet by prayers we obtain that which we ask.

So oft as we prepare ourselves to prayer, we must especially consider two things, partly that we may have entrance to God, partly that with full and perfect trust we may repose ourselves upon him, that is, his fatherly love towards us, and his great power. Wherefore let us not doubt but that God will willingly embrace us, but that he is ready to hear our prayers, and also that he is willing of his own accord to help us. He is called by the name of Father. Therefore Christ in this epithet does minister unto us much matter for the stay of our faith ; but because that we rest on the goodness of God only in part, in the next clause he commends to us his power. For when the Scripture says that God is in heaven, it declares that all things are under his power, and that the world and whatsoever is in it, is contained in his hand, that his power is spread in every place, and all things are ordained by his providence.

Nothing shall better encourage us to pray than a certain assurance of obtaining ; for it cannot be that they should pray diligently that doubt ; yea, prayer without

faith is but a vain and sporting ceremony ; Christ, therefore, that he might effectually stir us up to this part of
our duty, he does not only command us what we ought
to do, but promises that our prayers should not be in
vain. And this is diligently to be noted ; first, that we
might know that this law of prayer is appointed and pre-
scribed unto us, that we might be certainly persuaded
that God is so merciful to us that he will hear our desires.
Then so oft as we prepare ourselves to prayer, or as oft
as we feel that we are not earnest enough in this desire
to pray, that we should remember this so loving a bid-
ding, wherein Christ testifies unto us God's fatherly
affection. So it shall come to pass, that every one of us
enjoying the grace of Christ may boldly pray and freely
call upon God. And because we are more ready to distrust than is meet, Christ repeats the promise in divers
words, that he might also reprove this fault. But he
uses the metaphor of seeking, because that we think those
things which we have need of, to be far from us ; and of
knocking, because that the fancies of our flesh do imagine that those things are shut up from us, which we
have not ready at hand.

It is not enough to pray unto God in two or three
words, and as it were in post, but that we must continue
in praying without being weary ; and that is a point right
necessary to be marked. For whereas there are many
faults in us, this is one of the greatest, that we cannot settle ourselves unto prayer but that we are fleeting, so as our mouths are no sooner opened but our wits
are by and by wandering elsewhere ; and besides, that if
we have prayed unto God once, we think it enough, and
too much. Contrariwise, we see that Moses was forty
days together in continual mourning for the offence of
the people. Therefore, in our praying to God, let us
learn to have the perseverance whereunto our Lord Jesus
exhorts us, saying,—That we must be importunate, and
that it is not enough for us to have uttered our grief

unto God lightly, and once for all; but that we must resort to him still, until he has heard our requests.

As touching prayer and supplication, it is true that we ought to pray one for another, as long as we live upon the earth, and we have seen the example thereof in Moses; yea, and we have seen in such wise as suffices to show us that our prayers are not vain nor unprofitable, but that God makes them available, and hears them when we pray one for another; howbeit, that is but while we are alive. Moreover, if we fall to seeking of patrons and advocates upon our own heads, without any warrant of Holy Scripture, it is too great a despising of God; for we follow not the manner of praying which God has ordained, and therefore it is a devilish malapertness for men to presume to enter into the kingdom of heaven, there to appoint officers, as though God had made them lord great masters there. Now then let us learn that we must let our Lord Jesus Christ alone with the office of advocate; that he must be our spokesman for us, and give us access and means to be accepted at God's hand. Moreover, we must not imagine any meriting or deserving in any mortal creature, no, not even in the angels of heaven; but we receive the merits of Jesus Christ, which thing was not in the holy patriarchs, nor in David, nor in any of his successors, for God adopted them freely. But it was his will that in Jesus Christ our sins should be wiped out, and our debts discharged, and that by his obedience righteousness should be purchased unto us; that, therefore, is the thing that we must resort unto. Wherefore let us learn, that if the fathers of olden times, when they minded to obtain favour at God's hand, alleged Abraham, Isaac, and Jacob, and consequently David, in his order, because he was ordained to be a figure of our Lord Jesus Christ; if this were used in the time when things were yet dark, we ought to take good heed that we swerve not to the right hand nor to the left, now that God hath revealed himself fully unto us; but that we direct our faith

to Jesus Christ, assuring ourselves, that for his sake, God
his Father has adopted us, and likes well of us by his
means, and grants us our requests. Besides this, forasmuch as the Scripture says that he is given us to be our
advocate, that he makes intercession for us, and that for
his sake we may rest upon God's mercy, let us not doubt
but he will show himself favourable unto us. Seeing that
the Scripture fathers these things upon Jesus Christ, let
us beware that we rob him not of them, and that we play
not the Papists, who, by their praying to their he-saints
and she-saints, do well show that Jesus Christ suffices them
not, and that because they pretend the name of God, they
provoke his vengeance more and more against them. We
see also how God has blinded them and given them
up to a hellish rage, so as they think it not enough to
say, these are our patrons and advocates; but also
they make no difference between God and a saint which
they have forged out of their own brain. For they say,
Our Father which art in heaven, as well kneeling before
a puppet, as if they spoke to God himself. But yet, how
make they their prayers? I shall not need to speak here
neither of the Apostles nor of the Prophets, for they have
saints which never were in the world; and although they
take the Prophets and Apostles, yet they pray to them as
to God, and with the same speech and style. We see
then that they are utterly brutish, and that God has given
them up to a reprobate sense; and it is good reason, because they have robbed Christ of his dignity, wherein God
his Father had set him, and are not contented with him
as with their only advocate and intercessor, but are
run astray here and there; therefore it is meet that God
should withdraw himself from them and forsake them,
that they might fall into such extremity as we see they
have fallen into. Wherefore let us for our part beware
that we hold fast the simplicity which the Scripture
shows us, that in calling upon God we have our eye upon
the Lord Jesus Christ; and again, that inasmuch as God

has established his covenant for ever in his name, we doubt not but that we are heard as often as we come unto God by him, and that he is merciful unto us.

They that are cold and negligent to pray to God, show that they have no faith; for herein doth faith show itself. And this is a true touchstone, whereby we may know how we have profited in the word of God, the gospel: And this it is, if we have an earnest affection and desire to pray to God, and it be a thing our souls breathe and thirst after both day and night; for that man that will say he trusts in God, and believes the gospel, and in the meanwhile makes no account of prayer, shows himself to be but a scorner and a hypocrite: for if we receive the promises of God, and if we be assured of that that he says, we must seek him: as he promised to be our father and saviour;—he calls us unto him, he reaches out his hand to us, he seeks nothing, but that, as we are called to the knowledge of his truth, we come and pray him to accomplish those things which we have hoped for at his hands. They, therefore, that have their mouths stopped, and are so blockish and negligent, give great token that they have never tasted of God's promises.

How may we call upon God? It is sure that we are not worthy to come to him. And, indeed, who dare be so bold as to set one foot forward? We are as worms of the earth! And whither shall we go to call upon God? We must go out of the world, we must climb up above the heavens; the angels themselves of Paradise, are not worthy to come to God, unless they have some mean. What shall we do then? And so it is impossible to have our prayers grounded in faith, and for ourselves to be so bold as to come before God, unless Jesus Christ present himself to be our mediator, unless he reach us out his hand, and promise us to bring us unto him, as also in his person we pray to God, and have him here with us.

We have here no need of the sprinkling of the Pope's holy water, but the price which St Paul speaks of

must answer and make satisfaction for us before God: if
we have this we are assured and resolved, knowing of a
truth that God will not cast away the sacrifice which he
has shown that he was very well content withal, and
whereby he is reconciled and made at one with us, even
for ever.   But if when we pray, we do not ground ourselves upon the death and passion of our Lord Jesus
Christ, we must needs be in doubt and perplexity.   And
so shall all our prayers be vain and unprofitable, as the
Scripture also shows, that if we pray not in faith and
certainty, we shall never profit one whit.

If this doctrine be above your capacity, pray earnestly
to God that he would illuminate you by his holy Spirit.
For as this consideration alone is sufficient to mitigate
any bitterness of calamity whatsoever, namely, that what
is disagreeable to the flesh is salutary to the soul; so,
unless we be supported by such kind of comfort, we must
of necessity be overcome by impatience.   Thus we see
that God does not require of us those things which are
above our strength, without being also ready to assist us
if we ask him.   Wherefore, as soon as he lays any commandment upon us, let us learn to ask of him the power
to perform it.

God is so readily inclined to give, that he neither rejects nor contumeliously puts off any one: not like some
penurious close-fisted mortals, who bestow but little,
and with an ill-will, and, as it were, a half-shut hand; or
who retrench from what they were about to give, or
debate long with themselves whether they will give it or
not.

As we cannot open the mouth in prayer, but through
the medium of words, so, before we open our mouth in
prayer, we ought to believe.   By prayer we testify that
we expect from God the grace which he has promised;
but if any one has not faith in his promises, he prays as
a hypocrite.   Hence, also, we learn what true faith is:
as soon as James has directed us to ask in faith, he adds

this explanation—" Nothing wavering." Faith, then, is that principle, which, relying on the promises of God, gives us the assurance of what we ask: Whence it follows, that it is conjoined with a confidence in, and certainty of the divine love towards us. The word used in the original, properly signifies to enquire, or, after the manner of disputants, to search diligently on both sides. He would then have us to be so fully persuaded in our own minds of the certainty of what God has promised, as by no means to entertain doubt whether we shall be heard or not. " For he that wavereth." By this figure of speech, he elegantly points out the manner in which God punishes the infidelity of those who doubt concerning his promises. They inwardly torture themselves by their own inquietude ; for nowhere can they have peace or rest to their souls, but while they rely on the truth of God.

Let us hold this principle, that our prayers are not heard by God, unless we pray in the full confidence of obtaining what we ask : it is impossible, indeed, but that, in this infirmity of the flesh, we must be harassed by various temptations, which are as engines to shake our faith. Nor will any one be found, who, in his carnal man, would not totter and tremble under them : but such temptations must at length be overcome by faith : as the tree which hath struck its roots deep and firm in the earth is shaken indeed by the violence of the wind, yet is not torn up, but continues fixed and firm in its place.

It is the necessary effect of faith to fix the mind, and prevent it from wavering. The stronger our faith is, the more steady will be our minds, and the less liable to wavering, which is frequently connected with duplicity in religion. The faith which is here recommended, relates chiefly to prayer, and consists in a firm belief that God will afford us such aid under all our sufferings for his name's sake, as will enable us to bear them with magnanimity and patience. He who doubts of this must be very much agitated betwixt hope and fear; a state of mind not only very uneasy in itself, but also very unacceptable to God; inasmuch as it betrays a distrust of his goodness, truth, and mercy, and of consequence proves a very great hinderance to the success of prayer. There is no promise more explicit, or more often repeated as a ground of hope, than the promise of assistance from on high in the time of need. The condition of those for whose instruction and comfort James wrote, particularly required the exercise of faith in this promise. He therefore exhorts them neither to trust to their own understanding in preference to the word of God, nor to lean to their own strength, but to look up to heaven, and solicit the necessary aid of that divine Spirit, whose peculiar province it is both to enlighten and to succour the humble-minded, whose hope is in their God.

Learn to accustom yourselves to the exercise of prayer. Do it while health and strength continue. When sickness overtakes you, you will fly unto this refuge; but if you are negligent at present, you have cause to fear that God will not then regard you. Let not the fashion of the world tempt you to omit this duty. Remember the words of your Lord and Saviour, "Whosoever is ashamed of me before men, of him will I be ashamed before my Father and his holy angels." Let the resolution of Joshua be your resolution, " Whatever others may do, as for me and my house, we will serve the Lord." However occupied in business, however much in company, always reserve a portion of your time to bow at the footstool of mercy, and to pour out your hearts in gratitude to your Maker. Never betake yourselves to rest till you have committed your family to the protection of the Almighty. When you close your eyes for sleep, you know not if you shall open them again till you see the Lord coming in the clouds to judge the world.

Watch, therefore, and pray, for blessed is the servant, who, when the Lord cometh, shall be found watching.

Prayer for true Repentance.—Almighty God, while thou art calling us unto thee, suffer us not to slumber in our sins, nor to become insensible to thy correction; but in season let us arrest thy final judgment: and may we so humble ourselves under thy mighty hand, as in truth to testify, and in deed to prove our penitence. Thus may we know thy will more clearly, so as to profit more in newness of life, till at length being freed from all the pollutions of our flesh, we may attain unto the enjoyment of that blessed rest, which thine only begotten Son has purchased for us with his own blood. Amen.

For Teachableness.—O God, who hast thought us worthy of this blessing, that thy word daily sounds in our ears, let it not find stony hearts and iron minds, but so let us submit ourselves to thee with the humility which becomes us, that we may truly feel thee to be our Father; and being confirmed in the hope of our adoption, so long as thou continuest to speak to us, may at length enjoy not thy voice alone, but even the sight of thy glory in that heavenly kingdom, which thine only Son has purchased for us by his blood. Amen.

Against Sluggishness.—Almighty God, since by our dulness we are so intent upon the earth, that even when thou stretchest forth thy hand to us, we cannot attain unto thee; grant that being attracted upwards by thy Spirit, we may learn to raise our senses heaven-ward, and to strive against our sluggishness, till by a nearer approach thou mayest so perfectly become known to us, that at length we may attain to the fruition of full and perfect glory, laid up for us in heaven by Christ our Lord. Amen.

Against a Worldly Mind.—Grant, O Almighty God, since thou hast willed that we should be subject to so many changes, lest our souls should be satisfied to remain in this world, grant, we beseech thee, that as exposed to such an unstable state, we may seek our rest in heaven, and always aspire to the sight of thy glory; that it, which cannot be beheld by our eyes, may shine upon us, and that we may so acknowledge that the whole world is governed by thy hand and might, as to repose ourselves upon thy paternal care, until we come to the enjoyment of that blessed rest, which has been obtained for us by the blood of thine only begotten Son. Amen.

For Dependence upon God.—Grant, O Almighty God, that although we may wander far from thee, we may yet be taught by thy word to keep the right way, by which we may approach unto thee, and behold by faith the things which are hidden from us, so as to depend on thee alone ; and that we may so trust to thy Providence as not to doubt our safety, since life and salvation are thy care. Thus, when storms assault us, we shall still remain in peace, till we finally enjoy that blessed and eternal peace, which thou hast prepared for us in heaven, through Christ our Lord. Amen.

For Spiritual Sustenance.—Almighty God, who, of thine inestimable mercy hast hitherto sustained us, may we never abuse such goodness ! May we never provoke thy vengeance by our obstinacy, but rather turn away thy judgments ; and so cast ourselves upon thee that thou mayest receive us into thy faith, and protect us against all our enemies. Bountifully supply to us whatsoever we need; and if thou willest that we should live in straitness as to the flesh, yet never let thy spiritual food fail us, but refresh our souls therewith, till at length we enjoy it in that fulness, which is promised, and laid up for us, even in heaven, by Christ our Lord. Amen.

For Acceptance of God's Mercy in Christ.—Almighty God, whose only begotten Son has come among us, fulfilling every measure of thy grace, make us thankful that we refuse not this most precious blessing, but embrace, with true and heartfelt faith, the mercy which thou offerest to supply our daily need. Nor let thy spirit of regeneration leave us, but let our lives be so offered to thee in entire obedience, that we may at length attain to that glory, which now shines before us but darkly, till we enjoy the full sight thereof, through him who is one with thee, Christ our Lord. Amen.

For Spiritual Knowledge.—Hear us, Almighty God, since thou on every side dost spare us; from time to time reminding us by visible signs of thine anger, to repent ere it be so late, that sloth hath cumbered our minds, and put thy judgments out of our sight. Hear us, who pray for knowledge of thy word, and of all things belonging thereto; that we may arrest thy vengeance, and so strive to reconcile ourselves unto thee, that being henceforth regenerate by thy spirit, we may glorify thy name in Christ Jesus our Lord. Amen.

For Spiritual Guidance.—All-powerful God, who hast ordained that we should pass through this world but as travellers, till thou gatherest us to thy heavenly rest, with intent that we may bear in mind that eternal heritage, and turn all our desires towards it; so guide us in our journey, that we stray not, neither depart from the way; but ever looking forward to the mark which thou settest before us, pass we on, until our course being finished, we may enjoy that glory which thy Son hath prepared for us, by his own blood. Amen.

Against Hardness of Heart.—Almighty God, who, day after day, dost call us unto repentance, by indulgence and long-suffering, as well as by thy warnings and chastisements; take away from us all hardness of heart, that we may learn to submit ourselves unto thee, and not offer ourselves to be thy disciples merely with feigned penitence, but so in truth give up our whole hearts unto thee, that we may seek above all things to profit more and more in the knowledge of thine heavenly doctrine, till at the end, we enjoy the fulness of that light, which we hope for through our Lord Jesus Christ. Amen.

Against Pride and Vain-Glory.—Almighty God, who hast not only created us out of nothing, but creating us a second time through thy mercy in thine only Son—hast raised us from the darkness and shadow of death, and brought us unto the hope of thy kingdom in heaven ; guard us, lest pride assault, or vain-glory elate us, that we may embrace thy mercy, with the humility which becomes our estate ; and serve thee in a humble spirit, even until we are made partakers of that glory, which the same, thine only Son, hath purchased for us. Amen.

For Probity.—Almighty God, guide us in our doings towards each other, that as thou beholdest the mutual faith of men, none may deceive his brother; but each with sincere affection help all others, and with one consent offer unto thee that faith which thou requirest from us, and to keep which we are firmly bound; since thou hast not only deigned to make a covenant with us by thy Son, but even to seal it with his own blood. So may we have a part in that heritage which hath been obtained for us by the sacrifice of his death. Amen.

For Humility.—Almighty God, who, in thy great kindness, hast laid open the vast and inestimable treasures of thy grace ; make us to bewail the memory of our former state, calling to mind what we might have been hadst thou not adopted us as sons. How often and how variously we have provoked thee, and made thy covenant of none effect; let glory be to thee in this our shame. For ever let us glorify thy name in our humbleness of heart, even until we come to partake of that glory, which thine only begotten Son hath prepared for us by his blood. Amen.

For Mutual Peace.—Grant, we pray thee, Almighty

God, that as thy law hath set before us a just and perfect rule of living, so that we cannot plead our ignorance or error; grant, we pray thee, that we may take heed to the doctrine which thou dost teach us, and so carefully exercise ourselves therein, that each may live in peace with all his brethren. Thus, may we worship thee with one consent, and glorify thy name till we have passed through this life unto the blessed inheritance, which thou hast promised unto us in thine only begotten Son. Amen.

For the Love of God.—All-powerful God, who hast hitherto deigned to keep us in safety by thy might, who hast turned away the assaults of violence from our heads, and bringing to nought the evil devices of our enemies, hast saved us from innumerable troubles; so continue thy gracious favour to us, that we, in turn, may love thee above all things; and that we may so acquaint ourselves with thy will, that thy holy name may be glorified throughout our whole lives; through thine only begotten Son our Lord. Amen.

For a sense of God's Protection.—O Lord, who daily dost invite us to thee by the testimony of thy paternal care; grant that we be not like unto brute beasts, but calmly attach ourselves to thee. May we so follow, whither thou callest us, as to know thee for our Father by experience; and so live under the protection of thy hand while we wander in this world, that at length, being gathered into thine heavenly kingdom, we may entirely belong to thee, and to thine only Son, who is our joy and glory. Amen.

For Dependence upon God.— Since thou, O Almighty God, hast deigned so plainly to draw nigh unto us; give us a desire to draw nigh unto thee on our parts, and to continue with thee in firm and holy union; that while we persevere in the right worship which thou teachest us in thy word, thy blessings may be multiplied upon us; until thou bringest us to the fulness thereof, when we are called together into thy heavenly kingdom, through Christ our Lord. Amen.

For a Right Use of Warnings.—Fulfil, O Lord Almighty, who deignest to minister to our salvation, and awakenest thy servants, who are as eyes to us, by which we perceive thee watching lest we perish; fulfil our prayers, that we may be so aroused by the holy warnings which come from thee by their ministry and labour, that if we have turned from the right way, we may at once return therein, and go on in our course, and strive with such perseverance, that we may finally reach the fruition of that blessed rest, which hath been purchased for us, by the blood of thy Son. Amen.

For Acceptance of the Gospel.—Grant, Almighty God, who warnest us by so many signs how dreadful is thine anger, most chiefly against the perverse and disobedient, who refuse the offer tenderly made unto them; grant, we pray, that we may embrace that which is offered to us in thy name, with the humility and reverence which becometh thy sons, that so we may repent us of our sins, and beg of thee to pardon them; till having at length put off all the corruptions of our flesh, we may be partakers of that everlasting and heavenly glory, which the blood of thine only begotten Son hath obtained for us. Amen.

For Firmness in the Faith of Christ.—Grant, Almighty God, that as thou hast stretched forth thine helping hand to us by thine only begotten Son, not only binding thyself to us by an oath, but even sealing thine eternal covenant by the blood of the same, thy Son; grant that we in turn may keep our faith towards thee, so that we persevere in the undefiled worship of thy name, till we attain unto the reward of our faith in thine heavenly kingdom, through the same Christ our Lord. Amen.

For Progress in Obedience.—Grant, Almighty God, that as thou hast once redeemed us by the death of thine only Son, we may not stop the progress of thy mercy, by our ingratitude or obstinacy; but so lead us in the obedience of thy Gospel, that we may be brought to the perfection of that grace which has been begun within us, and profit the more in true piety as our days pass onward; till finally, we come together into thine heavenly kingdom, and enjoy the heritage, both promised and obtained, through the same Christ our Lord.   Amen.

For Grace to Profit under the Word.—Almighty God and heavenly Father, seeing it hath pleased thee so graciously to beckon us unto thee, and that thou hast consecrated thy word for our salvation; give us grace that willingly and heartily we may yield ourselves subject unto thee; that those things which thou hast ordained for our good and salvation, may not turn to our ruin and destruction; but that this incorruptible seed (by which thou begettest us again to a lively and heavenly hope) may take such deep rooting in us, and may bring forth such fruit that thy holy name may be glorified.   Grant, also, we may in such wise be planted in the courts of thine house, that we may flourish, and the fruit thereof may appear in the whole course of our lives, till at last we come to the enjoying of that blessed life, which is prepared for us in heaven by Jesus Christ our Lord.   Amen.

For Courage.—Almighty God and heavenly Father, since thou didst once in such wise vouchsafe to arm thy servant Jeremiah with the invincible power of thy holy Spirit, that at this day his doctrine humbles us, grant we may learn willingly to subject our necks to thy yoke, and so to receive, yea, and to embrace whatsoever thou hast taught us by this thine holy servant, that thou raising us up by thine hand, and being underpropped by thy power and defence, we may fight hand to hand against the world, and the prince thereof, Satan himself; that in the meanwhile each of us in our places and callings may so confidently rely upon thy power, that we may not doubt to expose our lives to all dangers, as oft as need shall require ; and that we may valiantly fight, and also persevere, till the last encounter be finished, when having run out our race, we may in the end attain to that blessed rest which is reserved for us in heaven, by Jesus Christ our Lord. Amen.

The Prayer which Calvin generally offered before his sermons.—Let us call upon our good God and Father, praying him to vouchsafe to turn away his face from the great number of faults and offences whereby we cease not to provoke his wrath against us ; and forasmuch as we are too unworthy to appear before his Majesty, it may please him to look upon us in the countenance of his well beloved Son our Lord Jesus Christ, accepting the desert of his death and passion for a still recompense of all sins, that by means thereof he may like well of us, and vouchsafe to enlighten us by his spirit in the understanding of his word, and grant us the grace to receive the same in true fear and humility, so as we may be taught thereby to put our trust in him, to serve and honour him by glorifying his holy name in all our life, and to yield him the love and obedience that faithful servants owe to their masters, and children to their fathers, seeing it hath pleased him to call us to the number of his servants and children. And let us pray unto him as our good master hath taught us to pray, saying, Our Father, &c.

The Prayer which Calvin generally offered after his sermons.—Let us fall down before the face of our good God, &c. (here he added as the subject treated of in the sermon gave him occasion to require at God's hands). That it may please him to grant this grace not only to us, but also to all people and nations of the earth, bringing back all poor ignorant souls from the miserable bondage of error and darkness, to the right way of salvation, for the doing whereof it may please him to raise up true and faithful ministers of his word, that seek not their own profit and vain glory, but only the advancement of his holy name, and the welfare of his flock ; and contrariwise root out all sects, errors, and heresies, which are seeds of trouble and division among his people, to the end we may live in good brotherly concord altogether ; and that it may please him to guide with his holy spirit all kings, princes, and magistrates that have the rule of the sword, to the end that their reigning be not by covetousness, cruelty, tyranny, or any other evil and disordered affection, but in all justice and uprightness, and that we also living under them may yield them their due honour and obedience, that by the means of good peace and quietness we may serve God in all holiness and honesty ; and that it may please him to comfort all afflicted persons whom he visits after divers manners with crosses and tribulations, all people whom he afflicts with plague, war, or famine, or other his rods, and persons that are smitten with poverty, imprisonment, sickness, banishment, or other calamity of body or vexation of mind ; giving them all good patience, till he send them full discharge of their miseries : and specially that it may please him to have pity upon all his poor faithful ones, that are dispersed in the captivity of Babylon, under the tyranny of Antichrist, chiefly which suffer persecution for the witnessing of his truth, strengthening them with true constancy, and comforting them, and not suffering the wicked and ravening wolves to execute their rage against them, but giving them such a true steadfastness as his holy name may be glorified by them, both in life and death : and finally, that it may please him to strengthen all churches that are nowadays in danger and assaulted for the quarrel of his holy name, and overthrow and destroy all the devices, practices, and attempts of all his adversaries, to the intent that his glory may shine over all, and the kingdom of our Lord Jesus Christ be increased and advanced more and more. Let us pray him for all the said things in such wise as our good Master and Lord Jesus Christ has taught us to pray, saying, Our

Father, &c. Also let us pray our good God to give us true continuance in his holy faith, and to increase it from day to 'day, whereof we will make confession, saying, I believe in God, &c.

A Morning Prayer.—My God, my Father, and Saviour, through whose mercy I have been brought through another night to see this new day; grant, also, that I spend it in the worship and service of thy most holy Divinity. May I neither think, nor say, nor do ought which has not obedience to thee for its object, and thy will as its animating principle; so that all my actions may show forth thy glory, and promote the well-being of my brethren, who, through my example, may be led to worship thee. And as by the splendour of thy sun thou enlightenest this world to the occupations of life, so by the effulgence of thy Spirit do thou illuminate my mind, and guide me in the path of righteousness. With whatsoever object my attention shall be engaged this day, may I ever purpose this to myself as my end, to be subservient to thee and thy glory. May I expect all my happiness from thy grace and loving-kindness only. May I undertake nothing but what is agreeable to thee. Grant, moreover, that while I labour for the sake of the things of time, and care for the sustenance and comfort of the body, I may raise my mind higher to the contemplation of that blessed and heavenly life which thou hast promised to thy children; and that thou mayest show thyself to be the protector, not only of my body, but also of my soul; strengthen and defend me against all the attacks of Satan, and from all the dangers which so continually impend over us in this life, do thou deliver me. Moreover, seeing it is a small thing that I begin the Christian course, if I do not persevere, therefore do I beseech of thee, O Lord, to be my guide and director, not for this day only, but even to the end of my life do thou take me into thy keeping, and under thy superintending care may my whole life be spent. And because we must be continually making progress, increase every day in me the gifts of thy grace, provided that I cleave altogether to thy Son Jesus Christ—whom rightly we call the true Son, shining for evermore in our minds. That I may obtain from thee all these great benefits, do thou forget my faults, and in thy infinite mercy forgive them all, even as thou hast promised to do to those who call upon thee in sincerity. Amen.

An Evening Prayer.—O Lord God! who hast appointed the night for repose, even as thou hast created the day for labour, grant, I pray thee, that my body may so rest this night that my soul may not, in the mean-time, cease to be watchful towards thee; that my heart may neither droop nor be overcome with sloth, but that it may always continue intent on thy love. Whilst I lay aside my ordinary cares, in order to give rest and refreshment to my soul, forbid that, in the mean-while, I should be forgetful of thee, or that the recollection of thy grace and goodness, which ought to dwell habitually on my mind, should ever be obliterated; whilst my body thus rests in peace, may my conscience also enjoy repose. Grant, moreover, that in taking the necessary sleep, I may not indulge in fleshly enjoyment, but may allow myself only that rest which the weakness of this nature demands, so that I may in consequence be better fitted to prosecute thy worship. Finally, mayest thou preserve me in purity both of soul and body, and safe from every danger, that even my sleep may redound to the glory of thy name. And since this day, now terminated, has not elapsed without my having offended in many ways against thee—for I am prone to sin continually—do thou forgive all such offences; and as this world is now buried in the shades of night, so may all my sins be buried and hidden from thee in thy mercy. Hear me, O God, my Father! and preserver, through Jesus Christ thy Son. Amen.

Grace before meat.—All things look to thee, O Lord! and thou givest them their meat in due season; what thou givest them they gather; thou openest thy hand, and all things are filled with abundance. O Lord! with whom is the fountain and unexhausted source of all good things, pour out thy blessing upon us, and sanctify to our use, the food and drink which are the gifts of thy bounty towards us, that using them with sobriety, as thou hast commanded, and with frugality, we may eat with a pure conscience. Grant also that with true gratitude we may now acknowledge, and with our lips ever praise thee, our Father, and the author of all good things, and that we may so enjoy the nourishment of the body, that, with the chief desire of our heart, we may aspire after the spiritual bread of thy truth, by which our souls may be nourished to the hope of everlasting life, through Jesus Christ our Lord. Man liveth not by bread alone, but by every word that proceedeth out of the mouth of God.

Grace after meat.—Let all nations praise the Lord :— Let all people sing praise to God, because his mercy is multiplied upon us, and his truth endureth for ever. We give thee thanks, O God and Father! for all the benefits which, in thy boundless loving-kindness, thou bestowest continually upon us. By bestowing upon us all things which we need for the maintenance of the present life, thou showest that thou carest even for our bodies ; and, inasmuch as thou hast revealed in thy Holy Gospel the hopes of a better life, thou hast indicated thy willingness that we should be regenerated. We pray thee, therefore, that thou mayest not suffer our souls, buried in our bodies, to be affected by earthly cares and thoughts. Moreover, do thou cause, that, rising above all grovelling desires, we may abide in the expectation of thy Son, Jesus Christ, until he appears from heaven to our redemption and complete salvation. Amen.

WHEN David meant to praise God as became him, he was not contented to apply all his wits and all his endeavour to the doing of it, nor to call men to bear him company; but he says also, ye heavens, thou earth, ye trees, ye hills, thou hail, thou snow, thou rain, and all ye senseless creatures, praise ye the Lord. We see what zealousness there ought to be in us when we mind to serve God in good earnest; that is to wit, we must desire not only that men and women, but also that the senseless creatures should with one common consent apply themselves to praise God with us, so as there may be nothing in this world, neither above nor beneath, which shall not bend itself wholly to glorify God. And herewith also let us pray God to give us the grace to be able to employ ourselves thereabouts, and to strengthen us against all temptations that may chance; not only against the assaults that shall be made upon us by our enemies from without, but also against the affections that are within us.

True it is, that we are glad if rain come when it may serve our turn; but in the mean-while we pass not to know how it is of God's sending: our minds are so tied to the earth that they cannot mount up thither. Also when we have fair weather, so as we see the sun, and are glad of his shining, yet notwithstanding we consider not how it is God that has kindled such a cresset to give us light. Thus have we no regard at all of God, which is a very great and overbeastly vice. But let us put the case that God come into our thought; yet is not that all. For there are many that should say, God be praised for this fair weather, but in the mean-while they forget all this, they never remember to say, It is God that gives us this fair weather to show himself a father toward us. Therefore it becomes us to be like-minded unto him, and behave ourselves as his true children, and therewithal to bethink ourselves thus : behold how all God's creatures obey him, and yet what obedience has he at our hand. Undoubtedly when we behold the order of nature, it must lead us to a certain fear of God, and to the present tasting of his goodness, to the end we may be given up unto him, and wholly dedicated to his obedience.

Lo ! how men can be quick enough to remember all that ever they have done in their life that may set forth their own glory, but in the mean-while we do wickedly forget the benefits of God. And yet works he in such wise toward us as ought to quicken us up to acknowledge his goodness, or else on the contrary part we do but thrust all under foot. He shall have delivered us from many after delays, and he shall have made us to have passed many great hinderances, so as we may have thought that we had been utterly shut out and undone, and he shall have reached us his hand ; and yet, for all that, we never think of it again. Now, then, whereas we see men to be reckless and slothful in following God, it is because they forget his benefits which they have had proof of, and become like the Jews.

It is one of the sacrifices which he requires of us, that we should do him homage for all his benefits, as holding them from him. But that cannot be done, except we be first put in mind that we cannot so much as eat one bit of bread without it be given us from above, not only for that he created all things, but also for that it behoves us to receive all things at his hand. Therefore whensoever we eat or drink, we must not only call to mind that God has created all things for man's use, but also that he feeds us, as a father cuts out meat to his little children, so as our having of things is, as it were, by his deliverance ; as if he should say to us, I do the office of a father, I have a care to nourish you. If we know not this it is impossible for us to thank God heartily and unfeignedly. True it is, that even they that have no such thought say grace, but that is just for fashion-sake and in way of hypocrisy. Will we, then, magnify God's goodness truly? Then must we be fully resolved not only that God created all things for man's use, but also that he still shows himself a father, and gives us assurance that he will sustain our bodies, and maintain us in this transitory life. Since it is so, is it not an encouragement unto us to yield him the thanks as he deserves?

If God is to be blessed in all his works, he ought especially to be so in man, in whom his image and glory particularly shine. The hypocrisy, therefore, is insufferable, when man employs the same tongue in the praise of God and in cursing of men. There can be no calling upon the name of God there—and there his praise must cease, where detraction reigns. For this is an impious profanation of the name of God, when the tongue, filled with virulence against mankind, unlawfully usurps his province of judging, under the pretence of praising him. Wherefore, in order that we may duly praise him, it is necessary that the vice of reproaching our neighbour should especially be corrected. Mean-while the particular doctrine is also to be observed, that those severe censurers of others ought to detect their own virulence, who, after they have sweetly praised God, suddenly vomit forth every imaginable reproach against their brethren. Should any one object that the image of God in human nature was destroyed by the transgression of Adam, it must be acknowledged that it was miserably disfigured; but yet some lineaments of it still appear. Justice and rectitude, with the liberty of desiring good, have been taken from us; but many excellent gifts, by which we excel the brutes, still remain. He, then, who worships and honours God in truth, will stand in awe to reproach men.

The heavenly host with one consent and with one voice give testimony to the son of God. Then what a perverseness were it not to credit the general testimony of the angels, whereby our salvation in Christ is witnessed ? whereby we gather how detestable this incredulity is unto God, which disturbs this sweet harmony both of heaven and earth ? Again, we are to be condemned of more than beastly blockishness, if this song which the angels with one consent have sung that they in words might begin to us, do not kindle in us a faith and an endeavour to praise God. Add this also, that the Lord would by this example of heavenly melody, commend unto us the unity of faith, and exhort us with one consent to sing his praises upon the earth.

The angels begin with thanksgiving, or with the praises of God, because that the Scripture every where teaches us that we are redeemed from death, to this end, that as well in tongue as in works we might testify our thankfulness to God. Let us therefore remember that this is the final cause wherefore God reconciled us to himself by his only begotten son, that the riches of his grace and great mercy being made known, his name might be glorified. And at this day how much every one of us is strengthened through the knowledge of grace to set forth the glory of God, so much has he profited in the faith of Christ; yea, as often as mention is made of our salvation, we must know that there is as it were a sign given us, to stir us up to giving of thanks and praises unto God.*

* The following information, given by Mr Shepherd, who passed a Sabbath at Geneva during a tour through Switzerland in 1816, may be interesting to the reader. " The service is performed here, and in other towns of Switzerland which have more than one church, by the ministers in rotation. It was conducted at the Temple Neuf, nearly as follows :—A clerk read the commandments ; the minister entered the pulpit, and repeated a form of confessional prayer ; a psalm was then sung ; the prayer which succeeded appeared to be extemporaneous, and was uttered with fervour ; this was followed by a discourse for half an hour ; then a prayer for all

XXVII —PARENTS AND CHILDREN

WE have to mark, that such as have children, ought not so to rejoice of the having of sons as to reject their daughters, as we see some vain-glorious fools do, who think that God does them great wrong, if he send them not men-children. And for what purpose? To the end to continue their houses, to purchase estimation, and to come in credit. Lo, after what manner men would as it were prolong their own life for ever. And yet in the mean-while, if God give them daughters, it is for their profit, and they know it not; and therefore they would have God to consent to their foolish fancies. Also God does oftentimes punish this presumptuousness. For he gives men-children to those that are too desirous of them, and they scratch out their eyes in the end, and are as sea-gulfs to swallow up their substance. The fathers are of opinion, that their children shall increase their house, when they have male-children. And yet most commonly it is an occasion to bring a house to confusion, so as it shall be pointed at with the finger. And what is the cause thereof? It is for that men apply not themselves to God and to his will. When men desire to have chil-

princes and magistrates, for the Helvetic Confederation, and for the Canton, for all Christian pastors, &c., concluding with the Lord's Prayer (which had been recited once before); next the Apostle's creed, preceded by the words ' Seigneur, nous croyons; fortifie notre foi ;' a psalm concluded the worship. With the benediction the people are reminded not to forget the poor; and a person stands at the church door, as in Scotland, to receive contributions. An organ was played here, but the psalmody is also, like that of Scotland, slow and heavy." The pious reader will be much affected to learn, that for nearly one hundred years Arianism and Socinianism have been spreading their poisonous influence amidst the pastors and academical professors of the once favoured city of Geneva.—S. D.

dren, that desire is good, so it be well ruled. But it must come to this point, Lord, if thou give me issue, let it be to the end that thy name may be honoured when I am gone. And if thou do me the worship to be a father, let me so bring up the children that thou shalt give me, as they may be rightly thine, so as they may learn to serve thee, and thou guide them according to thy good will. Behold, I say, how fathers and mothers must content themselves. When God sends them but one child, whereas they would have three or four ; and when God sends them a daughter, whereas they would have a son ; let them say, Even so, Lord, thou knowest what is meet for us, and we must frame ourselves thereafter. Behold, I say, wherein the blessing of God shows itself. But forasmuch as men are inordinate in their desires, it is meet that God should scorn them and their follies.

Such as have charge of others must be watchful, and that when any fault happens they must hold themselves blameworthy before God for the same. And this is well worthy to be marked ; for we see how ambition reigns in the world. If a man have many children, he is glad that he has so many reasonable creatures to be under him at his commandment. If he have wherewith to find a great household, he likes well of himself for it. But what ?— All is but mere ambition or vain-glory ; for there is no regard had of the charge that is matched with it. True it is that God does men great honour when he gives those whom he has created after his own image unto them to be their underlings ; But yet therewithal this honour carries a great bond with it ; namely, that such as have households to govern must always be watchful ; for if an offence be committed against God in any household, he that is the head and master of the house must think himself blameworthy. He must mourn before God as if himself were the party that had done the deed ; and although he be not consenting unto it, yet must he think thus with himself :—I have not discharged myself of my duty, albeit that I watch both night and day ; although I exhort as well my children as also my men-servants and my maid-servants to serve God ; yet is it impossible for me to do all that I ought to do, for I see my children offend, I see faults in my men-servants and maid-servants. Of whom take they it ? Although I take pains to instruct them, yet are there many things to be found fault with ; for I have not given them such example as I ought. Had I walked in the fear of God as becomes me, they must needs have followed my steps; and so it may be that their stepping aside from the right way has been through my default and offence, and therefore I must show them such example as I would have them to follow. If fathers and masters that have children and servants under their hand had this regard with them, things would be better ordered than they are.

Seeing that God has granted us the grace and privilege to be called to the hearing of his word, and to have it set forth in the pure simplicity among us, let us understand that we are the more bound to serve and honour him, not only severally for our own parts, but also by teaching our children ; and by taking pains to make them also live virtuously, so as the doctrine which they shall have heard in their youth be not lost nor marred, as we see too much by experience.

If a man see a despiser of God who has a daughter like her father, and he goes and matches himself with her, is it not as good as renouncing of God ? I go and give my daughter, and to whom ? To a wicked man ; to a naughty pack that has not one spark of honesty in him, whose life is wholly out of order. I make the silly sheep a prey, and cast it into the wolf's throat. And what a cruelty is that ? Is it not all as one, as if I sacrificed my daughter unto Moloch ? Yes, for he draws her away from obedience unto God, to put her into the hand of the devil, and to turn her into all naughtiness. Again, if a man match his son with a young woman that is evil condi-

tioned, and an idolatress, in whom he sees no religion
nor virtue, is it not as good as if he should go poison his
son? True it is that the wife, to men's seeming, has not
authority over her husband. But yet it is a deadly plague
for a man to be matched with a wicked wife. For surely
one woman of naughty behaviour, shall rather mar ten
men, than ten good husbands shall win one lewd woman
that is set upon wickedness, and that, does experience
show. The wife shall sooner mar her husband by her
allurements and temptations, I wot not how, than the
husband shall reclaim his wife, and bring her back again
to good. And, therefore, let us not think it strange that
God should tell the Jews here, that if they gave their
sons and daughters to the Ammorites, Hittites, Ca-
naanites, Hivites, Jebusites, and such like people, they
should by and by be turned away to idolatry.

If any of us would have a servant, he will seek a fit
one as nigh as he can, and such a one as is meet for him,
and if there be any great evil fault in him, all the world
shall not persuade him to take him. Is he a drunkard?
I will never trouble myself with him. Is he thought to
be a thief? Is he a loiterer? Is he a tell-tale? We
are wise enough to beware of those faults, that may
hurt or endamage us by any means, as we are sighty
enough to our own profit; and, therefore, we would
never take a naughty servant into our houses. In like
sort, if a man would have a herd for his beasts, he would
gladly have a diligent fellow, and honest withal. But if
a man should choose a schoolmaster for his children, it
fares so sometimes that he would be less careful in that
case, than in choosing a herd to see to his beasts. A
beastly blindness that men are possessed withal.

The most part have a care to nourish their children,
but where is instruction? Nay, there is worse than this;
we see a great number that seek nothing but to have their
children exceed in all wickedness; they are afraid to be
shamed, and that their children should be better than

themselves. See, there is a contemner of God's word among us, a naughty and wicked man, full of deceit, and traitorous, without conscience and faithfulness, who snatches where and how he can, and would have his children like him. He is a whoremonger and a vile caitiff; he is glad when he sees his children wicked imps at six or seven years of age. We see this commonly, and yet few men think upon it, to dedicate their children to God, to see that they live well, and that God be honoured by them, and that they serve their neighbours. How many are there that see to this? Truth it is that they will fast enough to advance their children, to bring them to credit, to make them rich; but always the principal wants, and the cart set before the horse.

They whom God has so far honoured as to give them children, let them consider that they are so much more bound to God to take pains that their children be well brought up. And if they will have them brought up well, they must always begin with religion. For children may in show have all the virtues in the world, but that is nothing unless they fear God and honour him. As we see a number that will take great pains to bring up their children in the affairs of this world; truth it is that they will have masters for their children, but it shall be to teach them some goodly fair show; they shall have some three words of Latin to make a show at table, to know how to talk, and make fair faces to the world, but to know God, there is no talk, no news of that. But this is not the way, this is to set the cart before the horse. Therefore, let us learn by St Paul's example, to begin at this end to instruct children. For if they love God, it is a good foundation to build upon; but without it, there is nothing but ruin and confusion; for if we take pains to instruct our children in religion, and in the true and pure knowledge of God, and of his truth, their life will be answerable to it; that is to say, they will be honest, they will not be dissolute, they will not be riotous, they will be so well bridled, that they will not give themselves to delicacies, nor to drunkenness, nor to lewd games, nor to such like things; there will be no such evil disposition in them.

It is to be lamented when we see rebellious children which cannot be tamed, do what we can, when they are but little ones, they cannot be made to taste of any goodness. And are they come to age? I say not to the age of men, as though they were at men's stature, but when they are past being little children, and are young striplings as we call them; yet they must needs be called men, and they think they have great wrong done them if they be called otherwise. They might well enough be kept at school yet ten years longer, and have the rod, and yet they will be taken for mighty fellows. And I have told them too often, away you lobs, must you be men? It were more needful for you to be under the rod, and be kept in coram. And if men would have been ruled quietly then, they needed not to have wept now, such rigour needed not to have been used as we see now, they needed not to have been punished so much to their shame as they are now, if there had been any wit and discretion in them. And, therefore, we must mark this, which St Paul says here, so much the better, and let fathers beware that they keep in their children well and straitly, and if they will needs be men when they are yet under the rod, let them not spare them. Truth it is, that parents may not grieve their children, nor give them occasion through their too over rough dealing to become naught, but yet they must fear, that their children being thus hard to govern, take not liberty to give themselves to all wickedness, and to become so lewd that they cannot be brought again to the right way; and therewithal, also, let young folks know, that unless they have this modesty in them, and this grace to suffer themselves quietly to be ruled by their superiors, we must say fie upon all their virtues; as indeed it is nothing, there is nothing but pride and filthiness in them, and God will also bring them to confusion.

It is a monstrous thing for children not to be obedient to their fathers, especially to such a one as never ceases to do them good, bestows his whole care as it were upon them. Lycurgus would not make any law against the unthankful, because it was a thing against nature not to acknowledge a benefit received. A child, then, that is unthankful to his father is a double monster, yea, rather a threefold monster against a liberal father who ceases not to do him good.

They are monsters and not men, that break the authority of parents with dishonour or stubbornness. Therefore the Lord commanded all the disobedient to their parents, to be slain, as men unworthy to enjoy the benefit of light, that do not acknowledge by whose means they came into it. And by many additions of the law it appears to be true what we have noted, that there are three parts of honour that he here speaks of, Reverence, Obedience, and Thankfulness. The first of these the Lord establishes when he commands him to be killed that curses his father or his mother, for there he punishes the contempt and dishonour of them. The second he confirms, when he appoints the punishment of death for the disobedient and rebellious children. To the third belongs that saying of Christ in the fifteenth of Matthew, that it is the commandment of God that we do good to our parents. And so often as Paul makes mention of a commandment, he expounds that therein obedience is required.

There is annexed a promise for a commendation, which does the rather put us in mind, how acceptable unto God is the submission that is here commanded. For Paul uses the same prick to stir up our dulness, when he says, that this is the first commandment with promise. For the promise that went before in the first table, was not special and properly belonging to one commandment, but extended to the whole law. Now this is thus to be taken : the Lord spake to the Israelites peculiarly of the land which he had promised them for their inheritance. If then the possession of the land was a pledge of God's bountifulness, let us not marvel, if it pleased God to declare his favour by giving length of life, by which a man might long enjoy his benefit. The meaning, therefore, is this—Honour thy father and thy mother, that by a long space of life thou mayst enjoy the possession of that land, that shall be unto thee for a testimony of my favour. But since all the earth is blessed to the faithful, we do worthily reckon this present life among the blessings of God. Therefore this promise does likewise belong unto us, forsomuch as the continuance of this life is a proof of God's good-will. For it neither is promised to us, nor was promised to the Jews, as though it contained blessedness in itself, but because it is wont to be to the godly a token of God's tender love. Therefore if it chance that an obedient child to his parents be taken out of this life before his ripe age, which is oftentimes seen, yet does God no less constantly continue in the performance of his promise, than if he should reward him with a hundred acres of land, to whom he promised but one acre. All consists in this, that we should consider that long life is so far promised us, as it is the blessing of God, and that it is his blessing so far as it is a proof of his favour, which he by death does much more plentifully and perfectly witness and show in effect to his servants.

Moreover, when the Lord promises the blessings of this present life to the children that honour their parents with such reverence as they ought, he does withal secretly say, that most assured curse hangs over the stubborn and disobedient children. And that the same should not want execution, he pronounces them by his law subject to the judgment of death, and commands them to be put to execution ; and if they escape that judgment, he himself takes vengeance on them by one means or other.

For we see how great a number of that sort of men are slain in battles and in frays, and some others tormented in strange unaccustomed fashions ; and they all in a manner are a proof that this threatening is not vain. But if any escape to old age, since, in this life being deprived of the blessing of God, they do nothing but miserably languish, and are reserved for greater pains hereafter; they are far from being partakers of the blessing promised to the godly children. But this is also by the way to be noted, that we are not commanded to obey them but in the Lord. And that is evident by the foundation before laid ; for they sit on high in that place, whereunto the Lord has advanced them, by communicating with them a portion of his honour. Therefore the submission that is used toward them, ought to be a step toward the honouring of that sovereign Father. Wherefore if they move us to transgress the law, then are they worthily not to be accounted parents, but strangers that labour to withdraw us from obedience to the true Father. And so is to be thought of princes, lords, and all sorts of superiors. For it is shameful, and against convenience of reason, that their pre-eminence should prevail to press down his highness, since theirs, as it hangs wholly upon it, so ought only to guide us unto it.

Let us treat of the duty of children to their fathers and mothers :—Indeed, it were to be wished above all things, that children were of themselves so well-advised, as not to vex their fathers and mothers in teaching them, and especially in chastising them for their faults. And were our nature as well ruled as it ought to be, a child would not tarry till he were rebuked or compelled, but rather he would think to what end do I live in the world ? And on the other hand he would consider thus,—God has set thee here to be served and honoured by thee; and, again, to obey my father and mother, whom he has given unto me to that end. Contrariwise, if they reap nothing but sorrow by my means, it had been better for me to have died before I was born, that the earth might have swallowed me up. After that manner ought a child to think. But forasmuch as youth lacks discretion, and children are not so reformable of themselves as were requisite, at leastwise let them suffer themselves to be governed by others. And if their father spy any vice in them, let them acknowledge it when they are put in mind of it, and not only confess the misdeed, but also reform it, for it is but hypocrisy when a child holds on in his unthriftiness after he has made pretence of repentance, by humbling himself before his father. If he change not his condition still in his unthriftiness, it is a lying before God, and mocking of his father. Therefore, if a child have done amiss, or see himself subject to any vice, and God is so gracious to him that he has a father or mother, let him consider thus with himself,—Go to, God reaches you his hand in this behalf, for what are my father and mother but the hands of God, and his instruments wherewith he intends to serve his turn, to guide you into the way of welfare? For when I see my father or mother go about to correct my vices, I must set myself against God, and defy him openly, if my stomach be not abated and pulled down to receive their correction. And surely children ought to understand that this superiority over us is the most amiable in all the world, I mean the superiority which our fathers and mothers have over us. For although kings, princes, and magistrates be but reverenced, yet is not that kind of superiority so amiable.

Young men ought to think, that although God hath given them some understanding, yet they want much, because they have not seen much. If a man want experience, surely he shall from time to time rashly overshoot himself: for he foresees not the end of things, neither knows he where to begin: and, moreover, the heat that is in young men, is always contrary to reason and good understanding. Though a young man be well-

stayed, and also have good knowledge therewithal: yet
notwithstanding youth drives him headlong, and there is
such boiling in his nature, as he cannot always rule himself. We see how Saint Paul warns Timothy, that he
should not be subject to the lusts of youth. And by
these lusts of youth, he means not disorderliness in play-
ing, whore-hunting, drunkenness, or other such loose behaviour: for Timothy was a mirror and pattern of all
holiness in himself, yea, and St Paul was fain to exhort
him to the drinking of wine, and yet notwithstanding he
speaks to him of the lusts of youth. And why? For
inasmuch as he was young of years, it was possible for him
to be overhasty in divers things. Now, if it behoved Timothy (who passed his elders in discretion and gravity)
to receive this warning, what had the common sort need
to do? Therefore, let young folks look well to themselves: for if they have not the honesty to hearken to
their elders, and to learn of them, and to follow their
counsel: surely, if they had all the virtues in the world,
that only one vice would stain and defile them all. And
there is not a more common vice than this presumption.
For inasmuch as young men have not been acquainted
with the difficulties that are in many things, therefore
they step forth boldly: they stick not at any thing;
nothing, as they think, is impossible unto them. Youth,
then, doth always carry presumption with it, as an over-
common and ordinary inconvenience: and yet is it not
therefore to be borne withal. For if a young man
have many virtues besides, and yet do trust in himself, yea, and despise his ancients, and bear himself in
hand, that he is able to lead all others: God will confound him with all his pride; and all the gifts that are in
him shall be defaced. And, therefore, so much the more
ought young folks, and such as have not yet seen much,
bridle themselves. Yea, and forasmuch as we see that
nowadays the world is so far out of order, that young
folks have gathered such a devilish pride, as they be past

receiving any manner of nurture or instruction at all: such of them as have any fear of God ought to fight so much the more against themselves, to the end they be not carried away after the common fashion.

True it is that modesty is a virtue convenient for all men ; but yet ought young folks to mark that which is said here, namely, that they must yield honour to their elders, acknowledging that they for their own part may have excessive passions which had need to be restrained by other men ; for they are not sufficiently staid of their own nature, and again, they have not experience to be so skilful as were requisite. Furthermore, when a young man has behaved himself so modestly, he must in time convenient utter the thing that God has given him, yea, even though it were among old men. For the order of nature lets not, but that when old men discharge not their duty, young men may supply the room in that behalf, yea, even to the shame of those that have lived long, and mispent the time that God has given them, or rather utterly lost it. You see then that the mean which we have to hold, is that the reverence which young folk bear to their elders, must not hinder the continual maintenance of the truth, that God should not be honoured and vices suppressed.

So then, if there be modesty in men, there must be also zeal and discretion, and we must not only not be bridled by the authority of such as have lived long, but also if the whole world were brought against us, yet ought not antiquity to prejudice the thing that is rightful and necessary. As how ? I have told you already that if all the old men in the Popedom had conspired against the gospel, and would have other men to stand to their accustomed fashion, it is not meant that their ancientness should shut God and his word out of the doors, or that young men should be hindered to maintain the truth, although that the old men set themselves against them, and would have all other men to hold

themselves to their customs, because they have maintained the evil a long time. For those to whom God
has given better grace, ought to step up against them.
Howbeit, it behoves us to pass further; and if any man
say unto us, how now? It is above a hundred years
ago since our fathers and forefathers have lived after
this sort; or it is five hundred years, yea, or a thousand
years ago since these things have been observed, and
since men have held them for a law and infallible rule;
I say, if men allege this antiquity of time, yea, or if a
man should allege from the creation of the world, yet
must not God's truth be oppressed under that shadow.

True it is, that nature may well stir up brethren to
love one another: but yet are men become so evil, as
there is very few that consider what brotherhood imports. For the proof hereof we shall see many brethren
that agree like cats and dogs. They are brethren, and
yet for all that they cease not to spite and malice one
another, as if one of them would eat another. We see,
then, by such (according as men grow out of kindness
into cruelty,) that brethren are not acquainted with concord and lovingness: and although it be not so with all of
them, yet is every man so addicted to himself, as there
are very few that love one another in such wise as God
teaches. Thus doth the Holy Ghost set a looking-glass
before our eyes, to make us to behold the good agreement and love that was among Job's children, and especially how they exercised themselves continually therein,
to the end they would not give any occasion of evil mistrust one to another.

CONSIDER what a virtuous mind was in Job, seeing his riches had not blinded him with pride, nor caused him to set too much by the world, or to discharge himself of the serving of God, as we commonly see that many men by reason of their great riches become so lofty that it is impossible to tame them, abusing their credit to the oppressing of poor folk ; and besides that they are full of cruelty, they are also stately and full of pomp ; so that riches are accompanied with many inconveniences. Therefore it is not in vain that it is told us here that Job, being so rich, had nevertheless always persisted in the serving of God, and held himself in the same singleness whereof mention is made here ; for by his example the rich men of this world are warned of their duty, which is, to take good heed that when God has put abundance into their hands, they are not entangled by them, according also as the Psalm exhorts them. And further, according as St Paul speaks to Timothy, that they be not puffed up with pride, nor put their trust in the transitory things of this world, wherein there is no certainty ; for he that is rich to-day may become poor by to-morrow, whensoever it pleases God. So then, seeing that the goods of this world are tickle, and that we may soon be bereft of them, rich men, says St Paul, ought to take good heed that they rest not themselves upon them, nor make an idol of them, as though they were sure to possess them and enjoy them ever, but must be ready to yield them up.

They who are advanced to high estate ought not to dazzle men's eyes, but rather acknowledge their own frail state ; and that forasmuch as the world and the shape thereof passes away, their riches, their credit, and their honour shall come to nought. Therefore, let them not besot themselves, but let them continually think upon death, and let those that have servants and subjects under them think thus with themselves:—we must come to account, we have one in heaven who is master of us all, as St Paul says, there will be no accepting of persons, there shall be no more bondage or mastership for men to allege before God. True it is that the earthly policy and also the state of magistrates is ordained of God. But all this concerns the world and worldly things, which shall take an end; and therefore must these things be transitory also. Then let us all take heed that we hold ourselves in lowliness and modesty, and that we attempt not any thing which God has not given us liberty to do.

They that are rich of the goods of the world, they that have lands and possessions, to live of their rents; the merchants that have good trade of traffic, these ought to be as rivers, and to water the places where they pass through, with the abundance that God has given them. But what?—they overflow their banks, and there is nothing else with them but of overthrowing one and of turning up another, and thereafter, as God has given every of them the more ability, so thinks he himself to have the more power to annoy and to grieve his neighbours. You see, then, after what sort men do through this default beguile those that have waited upon them; for they have a stream of water, as it were a flood, yea to destroy and turn up all things. When we see this gear, let us assure ourselves that such men are enemies to nature, and work spite unto God. But herewithal let us also mark that by this means God wakens us and draws us to him, to the intent we should learn to put all our trust in him.

This is it that is commonly to be seen in these jolly fellows that stand so much upon their reputation, and that make so great noise. Why so? for they hold not themselves in modesty, but they overflow their banks, and swell in such sort, as it should seem there were toto

an invincible strength in them. They spread out their
wings, and when they are at their ease they promise this
and that. But when it comes to the push, it is nothing
so nor so. For as a river is more requisite in the great
heat of summer, and in a dry coast, than it shall be in
winter and in moist grounds, so also must our virtuous-
ness show itself when it comes to the true trial. If God
afflict a man, it is the thing wherein he ought to show
himself patient ; and afterward, if it behove him to employ
himself upon his neighbours, you see wherein he ought to
show his charity. Then let us bear well in mind that
such as endeavour to make themselves renowned afar
off, do show themselves to be dry brooks in the end,
whereas they that walk by measure and compass, keeping themselves in modesty, making no great show nor
great noise, nor ranging far to enlarge their borders, shall
be as a well-spring that is covered and hidden, the which
will not cease to do well; and yet, howsoever it be, we
see it has not any great abundance, that a man might
say it were likely that it should never fail; howbeit this
same is more commodious and brings more profit, than
all these great brooks that make so great noise in over-
flowing their banks. And so they that make their great
shows and musters beforehand, are nothing else but little
apes' toys, and for our part let us take them to be so,
that we may shun them ; for God suffers this foolish vain-
gloriousness that is in men so given to vanity, to turn to
a mockery, and themselves to be put to shame. It is
certain, that all such as set such store by themselves and
would make themselves renowned, are led by vain-gloriousness ; and if there were not such windiness and swelling in them, they would be more still and quiet than they
are, and they would not hunt for so great reputation.
But forasmuch as they are so haughty in themselves,
that is to say, forasmuch as they are driven and led with
vain-gloriousness, it is good reason that God should
make them reproachful among men, and that in the end

we should know how there was nothing but leasing in their case.

If a man be rich, let him consider that he must not therefore occupy the whole earth. If he be in authority, he must not therefore despise the poor which are of no estimation. No, but they must support one another, and so behave themselves, that he which is rich may offer some means to the poor to live with him, and that they may get their living honestly when they travail for his advantage. Let him that is poor, although he have nothing of his own, content himself, seeing that it pleases God to make him able to get his living without doing injury to other men, and let them so deal one with another, as the common society may be maintained, and every man be nourished and sustained. Thus then are the rich men warned not to despise the poor so proudly as they were wont to do, and the poor also to walk according to their degree and small ability, and all men to live as though they were lodged in this world by the hand of God and nourished by his grace.

Here is special mention made of widows and fatherless children, because the Lord does specially commend them for that they have least succour. For the wife is under the shadow of her husband and under his protection so long as she has him alive, and he also that is come to man's state, is already able to maintain himself; but a poor widow has neither counsel nor means, and a poor fatherless child knows not what things mean. These, therefore, are more ready to be spoiled, and therefore our Lord would have them so much the more commended, for we are wont to pleasure them of whom we look for recompense. But contrariwise God intends to prove our charity, whether we will do good to them that are not able to requite us. And besides that, look where men be oppressed, there must we apply such means as God has given us. The same is to be seen in widows and fatherless children, and therefore God has commended them unto us. He joins also strangers with them, because they have not many kinsfolk, nor are allied or linked to a long train of friends by whom they might be maintained. So much the more it becomes the children of God to have pity upon such persons. To be brief, we see that God in his law and throughout the whole Holy Scriptures, declares himself to be more grievously offended when widows and fatherless children, and strangers are afflicted, than when any other men are hurt or harmed, because that they be destitute of all succour. And therefore, so much the more must we have pity on them; and because they have no means to requite us, we show ourselves to be the children of God, when we extend our charity to them; and also God does acknowledge the same, and puts it in his accounts, and therefore let us not doubt but it is much more profitable so to entreat the strangers, widows, and fatherless children, than if men had already recompensed us. Contrariwise, when we vex those that as now do lie open to so many injuries, and do add evil upon evil, we are come to the accomplishment of all mischief, and it is a token that we are void of all human judgment, and become like unto brute beasts.

Job compares the houses of wicked men to the houses of moths. How so? The moth mars and wastes all things to make himself a lodging; he eats cloth, he eats fur, he eats all that he finds, and to be short, wheresoever a moth lodges it is always to another body's cost and hinderance, and yet notwithstanding, there is nothing but corruption and vermin in his lodging. When a vinekeeper makes his cabin to watch the vineyards, it is but for three months; for as soon as the vintage is done, down goes the cabin; and although no man set hand to it, yet it falls down of itself. Even so it is said here that the wicked men do make them stately houses, and bear themselves in hand that when they have builded after that manner they shall dwell in them for ever. But what? What are they themselves? Even as a moth; that is to say, they have nothing but corruption, and that must they be fain to carry with them continually. Seeing it is so, surely their houses will not continue long. True it is that they shall make a great show for a time, but in the end God will beat down their houses, so as they shall not abide in them any long while.

Let us mark that it is an intolerable vice for a man to trust in his goods. And why? For is it not an exceeding heinous offence for a man to rob God of his due honour, and to give it to a dead and senseless creature? But does not he make a god of his riches which presumes so much upon them? You see, then, that God is bereft of his honour, and gold and silver, which are but dead creatures, have it. And is not that a monstrous thing? Wherefore let us learn that we cannot presume of ourselves under the colour of the goods which God gives us, but we must become rank traitors to God, and foul idolaters, as St Paul terms the covetous folk. And that is it which Job also meant to express in saying, " If I have set my heart upon gold, or if I have said to the wedge of gold, thou art my trust." Here Job brings in a talk between himself and his money. Verily a man will not talk unto his riches when he opens his chest and coffer; he will not enter communication with them as though he had some body to talk with him; but in this manner of speech Job does very well set forth the folly and overweening of rich men in trusting to their riches. And why? They have there, as it were, a secret conference and conspiracy with their gold and their silver. True it is that they speak not, but yet without speaking they cease not to have the thing which Job shows here. Wherefore as often as we are tempted to put our trust in creatures and earthly things, let us call to mind that it is a robbing of God of his honour, and a purloining of it from him to give it to a thing of nothing, and therefore let us abhor such dealing Therewithal also let us remember the condemnation that Job lays here upon us, and let us compare ourselves with him. What a shame is it that a man should advance himself, and gaze upon his feathers, and think himself to be a jolly fellow, because he is worth I wot not what ! Behold Job possessed great treasures, and had gathered gold and silver in heaps ; and yet notwithstanding he always held himself in such lowliness as if he had been a poor man. What a shame, then, is it for us to be lifted up with a little, seeing that Job was not blinded with all the great abundance that God had given him ! Mark that for one point. And furthermore let us mark, that it is a great trial of a man, when he is rich, and yet notwithstanding becomes not proud, but continues always mild, and without presuming of himself, walks as if he were no better than another man.

Mark here that Job rejoiced not in his riches, but in the goodness of God that made him rich. But yet could not this be sufficiently understood if it were not declared more familiarly. Not that the words are over-dark of themselves, but because we would always use some hypocrisy with God, as though we were wily enough to beguile him. Men then hope ever to escape by their starting holes, when they do but half know themselves ; and therefore, if a man say at one word that we must not rejoice in riches but in God that gives them, the veriest niggards and the veriest pinchpennies in the world will allege this excuse, and make protestation with full mouth, O, I, I rejoice not in my riches, but forasmuch as God has given me them ; I glory only in him that guides and governs me. Lo, how men, being full of hypocrisy, seek also some fair colours to varnish their filth withal ; and therefore I said, that it was needful to expound better this sentence, of rejoicing in God, and not in riches. What, then, does that im-

port? That having an eye to God, who has given us
the goods that we possess, we should understand that
therein he means to show himself a father towards us;
and that seeing he is our father, it is a good reason also
that we should be children on our sides towards him.
But God's children we cannot be, unless we use brotherly love towards men, bearing in mind that the goods
which we have are laid as a pledge in our hand by God,
for the relieving of our neighbours that have need.

Let us learn to trust unto God, and to lean upon him
in our abundance, and to give him thanks for vouch-
safing to make his creatures to serve our turn after that
fashion; and let us beware that we convey not over his
power and praise to any other thing. For that were to
make an idol of the bread God has ordained to do us
service; and he has put it in subjection to us—and shall
we notwithstanding go and worship it? If the bread of
itself do sustain us, has it not the office of God, so as
God must sit still like an idle and dead thing? Let us
beware that we make not idols of the benefits which
God has bestowed upon us, for that were an intolerable
unthankfulness. Thus much concerning abundance;
and therefore let not rich men think they can forbear
God's help, because they have their garners well stuffed
and stored, for if God do but blow upon them, all
vanishes away. When they have the morsels in their
mouths they shall stick fast in their throats, and when
they have their bellies crammed never so full, yet shall
they receive no nourishment by it, except God give it
them by his secret working. By this means shall all of
us live in humility, and such as are well stored shall not
cease to make this prayer, without hypocrisy, Give us
this day our daily bread. For otherwise, were it not a
mockery of God if a man should think himself well
enough provided, because he has great store of corn and
wine, because he has money in his purse and rents coming in, or because he perceives himself to be thoroughly

furnished and stored of all things? How shall he crave his daily bread at God's hand, unless he know that the things which he has are nothing, and that God must be fain to work, yea, and to continue his secret operations always? If that were not, a man might defy God, and hold scorn of him, as in very deed he might well enough forbear him. But if we are fully resolved of this lesson in our hearts, that nothing sustains us, but only God, it will put us in mind to pray him to continue his sustaining of us to-morrow, as well as he has fed us to-day, notwithstanding we have a whole year's provision before hand. For we must always consider that all that ever we have without him is nothing.

Let us learn to weigh better the value of this lesson concerning God's blessing, and let no man rest upon the things that he has in his own possession, nor put such trust in them as to say, This is my stay, this is the staff that I must lean upon. Let us beware of such trust, for it is devilish. Nay, rather, let us think thus : seeing that God has given me whereon to live, I am contented with that which I have, and I hope that he will also provide for me still hereafter. And in the mean-time I will so use it which he gives me, as I may succour those that have need, and therewithal I will put from me all things that may draw me from the obeying of my God, and from the trust which I ought to repose in his goodness. Thus you see how we ought to benefit ourselves by the promises of God's blessing, so as they may quicken us up not only to have recourse unto him, but also to use liberality towards those that have need of us. To the end that our Lord may be praised both of great and small, rich and poor, and all of us have our contentment in him alone, according to the grace that he shall have bestowed upon us.

If a man of wealth be so liberal as to endeavour to do good to such as have need of his help, and advance not himself through pride and stateliness, but always behave himself mildly, that is a very good proof. If another man, being poor, take patiently whatsoever it pleases God to send him, and moreover, be not led to any deceit or naughtiness, how much soever he suffer, or how hard soever his state be, that also is a good and profitable trial. Now, then, let us mark, that whereas there are both rich and poor in this world, God has so ordained it, and it comes of his providence, and that, therefore, we must hold it for a sure ground, that there shall never want poor folk.

Although the alms deeds be done to mortal creatures, yet does God well accept and well like thereof, and puts it to his accounts as though the things which we bestow upon the poor were delivered into his own hands. True it is, that as in respect of God the deed that we do is no alms deed, but an homage of the goods that he has given us, and for the which we are beholden to him ; yet nevertheless, there is, moreover, that besides his accepting of the acknowledgment which we yield unto him for the good that he does us, it is all one as if the mercy which we showed to our brethren extended itself unto him. And that is the case why it is said, that he which shuts his ears at the crying of the poor, shall cry himself unto God and not be heard. On the contrary part, if we be pitiful, and be moved to pity the poor when we hear of their wants, God also will use pity and compassion towards us, to succour us again at our need.

If we think to enrich ourselves any way we care not how, whether it be by hook or by crook, let us consider on the contrary side, that if God bereave us of his blessing, we may well do what we can, but what will be the issue thereof ? Verily, all must needs slip away like water, and we must go backward. And albeit God suffer a man for a time to increase his wealth beyond measure, yet shall that be turned in the end into a wo, both for him and for his children : and, therefore, let us not be enticed by such baits. When we see that many through filing and polling of others, do profit themselves greatly, and heap together much wealth, let not that move us to envy them, because the blessing of God is much more worth than all the riches in the world. And that is promised to none but unto them which hold themselves within their bounds, and abstain from all wicked dealings. And in very deed, if we would but open our eyes, we should be sufficiently warned of that which is here told us. But what? Every man is carried away so headlong, that we consider not of those things which might teach us plainly every day. Behold there is one which thinks he has swallowed up a great part of the world, and it would abash any man to see how suddenly he is consumed and brought to nothing. God, in so doing, does show, as it were, with his finger how he curses men's covetousness, extortion, and such like things, and yet we have no regard of them. Many complain and say, O, behold we thought to have advanced ourselves, and in the meantime we are fallen behind hand, yea, and that is because they considered not whether they depended still on the goodness of God, or whether they proceeded not any further than he gave them leave.

Therefore let us learn to fare the better by all those teachings which God bestows upon us. When we see that he causes such as snatch so to themselves on all sides, which play the ravenous wolves, which have nothing in them but craft and wiliness to circumvent and to snare the simple sort, when we see how God undermines them and consumes them ; again, on the other hand, when we see that he blesses those that walk soundly and uprightly, and that although they have no great abundance, yet he fails not to nourish them and have a care of their family; when we see this, let us desire rather to be blessed in this sort of God, than to have all the means in the world which are so accursed of him. And, indeed, the grace and favour of God shines forth much clearer when a man has not much to live upon, than when he has great revenues and a rich trade of merchandise, and money in his purse, and provisions of his own, both in his garners and in his cellars. Why so ? For if a man be well furnished of all things, he makes this reckoning, that God has no longer need to help him. But when a man must live from hand to mouth, or when he has not much to maintain himself withal, and that at least he might consume all that he has in the compass of one year, and that yet for all that he goes on without diminishing, and that yet knows not whence his wealth proceeds, but that he is certainly persuaded that God had pity of him ; when he thus drives away the time, and at the end of the year acknowledges that it was God only that sustained him and his, therein there is a much more manifest declaration of the goodness of God, and God by effect shows unto us how he blesses his, and how much his blessing avails.

If I constrain a poor man to labour for me, and pay but by halves, doubtless I defraud him of his labour. If I covenant with one to serve me, well, says he, you shall pay me thus much for my day's work; but in the end I cut his hire so short that the poor man, after having done all he was able, shall not have wherewith to feed himself. For why ? I will see. This man here must needs labour, he has not else whereon to live, and he must needs pass through my hands, therefore I will have him for what I list. After this manner do the rich often behave themselves in this behalf ; they espy some occasion or other to the intent they may cut off the one half of the poor man's wages, when he knows not what to set himself about. The poor folk offer themselves to labour ; they desire but to get their living if they could tell where. Hereupon you shall hear a rich man say, This fellow is now out of money and out of work, I may hire him for a morsel of bread ; for he must yield unto me spite of his teeth ; I will give him but half wages, and he shall be glad and fain of that ; therefore,

when we use such rigour, although we have not withheld
their hire, yet it is a point of cruelty, and we have de-
frauded the poor; and this cloak of paying the money
the same day will stand us in no stead before God. For
it is to be known whether the poor man be contented or
no. When a rich man has wares to sell, and one comes
unto him for them, he will say, you shall not have them
for any else. And why? His wares diminish not in
his shop. But if there is a poor man who lives from
hand to mouth, and has neither penny nor halfpenny in
his purse, he shall be forced to sell his ware for nought.
If one buy them at that price, and knows the necessity
which the poor man is driven unto, he is a manifest op-
pressor, and we can skill to say in a common proverb, It
is a holding of our foot upon a man's throat; it is a kind
of robbery. We have skill to speak thus of them who
buy such pennyworths of them that are in need, and are
so far pinched that they can be at no other choice, but
to do what they will have them. Let us note well then,
God commands us to pay not only without driving them
off from day to day, which have laboured or taken pains
for us, but also would have a due regard of every man's
need, and that when we set a poor man a-work about
our business, we should pay him his day's hire; yea, and
that every man should set a price of his own wares, so as
if we come to drive a bargain, the seller should not be
fain to say to us, make what price you yourself list. And
again, that when a poor man has wrought for us we
should not deal so unconscionably as to make no further
account of him than to have the fruit of his labour; but
rather enter into just trial with ourselves, whether, if we
were in his case, which pines away and has no other
means to sustain himself but this, we ourselves would be
contented to be so handled. We would have men to
use gentleness towards us, and relieve and succour us;
let us therefore do the like, or else we shall be accursed
before God.

If a man be rich, let him beware that he set not his heart upon his riches, but use them as if from this to-morrow he should be made poor, and let him make this account, that to have lands, or possessions, or gold, or silver in his purse, is not an everlasting inheritance, but that God gives him the use of them so long as it pleases him. And then let them that are poor, content themselves with this, that God does nourish them ; let them trust in him, both for themselves and for their children. They that have meanly wherewith, let them desire not to increase farther, but keep themselves in their mean estate. And in the meanwhile, let all of them see, they do good one to another, and help their neighbours. When we have this, Satan can get nothing of us ; though his nets be laid, yet we shall not be a prey to him. Cannot hatred, envy, unfaithfulness, perjury, treason, violence, imprisoning, corruption, cannot all these things come of covetousness ? For a man that seeks to enrich himself will first of all be given wholly to himself; insomuch as he will forget his neighbours, and make no count of any man but of himself; he is so carried away, that it is to no purpose to talk to him of right and just dealing ; he passes for nothing but for his own profit ; he eats and wastes other men's substance ; he spoils all. Thus we see in what sense St Paul says, that covetousness is the root of all evils. For if a man be covetous, being friend to himself, he will not care for his neighbours ; you will never see any favour of love in him ; he would all were his, and thinks the whole world not enough for him.

It is a thing too frequent and common, that delicacy, wantonness, and abundance of voluptuousness do easily follow great wealth and riches, which is very often seen in wealthy countries and cities of merchandise. For those that trade into far countries, contenting themselves nothing at all with things which are in their houses, do bring home with them new sumptuous and rich stuffs, which in former times were utterly unknown.

It is certain that men's manners are corrupted when they give their lusts the bridle thus to seek here and there for such unnecessary superfluities ; and we see that such deliciousness was the ruin of the empire of Rome. For, before the Romans travelled into Greece, they were very chaste, continent, and moderate ; but, in the end, having overcome Asia, they began to wax delicate, and to become more and more effeminate. But after they were once dazzled with golden pictures, vessels, precious stones, and tapestry, and that their nostrils were perfumed with ointments and odours, by the same means they became besotted in all their senses ; and, following the dissoluteness of eastern parts as a more gentlemanlike fashion of living, they began to overflow more and more in all disordered dissoluteness.

The ambition of those is reproved who desire to dwell in goodly palaces and spacious houses. It is not unlawful for him who has a great family to have also a large house ; but when men, puffed up with pride, will add to their houses without cause, only to be at more liberty, and that one alone takes up the dwelling-places which would suffice a great many, then it is merely ambition and vainglory which ought worthily to be reproved. For it is all one as if having condemned others, they only should be lodged, and that their poor brethren were worthy of no more than the covering of the firmament, or that they ought to go seek out some other habitation.

The Lord shows, as in a glass, how ridiculous the vanity of men is who lay out an infinite mass of money to build palaces, which yet will one day be nests and dens for night-crows, owls, mice, and such like beasts. These things are daily before our eyes, and yet we take none of them to heart, to grow the wiser by them. These fall out so many and sudden changes, so many houses desolate, so many cities wasted and laid on heaps ; lastly, so many other and so evident signs of God's judgments, and yet, notwithstanding, men cannot be withdrawn or weaned from this insatiable greediness of coveting.

Glorying in riches, which make to themselves wings and fly away, is foolish and preposterous. Philosophers teach the same doctrine; but it is like telling the story to a deaf man, until the Lord open the ear to understand the everlasting duration of the heavenly kingdom.

Wealth and honour frequently expose to vice; they too often puff up with pride, and lead to oppression, to the neglect of religion; and, despite of its great and glorious author,—" Do not rich men oppress you, and draw you before the judgment-seats; do not they blaspheme that worthy name by which you are called?" Are you rich? Be on your guard against those temptations to which your circumstances in life more immediately expose you. Remember that God resists the proud, but gives grace to the humble. Remember that the cries of the oppressed go up unto him, and he will, ere long, vindicate the cause of the injured. Oh! remember what is to be the portion of the profane and blasphemous· Are you poor? Be resigned to the will of Providence; yea, be thankful that hereby you are the less in danger of falling into wickedness. To be poor and wicked is most miserable indeed; yet this is too generally the case. A want of truth and honesty, merciless slander and detraction, cruel envy, much filthy speaking, and too much blasphemy even among the poor. O man! no wonder you are poor, when this is thy manner of life; when you are at so much pains to provoke God to make you wretched here, and miserable beyond expression, hereafter.

And nowadays, what hinders so many simple folk to come unto God's truth, and to frame themselves thereafter; but because they look upon the great ones of the world, saying, behold them that govern all, behold the rich men, behold all the noblemen? none of them will receive this doctrine, and therefore it is a token that

it is nothing worthy, and that it is doubtful, and not for us
to meddle withal. We see how rich men are put into the
balance, so as men think that wisdom is as it were tied
to them. But it is clean contrary. For you shall often see
the rich men so blinded with vain presumption, that their
riches bring nothing but folly to rock men asleep, and
to make men utterly brutish. As much is to be said of
great estate and dignity. A man of mean and low degree will know himself, and gather his wits to him, when
our Lord gives him discretion; and, contrariwise, he
that is highly advanced, forgets himself, and is blinded.
For like as he spreads out his wings in imagining himself to be more than he is, so our Lord suffers all his
reason to vanish away, and him to become as an idol.
We see this with our eyes, but we consider it not;
wherefore let us weigh well that which is said here; that
wisdom is not purchased with gold or silver, lest men
should trust too much to the things which they may attain to here beneath; and let us assure ourselves, that to
understand God's secrets is a special gift of his, and a
treasure that is shut up from us, till God of his own
mere goodness come to enlighten us, and give us thereof what seems good to him.

True it is, that poverty of itself brings store of temptations. For when a man is in necessity, he falls to
thinking in himself, what shall become of me? and the
Devil thrusts him forward to distrust. Hereupon he
shall be induced to murmur against God, according as
we see that many fall into a rage, and it seems to them
that God does them wrong, and they wot not on which
side to turn themselves, whereupon they conclude thus:
Since I cannot get my living by my labour, without
doing other men wrong, I must take another way to the
wood. Hereupon they take leave to rob and reave, and
they do many shrewd turns, harms, and damages to their
neighbours. Behold, I pray you, the temptations which
poverty brings.

We are warned, not to condemn riches in themselves, also like as we see how our Lord Jesus Christ has shown us, by matching the poor and the rich together in the kingdom of heaven, when he speaks of Lazarus in St Luke. He says there, that the angels carried Lazarus. For albeit that he was an outcast among men, and a poor creature of whom no account was made, insomuch that he was forsaken of all men, yet nevertheless behold how the angels carry his soul into Abraham's bosom. And what was this Abraham? A man rich both in cattle and in money, and in household, and in all other things, saving houses and lands, for those were not lawful for him to have, because it behoved him to tarry God's leisure, till he gave him the land of Canaan to inherit. True it is that he purchased a burying-place, but he had not any inheritance, notwithstanding that his movables were very great. Therefore when we see the soul of Lazarus carried by angels into the bosom of Abraham, who is the father of the faithful, we perceive that God, of his infinite grace and goodness, calls both rich and poor to salvation.

Again, in time of poverty, it is a great comfort unto us that we may resort unto God, and beseech him to have pity upon us, and be sure that although there were no bread in the world, yet he will not fail to sustain us by his power. Seeing, then, that we have this promise, it ought to be an encouragement to us to pray boldly, and to rejoice, and not to torment ourselves out of measure, as they that think there is no God at all in heaven, when they see the helps wherewith they are acquainted. And why is that? Because we tie all God's power to our eyesight and outward senses. Therefore let us beware of such fondness, and let us put this lesson in use. And truly God shows us the experience thereof, even still at this day, if we had our eyes open. We should perceive that this is not written in vain. For you see that even they which are best fed receive no benefit by their meat, whereas, in the meantime the children which are neither well fed nor well clad, are nevertheless both fat and lusty, and thrive well to see to.

XXIX — MINISTERS

CHRIST is gone up on high, that he might fulfil all things. This is the manner of fulfilling, that by his ministers, to whom he has committed that office, and has given the grace to execute that work, he disposes and distributes his gifts to the church, yea, and after a certain manner gives himself present, with extending the power of his spirit in this institution, that it should not be vain or idle. So is the restoring of the holy ones performed; so is the body of Christ edified; so do we by all things grow into him that is the head, and do grow together among ourselves; so are we all brought into the unity of Christ, if prophecy flourish among us, if we receive the Apostles, if we refuse not the doctrine ministered unto us. Therefore he goes about the dissipation, or rather the ruin and destruction of the church, whosoever he be, that either endeavours to abolish this order of whom we speak, and this kind of government, or diminishes the estimation of it as a thing not so necessary. For neither the light and heat of the sun, nor meat and drink are so necessary to nourish and sustain this present life, as the office of the Apostles and pastors is necessary to preserve the Church on earth.

Therefore I have above admonished, that God has oftentimes with such titles as he could, commended the dignity thereof unto us, that we should have it in most high honour and price, as the most excellent thing of all. He testifies that he gives to men a singular benefit, in raising them up teachers, where he commands the prophet to cry out, that fair are the feet, and blessed is the coming of them that bring tidings of peace ; and when he calls the Apostles the light of the world, and salt of the earth. Neither could this office be more honourably advanced, than it was when he said, he that hears you hears me; he that despises you despises me. But there is no place more plain, than in Paul's second Epistle to the Corinthians, where he, as it were of purpose, entreats of this matter. He affirms, therefore, that there is nothing in the church more excellent or glorious than the ministry of the Gospel, forasmuch as it is the administration of the Spirit, and of righteousness, and eternal life. These and like sayings serve to this purpose, that that order of governing and preserving the church by ministers, which the Lord has established for ever, should not grow out of estimation among us, and so at length by very contempt grow out of use.

Now remains the form of ordering to which we assigned the last place in the calling. It is evident that the Apostles used no other ceremony when they admitted any man to the ministry, but the laying on of hands. And I think that this usage came from the manner of the Hebrews, who did, as it were, present unto God, by laying on of hands, that which they would have blessed and hallowed. So when Jacob was about to bless Ephraim and Manasseh, he laid his hands upon their heads: which thing our Lord followed when he prayed over the infants. In the same meaning, the Jews, by the ordinances of the law, laid hands upon the sacrifices : wherefore the Apostles by laying on of hands did signify that they offered him to God whom they admitted into the ministry. Albeit they used it also upon them to whom they applied the visible graces of the Spirit. Howsoever it be, this was the solemn usage, so oft as they called any man to the ministry of the Church. So they consecrated pastors and teachers, and so also deacons. But although there is no certain commandment concerning the laying on of hands, yet because we see that it was continually used among the Apostles, their so diligently observing of it ought to be to us instead of a commandment. And truly it is profitable that by such a sign both the dignity of the ministry should be commended to the people, and also that he who is ordained should be admonished that he is not now at his own liberty, but made bound to God and that church. Moreover, it shall not be a vain sign if it be restored to the natural beginning of it; for if the Spirit of God has ordained nothing in the Church in vain, we must think that this ceremony, since it proceeded from him, is not unprofitable, so that it is not turned into a superstitious abuse. Last of all, this is to be held, that not the whole multitude did lay their hands upon the ministers, but the pastors only. Howbeit it was uncertain whether many did always lay on their hands or not; but it is evident that that was done in the deacons—in Paul and Barnabas, and a few others. But Paul himself, in another place, reports that he, and not many others, did lay his hands upon Timothy. I admonish thee, says he, that thou raise up the grace which is in thee by the laying on of my hands; for, as for that which in the other epistle is spoken of the laying on of the hands of the degree of priests, I do not so take it as though Paul did speak of the company of the elders, but I understand by that word the very ordinance itself: as if he had said,—Make that the grace which thou hast received by laying on of hands when I did create thee a priest, may not be void.

All are not fit for the ministry of the word, which requires a special calling; nay, it is the duty of those who consider themselves as possessing the best qualifications, to take care lest they hurry into it without a call. This evidently shows the folly of those "dumb dogs" who are distinguished for nothing else but a mitre, a crozier, and such like mummeries, while they yet boast of themselves as the successors of the Apostles.

Paul adds, that a constant mark and necessary distinction between false prophets and the servants of Christ, may be found in the former not paying the least regard to the glory of Christ, but minding only their own bellies. Since, however, they creep into the Church by craft, and conceal their own wickedness under a false and assumed character, he points out, at the same time, their arts, to prevent any one from being deluded by that smooth and flattering language which they use as a means for securing to themselves favour. The preachers of the Gospel are also distinguished by their own peculiar affability and pleasantness of manners, but combined, at the same time, with a freedom which prevents them from wheedling men by vain praises, or alluring them by the indulgence of their vices. But these impostors not only entice the affections of others by flattery, but spare and gratify their vices with a view to attach them more strongly to their own persons. He applies the term simple to those who want sufficient circumspection to avoid the fraudulent arts practised by such deceivers.

Kindness, prudence, or skill in giving advice, are the chief characters of a wise and good teacher and instructor; kindness inclines to assist the brethren by its counsels—by gentleness, and courtesy of language and demeanour; prudence, or skill in giving advice secures authority, and the means of affording valuable and useful information to all who are prepared to listen to its instruction. Malignity and arrogance are so entirely and completely opposed to brotherly kindness and instruction, that wanderers from the path of rectitude treat advice, when given in such a manner, with pride and contempt, and are prepared rather to manifest the pride, haughtiness, and ridicule of contempt, than to submit to correction from such a quarter. Harshness, whether in language or the appearance of the countenance, deprives instruction of its use and value. A combination of kindness, courteousness, prudence, and skill in business, is highly necessary in giving advice.

A heavenly command has destined and offered the gospel to the wise, by which the Lord may subject all the wisdom and all the ingenuity of the world to himself, and make every kind of science, and the sublimity of all the arts, yield to the simplicity of his doctrine; especially, because the learned are reduced into discipline with the ignorant, and become so tame as to endure those characters to be schoolfellows under Christ their Master, whom they would not before have deigned to receive as scholars.

Too many, while they boast of a certain rare knowledge of the gospel, abandon themselves to every kind of profligacy, as if the gospel was not a rule of life. That we may not so securely jest with the Lord, let us call to our recollection what dreadful judgments impend over such mere flourishers in words, who boast of the word of God by their prating alone, and mere babbling.

When the Jews proclaimed God to be their legislator, and were by no means careful to regulate their lives according to his rule, they declared themselves to pay little attention to the Majesty of their God, which they could so easily despise. Thus also, at the present time, such as idly prate concerning the doctrine of Christ, while at the same moment they trample upon it by their headstrong and libidinous course of life, dishonour the Messiah by the transgression of his gospel.

When a man is in any pre-eminence, he ought to consider, that all men look upon him, and that our Lord has set him as a candle on a cupboard, or a table, to give light. Therefore it stands him in hand to walk the more carefully, and to beware that he gives no occasion of stumbling unto any man. Thus you see how the honour which God gives us ought to be applied, not to our own vain-glory, but to the edifying of our neighbours. And, on the other side also, let us mark how St Paul says, that it behoves us to be thoroughly acquainted with reproaches, and to have our ears beaten with them. If men slander us, let us nevertheless take all in good part, and yet, notwithstanding, let us take good heed that their scoffing at us may not be for our faults. Furthermore, if our conscience be clear before God, so as we be sure that they which rail upon us and backbite us, do it of malice and without cause, let us put it over wholly unto God, and content ourselves with his allowance.

The matter consists not in knowing; but we must persevere in the same knowledge, to withstand temptations with it when they assail us. For if we have read the Holy Scripture, if we have hunted sermons, if we have been taught that which is requisite for a man's salvation, and yet for all that be negligent, and bend not our mind to bethink us of the things that we have heard before, it is all one as if a man being well furnished with corslet, morion, sword, and target, should hang them all up upon a spigot, and suffer his armour to rust, and his sword to stick fast to the scabbard, when he should come to have need of them. He may well say, I have armour and weapon ready, but what shall it boot him to look upon them? you see his furniture is unprofitable, because he hath suffered it to rust, and moreover he shall not know how to handle either sword or target at his need. Even so stands the case with us. We may well have known the thing that is good and convenient for our salvation, and yet for all that, when as we think ourselves to be handsome and well appointed men, we shall not have the skill how to apply all things to our behoof; but this knowledge of ours shall be as it were rusty, so as it shall not come to our remembrance when we have need of it, and when it might stand us in best stead. Then see we here a good lesson for us, which is, that it is not enough for us to have known the thing that God shows us for our profit, but we must also exercise it without ceasing, and our remembrance must be refreshed, to the intent we may know which is the true use of the Holy Scripture.

We that have the charge to bear about the word of God, shall be so much the more blameworthy, though we have faithfully taught that which God himself has

shed out upon us by the gift of his Holy Spirit, if we
have not begun to show the same at our own persons.
And so, must we amend others? Let us first amend
ourselves. Must we exhort others? Let us first exhort ourselves, and let us always be the first in leading
of the dance. Specially when we rebuke such as have
done amiss, let us practise that which Saint Paul says,
that is to wit, let us use all softness in reproving them
that have done amiss.

When a man meddles with teaching his neighbours, it
is not enough for him to be an honest man, and to have
a desire to live well, and to give good example to all
men. But he must also have a skilfulness, and God
must have given him wit and reason. Nevertheless if a
man were as skilful as could be wished, and had his
tongue ready to utter, so as there were no blemish in his
speech, and yet were of an evil conscience, so as he were
a scorner of God, or a heathenish man in his life, he deserves not to be heard ; for his life makes him suspected,
so as men can hardly take any taste of his doctrine. I
mean not that the wickedness of men's lives ought to
diminish the authority of God's word, but I speak of the
common infirmity that is in us, insomuch that if we see
a man that is wicked and froward, and without all uprightness, who in his doings scorns all virtue ; if such a
man speak as an angel, yet would not men vouchsafe to
hear him ; for they would think themselves deceived,
because they see he speaks not from his heart.

So therefore it is a requisite thing for him that deals
with teaching, to have the said uprightness, that men
may know he speaks from his heart, and not feignedly,
and that he tells not a tale in jest, like as a player may
play his part in an interlude, and yet when all is done, it
is but a jest. And this is the cause why I said that it is
not enough to speak well, but that he which minds to
teach others, must not only speak with his tongue, but
also deal so as men may know that the same comes from

his heart, and he must so ratify and seal his doctrine by his deeds, as men may see that the thing which he speaks is so settled in his heart, and so printed and engraven in him, that he speaks as it were in the presence of God.

When a man walks uprightly, and gives good assurance that his speech is not feigned, and that he is no dissembler that does but babble from the teeth outward, and has no affection at all in his heart : if a man be such a one, as that his whole life warrants that he intends to teach other men in good earnest, to the intent that God may be served and honoured, let us assure ourselves that we must take such a one for a mirror or looking-glass, for if we make no reckoning of the good life of such as ought to teach us, we reject the assurance that God gives us of his doctrine. True it is, as I have said, that men cannot bar the word of God from continuing in its full state, for it depends not upon the virtuous behaviour of men : but howsoever the world go, when God is so gracious unto us to teach us by such men as witness by their lives, that their only seeking is that men should serve God, I say when we have such a record, it is as it were a sealing of the doctrine, and it is alone as if God should relieve our infirmity by driving and pricking us forward, because he sees us so negligent and slow to come unto him. Is it not a sign that we be slothful beasts, if we make no accompt of this ?

The ministers of God's word can never edify the people, except they begin at that point of showing men that they be utterly destitute of all wisdom. And it behoves every one of us to receive the same admonishment in ourselves, acknowledging ourselves to be utterly destitute and void of all wisdom, and assuring ourselves that we shall find all wisdom in God's word. Wherefore let us not be afraid that we shall not be sufficiently taught in all perfection if we suffer God to declare his will unto us, and desire the same at his hand, being ready to receive whatsoever he shall say unto us. Then if we have the wit to suffer ourselves to be governed by God's mouth, we have the perfection of all wisdom, wherein there is no fault to be found. And why ? For the Holy Ghost lied not in saying, that the proper and very natural office of good doctrine is, to teach men wisdom and reason that want it.

Like as God's word is hated of the wicked sort, and of the despisers thereof, because it tells them of their destruction, so also they that are cast down in themselves, and are not advanced with pride, presumption or stubbornness, but are always lowly-minded, and to be short, all the scholars of Jesus Christ, must needs be cheered at his doctrine, according to his saying, come unto me all ye that labour and are heavy laden, and I will refresh you. So then, let such as have the charge to utter God's word, look well that they make the doctrine which they carry, to be sound, sweet, and amiable, to all such as are oppressed and overwhelmed in themselves through the knowledge of their own wants and miseries. And therewithal, if they deal roughly, let it be towards those that have need to be roughly handled and tamed by reason of the hardness that is in them.

Let such as have the office of preaching God's word look well to themselves, that they go soberly to work, and that they may always be able to protest that the things they teach are put into their mouths by God. When they be once sure that it is so, let them labour to make all their hearers to feel God's power, which is after a sort enclosed in his word, that it may be received as it deserves, and every man submit himself to it, and God by that means be worshipped of all men, and served with one accord. And, therewithal, let them despise all rebels and despisers when they see the heathenish sort fall to scoffing at the doctrine which they bear abroad ; let them assure themselves that the things which they have uttered shall suffice to send all these to the bottom of hell which do set themselves against them, according to the saying of St Paul, That the preachers of God's word are armed with such a sword as is able to confound all such as will not obey the doctrine.

The ministration of the church is not an easy and indulgent exercise, but a hard and severe warfare, where Satan is exerting all his power against us, and moving every stone for our disturbance.

Ministers should go up into the pulpit, to preach the word of God, in his name, with that strength of faith as to be assured that their doctrine can no more be overthrown than God himself. *

We that are appointed to preach the Gospel ought to know that God has honoured us, in that it pleased him that our mouths should bear them witness of salvation, and that we should be witnesses of his truth, and that we should offer salvation to them that were before condemned and castaways. Hereby we ought to be stirred up, first of all to praise God, for that it has pleased him to honour us in such sort, and then walk in greater fear and wariness. And this honour will cost them dear that use it not accordingly, especially them that shall walk negligently, and like blind bayards. When God has set them in place to dispense the treasures of salvation, and in the meanwhile they make no account of it, what unkindness and unthankfulness is it? And, therefore, let us take good heed to ourselves, and be we watchful, to execute the charge that is committed unto us faithfully.

* "It will greatly conduce to your object in endeavouring to preach the gospel of Christ, that you should reject all previously-conceived opinions and doctrines, and come to the Word of God alone, in the character of a learner and not of a teacher. They who apply to it only to seek support for their own opinions, will inevitably do it violence, and corrupt it; but they who come to it, that by its information they may become acquainted with the divine mind and will, to learn and not to teach it, their profiting will be great."—*Epistle of Zuingle to Peter Sebiville, preacher at Grenoble, December* 13, 1523.—S. D.

Men hate the light of God, and endeavour, as much as in them lies, to put it out, because it discovers their shamefulness, and filthiness, and they seek nothing else but liberty to do evil in darkness. So then, it cannot be, but wheresoever the word of God is preached, by and by there must needs be troubles and much sedition, for as we see the thunder moving in the air, because the water which is there cannot abide that the fire should mount up; and when there are two things joined together, which are such enemies one to the other, they must needs strike one the other, and so bring forth a great violence; even so fares it with the word of God. For there is such pride and arrogance in men that the heavens themselves ring of it. If a green and moist piece of wood cannot burn without much ado, what shall become of our nature, which is so contrary unto the righteousness of God, which shows itself in the Gospel? So then let us bear this well away, that all they that will serve God in preaching the Gospel, must first of all, and before all things, arm themselves, and prepare themselves to fight, being sure of this, that they can in no wise preach the word of God, but Satan on one side will do what he can to hinder them—the world will be in an uproar, and be full of scourges; but we must have this constancy to go on and achieve our purpose.

Although every Christian ought to be wise in governing his life, and very watchful that Satan take him not at unawares with his temptations, and must also take heed and prevent all dangers that compass us in on every side, yet is not this spoken in vain to the ministers of the word, for they are as a candlestick, set upon a cupboard or table, they must give light afar off. It is truly said to all Christians in general, because they bear the light of life, when God has lightened them with his word, that they must give good example, and walk wisely, to the end they may instruct the ignorant. But if this be required in all men without exception, what shall we say of them whom God has appointed to show the way to all the rest? So, then, there is a great deal less excuse in the shepherds that must preach the Word of God, if they walk disorderly, than in private men. Truth it is that all shall be condemned before God, but the vengeance shall be double upon our heads when we have no regard to the office that God has called us unto, and that, upon this condition, that our life shall be as it were a witness of the doctrine to give it more authority. And, therefore, we ought to muse well on this lesson and warning; if we do but only go up into the pulpit to preach, though we had the best grace that a man could wish for, it is nothing, it is no better than the sound of a brass pan. Truth it is that it may be heard afar off, it may well beat mens' ears as a bell that has a good pleasant sound. Such shall we be if we have good doctrine in our mouths, and our lives be wicked and naught. And, therefore, we must remember this lesson the better, that it is not enough for us to have preached the Word of God purely, and expounded the Holy Scripture faithfully, and applied that we have handled to the people's use; our life must speak as well as our tongues, and we must endeavour to walk uprightly, to the end that others may follow us.*

---

* " We exhort you, and in exhorting you exhort ourselves, to consider well in what a situation the Lord has placed us. How many look up to us; how many eyes are upon us; what enemies we have; what numbers will reproach us even when we live ever so innocently; how tender the flock is which we are set to keep; and how many dangers on all sides surround us. It is not our own business which we have to conduct, but Christ's. It is no common business, but such as is of the highest concernment—that which he himself undertook as the most important. Let us not underrate the service in which we are engaged. But we do even despise it, if we apply not to it with becoming gravity and purity. Not only do they corrupt the Word of God, who intermix with it false doctrines, but they also who admit their own passions into their preaching; and while they would draw odium upon their brethren, betray the envy which actuates their own

St Paul shows that he that is called to govern the
church must never be weary, whether it be in giving good
example by his life, or by preaching the Word of God,
to give food of salvation continually to his flock ; therefore, we must continue in it, for the word that St Paul
uses imports as much as to stay and rest ourselves upon
it. To be short, he means that God, when he calls a
man to be a minister of his Word, does not take him to
hire for three days, or for a little time, but will that he
give himself wholly to his service. Is it so ? Then we
must not be idle, nor negligent, but follow the order
that God has shown us ; and when we have taken pains

minds.   What place can there be for contention, where nothing
but the glory of Christ is sought in our preaching ? Is any man
wise ? let him first be wise to himself.   Has he any thing to propose for the profit of the Church ? let him propose it without prejudice to a brother who also faithfully labours in the same vineyard ;
lest, while he unseasonably and improperly sets himself to root up tares
(which may yet not be tares), he destroys the wheat, not another's
only but his own—or rather neither his nor another's, but Christ's. If
any thing of human infirmity, therefore, has crept in among us, we
beseech you, for Christ's sake, and for the sake of the service in
which you are engaged, and by all that we hold sacred and dear, let
us forgive one another after his example who has forgiven us ten
thousand talents ; let us hail one another, acknowledge one another,
respect one another, as friends and fellow-labourers of Christ ; and,
if any thing occurs in our preaching which displeases any of us, do not
let us presently contradict it before the people, but let us meet together
and examine the Scriptures upon it, and consider the arguments on one
side and on the other ; and let him who is shown from Scripture to
have been wrong yield to him who has convinced him, and return
thanks for the light he has received.   Where there is a humble heart,
a spirit remote from pride ; and when a man seeks to consecrate all
his attainments to the glory of God and not to his own ; this will be
easy.   For the source of envy is pride, which fears not being sufficiently honoured.   He who thinks humbly of himself and honourably
of his neighbour will be thankful that Christ should be preached, by
whomsoever or on whatsoever occasion it may be."—*Epistle by Œcolampadius, in the name of the pastors of Basle, to Otto (Binder),
Augustine, and James, pastors of Mulhausen.*—S. D.

one year or two, let us know that this is nothing if we continue not constantly to the end. And this warning is more than necessary, for we see what faintness there is in us. And on the other side we try but too much, that Satan goes about as much as he can to bring them out of fame that are courageous, and to break their hearts, to the end they may fail in the midst of their way. Though the charge we have were not so hard and burdensome, we are on our parts so weak, that the least thing in the world will make us leave off, and turn.

If there be a good teacher that does his duty thoroughly in preaching the word of God, and has a care to give good example by his life, that he is, as it were, a minister of salvation ; and on the contrary side, if a man is negligent in teaching, and be as the most part are, and have no zeal, and for his life is a naughty and wicked liver, and as it were a deadly plague amongst men : when we hear this, know we first of all, that God curses us, that it is a sign of his vengeance when we have not good pastors, but want men that should preach the doctrine of salvation, and have such as pass not which way the world goes. Therefore, if we have men that corrupt and falsify good doctrine, or else are of a wicked and slanderous life, it is as much as if God spake from heaven to tell us, that he withdraws himself from us, and that we are not worthy to be taught of him, nor to be governed by him : and we have not only this witness, but the gate of hell is as it were open to make us all fall into everlasting destruction.

We know there are very few that can abide to be rebuked, though they have done amiss, and feel themselves faulty. For, first of all, we are proud, and that hinders the most of us from submitting ourselves to correction : and then, we have a foolish kind of shamefacedness, so that we had rather abide still in our sins than to be told of them, to the end we might beware of them. For this cause it is requisite for him that must reprove sinners, to have some moderation and modesty in him, that he may somewhat sweeten his reproving and rebuking of them, which otherwise might seem sharp and bitter. As we see physicians use to do when they will give a sick man some drink, they will sweeten it, because the medicine of itself is unpleasant; and, therefore, they mix some sugar or syrup with it. So then is it profitable, by reason of that gainstriving which I spake of, if we will do good in warning them that have done amiss, to use some gentle and meek kind of dealing. And this is especially requisite toward old men, which are more forward and hard to rule. For they think they have lived long enough in the world to know what is good, and would exempt themselves from all rebuke, under a pretence or colour of their age, although they have more need than other, insomuch as when an old man giveth himself to do evil, it is less to be suffered a good deal than in a young man. But yet old folks are not very patient to be corrected. And, therefore, we must go wisely to work with them, to the end they may take our correction well in worth, and we must sweeten it, so that they may abide it and profit by it.

Let the pastors of the word then learn how they ought to behave themselves, when they have to deal with benumbed consciences, to wit, that being well awakened by the judgments of God, they learn to fear this judgment seat in good earnest. And, howsoever it often seems that we lose our labour in singing thus to deaf ears, yet will this terror of God's judgment pierce even into hearts of iron : at the least to leave them without excuse. And ofttimes, also, it comes to pass that some are healed ; and the faithful in like manner do profit by it, when they understand what shall befall the wicked and reprobate, by executing such horrible judgments upon them.

I remember I once saw in a renowned city two preachers: one of them reproved sin sharply, and with a shrill voice : the other studied altogether how to insi-

nuate himself into the good grace of his auditors by flatteries. He that was so plausible, expounded the prophecy of Jeremiah, and was then in hand with a very
sweet place that was full of consolation. Now, having
found a text, as he thought, fit for his turn, he began
sharply to inveigh against these vigorous and severe re-
provers, who are wont to terrify men by thundering out
the judgments of God against them. But on the next
day, because the prophet changed his style, and agreeable
to his vehemency, roughly rebuked the ungodly, this
vile flatterer was, to his shame, constrained to recant, as
it were, that which all had yet fresh in memory. And
thus the favour of the people, at which he so much aimed,
soon vanished away ; for himself had discovered his own
heart ; by means whereof he was loathed both of good
and bad. We must distinguish, then, as you see, between
the teachable and obstinate that we prostitute not this
our softness to all purposes.

Nothing can be more desirable than to rescue a soul
from eternal death. This he does who recalls a wandering brother into the right way. So glorious a work is
not to be neglected. To give meat to the hungry, and
drink to the thirsty,—we see at what rate Christ esti-
mated it, but the salvation of the soul is much more precious to him than the life of the body. We must be on
our guard, then, lest the souls redeemed by Christ,
should in some measure perish through our indolence ;
the salvation of whom God has, in some measure,
placed in our hands. Not that we ourselves can confer
salvation, but that God, through our ministry, preserves
and delivers what, otherwise, seemed approaching to
destruction.

Christ seems earnestly to apply his speech to the
ministers of the word, lest they should wax cold in their
office : because the fruit of their labour doth not presently appear. Therefore, he sets before them the hus-
bandmen to follow, which in hope of a time to reap, do

cast the seed into the earth, and are not vexed with greediness, which never is at quiet ; but they go to rest, and arise again : that is, they do ordinarily apply their daily labour, and refresh themselves with their nightly rest, until the corn wax ripe at length in due time. Therefore, though the seed of the word lie hid for a time, as if it were choked or drowned, yet Christ commands the godly teachers to be of good comfort, lest distrust should abate their diligence.*

XXX —HEARERS

BECAUSE God chooses men unto him for ministers, whose aid he uses in building of his church, together by them he works with the secret power of his Spirit, that their labour might be effectual and fruitful. As oft as the Scripture commends this efficacy in the ministry of men, let us learn to yield the thing received to the grace of the Spirit, without the which man's voice to no effect should be spread abroad in the air. So Paul, while he rejoices himself to be the minister of the Spirit, challenges nothing apart unto himself, as though with his voice he should pierce the hearts of men, but he de-

* " How faithfully you labour in the Lord's vineyard all good men testify. Go on, and never expect to find your labours less or lighter than they are. Grow not weary of your work ; nor look to have the triumph over a conquered world, and eternal glory awarded you, without your having here striven lawfully. The consciousness of having done all for the honour and glory of the universal Sovereign Lord is a mighty stay to the mind, to support its constancy. On the contrary, nothing so much converts the pillars of the Church into reeds shaken with the wind, as the desire of their own glory. I need not mention examples—you have them near you. May a merciful God grant to such that they may not always dissemble known truths."
—*Epistle of Œcolampadius to Conrad Somins of Ulm, February 9, 1526.—S. D.*

clares in his ministry the power and grace of the Spirit. These sayings are worthy to be noted; for Satan very artificially works to diminish the effect of doctrine, that he might weaken the grace of the Spirit joined to it. I grant that external preaching, separately by itself, can do nothing; but because it is an instrument of Divine power for our salvation, and an effectual instrument by the grace of the Spirit, let us not separate those things which God has joined; but that the glory of conversion and of faith may remain whole towards one God.

If it please God to teach us, and for the doing thereof to raise up meet men endued with the grace of his Holy Spirit, under whom we may profit, let us give ear to them with all reverence, and yield to their good doctrine without any constraint. True it is that we ought to examine Spirits, and that we must not at all adventure receive all doctrines that are set before us, until we are sure that they are of God; but when we know that it is God that speaks, that is to say, when we are sure that we are taught in his name, and, as it were, by his mouth, then is there no replying, but we must do him the honour to settle ourselves fully upon his word, so as we may yield ourselves obedient unto it, and it may have full course and authority among us. True it is that many can find in their hearts to suffer God to speak without kicking against him, so as they know the things to be good which are preached unto them; but yet do they strive against him in their life. And that is the thing wherein our Lord intends to try whether we are his or not. Have we heard God's word; We must not reply against it, but we must glorify God, assuring ourselves that there is nothing better for us than to obey him. Have we once acknowledged that? Let every one of us, when we are returned into our houses, show by our deeds that we have borne away the doctrine, and do allow it as good; for he that does contrary to that which he confesses is doubly condemnable. And surely, as there are folk that do much worse in secret than if their wickedness were opened to the world, so also, their replying against God extends not only to the mouth, but also to the life. Therefore, when folk live not as they are taught by the Gospel, their works reply sufficiently against God. When any man troubles his neighbour, so as he rises up openly against him and does him any violence, it is certain that such outrage shall not be borne withal, but shall be punished at God's hand, how long soever he tarries. And although our going about to annoy our neighbours be by subtlety, and, as it were, by undermining, so as our slights are chiefly conveyed and covered, and we cannot be reproved of men, neither can any man to our seeming find fault with us; yet, notwithstanding, the cry mounts up to heaven, and craves vengeance at God's hand for the extortion that we have so committed in secret. Wherefore let us mark well that although we have yielded such reverence unto God's word, as to hear it as good and holy doctrine, and to receive it as the very food of our souls, and as the means to bring us to the everlasting life and the salvation which we pretend to desire, yet it behoves every one of us to take good heed to himself that he replies not against it by his life.

When God created us, he gave us a mouth to taste meats, to the intent we should receive food daily at his hand. And the same is a benefit which we ought to esteem, in that our Lord nourishes us by it; but that is not the principal benefit; for he gave us ears also. And to what purpose? For to be taught by. They are not to communicate one with another only about the buying of boots, shoes, caps, bread, and wine: the use of the tongue and of the ears is yet more noble; that is to wit, to lead us into truth by the means of God's word, that we might know how we were created incorruptible, and that when we are passed out of this world there is an heritage prepared for us above, and, to be short, to bring us unto God. Faith comes by hearing, as says St Paul.

Seeing, then, that God has ordained our ears to so excellent an use as to lift us up to heaven to behold our God, and to behold him as our father, and to witness unto us that he receives us as his children, and to sow the seed of the incorruptible life in us in the midst of the corruptions that are in us : seeing that we may obtain such a benefit by the ear, should we play the deaf men, or stop our ears when men speak unto us and tell us of the truth which we know to be for our salvation ?

Such as would fain be wise and full of understanding, do give themselves to many vain curiosities, they gaze about them, they trudge up and down, they are insatiable, they are desirous to know this and that, and they are never at any rest, because they labour always for vain and unprofitable things. Behold here a very evil extremity, when men cannot know their own ability, but flutter in the air, and plunge themselves into so deep dungeons as they can never get out again. On the contrary part, what do such as mind not to trouble themselves in vain after that sort ? They become brutish, as we see, by experience, especially in the Papacy. I pray you have we not there a fair mirror of this doltishness which is in men, that to hold themselves within modesty they will know nothing at all, but shut themselves from that which ought to be common to all men ? To be short, for fear to overshoot themselves in curiosity, they become as calves, or other brute beast, without any other understanding.

Whereas we desire our own welfare, and God is ready to show us the way, and calls us to him, to the end we should find the fulness of all welfare in him, we vouchsafe not to come, but turn our backs upon him. Again, when he teaches us, it is to the end we should know him, and be as it were transformed into him; and we know that his image and glory are to be preferred before all things. Therefore, when we cannot abide to be taught, it is as much as if we would turn light into darkness, and deface God's glory, that it might not be seen nor known any more. And must not men needs become terrible monsters and devils incarnate, when they labour so to abolish God's glory, and to quench the light, even the light that was their whole welfare, soul, health, and joy? But yet is this vice too common; so then let us learn to esteem this benefit that God does for us when he vouchsafes to call us to his school, and opens us the door, to the end we should learn of him; and whereas of nature we were bereft of the said wisdom, he comes to set it before our eyes, and offers it us familiarly; yea, and tarries not till we seek it, but knocks at our doors, and calls upon us, desiring nothing but to win us to himself. Seeing then that our Lord uses such gentleness towards us as to allure us so courteously, let us learn to make account of that honour, and let us not be so unkind, when he would have us to come unto him.

All they which will not submit themselves to the doctrine of salvation, fight against God to the uttermost of their power, and would banish him out of the world, and cannot abide that he should reign, and enjoy his authority; you see what the Holy Ghost says of them. Forasmuch, then, as the case stands so, if we will not be guilty of such a sacrilege, let us learn to humble ourselves, and whensoever God sends his word amongst us, let us tremble at it, and thereby declare that we seek nothing else but to be present with our God, always to behold him, and to walk as they that know very well that we must make an account of our whole life before him, and that we cannot escape his hands. And moreover let us long for the presence of God. For it is not enough that we have our eyes upon God, but we must desire to be always in his sight and under his guiding, for sometimes the most wicked will have an eye unto God, but it shall be as the galley slaves do, who fall to rowing when they see themselves fast chained and surely beaten; then they must needs do it, but it is of force and constraint. So the wicked, when God speaks, do know that he is present there; but if it lay in them they would destroy his Godhead which is against them; they would also thrust God out of his kingdom, or else they would flee from him, as the Holy Scripture reports of them, that they shall say unto the mountains, cover us. You see how the wicked do always flee from the presence of God, because it is terrible unto them. Now on our behalf, as I have said, we must not only know that he is near unto us, but we must desire always to be in his presence, knowing that our state and condition is miserable, when God does not behold us. Whether can we go but into destruction, when God is not our safeguard. For if we think to save ourselves, where is our assurance; what guides are we? So then let us learn to pray unto our God, that he never depart from us, whatsoever happen; and that we may so do, let us pray him to make us feel and taste the infinite goodness which is in him, that through his enlightening of us by his word, we may know that he is the judge of the whole world, and that we must render an account before him, not only of all our doings, but also of all our thoughts.

God's will is, that every man should seek after him; but yet, therewithal, his will is also that men should hold the way which he shows them; that is, to wit, that they should, with all humility, follow that which is contained in the Holy Scripture. Now, when we have learned that which God teaches us in his school, let us hold ourselves to it; and if there come in any toy in our head to the contrary, so as our hearts be tickled to seek for more than is meet for us to know, let us beware that we have the wisdom and modesty to say,—Poor creature, is it meet that you should presume to have a larger instruction than that which God gives you in the Holy Scripture?

The command of God is obstinately resisted, and his whole order perverted, by those who reject, in an irreverent and contemptuous manner, the preaching of the gospel, for its very design is to compel us to obey God.

Wherever the voice of God sounds, or any of his precepts are given, if men receive them not with sincere affection of the heart, they remain in the letter, in cold dead writing; but if they penetrate the mind, they are in some measure transformed into the spirit.

Because the eyes of men are fixed upon mere appearances, we ought not to be contented with what is only commended by human opinion, which is so apt to be deceived by external splendour; but to be satisfied with the eyes of God, from which the most hidden secrets of our hearts are not concealed.

If, while the Lord deigns to communicate his word to any nation, it is to be regarded as so great a favour, we can never sufficiently detest our own ingratitude for receiving his oracles with so much negligence and indolence, not to say scorn.

Seeing, then, that God has uttered so great majesty in the gospel, and his preaching of it unto us has not been for once and away, but we have our ears beaten with it every day, let us see if we are good scholars, and whether we bear in mind the things that have been told us, so as God is honoured at our hands. Are we linked unto him? Alas, it is nothing so, for continue God never so much in setting forth his doctrine unto us, wherein we do, as it were, see his heart laid open unto us, yet are we locked up on our part, and we give him no entrance, but rather we are gadding and full of vanity, and we are so far off from being touched with his doctrine, and from receiving it to hold ourselves wholly to it, and to set our minds upon it, and to be settled in right obedience to it, that rather the clean contrary is to be seen. And so we see that the Jews are as a looking-glass wherein we may behold our own rudeness, frowardness, unthankfulness, and wilful stubbornness against God. Yea, and we are more blame-worthy than the Jews for giving so slender ear to our God. For as I have told you already, the people of old time ought to have thought themselves bound unto God, and to have yielded and given over themselves wholly to his service, because he had delivered them from the thraldom of Egypt. And what is it that God has rid us from now at this time? Is it but from the tyranny of a mortal man, or of earthly people? No, but we know that he has ransomed us from the chains of sin and of the devil; he has pulled us out of the gulf of death; he has drawn us out of the dungeon of hell; and he has not only promised us the land of Canaan for an inheritance, but also opened the heavens unto us in the person of our Lord Jesus Christ, who has taken possession thereof for us, to the end we might be sure that our abiding place and everlasting rest is made ready for us there. Seeing then that God has bound us in such wise unto him, is not our unthankfulness double, yea, or rather an hundredfold more shameful, than the unthankfulness of the people of the old time?

Men have itching ears, and are desirous to hear always new things, and if the doctrine be preached and set forth to them every day, it becomes irksome to them, and they must wax weary of it. For to their seeming it is enough to speak of it once or twice, and they consider not how they forget the things which they ought to have borne away. So then, to the end we wax not weary of the doctrine that is preached unto us, let us mark that it is needful for us, that God should put us still in mind of the things that he has taught us already, for our wits are short towards him. And, therefore, let us bethink ourselves well, and whensoever it is told us, that there is but one God in whom we are, and that he is not only our Maker, but also our Father, and has adopted us to be his children, and moreover tied us to him by a much straiter band, in that he has redeemed us with the blood of his own Son, whensoever we are put in mind of these things, although we have heard of them before, yet let us not say, tush, these things have been preached to us long ago, but let every one of us enter into himself, and examine himself, and see whether the things that we have heard here before be well principled in our hearts.

If we subdue not ourselves to the hearing of our God, and suffer ourselves to be taught by him all the time of our life, let us be afraid lest he execute the vengeance upon us which he threatened once to the people of Israel by his prophet Isaiah, saying, his law should be to them as a book shut up and sealed, so as if it were offered to men of skill, they should say, the letters are not to be seen, there is a seal upon them, I cannot tell what is within it. And if it were offered to ignorant and unlearned men, they should answer, we are not book-learned, we never went to school, we cannot read. Lo, how God punishes all such as walk on in their own brutishness, and will never submit themselves unto him. True it is that God bears with us for a time, and that, although we be worthy to be cut off from his house, and to be bereft of his truth, so as he should give us up into Satan's hands, to be blinded with his, and to be poisoned by him, yet, notwithstanding, our God having pity upon us, essays still to win us to himself. But if we continue still in refusing the good doctrine, and become never the better for it at the year's end than we were at the first day, at length, this threat must needs light upon us; namely, that we shall take the Holy Scripture into our hands, and have it preached unto us, and yet we shall understand never a whit of it, though we are never so witty; and that, when as the unlearned would say, I wot not what it means, it shall be as a letter folded up, and fast sealed, even to them that are skilfullest and sharpest-witted. Wherefore let us stand in fear of such threatenings, and lest our light be turned into darkness, let us take hold of the opportunity which God offers us nowadays that we may fare the better by his continual speaking after that sort.

God directs his speech to us at this day, therefore we must have our ears open to hearken unto him; we must not drive off from morrow to morrow. We must seek no delay; as soon as God speaks we must be ready to learn, and not harden our hearts against him. Whereby we are put in mind that there is nothing which hinders our obedience unto God but our own resisting of him, through a certain wilful frowardness. For he, for his part, applies himself in such wise unto us, as he bears with our rudeness and infirmity. So then, all they that are taught by the gospel shall obey God without gainsaying, if they poison not themselves through a certain wilful frowardness to withstand God and to drive back his grace. That is the cause why we are expressly warned not to harden our hearts. Yea, verily, for we must not think that God will suffer his grace to be scorned and dallied with and set light by. If he were inflamed with anger against the Jews for refusing to enter into the land of Canaan, if we nowadays do play the restive jades, and fall to kicking, let us not think that such unthankfulness shall escape unpunished.

Let us understand that it is greatly to our profit to be told that when God's ministers speak, they cast not forth a fading sound, but such a one as is matched with effect, and therefore let us be edified to our salvation. Since we know that the remission of sins is not preached unto us in vain, it ought to assure us. Come we to a sermon? Is God's grace offered us? Is it told us that Jesus Christ has made amends for us, to rid us out of the cursedness wherein we were? When we are certified of these things it is all one as if they were put into our hands. Why so? For when God sends messengers to tell us his will, he matches such force therewithal as that the effect is joined to the word. Likewise, when he threatens us, let us assure ourselves that vengeance is in readiness, as says St Paul. Let us not think it a sport and dalliance when we are told of God's curse and wrath against the despisers of the gospel, and against the disobeyers of the same. Hereby we see with reverence we ought to resort to sermons. Also we see in what taking all these heathenish sort, which come to sermons, as it were, in scorn of God, with such brutishness as even little children are ashamed of them, insomuch that there is neither fear of God nor honesty in them; let us be well advised to shun such men's company, and to abhor them, assuring ourselves that if we learn not to mislike of them, we shall be entangled with them by becoming like them.

If at the end of twenty years, when we have had our ears continually beaten with the gospel, so as God has spoken to us early and late, and cried out unto us to waken us, we abide still at our A, B, C, and wot not what rule or doctrine means, must it not needs be said that we be of too untoward a nature? Yes; and that is it which the Apostle means in saying, ye ought by this time to have been great doctors, in respect of the time that ye have gone to school, and behold ye are still raw and unlearned, so as it should seem God never spake to you. According, then, to the time that God, of his grace, shall have bestowed in teaching of us by his Word, let us learn to yield ourselves the more teachable, and to show that he has not lost his labour, but that we have profited well in his school.

Our ears itch to hear this and that, we make discourses, we have our imaginations, and a number of things do run in our heads. Why should not this be good, say we? Why should not this be lawful? Because then that curiosity has taken so deep root in our minds, therefore cannot God hold us to the pure simplicity of his Word? Besides this, we have a sort of naughty affections, which turn us away from God, and are all of them enemies to make war against God, as we cannot so much as think a good thought, but we are full of vice and corruption. That is the cause why we cannot hold ourselves in obedience unto God.

What fares man the better for seeing of himself in a glass? As soon as he turns away his face, his shape vanishes away. Even so is it with us. Whereas, our coming to God's Word should be to be transformed into the likeness of God, as St Paul teaches in the second to the Corinthians; and, whereas it is the power and property of the Gospel to transform us into the glory of God, by beholding him in the person of Jesus Christ; we come to it but to make a pastime of it, so as anon all slips away again, and there remains no substance or power of it in us. And by that means the precious seed of the gospel perishes, for it lights among stones, so as it can take no root. A man may lose a good deal of corn if he cast it upon the dry ground, or in a footpath, or upon stones, for the birds will pick it up by and by. Even so let us not marvel though God's words enter not into us, for whereas our hearts ought to be tilled as when a plough has eased a piece of land, they lie still unopened and unbroken up at all. By reason whereof God's Word may well be given us as a seed, but it shall do us no good, the devil will catch it away by and by, because it sinks not into our hearts and into our souls.

If a husbandman will have his seed to thrive, he must first till the ground, and if there come up any shrewd weeds he must pull them up or cut them off. After the same manner doth God deal with us, to the intent his word may have entrance into us, and be received without any hinderance, he rids us from all evil and vice that is in us. For all our own seeking is to give ourselves to folly. And the devil is so wily and subtle, that he finds means to attain to his purpose, because he knows that our minds are so fickle that our whole seeking is to be beguiled.

Let us bear well in mind that we must be disposed to receive whatsoever God enjoins us, before we can benefit ourselves by any one sentence of the Holy Scripture. As for example, when a man comes to a sermon, though he hear the matter, yet it shall not touch him to the quick, unless he know beforehand that God's truth must be received, and that it is not to be encountered with disputing. And surely we see many that are sufficiently convinced that the things which are told them are true, and that they are not able to reply against them, and yet pass not to make a mock at them. And why is that? Because they are not touched with the majesty of God, and therefore they cannot think that we ought to submit ourselves to him that made us and fashioned us, to be obedient to him and to his commandments. But on the contrary part, when we are urged to receive the things which we know to come from God, his truth will bear sway with us. As soon as we hear that it is God that speaks, we tremble at his speech, as is said by the prophet Isaiah, And so ye see now why God gives this general rule to his, that they must hold themselves to his pure and simple will. But forasmuch as men are naturally given to superstition, and seem to seek even wilfully to be beguiled, God here does first withdraw us from all errors and abuses, and afterwards gives us a foundation whereon to stay and to be builded by hearkening unto him, and by sticking to that which he says.

So often as we are assembled in the name of our Lord Jesus Christ, he is in the midst of us ; it is as much as if he spoke to us in his own person, and it is our duty to be answerable again that we seek nothing but to be his, and to give ourselves over to him. Therefore, if there be any counterfeiting, let us not think to hide it ; it must needs come to reckoning. For whosoever comes not to him with right soundness, doth plainly mock the Son of God. Wherefore, let us consider well that we must not be double-minded when we come to a sermon, lest Jesus Christ blame us for falsifying our faith and promise, by our wicked abusing of his word, and by turning of a thing of such holiness and majesty to a jest and scoff. For when he calls us to be members of his body, and would have us to do him homage, it is an excellent benefit, and such a one as cannot be sufficiently esteemed. And therefore so much the more diligent ought we to be to subdue ourselves unto him. To be short, as often as we go to the church, if we step but one step thitherward whensoever the bell calls us, it ought to come to our remembrance, that our Lord Jesus Christ comes thither himself to receive the obedience which we yield unto him, and that we come hither to make our musters before him, thereby to show that we are his people, yea, and his very body. Now, as it imports an infinite rejoicing when our Lord Jesus Christ is near unto us, so ought we also to tremble before his royal majesty, which was given him of God his Father, and to resort thither with a true and right meaning heart.

If the matter be no more but to bow down the ears, Christ shall have a great company of scholars; at the least, he shall have a good sort; but if there be no more in it than listening with the ears, asses will be taken to be as wise as we. Our Christ is not content with this; for he will have us show by our life that we have received his word, and that it dwells in our souls; otherwise it will serve us to small purpose to protest that we will stick to the truth,—our life will prove us liars; and that must needs be fulfilled that is spoken in another place, that such hypocrites having indeed professed the name of God with their tongues, renounce him in their whole life.

When any of us comes to a sermon, let it not be to hear some pleasant matter, and to have our ears tickled, and to have him make brave discourses; but let us do it to grow in the fear of God and humbleness, and to stir us up to call upon him, and to confirm ourselves in patience. And so if we have heard one exhortation to-day, and hear the same to-morrow again, let us not think it needless, let us not be grieved at it; for if every one of us will rightly examine himself, he shall perceive that he is far wide, and has not well remembered his lesson to practise it aright.

The Prophet has shown heretofore that the cause of this blindness was in themselves. For in commanding them to hearken he testifies that there is a doctrine fit for their instruction, if they would show themselves teachable : and that the light is offered to enlighten and lead them, if so be they would open their eyes.

All the fault, then, is imputed unto the people, because they rejected so wonderful a blessing of God. Whence the solution of the difficulty which we touched a little before, is more apparent. I grant it seems very hard at the first blush, that the Prophets should make the hearts of men more hard, seeing they bring the word of God in their mouth, by which, as by a light, men should lighten and order their paths ; and we know that David gives it this title. It is not the office of the Prophets, then, to blind the eyes, but rather to open them. And hereafter this word is called perfect wisdom. How comes it to pass, then, that it takes away men's understanding, and makes them dullards ? Rather the hearts which were before of stone, iron, and steel, should hereby be mollified : how can it be, then, that they should become the more obdurate ? I answer, as I have touched already, that such blindness and hardening proceeds not from the nature of the word, but is by way of accident: and it ought to be attributed to the wickedness of men. For even as they that have sore eyes cannot accuse the sun for hurting them with the light thereof: nor he who has a weakness and fault in his hearing, a clear and very loud voice which he cannot hear: lastly, as he that is of a weak capacity, is not to be offended with high and difficult things which he is unable to comprehend : so, likewise, the wicked cannot accuse the word of God that they become the worse after the hearing of it. Seeing, then, that all the fault is in themselves, because they do not give it access into their hearts, what wonder is it if that which was appointed for their food do become their bane. For it must needs be, that the disloyalty and infi-

delity of men should be punished in this manner, to the
end they should feel death from that, whence they might
have received life; and darkness from thence, whence
they might have received light: lastly, all noisome and
hurtful things from thence, whence they might have had
the fulness of all blessings to salvation. Which is diligently to be noted ; because there is nothing more common with men, than to abuse the gifts of God: and
whilst they make themselves believe they are very innocent, anon they deck themselves with other men's
feathers. But they are doubly wicked, inasmuch as they
apply not those things to their true use which the Lord
hath given them in trust, but have also profanely and
miserably corrupted them.

There is none, however weak, in the church of Christ,
who cannot be of some use for our advance in grace, but
malignity and pride prevent us from deriving such fruit
by mutual and reciprocal instructions. Such is the nature of our pride, such the inebriating effect of our foolish
boasting, that each of us, while he despises and bids adieu
to others, considers he has a sufficient abundance in
himself.

We ought to study to instruct our neighbours substan-
tially, that the thing which we have learned may not slip
away like wind. And, furthermore, every one of us must
also bend to such teaching, that we covet not to be filled
with wind, as we see many curious folks are, who would
fain have men listen unto them, that they might feed
their cares and satisfy their fond fancies. They imagine
this and that, and would fain have men to listen to their
complaints, to dispute of matters that are to no edifying.
And the mind of man is over much inclined to this vice,
yea, and wholly given unto it. For that if every one of us
should follow his own appetite, it is certain that there
would be none other question among us but how we
might hold unprofitable talk of this and that, which
should spread into the air, and have no substance in it,

nor aught at all but wind. And, therefore, learn to
seek that which is good and convenient to edify us in
the fear of God, and in faith and patience, and in all
good and profitable things.

XXXI — GOOD ANGELS

THAT the angels, forasmuch as they are the ministers
of God ordained to execute his commandments, are also
his creatures, it ought to be certainly out of all question.
To move doubt of the time and order that they were
created in, should it not rather be a busy waywardness
than diligence? Moses declares that the earth was made,
and the heavens were made, with all their armies. To
what purpose then is it curiously to search what day the
other more secret armies of heaven, beside the stars and
planets, first began to be? But because I will not be long,
let us as in the whole doctrine of religion so hear, also remember that we ought to keep one rule of modesty and
sobriety, that of obscure things we neither speak nor think,
nor yet desire to know any other thing than has been
taught us by the Word of God; and another point, that
in reading of Scripture we continually rest upon the
searching and studying of such things as are certain to
edification, and not give ourselves to curiosity or study
of things unprofitable. And because it was God's pleasure to instruct us not in trifling questions but in sound
godliness, fear of his name, true confidence, and duties
of holiness, let us rest upon such knowledge. Wherefore, if we will be rightly wise, we must leave those
vanities that idle men have taught without warrant of
the Word of God, concerning the nature, degree, and
multitude of angels. I know that such matters as this are
by many more greedily taken hold of, and are more plea-

sant unto them than such things as lie in daily use. But
if it grieve us not to be the scholars of Christ, let it not
grieve us to follow that order of learning that he hath
appointed. So shall it so come to pass, that being contented with his schooling, we shall not only forbear, but
also abhor superfluous speculations, from which he calls us
away.

It is commonly read in the Scripture that the angels
are heavenly spirits, whose ministration and service God
uses for putting in execution of those things that he has
decreed; for which reason that name is given them, because God uses them as messengers to show himself unto
men; and upon like reason are derived the other names
that they are called by. They are named armies, because
they do, like a guard, environ their prince, and do adorn
and set forth the honourable show of his majesty, and,
like soldiers, they are always attending upon the engine
of their captain, and are ever so prepared, and in readiness to do his commandments, that so soon as he does
but beckon to them, they prepare themselves to work, or
rather, are at their work already. Such an image of the
throne of God to set out his royalty, the other prophets
do describe, but principally Daniel, where he says,—That
when God sat him down in his throne of judgment, there
stood by a thousand thousand, and ten thousand companies of ten thousands of angels. And because God
does by them marvellously show forth and declare the
might and strength of his hand, therefore they are named
strengths; because he exercises and uses his authority in
the world by them, therefore they are sometimes called
principalities, sometimes powers, sometimes dominions;
finally, because in them, as it were, sits the glory of God,
for this cause also they are called thrones. Though of
this last name I will not certainly say, because another
exposition does either as well or better agree with it.
But, speaking nothing of that name, the Holy Ghost
often uses those other former names to advance the dig-

nity of the ministry of angels. For it were not reason that those instruments should be let pass without honour, by whom God does specially show the presence of his majesty; yea, for that reason, they are many times called gods, because in their ministry, as in a looking-glass, they partly represent unto us the godhead. Although indeed I mislike not this that the old writers do expound, that Christ was the angel, where the Scripture says, that the angel of God appeared unto Abraham, Jacob, Moses, and others, yet oftentimes where mention is made of all the angels indeed, this name is given unto them; and that ought to seem no marvel. For if this honour be given unto princes and governors, that in their office they stand instead of God that is sovereign King and Judge, much greater cause there is why it should be given to the angels, in whom the brightness of the glory of God much more abundantly shines.

But the Scripture stands most upon teaching us that which might most makes to our comfort and confirmation of faith: that is, to wit, that the angels are the distributors and administrators of God's bounty towards us. And therefore the Scripture recites that they watch for our safety; they take upon them the defence of us, they direct our ways, they take care that no hurtful thing betide unto us. The sentences are universal, which principally pertain to Christ the Head of the Church, and then to all the faithful. He has given his angels charge of thee, to keep thee in all thy ways. They shall bear you up in their hands, lest you chance to hit your feet against a stone. Again, the angel of the Lord stands round about those that fear him, and he does deliver them ; whereby God shows that he appoints to his angels the defence of those whom he has taken in hand to keep. After this order the angel of the Lord did comfort Hagar when she fled away, and commanded her to be reconciled to her mistress. God promises to Abraham, his servant, an angel to be the guide of his journey. Jacob, in blessing of Ephraim and Manasseh, prays that the angel of the Lord, by whom he himself had been delivered from all evil, may make them prosper. So the angel was set to defend the tents of the people of Israel. And so often as it pleased God to rescue Israel out of the hands of their enemies, he raised up revengers by the ministry of angels. So, finally, to the end I need not rehearse many more, the angels ministered to Christ and were ready assistants to him in all necessities; they brought tidings to the women of his resurrection, and to the disciples, of his glorious coming; and so, to fulfil their office of defending us, they fight against the devil and all enemies, and do execute the vengeance of God upon them that are bent against us; as we read that the angel of God, to deliver Jerusalem from the siege, slew in one night an hundred fourscore and five thousand in the camp of the King of Assyria.

But whether to every one of the faithful be a separate angel assigned for his defence, I dare not certainly affirm. Surely when Daniel brings in the angel of the Persians and the angel of the Grecians, he shows that he means that there are two kingdoms and provinces, and certain angels appointed as governors; and when Christ says that the angels of children do always behold the face of the Father, he seems to mean that there are certain angels to whom the preservation of them is given in charge. But I cannot tell whether we ought thereby to gather that every one has his angel set over him; but this is to be held for certain, that not one angel only has care of every one of us, but that they all, by one consent, do watch for our safety. For it is spoken of all the angels together, that they rejoice more of one sinner converted to repentance, than of ninety-and-nine just that have stood still in their righteousness. And it is said of more angels than one, that they conveyed the soul of Lazarus into the bosom of Abraham ; and not without cause did Elijah show to his servant so many fiery chariots that were peculiarly appointed for him. But one place there is that seems more plain than the rest to prove this point. For when Peter, being brought out of prison, knocked at the door of the house where the brethren were assembled, when they could not imagine that it was he, they said it was his angel. It should seem that this came in their mind by the common opinion, that to every of the faithful are assigned their angels for governors. Albeit, yet here it may be answered, that it may well be, notwithstanding any thing that there appears, that we may think it was any one angel, to whom God had given charge of Peter for that time, and yet not to be his continual keeper, as the common people do imagine that there are appointed to every one two angels, as it were divers ghosts, a good angel and a bad. But it is not worth travail curiously to search for that which does not much import us to know. For if this do not content a man, that all degrees of the army of heaven do watch for his safety, I do not see what he can be the better, if he understand that there is one angel peculiarly appointed to keep him. And they which restrain unto one angel the care that God hath to every one of us, do great wrong to themselves, and to all the members of the church, as if that power to succour us had been vainly promised us, wherewith being environed and defended, we should fight the more boldly.

They that dare take upon them to define of the multitude and degrees of angels, let them look well what foundation they have. I grant Michael is called in Daniel the great Prince, and with Jude, the Archangel ; and Paul says, it shall be an Archangel that shall with sound of trumpet call men to the judgment. But who can thereby appoint the degrees of honours between angels, or discern one from another by special marks, and appoint every one his place and standing ? For the two names that are in Scripture, Michael and Gabriel, and if you list to add the third out of the history of Tobit, may, by their signification, seem to be given to the angels, according to the capacity of our weakness, although I had rather leave that exposition at large. As for the number of them, we hear by Christ's mouth of many legions; by Daniel many companies of ten thousands; the servant of Elisha saw many chariots full; and this declares that they are a great multitude, that, it is said, do camp round about them that fear God. As for shape, it is certain, that spirits have none, and yet the Scripture, for the capacity of our wit, do not in vain, under cherubim and seraphim, paint us out angels with wings, to the intent we should not doubt that they will be ever, with incredible swiftness, ready to succour us, so soon as need shall require, as if the lightning sent from heaven should fly unto us with such swiftness as it is wonted. Whatsoever more than this may he sought of both these points, let us believe it to be of that sort of mysteries, whereof the full revelation is deferred to the last day. Wherefore let us remember to take heed both of too much curiosity in searching, and too much boldness in speaking.

But this one thing which many troublesome do call in doubt, is to be held for certainty, that angels are ministering spirits, whose service God uses for the defence of his, and by whom he both distributes his benefits among men, and also puts his other works in execution. It was in the old time the opinion of the Sadducees, that by angels is meant nothing else but either the motions that God doth inspire in men, or the tokens that he shows of his power. But against this error cry out so many testimonies of Scripture, that it is marvellous that so gross ignorance could be suffered in that people. For to omit those places that I have before alleged, where are recited thousands and legions of angels; where joy is given unto them; where it is said that they uphold the faithful with their hands, and carry their souls into rest; that they see the face of the Father, and such like; there are other places whereby it is clearly proved that they are indeed spirits of a nature that has substance. For whereas Stephen and Paul do say, that the law was given by the hand of angels, and Christ says, that the elect, after the resurrection, shall be like unto angels—that the day of judgment is not known to the very angels—that he shall then come with his holy angels; howsoever they be writhed, yet must they so be understood. Likewise, when Paul charged Timothy before Christ and his chosen angels to keep his commandments, he means not qualities or inspirations without substance, but very spirits. And otherwise it stands not together that is written in the Epistle to the Hebrews, that Christ is become more excellent than angels, that the world is not made subject unto them ; that Christ took upon him not their nature, but the nature of man. If we mean not the blessed spirits, to whom may these comparisons agree ? And the author of that Epistle expounds himself, where he places in the kingdom of heaven the souls of the faithful and the holy angels together. Also the same that we have already alleged, that the angels of children do alway behold the face of God, that they do rejoice at our safety, that they marvel at the manifold grace of God in the church, that they are subject to Christ, the head. To the same purpose serves this, that they so oft appeared to the holy fathers in the form of men, that they talked with them, that they were lodged with them. And Christ himself, for the principal pre-eminence that he has in the person of the Mediator, is called an angel. This I thought good to touch by the way, to furnish the simple with defence against those foolish and reasonless opinions that, many ages ago raised by Satan, do now and then spring up again.

Now it rests that we seek to meet with that superstition which is commonly wont to creep in, where it is said, that Angels are the ministers and deliverers of all good things unto us. For by and by man's reason falls to this point, to think that, therefore, all honour ought to be given them. So comes it to pass, that those things which belong only to God and Christ, are conveyed away to angels. By this means we see that in certain ages past, the glory of Christ has been many ways obscured, when angels, without warrant of God's word, were laden with immeasurable titles of honour. And of all the vices that we speak against, there is almost none more ancient than this. For it appears that Paul himself had much to do with some which so advanced angels, that they in manner would have brought Christ under subjection. And therefore he does so carefully press this point in his Epistle to the Colossians, that Christ is not only to be preferred before all angels, but that he is also the author of all the good things that they have ; to the end we should not forsake him and turn unto them, which cannot sufficiently help themselves, but are fain to draw out of the same fountain that we do. Surely forasmuch as there shines in them a certain brightness of the majesty of God, there is nothing whereunto we are more easily inclined, than with a certain admiration to fall down in worshipping of them, and to give unto them all things that are due only to God. Which thing John, in the Revelation, confesses to have chanced to himself, but he adds withal, that he received this answer, See thou do it not ; for I am thy fellow-servant : Worship God.

But this danger we shall well beware of, if we do consider why God uses rather by them than by himself without their service to declare his power, to provide for the safety of the faithful, and to communicate the gifts of his liberality among them. Surely he does not this of necessity, as though he could not be without them ; for so oft as pleases him, he lets them alone, and brings his work to pass with an only beck ; so far is it off that they be any aid to him, to ease him of the hardness thereof. This, therefore, makes for the comfort of our weakness, so that we want nothing that may avail our minds either in raising them up in good hope, or confirming them in assurance. This one thing ought to be enough and enough again for us, that the Lord affirms that he is our protector. But while we see ourselves besieged with so many dangers, so many hurtful things, so many kinds of enemies, it may be (such is our weakness and frailty) that we are sometime filled with trembling fear, or fall for despair, unless the Lord, after the proportion of our capacity, do make us to conceive his presence. By this means he not only promises that he will have care of us, but also that he has an innumerable guard to whom he has given in charge to travail for our safety, and that so long as we are compassed with the garrison and support of them, whatsoever danger betides, we are without all reach of hurt. I grant we do amiss that, after this simple promise of the protection of God alone, we still look about from whence other help may come unto us. But forasmuch as it pleases the Lord, of his infinite clemency and gentleness, to help this our fault, there is no reason why we should neglect his so great benefit. An example thereof we have in the servant of Elisha, who, when he saw the hill besieged with the army of the Syrians, and that there was no way open to escape, was stricken down with fear, as if his master and he were then utterly destroyed. Then Elisha prayed God to open his servant's eyes, and by and by he saw the hill furnished with horses and fiery chariots, that is, with a multitude of angels to keep him and the prophet safe. Encouraged with this vision, he gathered up his heart again, and was able with a dreadless mind to look down upon his enemies, with sight of whom he was before in a manner driven out of his wits.

Wherefore, whatsoever is said of the ministry of angels, let us apply it to this end, that overcoming all distrust, our hope may be the more strongly established in

God. For these succours are therefore provided us of God, that we should not be made afraid with multitudes of enemies, as though they could prevail against his help, but should fly unto that saying of Elisha, that there are more on our side than are against us. How much, then, is it against order of reason, that we should be led away from God by angels, which are ordained for this purpose, to testify that his help is more present among us? But they do lead us away indeed, if they do not straight lead us, as it were, by the hand to him, that we may have eye unto, call upon, and publish him for our only helper; if we consider not them to be as his hands that move themselves to no work but by his direction; if they do not hold us fast in the one Mediator Christ, so that we may hang wholly of him, lean all upon him, be carried to him, and rest in him. For that which is described in the vision of Jacob, ought to stick and be fastened in our minds, how angels descend down to the earth unto men, and from men do go up to heaven by a ladder, whereupon stands the Lord of hosts. Whereby is meant, that by the only intercession of Christ it comes to pass, that the ministries of the angels do come unto us, as he himself affirms, saying, Hereafter ye shall see the heavens open, and the angels descending to the Son of Man. Therefore the servant of Abraham being committed to the custody of the angel, does not therefore call upon the angel to help him, but helped with that commendation, he prays to the Lord, and beseeches him to show his mercy to Abraham. For as God does not, therefore, make them ministers of his power and goodness, to the intent to part his glory with them, so does he not, therefore, promise us his help in their ministration, that we should divide our confidence between him and them. Let us, therefore, forsake that Platonical philosophy, to seek the way to God by angels, and to honour them for this purpose, that they may make God more gentle unto us, which superstitious and curious men have from the beginning gone about, and to this day do continue to bring into our religion.

Certain it is, as the Scripture shows in many other places, that the angels are evermore before God, notwithstanding that they execute his commandments, according as it is said that they pitch their tents round about us to guard us, and that God has appointed them to guide us, to the end we should be as it were under their protection. Also it is said, that they execute his wrath and vengeance upon the wicked. But yet for all this, the angels being spirits, are not hindered to serve God, and to obey him, nor to execute his judgment here below, albeit that they be all the while continually in his presence. And therefore, when our Lord Jesus Christ says, that the angels which have the keeping of little infants, do continually see and behold the face of his father, thereby it is given us to understand, that although the angels assist us, and that we feel their virtue in maintaining us, yet notwithstanding they joy still all the while in the glory of God, and are not separated from him. And therefore, whereas it is said that they appeared, it is not meant, that when God sends them forth they are separated from his majesty and deprived of the heavenly life during the time that they are in their voyage; but forasmuch as we are rude and gross, the Scripture meant to liken God to earthly princes, to the end that, by a more homely and familiar manner, we might know how the angels do not any thing of their own proper moving, but that it is God that commands them, who has all dominion over them, and they come to yield him account, and nothing is hid from him, insomuch as the angels have not any proper or peculiar authority in themselves; and that although they be called powers, principalities, and virtues, it is not for that God has resigned his own office unto them, it is not for that he has despoiled himself of his own power, it is not for that he himself abides idle in heaven, but it is for that the angels are instruments of his power, to the end it should be spread out over all.

St Paul says, that Jesus Christ is come to gather together the things that are in heaven and earth. And thereby he shows, that the angels have their steadfastness in the grace of our Lord Jesus Christ, forasmuch as he is the Mediator between God and his creatures. True it is that Jesus Christ redeemed not the angels, for they needed not to be ransomed from death, whereunto they were not yet fallen ; but yet was he their Mediator. And how so? To the intent to join them unto God in all perfection, and afterwards to maintain them by his grace, that they may be preserved from falling.

When men utter all the force which they have, practising this and that to destroy us, yea, and when the devil himself rises up against us, we must not be afraid. Why so? Because God has his heavenly armies to defend us, according as it is said that the angels encamp themselves round about us, and that he has appointed his angels to guide us, so as the faithful person shall not stumble. We see then that the infinite number of angels serves to comfort us, to the end we might be sure that God will succour us at our need, and that he has wherewith to do it. But like as the faithful that lean unto God, and submit themselves to him with all humility, are preserved by the multitude of the angels ; even so, all they that strive against him, all they that are proud, and all they that are sturdy, must be enforced to fear him, and to understand that when they set themselves after that fashion against God, they have to do with many enemies besides, insomuch that all the power that is in the angels shall fall upon them to overwhelm them, and all creatures shall serve to maintain the glory of him by whose power they have their being. And therefore let us remember well this sentence, where it is said, that the armies of God are without number, and thereupon let us assure ourselves, that it is to no purpose for men to conspire against us, for when they shall have assembled all their forces together, yet shall they not be too strong for us, but God shall always get the upper hand of them. Wherefore let us not deceive ourselves when we see ourselves well accompanied, and a great number of people gathered about us. And why? For we may all be confounded in one moment by the hand and power of God. Again, although he alone be enough, either to save us or to destroy us, yet moreover he hath his armies ready furnished after an incomprehensible manner, which shall set upon us whensoever he thinks good. Therefore, let us stand in fear, and let us learn not to be proud when we see the world hold on our side, and a great power to maintain us. For all that gear shall stand us in no stead, considering the great power of God that is declared here. And hereby a man may see how sore the unbelief of men is blinded. For it is put to our choice whether we will have the angels of heaven to watch about us, and to guard us, and to be servants of our welfare; or whether we will have them against us, and to be our deadly enemies. Behold, God uses such goodness and grace towards us, that he appointed his angels to do us service, as the Scripture vouches, he will have us guarded by them, and therewithal he affirms them to be powers, as who should say, he stretches out his hand over us to the end he might maintain us. Of whom then is it long that we be not guided by the angels, and that they guard us not from all harm? It is even long of ourselves who cannot take the benefit that is offered us. We needed no more but to receive it, and what do we? We are so far off from receiving the good turn that God offers us, that in derogation of his majesty we fall to provoking of his angels to arm themselves to our ruin and confusion. Needs then must we be bereft of our right mind, and as it were bewitched of the devil, when we had rather to have the angels to be our enemies, than the ministers of our welfare, for they be ready to help us and to guide us, so we be members of our Lord Jesus Christ, and yield obedience unto him as our head.

If the angels do rejoice among themselves in heaven, when they see restored into their company that which was lost, it becomes us that are in the same and like estate with them to be partakers of the same joy. But how is it that he says that the angels do rejoice more at the repentance of one wicked man, than at the perseverance of many righteous, whom nothing more delights than a continual and just course of righteousness ? I answer, though it should more agree with the desires of the angels, as it is also more to be desired, that men should always continue in pure integrity, yet, because the mercy of God does more appear in the deliverance of a sinner, who now had been given over to destruction, and had fallen off as a rotten member from the body, he attributes to the angels, after the manner of men, the greater joy for this good unlooked or unhoped for.

It ought to make our hair stand on end to see men revolt and slide back from God, and forsake the faith and allegiance which once they promised him. Neither can it be, but men of any good heart will be deeply touched with extreme sorrow at the beholding of such a woful spectacle. We read how the angels rejoice at the conversion of a sinner, and, therefore, they are much grieved at the perdition of any one of them. But how much more heavy and sorrowful are they when they behold the ruin and destruction of a whole city and church.

XXXII —BAD ANGELS

As FOR such things as the Scripture teaches concerning devils, they tend in a manner all to this end, that we may be careful to beware beforehand of their awaits and preparations, and furnish ourselves with such weapons as are strong and sure enough to drive away even the strongest enemies. For whereas Satan is called the god and prince of the world, whereas he is named the strong armed man, the spirit that has power of the air, and a roaring lion, these descriptions serve to no other purpose but to make us more wary and watchful, and readier to enter into battle with him. Which is also sometimes set out in express words. For Peter, after he had said that the devil goes about like a roaring lion seeking whom he may devour, by and by adds this exhortation, that we strongly resist him by faith. And Paul, after he had given warning that we wrestle not with flesh and blood, but with the princes of the air, the powers of darkness, and spiritual wickedness, by and by bids us put on such armour as may serve for so great and dangerous a battle. Wherefore let us also apply all to this end, that being warned how there doth continually approach upon us an enemy, yea, an enemy that is in courage most hardy, in strength most mighty, in policy most subtle, in diligence and celerity unweariable, with all sorts of engines plenteously furnished, in skill of war most ready, we suffer not ourselves, by sloth and cowardice to be surprised, but on the other side with bold and hardy minds set our foot to resist him and (because this war is only ended by death), encourage ourselves to continue. But specially, knowing our own weakness and unskilfulness, let us call upon the help of God, and enterprise nothing but upon trust of him, for as much as it is in him only to give us policy, strength, courage, and armour.

And that we should be the more stirred up and enforced so to do, the Scripture warns us that there are not one or two, or a few enemies, but great armies that make war with us. For it is said, that Mary Magdalene was delivered from seven devils, wherewith she was possessed. And Christ says, that it is the ordinary custom, that if, after a devil be once cast out, a man make the place open again, he brings seven spirits worse than himself, and returns into his possession, finding it empty. Yea it is said that a whole legion besieged one man. Hereby, therefore, we are taught, that we must fight with an infinite multitude of enemies, lest, despising the fewness of them, we should be more slack to enter in battle, or thinking that we have some respite in the meantime granted, we should give ourselves to idleness. Whereas many times Satan or the devil is named in the singular number, thereby is meant that power of wickedness which stands against the kingdom of justice. For as the church and the fellowship of saints have Christ to their head, so the faction of the wicked is pointed out unto us with their prince, that has the chief authority among them. After which manner this is spoken, Go, ye cursed, into eternal fire that is prepared for the devil and his angels.

Here, also, this ought to stir us up to a perpetual war with the devil, for that he is every where called the enemy of God and of us. For if we have regard of God's glory, as it is meet we should, then ought we with all our force to bend ourselves against him that goes about to extinguish it. If we are affectioned to maintain the kingdom of Christ as we ought, then must we needs have an unappeasable war with him that conspires the ruin thereof. Again, if any care of our own safety do touch us, then ought we to have neither peace nor truce with him that continually lies in wait for the destruction of it. Such a one is he described in the third chapter of Genesis, where he leadeth man away from the obedience that he did owe to God, that he both robs God of his due honour, and throws man himself headlong into destruction. Such a one, also, is he set forth in the Evangelists, where he is called an enemy, and is said to scatter tares to corrupt the seed of eternal life. In sum, that which Christ testified of him, that from the beginning he was a murderer, and a liar, we find by experience

in all his doings. For he assails the truth of God with
lies, obscures the light with darkness, entangles the
minds of men with errors, raises up hatreds, kindles contentions and strifes, does all things to this end to overthrow the kingdom of God, and drown men with himself in eternal destruction. Whereby it appears, that he
is of nature froward, spiteful, and malicious. For needs
must there be great frowardness in that wit that is made
to assail the glory of God and salvation of men. And
that doth John speak of in his Epistle, when he wrote,
that he sinned from the beginning. For he means that
he is the author, captain, and principal workman of all
malice and wickedness.

But forasmuch as the devil was created by God, let us
remember that this malice which we assign in this nature, is not by creation, but by depravation. For whatsoever damnable thing he has, he has gotten to himself by
his own revolting and fall. Which the Scripture therefore
gives us warning of, lest thinking that he came out such a
one from God, we should ascribe that to God himself which
is farthest from him. For this reason does Christ say
that Satan speaks of his own when he speaks lies, and
adds a cause why, for that he stood not still in the truth.
Now, when he says that he stood not still in the truth,
he shows that once he had been in the truth. And when
he makes him the father of lying, he takes this from him,
that he cannot lay that fault to God whereof he himself
is cause to himself. Although these things be but shortly
and not very plainly spoken, yet this is enough for this
purpose, to deliver the majesty of God from all slander.
And what makes it matter to us, to know more or to
any other purpose concerning devils? Many, perhaps,
do grudge that the Scripture does not orderly and dis-
tinctly in many places set forth that fall, and the cause,
manner, time, and fashion thereof. But because these
things do nothing pertain to us, it was better, if not to
be suppressed wholly, yet to be but lightly touched,

and that partly because it was not beseeming for the Holy Ghost to feed curiosity with vain histories without any fruit: and we see that it was the Lord's purpose to put nothing in his holy oracles, but that which we should learn to edification. Therefore, lest we ourselves should tarry long upon things superfluous, let us be content shortly to know thus much concerning the nature of devils, that at the first creation they were the angels of God: but by swerving out of kind, they both destroyed themselves, and are become instruments of destruction to others. Thus much, because it was profitable to be known, is plainly taught in Peter and Jude. God spared not his angels which had sinned, and not kept their beginning, but had forsaken their dwelling-place. And Paul, naming the elect angels, does, without doubt, secretly by implication set the reprobate angels in comparison against them.

Because God bows the unclean Spirits hither and thither as pleases him: he so tempers this government that they exercise the faithful with battle, they set upon them out of ambushes, they assail them with invasions, they press them with fighting, and oftentimes weary them, trouble them, make them afraid, and sometimes wound them, but never overcome nor oppress them. But the wicked they subdue and draw away, they reign upon their souls and bodies, and abuse them as bond-slaves to all mischievous doings. As for the faithful, because they are unquieted of such enemies, therefore they hear these exhortations:—Do not give place to the devil; the devil your enemy goes about like a roaring lion seeking whom he may devour, whom resist ye, being strong in faith, and such like. Paul confesses that he himself was not free from this kind of strife, when he says, that for a remedy to tame pride, the angel of Satan was given to him, by whom he might be humbled. This exercise, therefore, is common to all the children of God: but because that same promise of the breaking of Satan's head pertains generally to Christ and to all his members, therefore the faithful can never be overcome nor oppressed by him. They are many times stricken down, but they are never so astounded withal but that they recover themselves. They fall down many times with violence of strokes, but they are after raised up again; they are wounded, but not deadly. Finally, they so labour in all the course of their life, that in the end they obtain the victory. But I speak not this of every doing of theirs; for we know that by the just vengeance of God, David was for a time given over to Satan, by his motion to number the people: and not without cause, Paul said, there is hope of pardon, although many have been entangled with the snares of the devil. Therefore, in another place, the same Paul says, that the promise above alleged is begun in this life, wherein we must wrestle, and is performed after our wrestling is ended, when he says the God of peace shall shortly beat down Satan under your feet. This victory has always fully been in our head, Christ, because the prince of the world had nothing in him; but in us that are his members it does now partly appear, and shall be perfected, when, being unclothed of our flesh, by which we are yet subject to weakness, we shall be full of the power of the Holy Ghost. In this manner, when the kingdom of Christ is raised up and advanced, Satan with his power falls down, as the Lord himself says,—I saw Satan fall as lightning down from heaven; for by this answer he confirms that which the Apostles had reported of the power of his preaching. Again, when the prince possesses his own palace, all things that he possesses are in peace, but when there comes a stronger, he is thrown out, &c. And to this end Christ, in dying, overcame Satan, who had the power of death, and triumphed upon all his armies, that they should not hurt the Church, for otherwise they would every moment a hundred times destroy it; for, considering what is our weakness and what is his furious strength, how could we stand, yea, never so little time against his manifold and continual assaults, but being supported by the victory of our captain? Therefore, God suffers not the devil to reign over the souls of the faithful, but only delivers him the wicked and unbelieving to govern, whom God does not vouchsafe to have reckoned in his flock. For it is said that he possesses this world without controversy till he is thrust out by Christ. Again, that he does blind all them that believe not the Gospel. Again, that he performs his work in the stubborn children, and worthily, for all the wicked are the vessels of his wrath. Therefore, to whom should they be rather subject than to the minister of God's vengeance? Finally, they are said to be of their father the devil, because as the faithful are hereby known to be the children of God because they bear his image, so they are the image of Satan, into which they have gone out of kind, and are properly discerned to be his children.

As we have before confuted that trifling philosophy concerning the Holy Angels which teaches that they are nothing else but good inspirations or motions which God stirs up in the minds of men; so in this place must we confute them that fondly say that devils are nothing else but evil affections and perturbations of the mind that are thrust into us by our flesh. That may we shortly do, because there are many testimonies of Scripture, and those plain enough upon this point. First, where the unclean spirits are called angels, apostates, which have swerved out of kind from their beginning; the very names do sufficiently express that they are not motions or affections of minds, but rather, indeed, as they are called minds, or spirits endued with sense and understanding. Likewise, whereas both Christ and John do compare the children of God with the children of the devil: were it not an unfit comparison, if the name of the devil signified nothing else but evil inspirations? And John adds, somewhat more plainly, that the devil sins from the beginning. Likewise, when Jude brings in Michael the archangel fighting with the devil, doubtless he sets against the good angel an evil and rebellious angel. Wherewith agrees that which is read in the history of Job, that Satan appeared with the holy angels before God. But most plain of all, are those places that make mention of the punishment which they begin to feel by the judgment of God, and specially shall feel at the resurrection. Son of David, why art thou come before the time to torment us? Again, go, ye cursed, into the eternal fire that is prepared for the devil and his angels. Again, if he spared not his own angels that had sinned, but cast them down into hell, and delivered them into chains of darkness to be kept unto damnation, &c., how fond should these speeches be,— that the devils are ordained to eternal judgment, that fire is prepared for them, that they are now already tormented and vexed by the glory of Christ, if there were no devils at all? But because the matter needs no disputation among them that believe the word of the Lord, and little good is done with testimonies of Scripture among those vain students of speculation whom nothing pleases but that which is new, I suppose I have performed that which I purposed; that is, that the godly minds should be furnished against such fond errors, wherewith unquiet men trouble both themselves and others that are more simple. But it was good to touch this, lest any entangled with that error, while they think they have none to stand against them, should wax more slow and unprovided to resist.

If we may receive conjectures, it is more likely that he was moved with a certain outrageous madness, as commonly the desperate sort of men are, that he might carry man with him for company into everlasting destruction. But we ought to content ourselves with this reason, that he being the enemy of God, went to overthrow the order which he had set; because he could not pull God out of his throne, he assailed man, in whom his image shined. Man being overthrown, he knew that the horrible confusion of the whole world should follow, even as it came to pass. Therefore, he sought to oppress the glory of God in the person of man.

The Holy Ghost meant to do us to understand, that not only the angels of heaven which obey God willingly, and are holy inclined, and given that way, do yield account unto him, but also the devils of hell, which are enemies and rebels to him to the uttermost of their power, which labour to subvert his Majesty, and practise to confound all things, so as they may be forced, spite of their teeth, to be subject unto God, and to yield him account of all their doings, and cannot do any thing without his permission and leave. Thus ye see in what wise Satan appeared among the angels; but yet, by the way, the manner of their dealing is divers. For when the angels guide us, and do the thing that God has commanded, they have the nature to apply themselves unto him, and have none other inclination but to obey him, and he on the other side dwells and reigns in them by his Holy Spirit. Lo, here the cause why we say, Thy will be done on earth as it is in heaven. Because we see so much counterfeiting, and so many horrible rebellions against God here below, we desire him to settle his kingdom peaceably here as it is aloft, where his angels are wholly obedient unto him. But the devils obey him as enforced, that is to say, not of their own good will, but because God compels them. They would with all their heart resist his power, and oppress him if they could, but they are fain to follow him in all points whithersoever he lists to lead them.

True it is that we see not Satan, nor perceive not by eyesight what he prepares and practises to our destruction, and therefore have we so much the more cause to be afraid of his guiles and policies. Lo, here the cause why Saint Paul says, that our fighting is not against flesh and blood. For hereby he means, that if we had to deal with visible enemies, we might well escape their hands by some shift or other, and we might find the means to resist them. But behold, says he, they be spiritual guiles that fight against us, of whom we have no sight at all, except God give us the eyes of faith to espy how Satan is against us, specially by the temptations that he triumphs in our way, whereby he urges us to evil, and labours to mar us. So then we must fully resolve ourselves of this point, namely, that the devils are always busy to procure our destruction, that they go about the earth, that they are never away from us, that they are ever seeking means to get unto us, and that as soon as they find never so small a breach, they enter unto us to throw us into endless destruction, and we are surprised before we mistrust that we are assailed, according as every man knows by experience, that we perceive not when the devil is near us, and yet in the mean-while we see ourselves wounded to death. Wherefore, when we feel any wicked desire in ourselves, so as we are carried, some to one lewd lust, and some to another, we must mark that it is the enemy that works so craftily. And thus we find by experience, that the devils are ever practising against us, specially against those to whom God has given wisdom and knowledge. For although the devil possess the wicked and reprobates, and work in them with all effectualness, as Saint Paul speaks to the Thessalonians, yet perceive they not that the devil is any thing, and they make but a sport of their vices ; they are so bewitched in evil, as they feel it not a whit, for they are become blockish, as Saint Paul says in another place. But when the faithful find their minds attainted with any evil affection, and that Satan has prevailed so much as to make entrance into them, they know that Satan has prevented them unawares, and that they perceived not when he gave them battle or alarm. We must not tarry till we have such an assault, but we must be afraid, and take heed to that which is said. For God shows the care which he has of us, and how it is not his will we should be taken unawares for want of knowing our adversaries, when he says that the devils go about the earth continually hunting after their prey. If a man should tell us that enemies were at hand, and that there were certain bands coming upon us, every one of us would stand upon his guard, and devise all means possible to defend ourselves and to withstand them. And why so? Because we are fleshly, and have a care to preserve this transitory life. But behold, our enemy Satan has store of wiles and subtleties more dangerous and mischievous than all the enemies in the world; his desire is to cast us all headlong into destruction; we know what strength he is of; as has been declared already, it is expressly said that he is at hand with us, and that he besieges us on all sides, and that he has a thousand ways to wind about us. When all this is told us, and yet we are never the worse, is it not a token of more than beastly blockishness, and that we have no mind at all of the heavenly life, and that we conceive no more than we see, like as the brute beasts do? But when it is told us that Satan ceases not to go about the world, but continually follows the chase, and is never idle, we must profit ourselves by that doctrine. And why? Because he being the enemy of our welfare, desires nothing else but to lead us into the same destruction whereunto he himself is come.

We must also mark, that the devil is always at our elbow to overthrow us if he can, so as if we escape from him on the one side, he stirs up a new temptation again on the other side. To be short, that which is said in one word in Zechariah, is declared to us here at large, that is to wit, that Satan is the accuser and the adversary of all the children of God; according also, as in the Apocalypse it is said, that he is the accuser of our brethren. And it is expressly shown unto Zechariah in that vision, that

Satan did set himself to accuse Joshua the high priest as the head of the Church, and as a figure of our Lord Jesus Christ, whom he came thither to accuse before God. And so, considering that we have so strong a party, and that Satan labours by all means possible to throw us down, notwithstanding that we have been long time fenced by the hand of God, we perceive we have great need that Jesus Christ should be our advocate, and that he should maintain us by his power against Satan, that we are not entrapped by his wiles and policies. Thus we see whereof we are warned in this sentence, to the end we should betake ourselves to God, beseeching him to strengthen us against the temptations of Satan, in such wise as we may never be vanquished, forasmuch as the Lord shall establish us in the invincible power of his Holy Spirit.

We see then how we ought to keep good ward and watch, and to stand upon our guard, to pray unto God that he suffer us not to be left up for a prey unto Satan. For if Satan durst be so hardy as to offer battle to the Saviour of the world, according as we see how our Lord Jesus Christ was assailed, we may be sure he will be more hardy to run upon us. And therefore, let us take the armour that God has given us to resist him withal, which is his word, whereunto Saint Paul sends us, when he means to arm us thoroughly against all the temptations of the world and the devil.

We must not be afraid although Satan have such a power, and that he be called the prince of the world. I say we need not be afraid that he should overwhelm us, so long as we are armed with faith. For we shall have strength enough, and we shall be sure of the victory, if we rest upon God, and lean unto the grace of our Lord Jesus Christ. The Father, says he, which has put you into my hand, is stronger than all. Fear you not that Satan shall overcome his Maker. For God has put us into the hands of our Lord Jesus Christ, to the intent that he should be the good and faithful keeper both of

our souls and of our bodies. Therefore let us rest ourselves upon him : but yet let us not cease to be still
wary and careful. Such as are negligent shall find themselves overtaken at every blow. For as for the sureness
which we have in God, it makes us not dull, nor to forget our own dangers, wherein we are ; but only upholds
us that we quail not in fighting. But as for them that
are drowsy and flatter themselves, they despise God's
aid and relief. Our Lord says, I will hold you up, be
not afraid, for although Satan give charge upon you with
thundering assaults, and that it seems to you that all
shall go to wreck, yet shall you be safe under me, and
under my hand. But when he says so, his meaning is
not that men should presume upon themselves and go no
further; but, contrariwise, he says, come to me, retire
yourselves under my protection, that I may be your fortress against them that devise mischief towards you.
And since we find ourselves assailed of so many enemies,
it behoves us so much the more to know what great
need we have of God's help, and that when we are under
his protection, we are sure, that neither Satan nor all
the wicked men in the world can bring that thing about
which they have enterprised against us. Let us mark,
then, how the devil is painted out lively unto us, and
that when the Holy Ghost says, that he ceases not to
keep his courses and circuits about the earth, it stands
us on hand to keep always sure watch, and to be evermore awake of purpose to pray unto God, and to have our
recourse unto him, and also to arm ourselves more and
more with faith, that we may enter into the field of
battle to fight courageously, until such time as God
grant us to enjoy the victory that he has promised us.

Christ assaults the devil with open defiance, so that
he casts him clean out, and leaves him not any place to
rest in. He overthrows him not on the one side, that he
may be stronger on the other, but he utterly overthrows
all his devices. Therefore Christ reasons aptly that he

has no fellowship with him; for this father of deceit has no other purpose but to uphold and maintain his kingdom.

We know that the devil is called, in divers places, the prince of the world. And the tyrannous government which he holds is fortified on every side with strong defences; for there are many snares to entrap men with, and he holds them that are now subject unto him in such bands, so that they rather nourish that servitude, wherein they are bound, rather than by any means aspire to liberty. Also, there are innumerable sorts of dangers, by the which he holds them miserably overwhelmed under his feet. To be short, there is nothing to the contrary, but that he may without resistance rule as a tyrant in the world, not that he can do any thing without the will of the Maker, but because that Adam, by estranging himself from the power of God, brought himself and his posterity under this strange and miserable servitude. But though the devil reigns against nature, and that by the just judgment of God, men are subject to his tyranny for their sins; yet he holds that kingdom in quiet possession, so that he triumphs over us without resistance until a stronger than he shall arise. But there is not a stronger to be found on earth, for there is no power in men to help themselves, therefore a Redeemer was promised from heaven. Now Christ shows that this manner of redemption is necessary, that he should by strong hands wrest from the devil that which he will never let go, except he be enforced.

Before that Christ makes us partakers of his power, the enemy reigns in us, as it were in play and sport. But being driven out, he sorrows the loss of his prey, he gathers new forces, and stirs all the powers he has, that he may overthrow us again. Therefore it is said metaphorically, that he walks through dry places; for his banishment is grievous to him, and his dwelling out of men is like to a filthy desert. In the same sense, also, he says, that he seeks rest so long as he is out of men; because that then he frets and torments himself, and he ceases not to try every way until he recover that he has lost. Wherefore let us learn, as soon as Christ calls us, there is a hot and a sharp combat prepared for us; for though he attempts to destroy all men, and that saying of Peter appertains to all without exception, that he goes about like a roaring lion, seeking whom he may devour, yet we are plainly taught by these words of Christ, that he burns with greater hatred, and is carried with more envious force, against them which are taken out of his snares. But this admonition ought not to make us afraid, but to stir us up, to make us diligent in keeping our watches, and that being armed with spiritual armours, we may be strong to resist him.

XXXIII —TEMPTATIONS

THERE are three degrees of faultiness in a sin, although it come not to the outward deed. The first is a fleeting imagination or thought which a man conveys by the beholding of any thing; for thereupon some one toy or other will come in his head, or else, although he see nothing, yet notwithstanding his mind is so tickle unto evil, as it carries him here and there, and makes many fancies to run in his head. And out of doubt the same is a faultiness, but yet is not that imputed unto us for sin. The second degree is, that upon the conceiving of such a fancy we are somewhat tickled, and feel that our will sways that way, and although there be no consent or agreeing unto it, yet notwithstanding there is some inward pricking to provoke us unto it; now that is a wicked sin, and as it were already conceived; afterward follows consent when we settle our will upon it, so as there is no hinderance in us for the performance of the evil but the want of occasion and opportunity ; there ye see the third degree, and then is the sin fully shapen in us, although there be no outward deed at all.

Hereby we are warned to look well to ourselves, that we are not so swallowed up of sorrow as to be cast into despair, by considering too much our own frailty. And it is a very profitable lesson ; for there is nothing that we ought to desire so much as to humble ourselves. And why so ? For it is the only wicket that we have to receive all God's graces in at. So long as men are sore possessed with pride, so as they ween themselves worth any thing, you shall see them so locked up as the grace of God can never enter into them. Then must humility go before ; and the chief of our studies ought to be to bethink ourselves well what we are, to the end we may have no trust nor self-liking in ourselves. For behold the craftiness of Satan ; the thing that is most profitable and available for men's salvation, he takes and makes it a rank poison against them. For he finds a way to make men, as it were, brutish, by knowledge of their miseries, insomuch as they become so mad that they cast themselves into despair. True it is that the devil, if he could, would continually sot us with the folly of overweening ; he would make us to believe wonders of ourselves ; he will never suffer men to humble and abase themselves ; he will hinder them from that as much as he can. But when he sees that he cannot hinder men from being abashed in themselves by knowing their own state, then he goes to the other shift. And here I see you are overmastered ; for he will set his feet upon men's bellies, yea, and upon their throats, and hold them still at that point, even till he have forced them to despair. For this cause, when we enter into the consideration of our own wants, let us be well advised, that after we have bethought us of them, we are not utterly overwhelmed so as we should not in the mean-while always acknowledge the good things that God has done

for us and put into us, and which he bestows upon us
continually, together with the remedies which he has given us to relieve those wants wherein we should have
rotted, had not God's extraordinary goodness been.
Then let us learn to know this, to the end we may take
our breath.

Let every one of us consider advisedly the good turns
that God has done him, and let him mark them, and note
him, that he may bear them in mind. Very well, God
has succoured me at such a pinch, I have felt his help
in such a case, I have been aided at his hand, and he has
made me to perceive his mighty power after such and
such fashion. After this manner must we make rehearsal
of God's benefits, and of his helping of us all the time
of our life. And after as he has uttered himself unto us,
so must we be the more confirmed to trust to his promises, and to rest wholly upon them. Herewithal let
us be established in invincible constancy to go which
way soever he leads us, without fear of any distress.
Why so? For my God, who has never forsaken me to
this day, will not give me over now. As I have felt,
heretofore, that he gives strength to those that are his,
so am I sure that he will reach me his hand and succour
me still. So then there is no more for me to do but to
commit myself unto him. I see that this thing and
that thing may cumber me; there are a number of temptations which may make me turn head; but yet forasmuch as my God has succoured me hitherto at my need,
I doubt not but that he will do the like unto the end.
Thus you see that the way for us to eschew the blame
of unthankfulness is to call God's benefits oftentimes to
our remembrance, thereby to strengthen ourselves still
in trust that he will never fail us unto the end. Also,
this will serve to make us overcome all temptations;
and although the devil have never so many means and
stops to turn us out of the right way, yet shall we not
cease to go on still. And why? Because the hope

which we shall have gathered of God's former making of us to feel his goodness will serve to carry us over all tempests in the midst of the sea; it will be as a boat, or as a ship, or as a bridge, to convey us safely over.

Let us learn, then, to make such account of the strength of our God, as that we may, by the power of his Spirit, get the upper hand in all encounters that he brings us unto, for he will not have us to be idle in this present life. He could well enough set us in quiet at the first instant, so as we should not be troubled any manner of way, nor the world make war against us, nor we be tempted at all by our own flesh, and that Satan should be far off from us. God, I say, could well maintain us in ease at the first instant : but he intends to try our patience ; for he will have us to be men of war. Wherefore, let us on our side fight, yea, let us fight lustily, and if our enemies be too strong for us, let us flee for refuge to the help that our Lord has promised us, and we shall overcome all hinderances if we fight in the strength of God. But yet let us mark that we must fight unto death, and not die once only ; but have death present daily.

This is a very perilous temptation when we are persuaded that we ought not to obey God, but so far as we have a reason of the commandment. For it is a true rule of obedience, when we, being contented with the bare commandment, persuade ourselves that all which he commands is just and right. But whosoever desires to be wise beyond measure, first shakes off the reverence of God, and then is by and by carried by Satan into open rebellion.

They are idle triflers who endeavour to lay the blame of their vices upon God ; for all evil, of whatever nature, springs from no other foundation than the perverse lust of man. And thus it is evident that every one's own wicked passions are his instigators to sin, and guide him in the commission of wickedness. And he proves that

God tempted no man from this, that God is not tempted with evil. For it is on this account that the devil entices to sin, because he is wholly inflamed with a furious desire of sinning, but God desires not evil, neither can he be the promoter of wicked conduct in us.

XXXIV — AFFLICTIONS

God trys those that are his, sifting them by afflictions, and casting them as it were gold into a furnace, not only to purge them, but also to make them known, for to those two purposes do afflictions serve, that is to wit, God kills the vices that are in us. For when he punishes us, then are we tamed, and he commands us to withdraw ourselves from the world, and not to be given to our pleasures and fleshly delights. But there is yet a further thing, that is to wit, that like as in a furnace, gold is tried to know whether it have any dross in it, so also God shows what we are by afflicting us; for men know not themselves before they have been so proved. Before we have passed through the sieve, we seem to ourselves to fear God, and that there is nothing to be misliked in us, and yet all the while there are many vices in us, that we know not of. It is God that shows them unto us, it is he that makes us to perceive them; when he sends us any trouble, or any adversity, then find we what our infirmity is. Now if God make the afflictions of his faithful ones to serve them as a mirror wherein to behold themselves, it is much more likely that they will show what is in other men, whether they have faith and obedience in their hearts or no, and whether they be hypocrites, or whether they serve him in truth.

We see how the present afflictions blind us. If it be summer, and that we be over hot, for we must take these familiar examples, it seems one of the painfullest troubles that a man can endure, especially if a man be so overladen that he faint, and be not able to hold out any further, he would have a frost that should cleave the stones, and he thinks he should be well refreshed, and that he should be the more at his ease. And if it be winter, we will think that no heat can be too great for us. Lo how the present passions carry us away; and this befals to all men. Yet notwithstanding, some are much more tender and nice to suffer adversity than others are. Therefore, according as each man's nature and complexion is, thereafter doth he torment himself with the adversity that he endures, and thereafter doth he martyr himself to the uttermost. Forasmuch as we see such experiences, we know that men are carried away by their affections, in such ways as they think upon nothing but the thing that grieves and torments them.

If we mind to comfort our neighbours in their heaviness and troubles, we must not go to it at random as many men do, which have no more songs but one, and have no regard at all to whom they sing it. For some men must be handled after one fashion, and some men after another. As for example, if there be one that is stubborn against God, in that case a man must speak with another manner of style and terms, than to a poor creature that hath walked always in simplicity. And so according as the malady is, it is needful that a man be warned to proceed thereafter. As for example, if men be dullards, they must be cried unto, and their negligence must be rebuked, to the intent they may feel the hand of God, and humble themselves under the same. Therefore we have need of great wisdom if we will comfort those whom God afflicts as we ought to do.

Let us be sure that whensoever we endure any afflictions, the same is God's punishment for our sins, and, therefore, that we may bear them patiently, let us assure ourselves we have deserved much more. Nevertheless let us be bold to flee unto our God, praying him to vouchsafe to cleanse us from all our unrighteousness, which is the cause of the miseries that we endure in this present life ; and that it may please him to bear with our infirmities, and make us feel his goodness, to the end we may always have occasion to glorify him even until he has despatched us out of this flightful life, to make us partakers of his everlasting glory.

And let us pray to this good God that it may please him to have always regard of our infirmities whensoever he shall afflict us ; and that forasmuch as it is good reason that we should be inured unto patience so long as we are in this world, although we are forced to pass through many thorns and divers heart-griefs and vexations of mind, yet nevertheless our good God will so arm us with his strength as we may not quail. And that forasmuch as our life is a corruptible and ruinous cabin, he will hold us up in our feebleness even unto the end, and until such time as he has rid us quite and clean of the infirmities of our flesh; and that therewithal, we also having our recourse unto the fatherly goodness which he uses towards us, may be succoured by him in all our necessities, not doubting at all but he will bring us to the salvation which he has promised us, assuring ourselves, that if we persist in his obeisance, we shall never be disappointed; and that if we stick unto his promises, he will never fail to have his hand stretched out over us to succour us.

Whensoever God sends a man any affliction, let him bethink himself, that besides the common miseries of this flightful life, God intends to give him particular instruction. And let us not say, why does not this man or that man deserve to be chastised as well as I, according to the common manner, which is, that every man would be privileged above others. Nay, let every one of us yield to receive the rod patiently at God's hand, assuring ourselves that he chastises us measurably, and as he knows to be for our profit.

Let us be admonished, therefore, that the faithful are subject unto divers temptations, so as they are first tried by war, then by sicknesses; yea, sometimes afflictions come in so thick and threefold upon them without intermission, that they endure combats all their life long? Why so? To teach them, that when one billow is over, they must expect another to follow presently. For they ought to be in such readiness, that if the Lord should be pleased to heap sorrow upon sorrow, yet they must not break in sunder, nor yet be discouraged under any calamity whatsoever. If he give them leave a little to take breath, let them know he does it in respect of their weakness; but I advise such not to imagine that these short truces should presage any time of peace unto them; no, let them rather in the mean-while gather more strength, that having finished their course, they may look for rest when they have attained the quiet haven of God's kingdom.

We see man die, we see the faithful persecuted here below, subject to a thousand afflictions, and yet a man should persuade himself that there is no more hope of salvation, all is accomplished and done, and we do in vain look for the coming of our Lord Jesus Christ, and have this hope, that he will deliver us out of this corruptible life to make us partakers of his heavenly glory, —that all this is beaten down and come to nothing, is not this an horrible and cursed thing?

This is our highest and incomparable dignity, that we are admitted into the society of angels, yea, made joint heirs with Christ. Those who set a proper value on this great kindness of God will lightly esteem all other things. Therefore neither poverty, nor contempt, nor nakedness, nor hunger, nor thirst, shall so distract their minds, but they may support themselves with this consolation—since the Lord has bestowed on me the chief good, it becomes me to bear the want of inferior blessings with resignation and a patient mind.

WHATSOEVER we do, we should always have death before our eyes, and be provoked to think upon it. This is well known among men—the very heathen had skill to say so. But what for that? Every man can play the doctor in teaching other men that, which is contained here, and yet in the mean-while there is never a good scholar of us all in this behalf. For there is not any man which shows by his doings, that ever he knew what it is to be consumed from morning to evening; that is to wit, that all his lustiness is but feebleness, and that there is no steadfastness in us, to hold ourselves in one continual state ; but that we always haste towards death, and death towards us, so as we must needs come thither at length. Verily if we had no more but this single doctrine alone, it would stand us in no stead, but to make us storm and torment ourselves ; like as when the Paynims knew that our life was so flightful, they concluded thereupon, that it was best never to be born, and that the sooner we died the better it was for us. Lo how the Paynims rejected the grace of God, because they knew not the honour that he does us when he sends us into this world, even to show himself a father towards us. For inasmuch as we are reasonable creatures, and have the image of God printed in our nature, we have a record that he holds us here as his children. And to despise such a grace, and to say, it had been better for us never to have been created, is it not apparent blasphemy ?

It is a melancholy matter, insomuch that if a man speak of death, every man is grieved at it, and falls into his dumps. Nevertheless the case so stands, that if men set not their minds upon it, they must needs overshoot themselves in all their devices, and in all their consultations, and all the greatest wisdom that they wish to have must needs be turned into foolishness. And wherefore; for is there any greater folly than for a man not to know himself—to what purpose serve all our wisdom and discretion, but to look to ourselves? And so they that think not upon death, nor put themselves in mind of it, overshoot themselves as much as is possible for them. Yea, they could find in their hearts to play the wild colts in forgetting themselves. We see then how it is all one, as if men meant to bury all the wit and reason that God has given them.

If a faithful man die at the age of thirty years, what does he? It seems not that he is greatly sorry for it, he makes no great struggling against it as we see the unbelievers do; yea, when they are even as stale as earth, as the Proverb says, behold a despiser of God and a worldling who never thought upon death; and when it comes to the point that God will pinch him in good earnest, it will make him grind his teeth and fret with himself, wishing to withstand death, and saying, can I not prolong my life one year longer? He takes himself to be a piece of green wood that crackles on all sides. Contrariwise, when a faithful person dies, although he endures much, yet he betakes himself unto God, and comforts himself in him; and although there is striving seen in his body, yet has he his mind quiet, and he desires nothing but to frame himself to God's good will, choosing rather to die when God calls him than to live here. To be short, he desires nothing but to obey his good heavenly father. We see, then, how God does always ripen his servants before he call them out of the world, so as they are fully satisfied when they come to their graves; and he that brings but twenty years to his grave is more ripe than another that shall bring (as you would say) a million of years with him; according as we see how the unbelievers do fret and chafe themselves against God when he calls them, so as they are never ripe nor old enough.

Let every body submit themselves to this order of

God's, that we may be able to say, that like as he has set us in the world, so also it is good reason he should take us hence again, not at our pleasure but at his. For it is not without cause that he hath limited the race of our life, and that it pleases him to take away one rather than the other. We being mortal before we come into this world, for a young babe may die as well in his mother's womb as after it is born. Since it is so, as soon as God gives us discretion let us apply our endeavours to understand that death besieges us every minute of an hour, and that we must not promise ourselves life till the next morrow, nor set any term to God: for his daily prolonging our life is but so much respiting of us. But howsoever we fare, let us be mindful of our own frailty, and let the same lead us to consider that if God take us out of this world, sooner than we looked for, it is meet that he should have us at commandment, and that every one of us should offer up our own bodies to him in that manner of sacrifice, in suffering God to separate us asunder, that what friendship or bond of kindred there have been betwixt us, yet we may not fail to glorify God when he takes away our kinsfolk and friends, nor use this beastly impatience, in pulling ourselves by the hair of our heads, and in scratching and disfiguring our faces, as though we knew not what it were to live in the obedience of God, and to die in the same likewise.

Again, have we not Jesus Christ for our guide? Then let us go to death. Do we not know how it is the entry whereby to come to the glory of heaven? Seeing that the resurrection was joined to the death of God's son, was not that also to assure us that God will not suffer us to continue in rottenness? Know we not that that which is written in the sixteenth Psalm was fulfilled in him? Namely, that God preserved him from rotting, to the end that we should be made free from it and drawn quite out of it at length. Seeing, then, that we have such promises at God's hand, and such assurance in the person of our Lord Jesus Christ, we ought to fight manfully against the dreadfulness of death.

It cannot be that he should forget them who do commend their salvation to him. If the thief had so easy a passage into heaven because that, when all things were in greatest extremity, he rested upon the grace of Christ, much more shall Christ, the conqueror of death, at this day reach forth his hand out of his throne to us, that he may gather us into the fellowship of life ; for it were absurd, since the time that he nailed to the cross the handwriting which was against us, and has put death and Satan to flight, and in his resurrection has triumphed over the prince of the world, that there should not be as easy and as ready a passage from death to life for us as for the thief. Therefore, whosoever, being ready to die, shall with a true faith commit the custody of his soul to Christ, he shall not be driven off any long time to languish in suspense, but Christ will accept his desire with the same kindness that he used towards the thief.

XXXVI—RESURRECTION

It is a thing hard to be believed that bodies, when they have been consumed with rottenness, shall at their appointed time rise up again. Therefore, where many of the philosophers have affirmed souls to be immortal, the resurrection of the flesh has been allowed of few ; wherein, although there was no excuse, yet we are thereby put in mind that it is too hard a thing to draw man's senses to believe it. That faith may overcome so great a stop, the Scripture ministers two helps ; the one is in the likeness of Christ, the other is the almightiness of God. Now, so oft as the resurrection is thought of, let the image of Christ come into our minds, who, in the nature that he took of us, so ran out the race of mortal life, that now, having obtained immortality, he is to us a pledge of the resurrection to come; for in the miseries wherewith we are besieged we carry about his mortifying in our flesh, that his life may be openly shown in us. And we may not sever him from us, neither can we possibly, but that he must be torn in sunder. Whereupon comes that argument of Paul,—— If the dead do not rise again, then neither is Christ risen again; because, verily, he takes that principle for confessed, that Christ was not made subject to death, nor obtained victory of death by rising again privately for himself, but that that was begun in the head which must needs be fulfilled in all the members, according to the degree and order of every one; for it were not right that they should in all points be made equal with him. It is said in the Psalm, Thou shalt not suffer thy meek one to see corruption; although a portion of this trust pertain to us according to the measure of gift, yet the full effect has not appeared but in Christ, who, being free from all rotting, has received again his body whole. Now, lest the fellowship of a blessed resurrection with Christ should be doubtful to us, that we may be contented with this pledge, Paul expressly affirms that he therefore sits in heaven, and shall come at the last day a judge, that he may make our base and vile body like fashioned to his glorious body. In another place, also, he teaches that God raised not up his Son from death to the intent to show a token of his power, but to stretch out the same effectual force of the Spirit towards us who are faithful, whom he therefore calls life, while he lives in us, because he was given to this end that he should make alive that which is mortal in us. I knit up in a brief abridgment those things which might both be more largely handled, and are worthy to be more gorgeously set out; and yet I trust that the godly readers shall in few words find matter enough which may suffice to edify their faith. Christ therefore is risen again, that he might have us companions of the life to come. He was raised up of the Father, in so much as he was the head of the Church, from which he does in no wise suffer himself to be plucked away. He was raised up by the power of the Spirit, which is common to us, unto the office of quickening. Finally, he was raised up that he should be resurrection and life. But as we have said that in this mirror there is to be seen of us a lively image of the resurrection, so let it be to us a sure substance to stay our mind, so that yet we be not loathful or weary of long tarrying, because it is not our part to measure the seasons of times by our will, but patiently to rest till God at his own fit time repair his kingdom.

We must come to the highest point, that is to wit, to the resurrection which is promised us. And where shall we find that? Not in our own nature. But we must rise up above the world, and we must understand that there is none but only Jesus Christ, which is the true mirror wherein to see that thing. There we see that God will raise us up again to glory, that he will pluck us out of the corruption and rottenness wherein we now walk, and wherein we should abide for ever, were it not for this extraordinary remedy whereby he helps the matter. Ye see then how we must be fain to come to Jesus Christ, to know whereat it behoves us to look, when we hope to be raised up again at the last day. Verily, Saint Paul uses certain similitudes which he takes of the common order of nature, to show the resurrection : as when he says, ye see how the grains of corn and other seeds are cast into the ground, and there rotting do grow up again. Now, in that men sow the bare corn, and afterward the same grows up again out of the rottenness whereunto it behoved it to be first turned : ye have a figure and image of the resurrection. But yet is not this as much to say as that we see our resurrection there. It serves only to show, that the faithless are unthankful and overlewd to Godward when they dispute how it is possible that our bodies should rise again after they be so rotted and turned into dust. If such as will be so wise in their own conceit, do shoot out their subtle devices, and thereupon conclude that it is impossible for God to raise us up again : Saint Paul shows that such folk are malicious, and that it is nothing else but their own un- thankfulness that turns them away from the receiving of this power of God, whereby he promises to set us in a per- fect state again. And why so ? For he gives us certain familiar likelihoods in the order of nature, to assure us of his good purpose. So then, when Saint Paul uses the foresaid manner of reasoning, it is not meant that our re- surrection shall be as a natural thing, but it is to make us understand the infinite power of God, and to ho- nour him, and to yield him the praise that belongs unto him : and therewithal to look upon the promise which he has made us, which is, that although it far surmount all our understanding, and be a very strange thing, that God should make us new again when we are turned unto dust : yet, notwithstanding, he will restore us, even when we shall have been turned to nothing. Although that this be hard to be believed, yet must we trust that God is nevertheless able to do it, by his power, wherethrough he is able to do all things.

What is our true resurrection and renewment ? Even that God should reserve us and set us in his kingdom : that when he has made us to wayfare through this world, and to pass through fire and water and all other afflictions, we may in the end be exempted from all the miseries of this world, and be made partakers of his life and glory. And so let us bear in mind how Saint Paul says unto us, that our life is hidden in Jesus Christ, and that we shall not see the true and perfect manifes- tation of it, until our Lord Jesus come from heaven. To be short, let us mark one other similitude which we ought to be well acquainted with. Truly in winter time the trees seem to be dead ; we see how the rain does as it were rot them; they are so swoln that they be ready to burst; and thus ye see well one kind of rottenness : Afterwards cometh the frost, as it were to sear them, and to dry them up. We see all these things, and we see not so much as one flower : and this is a cutting us off. Behold here a kind of death, which lasts not for a day or two, but for four or five months. Nevertheless, although the life of the trees be unseen, yet is their sap in their root, and in the heart of the wood. Even so is it with us, that our life also is hidden, howbeit not in ourselves. For that were a poor kind of hiding. There should need no great frost to starve it up, nor great wet to mar it. For we carry fire and frost enough in ourselves to consume it. But our life is hidden in God, he is the keeper of it, and we know that Jesus Christ is the party from out of whom we draw all our life. So then let us content ourselves with the said headiness. True it is, that if a man take up a tree and purpose to set it again, he had need to make haste. For if a tree tarry any long time above the ground, it will never take root any more, though it be planted new again. But God hath another manner of power, than the labourers of the earth have. Nevertheless, we see sometimes that men are cunning, and can well keep a tree alive for a time. They will lay it in a shady place where neither wind nor sun shall come at it to dry it, so as the sap shall always be kept close in it : men will find some means or other, and although they cannot save the lives of trees for ever, yet will they help them in some sort. And let not us think that when God lists to keep us unplanted a long time, he cannot for all that preserve us, yea, even in such wise as it shall not be hard for him to make us take new roots again, whensoever it pleases him.

As the Son of God abased himself so far as to be subject to our curse and to feel God's hand against him, that was to the end to deliver us from death, and to assure us that the victory which he has purchased is for us. Seeing,

then, that he has power over death, let his resurrection
always come before our eyes, and let us assure ourselves
that God has stretched out his strong and victorious
hand to deliver us from the bondage of Satan.   And
therein let us consider, that although we have many
adversities to suffer in this mortal life, and that it please
God to exercise us, we must not think it strange, nor
enter into the wailings and complaints which are made
here, to say yea, what am I? when I have passed through
this world, I must go to the grave, and no man can rescue me.   But we shall be rescued well enough, if we
have Jesus Christ for our Redeemer, who is ordained to
be our pledge and warrant, and has abolished the pains
of death, broken the bands of Satan, and burst open the
brazen gates to set us free. Seeing we know this, let us
be patient in the midst of all the adversities of this world,
assuring ourselves that although we have battles here
below, we have a rest prepared for us above in heaven,
and if we fight manfully here, let us assure ourselves
that we cannot but triumph in heaven.

XXXVII —HELL

THE souls of the faithful, when they do go out of the
body, do lead a joyful and a blessed life out of the world ;
and there are horrible torments prepared for the reprobate, which can no more be conceived in our minds
than can the great glory of the heavens. For, as we
only in very small measure, to wit, as we are lightened
by the Spirit of God, do taste by hope the glory promised
to us, which far exceeds all ourselves ; so let it suffice
that the incomprehensible vengeance of God, which remains for the wicked, is known darkly of us ; even so
as it is meet to strike a terror into us. So the words of
Christ do give a taste and a small knowledge of these
things, and yet such as may suffice to bridle curiosity ;

to wit, that the wicked are cruelly tormented with the feeling of their own misery, that they should desire some refreshing, yet all hope being taken away, they feel double torment; yea, and they are the more tormented, while they are enforced to remember their own sins, and to compare the present blessedness of the faithful with their own miserable and damnable estate.

XXXVIII.—HEAVEN

Let us always have in mind the eternal felicity, the end of the resurrection; of the excellency whereof, if all things were spoken which the tongues of men were able to speak, yet scarcely the smallest parcel thereof should be expressed. For howsoever we truly hear that the kingdom of God shall be stuffed full with brightness, joy, felicity, and glory; yet those things that are spoken of are most far removed from our sense, and remain, as it were, wrapped in dark speeches, until that day come when he himself shall give to us his glory to be seen face to face. We know, says John, that we are the children of God, but it has not yet appeared. But when we shall be like to him, then we shall see him such as he is. Wherefore the prophets, because they could by no words express the spiritual blessedness in itself, did in a manner grossly portray it out, under bodily things. But forasmuch as the ferventness of desire must, with some taste of that sweetness kindled in us, let us chiefly continue in this thought, that if God does, as a certain fountain which cannot be drawn dry, contain in him the fulness of all good things, nothing is beyond him to be coveted of them that tend toward the sovereign good and the full perfection of felicity, as we are taught in many places,— Abraham, I am thy exceeding great reward. With which saying accords David,—The Lord is my portion, the lot has very well fallen to me.

As God, diversely distributing his gifts to the saints in this world, does unequally enlighten them, so the measure of glory shall not be equal in heaven where God shall crown his gifts. For neither does this belong indifferently to all which Paul says,—You are my glory and crown in the day of Christ; nor also that saying of Christ to the Apostles,—You shall sit judging the twelve tribes of Israel. But Paul, who knew that as God enriches the holy ones with spiritual gifts on earth, so he beautifies them with glory in heaven, doubts not that there is a peculiar crown laid up for him according to the rate of his labours. And Christ, to set forth to the Apostles the dignity of the office which they did bear, tells them that the fruit thereof is laid up for them in heaven. So Daniel also says,—But the wise shall shine as the brightness of the firmament, and they which justify many, as stars to the world's end, and for ever. And if a man heedfully consider the Scriptures, they do not only promise eternal life to the faithful, but also special reward to every one. Whereupon comes that saying of Paul,—The Lord render to him in that day; which the promise of Christ confirms,—Ye shall receive a hundred in the eternal life. Finally, as Christ begins in this world the glory of his body with manifold diversity of gift, and increases it by degrees, so he shall also make it perfect in heaven.

Men love better to be inquisitive what is done in Paradise than to know which is the way to come thither. Behold, God himself tells us, saying,—Come to me; he shows us how we may come thither, and we pass not for it. You would marvel to see how cold we are when it stands upon the point of going unto him by the means that he has given us; and yet, in the mean-while, we are busy in demanding what is done here; and what is done there; what is this; and what is that? We are desirous to know that which God has hidden from us; for he will not have us to know ought as now, but only in part.

INDEX